RED STAR OVER CHINA

RED STAR OVER CHINA

by

EDGAR SNOW

LONDON
VICTOR GOLLANCZ LTD

Printed in Great Britain by
The Camelot Press Ltd., London and Southampton

To
NYM

CONTENTS

PART ONE
IN SEARCH OF RED CHINA

PART TWO
THE ROAD TO THE RED CAPITAL

PART THREE
IN " DEFENDED PEACE "

PART FOUR
GENESIS OF A COMMUNIST

PART FIVE

THE LONG MARCH

PART SIX

RED STAR IN THE NORTH-WEST

PART SEVEN

EN ROUTE TO THE FRONT

PART EIGHT

WITH THE RED ARMY

PART NINE

WITH THE RED ARMY

PART TEN

WAR AND PEACE

PART ELEVEN

BACK TO PAO AN

PART TWELVE

WHITE WORLD AGAIN

ACKNOWLEDGMENT

I have incorporated in this book a few passages which have appeared in the *Daily Herald*, and I wish to make acknowledgment to the courtesy of the editor of that paper for permission to reprint them here.

PUBLISHER'S NOTE

For the convenience of English readers, it should be explained that in 1928 the name " Pekin " was changed to " Peiping ", and the author uses both forms in the course of his narrative.

ILLUSTRATIONS

Sixteen photographic plates will be found after page 224. Detailed descriptions of these plates will be found at the end of the book, before the index.

THE MAP OPPOSITE

shows the route of
the main forces of
the Red Army on its
Long March

SCALE
ENGLISH MILES

| 0 | 100 | 200 | 300 | 400 |

PART ONE

IN SEARCH OF RED CHINA

1

Some Unanswered Questions

DURING my seven years in China, hundreds of questions had been asked about the Chinese Red Army, the Soviets, and the Communist movement. Eager partisans could supply you with a stock of ready answers, but these remained highly unsatisfactory. How did they *know*? They had never been to Red China. The fact was that there had been perhaps no greater mystery among nations, no more confused an epic, than the story of Red China. Fighting in the very heart of the most populous nation on earth, the Celestial Reds had for nine years been isolated by a news blockade as effective as a stone fortress. A mobile Great Wall of thousands of enemy troops constantly surrounded them; their territory was more inaccessible than Tibet. No one had voluntarily penetrated that wall and returned to write of his experiences since the first Chinese Soviet was established at Ch'alin in south-eastern Hunan, in November 1927.

Even the simplest points were disputed. Some people denied that there was such a thing as a Red Army. There were only thousands of hungry brigands. Some denied even the existence of Soviets. They were an invention of Communist propaganda. Yet Red sympathizers extolled both as the only salvation for all the ills of China. In the midst of this propaganda and counter-propaganda, credible evidence was lacking for dispassionate observers seeking the truth. Here are some of the unanswered questions that interested everyone concerned with politics and the quickening history of the Orient:

Was or was not this Red Army of China a mass of conscious Marxist revolutionaries, disciplined by and adhering to a centralized programme, a unified command under the Chinese Communist Party? If so, what was that programme? The Communists claimed to be fighting for agrarian revolution, and against imperialism, and for Soviet democracy and national emancipation. Nanking said that the Reds were only a new type of vandals and marauders led by " intellectual bandits." Who was right? Or was either one?

Before 1927, members of the Communist Party were admitted to the Kuomintang, but in April of that year began the famous " purgation." Communists, as well as unorganized radical intellectuals, and thousands of organized workers and peasants, were executed on an extensive scale under Chiang Kai-shek, the leader of a Right *coup d'état* which seized power at Nanking. Since then it had been a crime punishable by death to be a Communist or a Communist sympathizer, and thousands had paid that penalty. Yet thousands more continued to run the risk. Thousands of peasants, workers, students and soldiers joined the Red Army in its struggle against the military dictatorship of the Nanking régime. Why ? What inexorable force drove them on to support suicidal political opinions ? What were the fundamental quarrels between the Kuo-Min-Tang and the Kung-Ch'an-Tang ?[1]

What were the Chinese Communists like, anyway ? In what way did they resemble, in what way were they unlike, Communists or Socialists elsewhere ? The tourist asked if they wore long beards, made noises with their soup, and carried home-made bombs in their brief-cases. The serious-minded wanted to know whether they were " genuine " Marxists. Did they read *Capital* and the works of Lenin ? Had they a thoroughly Socialist economic programme ? Were they Stalinites or Trot-skyites ? Or neither ? Was their movement really an organic part of the World Revolution ? Were they true internationalists ? " Mere tools of Moscow," or primarily nationalists struggling for an independent China ?

Who were these warriors who had fought so long, so fiercely, so courageously, and—as admitted by observers of every colour, and privately among Generalissimo Chiang Kai-shek's own followers—on the whole so invincibly ? What made them fight like that ? What held them up ? What was the revolutionary basis of their movement ? What were the hopes and aims and dreams that had made of them the incredibly stubborn warriors —incredible compared with the history of compromise that is China !—who had endured hundreds of battles, blockade, salt-

[1] The Kuo-Min-Tang, or " National People's Party," founded by Dr. Sun Yat-sen and others, held the hegemony of power in the so-called Nationalist Revolution, 1924–7. The Kung-Ch'an-Tang, " Share Production Party," or the Communist Party of China, founded in 1921, was the chief ally of the Kuo-Min-Tang during the Nationalist Revolution.

shortage, famine, disease, epidemic, and finally the historic Long March of 6,000 miles, in which they crossed twelve provinces of China, broke through thousands of Kuomintang troops, and triumphantly emerged at last into a powerful new base in the North-west?

Who were their leaders? Were they educated men with a fervent belief in an ideal, an ideology, and a doctrine? Social prophets, or mere ignorant peasants blindly fighting for an existence? What kind of man, for instance, was Mao Tse-tung, No. 1 " Red-bandit " on Nanking's list, for whose capture, dead or alive, Chiang Kai-shek offered a reward of a quarter of a million silver dollars? What went on inside that highly priced Oriental head? Or was Mao really already dead, as Nanking officially announced? What was Chu Teh like—this man called Commander-in-Chief of the Red Army, whose life had the same value to Nanking? Who was this Lin Piao, the twenty-eight-year-old Red tactical genius whose famous First Red Army Corps was said to have never suffered a defeat? Where did he come from? Who were the many other Red leaders repeatedly reported dead, only to reappear in the news—unscathed and commanding new forces against the Kuomintang?

What explained the Red Army's remarkable record of resistance for nine years against vastly superior military combinations? Lacking a big industrial base, big cannon, gas, aeroplanes, money, and the modern technique which Nanking had utilized in its wars against them, how had these Reds survived, and increased their following? What military tactics did they use? How were they instructed? Who advised them? Were there some Russian military geniuses among them? Who led the outmanœuvring, not only of all Kuomintang commanders sent against them, but also of Chiang Kai-shek's large and expensive staff of foreign advisers, formerly headed by the late General Von Seeckt, chief of Hitler's Reichswehr?

What was a Chinese Soviet like? Did the peasants support it? If not, what held it together? To what degree did the Reds carry out " Socialism " in districts where they had consolidated their power? Why hadn't the Red Army taken big cities? Did this prove that it wasn't a genuine proletarian-led movement, but fundamentally remained a peasant rebellion?

Anyway, how was it possible to speak of " Communism " or
" Socialism " in China, where over 80 per cent of the population was still agrarian, where industrialism was still in infant
garments—if not infantile paralysis ?

How did the Reds dress ? Eat ? Play ? Love ? Work ? What
were their marriage laws ? Were women " nationalized," as
Kuomintang publicists asserted ? What was a Chinese " Red
factory " ? A Red Dramatic Society ? How did they organize
their economy ? What about public health, recreation, education,
" Red culture " ?

What was the strength of the Red Army ? Half a million, as
the Comintern publications boasted ? If so, why didn't it seize
power ? Where did it get arms and munitions ? Was it a disciplined army ? What about its morale ? Was it true that officers
and men lived alike ? If, as Generalissimo Chiang announced
in 1935, Nanking had " destroyed the menace of Communist-
banditry," what explained the fact that in 1937 the Reds
occupied a bigger single unified territory (in China's most
strategic North-west) than ever before ? If the Reds were
finished, why did Japan demand, as the famous Third Point of
Hirota, that Nanking form an anti-Red pact with Tokyo and
Nazi Germany " to prevent the bolshevization of Asia " ?
Were the Reds really " anti-imperialist " ? Did they really want
war with Japan ? Would Moscow support them in such a war ?
Or were their fierce anti-Japanese slogans only a trick and a
desperate attempt to win public sympathy, the last cry of
demoralized traitors and bandits, as the eminent Dr. Hu Shih
nervously assured his excited students in Peiping ?

What are the military and political perspectives of the Chinese
Communist movement ? What is its historic development ?
Can it succeed ? And just what would such success mean to us ?
To Japan ? What would be the effect of this tremendous mutation upon a fifth of the world's inhabitants ? What changes
would it produce in world politics ? In world history ? How would
it affect the vast British, American and other foreign investment in China ? Indeed, have the Reds any " foreign policy " at
all ?

Finally, what was the meaning of the Communists' offer to
form a " National United Front " in China, and stop civil war ?

For some time it had seemed ridiculous that not a single non-Communist observer could answer those questions with confidence, accuracy, or facts based on personal investigations. Here was a story, growing in interest and importance every day; here was *the* story of China, as newspaper correspondents admitted to each other between dispatches sent out on trivial side-issues. Yet we were all woefully ignorant about it. To get in touch with Communists in the " White " areas was extremely difficult.

Communists, over whose heads hung the sentence of death, did not identify themselves as such in polite—or impolite—society. Even in the foreign concessions, Nanking kept a well-paid espionage system at work. It included, for example, such vigilantes as C. Patrick Givens, former chief Red-chaser in the British police force of Shanghai's International Settlement. Inspector Givens was each year credited with the arrest—and subsequent imprisonment or execution, after extradition from the settlement by the Kuomintang authorities—of scores of alleged Communists, the majority of them between the ages of fifteen and twenty-five. This famous flatfoot's services were recognized by Nanking in 1934, when he was awarded the Order of the Brilliant Jade, and generous gifts in cash. But he was only one of many foreign sleuths hired to spy upon young Chinese radicals and hunt them down in their own country.

We all knew that the only way to learn anything about Red China was to go there. We excused ourselves by saying, " *Mei yu fa-tzu* "—" It can't be done." A few had tried and failed. It was believed impossible. People thought that nobody could enter Red territory and come out alive. Such was the strength of years of anti-Communist propaganda in a country whose Press is as rigidly censored and regimented as that of Italy or Germany.

Then, in June 1936, a close Chinese friend of mine brought me news of an amazing political situation in North-west China—a situation which was later to culminate in the sensational arrest of Generalissimo Chiang Kai-shek, and to change the current of Chinese history. More important to me then, however, I learned, with this news, of a possible method of entry to Red territory. It necessitated leaving at once. The opportunity was unique and not to be missed. I decided to take it, and attempt to break a news blockade nine years old.

It is true there were risks involved, though the reports later published of my death—" killed by bandits "—were probably exaggerated. But, against a torrent of horror-stories about Red atrocities that had for many years filled the subsidized vernacular and foreign Press of China, I had little to cheer me on my way. Nothing, in truth, but a letter of introduction to Mao Tse-tung, chairman of the Soviet Government. All I had to do was to find him. Through what adventures ? I did not know. But thousands of lives had been sacrificed in these years of Kuomintang-Communist warfare. Could one foreign neck be better hazarded than in an effort to discover why ? I found myself somewhat attached to the neck in question, but I concluded that the price was not too high to pay.

In this melodramatic mood I set out.

2

Slow Train to " Western Peace "

It was early June and Peking wore the green lace of spring, its thousands of willows and imperial cypresses making of the Forbidden City a place of wonder and enchantment, and in many cool gardens it was impossible to believe in the China of breaking toil, starvation, revolution and foreign invasion that lay beyond the glittering roofs of the palaces. Here the well-fed foreigners could live in their own little never-never land of whisky-and-soda, polo, tennis and gossip, happily quite unaware of the pulse of humanity outside the great city's silent, insulating walls—as indeed many did.

And yet, during the past year, even the oasis of Peking had been invaded by the atmosphere of struggle that hovers over all China. Threats of Japanese conquest had provoked great demonstrations of the people, especially among the enraged youth. A few months earlier I had stood under the bullet-pitted Tartar Wall and seen ten thousand students gather, defiant of the gendarmes' clubbings, to shout in a mighty chorus : " Resist Japan ! Reject the demands of Japanese imperialism for the separation of North China from the South ! "

All Peking's defensive masonry could not prevent reverberations of the Chinese Red Army's sensational attempt to march through Shansi to the Great Wall—ostensibly to begin a war against Japan for recovery of the lost territories. This somewhat quixotic expedition had been promptly blocked by eleven divisions of Generalissimo Chiang Kai-shek's crack new army, but that had not prevented patriotic students from courting imprisonment and possible death by massing in the streets and uttering the forbidden slogans: " Cease civil war ! Co-operate with the Communists to resist Japan ! Save China ! "

One midnight I climbed aboard a dilapidated train, feeling a little ill, but in a state of high excitement. Excitement because before me lay a journey of exploration into a land hundreds of years and hundreds of miles removed from the medieval splendours of the Forbidden City: I was bound for " Red China." And " a little ill " because I had taken all the inoculations available.

A microbe's-eye view of my blood-stream would have revealed a macabre cavalcade, with my arms and legs shot with smallpox, typhoid, cholera, typhus and plague germs. All five diseases are prevalent in the North-west. Moreover, alarming reports had lately told of the spread of bubonic plague in Shensi province, one of the few spots on earth where it is endemic.

My immediate destination was Sianfu—which means Western Peace. Sianfu is the capital of Shensi province, it is two tiresome days and nights by train to the south-west of Peking, and it is the western terminus of the Lunghai railway. From there I planned to go northward and enter the Soviet districts, which occupied the very heart of *Ta Hsi-pei*—China's Great North-west. Lochuan, a town about a hundred and fifty miles north of Sianfu, then marked the beginning of Red territory in Shensi. Everything north of it, excepting strips of territory along the main highways, and some points which will be noted later, was already dyed Red. With Lochuan roughly the southern, and the Great Wall the northern, extremities of the Red control in Shensi, both the eastern and western Red frontiers were formed by the Yellow River. Coming down from the fringes of Tibet, the wide muddy stream flows northward through Kansu and Ninghsia, and above the Great Wall into the province of Suiyuan—Inner Mongolia. Then after many miles of uncertain wandering toward the east it turns southward again, to pierce the Great Wall and form the boundary between the provinces of Shensi and Shansi.

It was within this great bend of China's most treacherous river that the Soviets then operated—in northern Shensi, north-eastern Kansu, and south-eastern Ninghsia. And by a strange sequence of history this region almost corresponds to the original confines of the birthplace of China. Near here the Chinese first formed and unified themselves as a people, thousands of years ago.

In the morning I inspected my travelling companions and found a youth and a handsome old man with a wisp of white beard sitting opposite me, sipping bitter tea. Presently the youth spoke to me, in formalities at first, and then inevitably of politics. I discovered that his wife's uncle was a railway official and that he was travelling with a pass. He was on his way back to Szechuan, his native province, which he had left seven years before. But he was not sure that he would be able to visit his home-town, after all. Bandits were reported to be operating near there.

" You mean Reds ? "

" Oh, no, not Reds, although there are Reds in Szechuan, too. No, I mean bandits."

" But aren't the Reds also bandits ? " I asked out of curiosity. " The newspapers always call them Red-bandits or Communist-bandits."

" Ah, but you must know that the editors must call them bandits because they are ordered to do so by Nanking," he explained. " If they called them Communists or revolutionaries that would prove they were Communists themselves."

" But in Szechuan don't people fear the Reds as much as the bandits ? "

" Well, that depends. The rich men fear them, and the land-lords, and the officials and tax-collectors, yes. But the peasants do not fear them. Sometimes they welcome them." Then he glanced apprehensively at the old man, who sat listening intently, and yet seeming not to listen. " You see," he continued, " the peasants are too ignorant to understand that the Reds only want to use them. They think the Reds really mean what they say."

" But they don't mean it ? "

" My father wrote to me that they did abolish usury and opium in the Sungpan [*Szechuan*], and that they redistributed the land there. So you see they are not exactly bandits. They have principles all right. But they are wicked men. They kill too many people."

Then surprisingly the greybeard lifted his gentle face and with perfect composure he made an astonishing remark. " *Sha pu kou !* " he said. " They don't kill enough ! " We both looked at him flabbergasted.

Unfortunately the train was nearing Chengchow, where I had to transfer to the Lunghai line, and I was obliged to break off the discussion. But I have ever since wondered with what deadly evidence this Confucian-looking old gentleman would have supported his startling contention. I wondered about it all the next day of travel, as we climbed slowly through the weird levels of loess hills in Honan and Shensi, and until my train—this one still new and very comfortable—rolled up to the recent and handsome railway station at Sianfu.

Soon after my arrival I went to call on General Yang Hu-ch'eng, Pacification Commissioner of Shensi province. General Yang was until a couple of years ago undisputed monarch of those parts of Shensi not controlled by the Reds. A former bandit, he rose to authority via the route that has put many of China's ablest leaders in office, and on the same highway he is said to have accumulated the customary fortune. But recently he had been obliged to divide his power with several other gentlemen in the North-west. For in 1935 the " Young Marshal," Chang Hsueh-liang, who used to be ruler of Manchuria, brought his army into Shensi, and assumed office in Sianfu as supreme Red-chaser in these parts—Vice-Commander of the National Bandit-Suppression Commission. And to watch the Young Marshal had come Shao Li-tzu, an acolyte of Generalissimo Chiang Kai-shek. The Hon. Shao was Governor of Shensi.

A delicate balance of power was maintained between these figures—and still others. Tugging strings behind all of them was the redoubtable Generalissimo himself, who sought to extend his dictatorship to the North-west, and liquidate, not only the struggling Soviet democracy, but also the troops of old Yang Hu-ch'eng and young Chang Hsueh-liang, by the simple process of using each to destroy the other—three acts of a brilliant politico-military drama the main stratagem of which Chiang evidently believed was understood only by himself. And it was this error in calculation, a little too much haste in pursuit of the purpose, a little too much confidence in his adversaries' stupidity, which was in a few months to land Chiang Kai-shek a prisoner in Sianfu, at the mercy of all three ! Later on I shall tell of this amazing arrest of the Generalissimo, and show how it canalized the history of China in new directions.

I found General Yang in a newly finished, stone mansion, just completed at a cost of $50,000. But he was living in this many-chambered vault—the official home of the Pacification Commissioner—all alone. Yang Hu-cheng, like many Chinese in this transitional period, was burdened with domestic infelicity, for he was a two-wife man. The first was the lily-footed wife of his youth, betrothed to him by his parents in Pucheng. The second, as vivacious and courageous a woman as Mme Chiang Kai-shek, was a pretty young mother of five children, modern and progressive, a former Communist, they say, and the girl that Yang had chosen himself. It seemed, according to the missionaries, that when he opened his new home each of his wives had presented him with the same minimum demand. Each detested the other; each had borne him sons and had the right to be legal wife; and each resolutely refused to move into the stone mansion unless the other stayed behind.

To an outsider the case looked simple: a divorce or a third wife was the obvious solution. But General Yang had not made up his mind, and so he still lived alone. His dilemma was a not uncommon one in modern China. Chiang Kai-shek had faced a similar issue when he married rich, American-educated, Christian Soong Mei-ling, and had solved it by pensioning off his two old-fashioned wives. The decision was highly approved by the missionaries, who have ever since prayed for his soul. Nevertheless, this way out—a new-fangled idea imported from the West—is still frowned upon by many Chinese. Old Yang, having risen from the people, was probably less concerned over the disposal of his soul than the traditions of his ancestors.

And it must not be supposed that Yang's early career as a bandit necessarily disqualified him as a leader. Such assumptions cannot be made in China, where a career of banditry in early youth often indicates a man of strong character and purpose. If you look through Chinese history you will find that some of China's ablest patriots were at one time or another labelled bandits. The fact is that many of the worst rogues, scoundrels and traitors have climbed to power under cover of respectability, the putrid hypocrisy of Confucian maxims, and the priestcraft of the Chinese classics—though they have very often utilized the good strong arm of an honest bandit in doing so—and all this is still more or less true to-day.

General Yang was in any case in bad repute among most of the foreign missionaries, so he could not have been a really wicked fellow. His history as a revolutionary suggests a rugged peasant, who once may have had high dreams of making a big change in his world, but who, finding himself in power, looked vainly for a method, and grew weary and confused, listening to the advice of the mercenaries who gathered round him. But if he had such dreams he did not confide them to me. He declined to discuss political questions, and courteously delegated one of his secretaries to show me the city. He was also suffering from a severe headache and rheumatism when I saw him, and in the midst of his sea of troubles I was not one to insist upon asking him nettling questions. On the contrary, in his dilemma he had all my sympathy. So after a brief interview with him I discreetly retired, to seek some answers from the Honourable Governor, Shao Li-tzu.

Governor Shao received me in the garden of his spacious yamen, cool and restful after the parching heat of Sian's dusty streets. I had last seen him six years before, when he was Chiang Kai-shek's personal secretary, and at that time he had assisted me in an interview with the Generalissimo. Since then, he had risen rapidly in the Kuomintang. He was an able man, well educated, and the Generalissimo had now bestowed upon him the honours of a governorship. But poor Shao, like many another civil governor, did not rule much beyond the provincial capital's grey walls—the outlying territory being divided by General Yang and the Young Marshal.

It is perhaps impolite to mention it, but the Hon. Shao was once a " Communist-bandit " himself. He was in fact a founder of the Chinese Communist Party. But he should not be judged too harshly : in those days it was fashionable to be a Communist and nobody was very sure exactly what it meant, except that all bright young men were Communists. Later on he had recanted, for after 1927 it had become very clear what it meant, and you could have your head removed for it. Shao then became a devout Buddhist, and subsequently displayed no further signs of heresy.

" How are the Reds getting along ? " I asked him.

" There are not many left. Those in Shensi are only remnants."

" Then the war continues ? " I asked.

" No, at present there is little fighting in north Shensi. The Reds are moving into Ninghsia and Kansu. They seem to want to connect with Outer Mongolia."

He shifted the conversation to the situation in the South-west, where insurgent generals were then demanding an anti-Japanese expedition. I asked him whether he thought China should fight Japan. " Can we ? " he demanded. And then the Buddhist governor told me exactly what he thought about Japan—not for publication—just as every Kuomintang official will tell you his opinion of Japan—not for publication.

A few months after this interview poor Shao was to be put in a spot on this question of war with Japan—along with his Generalissimo—by some rebellious young men of Marshal Chang Hsueh-liang's army, who refused to be reasonable and take " maybe some day " for an answer any longer. And Shao's fat little wife—a returned student from Moscow and a former Communist who had also " betrayed "—was to be cornered by some of the insurrectionists and make a plucky fight to resist arrest.

But Shao revealed no premonition of all this in our talk, and an exchange of views having brought us perilously near agreement, it was time to leave. I had already learned from Shao Li-tzu what I wanted to know. He had confirmed the word of my Peking informant, that fighting had temporarily halted in north Shensi. Therefore it should be possible to go to the front, if properly arranged. I proceeded to make the arrangements.

3

Some Han Bronzes

SOME six months after my arrival in Sianfu the crisis in the North-west was to explode in a manner nobody had anticipated, so that the whole world was made dramatically aware of an amazing alliance between the big army under Marshal Chang Hsueh-liang, and the " bandits " which he had been ordered, as deputy Commander-in-Chief of the Communist-Suppression Forces, to destroy. But in June 1936 the outside world was still in complete ignorance of these strange developments, and even in the headquarters of Chiang Kai-shek's own Blueshirt gendarmes, who controlled the Sianfu police, nobody knew exactly what was taking place. Over 300 Communists were imprisoned in the city's jail, and the Blueshirts were hunting for more. An atmosphere of extreme tension prevailed. Spies and counter-spies were everywhere.

But there is now no longer any necessity to remain covert about those exciting days, with the secrets of which I was perforce entrusted, so here it can be told.

I had never seen a Red Army man before I arrived in Sianfu. The man in Peiping who had written for me in invisible ink the letter addressed to Mao Tse-tung was, I knew, a Red commander; but I had not seen him. The letter had reached me through a third person, an old friend: but besides this letter I had only one hope of a connection in the North-west. I had been instructed simply to go to an hotel in Sianfu, take a room there, and await a visit from a gentleman who would call himself Wang, but about whom I knew nothing else. Nothing—except that he would arrange for me to enter the Red districts by way of the private aeroplane, I was promised, of Chang Hsueh-liang !

A few days after I put up in the hotel a large, somewhat florid and rotund, but strongly built and dignified Chinese, wearing a long, grey-silk gown, entered my open door and greeted me in excellent English. He looked like a prosperous merchant, but he introduced himself as Wang, mentioned the name of my Peiping friend, and otherwise established that he was the man I awaited.

In the week that followed I discovered that Wang alone was

worth the trip to Sianfu. I spent four or five hours a day listening to his yarns and reminiscences and to his more serious explanations of the political situation. He was wholly unexpected. Educated in a missionary school in Shanghai, he had been prominently identified with the Christian community, had once had a church of his own, and (as I was later to learn) was known among the Communists as Wang Mu-shih—Wang the Pastor. Like many successful Christians of Shanghai he had been a member of the Ch'ing Pang, the Tammany of that city, and he knew everyone from Chiang Kai-shek (also a member) down to Tu Yueh-sheng, the Ch'ing Pang chieftain. He had once been a high official in the Kuomintang, but I cannot even now disclose his real name.

For some time, Pastor Wang, having deserted his congregation and officialdom, had been working with the Reds. How long I do not know. He was a kind of secret and unofficial ambassador to the courts of various militarists and officials whom the Communists were trying to win over to understanding and support of their " anti-Japanese national front " proposals. With Chang Hsueh-liang, at least, he had been successful. And here some background is necessary to illuminate the basis of the secret understanding which had at this time been reached.

Chang Hsueh-liang, as everyone knows, was until 1931 the popular, gambling, generous, modern-minded, golf-playing, dope-using, paradoxical warlord-dictator of the 30,000,000 people of Manchuria, confirmed in the office he had inherited from his ex-bandit father Chang Tso-lin by the Kuomintang Government at Nanking, which had also given him the title Vice-Commander-in-Chief of the Armed Forces of China. In September 1931, Japan set out to conquer the North-east, and Chang's reverses began. When the invasion commenced, Young Marshal Chang was in the Peking Union Hospital, below the Wall, recovering from typhoid, and in no condition to meet this crisis alone. He leaned heavily on Nanking and on his blood-sworn " elder brother," Chiang Kai-shek, the Generalissimo. But Chiang Kai-shek, who wanted to avoid war at all costs, urged non-resistance, withdrawal, and reliance on the League of Nations. Sick, young (he was only thirty-three), inexperienced, and surrounded by corrupt and incompetent retainers, Chang Hsueh-liang took the

Generalissimo's counsel and Nanking's orders. As a result he lost his homeland, Manchuria, with scarcely a shot having been fired in its defence, while the sacrifice enabled the Generalissimo to hold his own tottering régime together in Nanking and begin a new annihilation campaign against the Reds.

This is how the bulk of the Manchurian troops, known in China as the Tungpei (meaning " North-eastern ") Army, moved south of the Great Wall into China Proper. The same thing happened when Japan invaded Jehol. Chang Hsueh-liang was not in the hospital then, but he should have been. Nanking sent no support to him, and made no preparations for defence. The Generalissimo, to avoid war, was ready to see Jehol fall to Japan, too—and so it did. But Chang Hsueh-liang got the blame, and docilely played the goat when somebody had to resign to appease an infuriated populace. It was Chiang or Chang—and the latter bowed and departed. He went to Europe for a year " to study conditions."

Now the most important thing that happened to Chang Hsueh-liang while he was in Europe was not that he saw Mussolini and Hitler and met Ramsay MacDonald and was stupidly refused permission to visit Soviet Russia, but it was this: that he cured himself of the dope habit. Some years before he had taken up opium, as many Chinese generals do, between battles. To break himself of the habit was not easy: he had no time for the long cure necessary: but a doctor in whom he naïvely placed confidence had assured him he could cure him by injections. He freed him of the craving for opium all right, but when he got through with him the Young Marshal was a morphine addict.

When I first met Chang at Mukden, in 1929, he was the world's youngest dictator, and he still looked fairly well. He was thin, his face somewhat drawn and jaundiced-looking, but his mind was quick and energetic, he seemed full of exuberance, he was openly, bitterly anti-Japanese, and he was eager to perform miracles in driving Japan from China and modernizing Manchuria. Several years later his physical condition was much worse. One of his doctors in Peiping told me that he was spending $200 a day on " medicine "—a special preparation of morphine which theoretically could be " tapered off."

But, in Europe, Chang Hsueh-liang won a great victory. He

conquered himself of the drug habit. When he returned to China in 1934 his friends were pleased and amazed: he had put on weight and muscle, there was colour in his cheeks, he looked ten years younger, and people saw in him traces of the brilliant vertebrate leader of his youth again. He had always possessed a quick, realistic mind, and now he gave it a chance to develop. At Hankow he resumed command of the Tungpei Army, which had been shifted to Central China to fight the Reds. It was a tribute to his popularity that, despite his errors of the past, his men enthusiastically welcomed him back.

Chang adopted a new routine—up at six, hard exercise, daily drill and study, simple food and spartan habits, and direct personal contact with the subalterns as well as officers of his troops, which still numbered about 140,000 men. A new Tungpei Army began to emerge. Sceptics gradually became convinced that the Young Marshal had again become a man worth watching, and took seriously the vow that he had made on his return: that his whole life was to be devoted to the task of recovering Manchuria, and erasing the humiliation of his people.

Meanwhile, Chang had not lost faith in the Generalissimo. In their entire relationship Chang had never wavered in his loyalty to the older man, whose régime he had three times saved from collapse, and in whose judgment and sincerity he placed full confidence. He evidently believed Chiang Kai-shek when he said he was preparing to recover Manchuria, and would yield no more territory without resistance. But, in 1935, Japan's militarists continued their aggression: the puppet régime of east Hopei was set up, part of Chahar was annexed, and demands were made for the separation of North China from the South, to which Nanking partly acquiesced. Ominous discontent rumbled through the Young Marshal's officers and men, especially after his troops, to their disgust, were shifted to the North-west to continue to wage an unpopular civil war against the Red Army, while not a shot was fired against Japan.

After months of fighting the Reds in the South, several important realizations had come to the Young Marshal and some of his officers: that the " bandits " they were fighting were in reality led by able, patriotic, anti-Japanese commanders; that this process of " Communist extermination " might last for many

Bc

more years; that it was impossible to resist Japan while the anti-Red wars continued; and that meanwhile the Tungpei Army was rapidly becoming proletarianized, was gradually being reduced and disbanded in battles which were to it devoid of meaning.

Nevertheless, when Chang shifted his headquarters to the North-west, he began an energetic campaign against the Reds. For a while he had some success, but in October and November 1935 the Tungpei Army suffered great defeats, losing two whole divisions (the 101st and 109th) and part of a third (110th). Thousands of Tungpei soldiers turned over to the Red Army. Many officers were also taken captive, and held for a period of " anti-Japanese tutelage."

When these officers were released, and returned to Sian, they brought back to the Young Marshal glowing accounts of the morale and organization in the Soviet districts, but especially of the Red Army's sincerity in wanting to stop civil war, unify China by peaceful democratic methods, and unite to oppose Japanese imperialism. Chang was impressed. He was impressed even more by reports from his divisions that the sentiment throughout the whole army was turning against war with the Reds, whose slogans—" Chinese must not fight Chinese ! " and " Unite with us and fight back to Manchuria ! "—were infecting the rank and file of the entire Tungpei Army.

In the meantime, Chang himself had been strongly influenced to the Left. Many of the students in his Tungpei University had come to Sian and were working with him, and among these were some Communists. After the Japanese demands in Peking of December 1935, he had sent word to the North that all anti-Japanese students, regardless of their political beliefs, could find haven in Sianfu. While anti-Japanese agitators throughout China were being arrested by Nanking, in Shensi they were encouraged and protected. Some of Chang's younger officers had been much influenced by the students also, and when the captured officers returned from the Red districts and reported that open anti-Japanese mass organizations were flourishing there, and described the Reds' patriotic propaganda among the people, Chang began to think more and more of the Reds as natural allies rather than enemies.

It was at this point, early in 1936, Pastor Wang told me, that he one day called on Chang Hsueh-liang and opened an interview by declaring: " I have come to borrow your aeroplane to go to the Red districts."

Chang jumped up and stared in amazement. " What? You dare to come here and make such a request? Do you realize you can be shot for this? "

The Pastor elaborated. He explained that he had contacts with the Communists, and knew things which Chang should know. He talked for a long time about their changing policies, about the necessity for a united China to resist Japan, about the Reds' willingness to make big concessions in order to influence Nanking to resist Japan, a policy which the Reds realized they could not, alone, make effective. He proposed that he should arrange for a. further discussion of these points between Chang and certain Red leaders. And to all of this, after his first surprise, Chang listened attentively. He had for some time been thinking that he could make use of the Reds: they also evidently believed they could make use of him: very well, perhaps they could utilize each other on the basis of common demands for an end to civil war and resistance to Japan.

The Pastor did after all fly to Yenan, north Shensi, in the Young Marshal's private aeroplane. He entered Soviet China, and returned with a formula for negotiation. And a short time later Chang Hsueh-liang himself flew up to Yenan, met Chou En-lai, a Red commander (of whom more later), and after long and detailed discussion with him became convinced of the Reds' sincerity, and of the sanity and practicability of their proposals for a united front.

First steps in the implementation of the Tungpei-Communist agreement included the cessation of hostilities in Shensi. Neither side was to move without notifying the other. The Reds sent several delegates to Sianfu, who put on Tungpei uniforms, joined Chang Hsueh-liang's staff, and helped reorganize political training methods in his army. A new school was opened at Wang Ch'u Ts'un, and here Chang's lower officers went through intensified courses in politics, economics, social science, and detailed and statistical study of how Japan had conquered Manchuria and what China had lost thereby. Hundreds of radical students flocked to Sian, and entered another anti-Japanese political training school, to which the Young Marshal also gave frequent lectures. Something like the political commissar system used in Soviet Russia and by the Chinese Red Army was adopted in the Tungpei Army. A number of old and feudal-minded higher officers inherited from the Manchurian days were sacked; to replace them Chang Hsueh-liang promoted more radical, younger officers, to whom he now looked for his main support in building a new army. Many of the corrupt sycophants who had surrounded Chang during his " playboy " years were also given the gate and were replaced by eager and serious-minded students from the Tungpei University.

But most of these changes developed in an atmosphere of close secrecy. Although the Tungpei troops no longer fought the Reds, there were Nanking troops along the Shansi–Shensi border, and also in Kansu and Ninghsia, and stiff fighting continued in these regions. No word of the real relations between Chang and the Communists crept into the Press. And, although Chiang Kai-shek's spies in Sian knew that something was fermenting, they could get few details of its exact nature. Occasional trucks arrived in Sian, carrying Red passengers, but they looked innocuous enough, for they all wore Tungpei uniforms. And the occasional departure of other trucks from Sian to the Red districts aroused no suspicion, for they resembled any other Tungpei truck setting off for the front.

It was indeed on such a truck, Pastor Wang confided to me soon after my arrival, that I would myself be going to the front. The journey by plane was " off ": too much risk of embarrassment to the Young Marshal was involved, for his American pilots might not hold their tongues if a foreigner were dumped on the front and not returned.

One morning the Pastor called on me with a Tungpei officer— or at any rate a youth wearing the uniform of a Tungpei officer— and suggested a trip by car to the ancient Han city, outside Sian. A curtained car waited for us in front of the hotel, and when we got in I saw in a corner a man wearing dark glasses and the Chung Shan uniform of a Kuomintang official. We drove out to the site of the old palace of the Han dynasty, and there we walked over to the raised mound of earth where the illustrious

Han Wu Ti once sat in his Throne Room and ruled the earth. Here you can still pick up fragments of tile from those great roofs of over 2,000 years ago.

Pastor Wang and the Tungpei officer had some words to exchange, and stood apart, talking. The Kuomintang official, who had sat without speaking during our long dusty drive, came over to me and removed his dark glasses and his white hat. I saw that he was quite young. Under a rim of thick, glossy hair a pair of intense eyes sparkled at me. A mischievous grin spread over his bronzed face, and one look at him, without those glasses, showed you that the uniform was a disguise, that this was no sedentary bureaucrat, but an out-of-doors man of action. He was of medium height and looked slight of strength, so that when he came close to me and suddenly took my arm in a grip of iron I winced with surprise. There was a pantherish grace about the man's movements, I noticed later, a lithe limberness under the stiff formal cut of the suit.

He put his face close to mine and grinned and fixed his sharp burning eyes on me and held my two arms tightly in that iron grip, and then wagged his head and comically screwed up his mouth—and winked ! " Look at me ! " he whispered with delight of a child with a secret. " Look at me ! Look at me ! Do you recognize me ? "

I did not know what to think of the fellow. He was so bubbling over about something that his excitement infected me, and I felt foolish because I had nothing to say. Recognize him ? I had never met a Chinese like him in my life ! I shook my head apologetically.

He released a hand from my arm and pointed a finger at his chest. " I thought maybe you had seen my picture somewhere," he said. " Well, I am Teng Fa," he offered—" *Teng Fa !* " He pulled back his head and gazed at me to see the effect of the bombshell.

Teng Fa ? Teng Fa . . . why, of course, Teng Fa was chief of the Chinese Red Army's Gaypayoo. And something else, good heavens, there was $50,000 on his head !

Teng danced with pleasure when he disclosed his identity. He was irrepressible, tickled with amusement at the situation: he, the notorious " Communist-bandit," living in the very midst of the enemy's camp, thumbing his nose at the spies that hovered everywhere. And he was overjoyed at seeing me—he literally hugged me repeatedly—an American who was voluntarily going into the " bandit " areas. He offered me everything. Did I want his horse ? Oh, what a horse he had, the finest in Red China ! His pictures ? He had a wonderful collection and it was all mine. His diary ? He would send instructions to his wife, who was still in the Soviet areas, to give all this and more to me. And he kept his word.

What a Chinese ! What a Red-bandit !

This Teng Fa, a Cantonese, was the son of a working-class family, and had once been a foreign-style cook on a Canton–Hongkong steamer. He had been a leader of the great Hongkong shipping strike, when he was beaten in the chest, and most of his ribs broken, by a British constable who did not like pickets. And then he had become a Communist, and entered Whampoa, and taken part in the Nationalist Revolution, until after 1927 he had joined the Red Army in Kiangsi.

We stood for an hour or more on that height, talking and looking down on that green-shrouded grave of an imperial city, and I cannot describe to you the strange emotional impact of that moment—so much intensified by our surroundings, so queerly premonitional, so oddly detached from me somehow, and part of the variegated history of China; for how incongruous and yet how logical that this place should seem to these Communists the one safe rendezvous where we four could safely meet, and after all how appropriate to greet this breath-taking young warrior of the revolution of to-day on the exact spot where, over two millenniums ago, the great Hans, radical enough in their own way and in their time, had ruled a united and then progressive China, and so successfully consolidated a people and a culture from the chaos of warring States that their descendants, ever since, have been content to call themselves Sons of Han.

It was here that Teng told me who would escort me to the Red districts, how I would travel, how I would live in Red China, and assured me of a warm welcome there.

" Aren't you afraid for your head ? " I asked as we drove back to the city.

" Not any more than Chang Hsueh-liang is," he chuckled; " I'm living with him."

4

Through Red Gates

WE left Sianfu before dawn, the high wooden gates of the once " golden city " swinging open and noisily dragging their chains, before the magic of our military pass. In the half-light of pre-dawn the big army truck lumbered past the aerodrome from which expeditions set out for daily reconnaissance and bombing over the Red lines.

To a Chinese traveller every mile of this road northward from Sianfu evokes memories of the rich and colourful pageant of his people. It seems not inappropriate that the latest historical mutation in China, the Communist movement, should choose this locale in which to work out a destiny. In an hour we were being ferried across the Wei River, in whose rich valley the wild dark men who were Confucius's ancestors developed their rice-culture, and formulated traditions still a power in the folk-myth of rural China to-day. And toward noon we had reached Ta'un Pu. It was near this battlemented city that the towering and terrible figure who first " unified " China—the Emperor Ch'in Shih Huang Ti—was born some 2,200 years ago. The Emperor Ch'in first consolidated all the ancient frontier walls of his country into what remains to-day the most stupendous masonry on earth—the Great Wall of China.

Opium poppies nodded their swollen heads, ready for harvest, along the newly completed motor road—a road already deeply wrinkled with washouts and ruts, so that at times it was scarcely navigable even for our six-ton Dodge truck. Shensi has long been a noted opium province. During the great North-west Famine which a few years ago took a toll of 3,000,000 lives, American Red Cross investigators attributed much of the tragedy to the cultivation of the poppy, forced upon the peasants by tax-greedy militarists. The best land being devoted to the poppy, in years of drought there is a serious shortage of millet, wheat and corn, the staple cereals of the North-west.

I spent the night on a clay *k'ang*,[1] in a filthy hut at Lochuan,

[1] A *k'ang* is a raised earthen platform built in Chinese houses, with a fireplace at one end. The flue is arranged in a maze beneath, so that it heats the clay platform, if desired.

with pigs and donkeys quartered in the next room, and rats in my own, and I'm sure we all slept very little. Next morning, a few miles beyond that city, the loess terraces rose higher and more imposing, and the country was weirdly transformed.

The wonderful loess lands, which cover much of Kansu, Shensi, Ninghsia and Shansi provinces, account for the marvellous fertility of these regions (when there is rainfall), for the loess furnishes an inexhaustible porous top-soil tens of feet deep. Geologists think the loess is organic matter blown down in centuries past from Mongolia and from the west, by the great winds that rise in Central Asia. Scenically the result is an infinite variety of queer embattled shapes—hills like great castles, like rows of mammoth, nicely rounded scones, like ranges torn by some giant hand, leaving behind the imprint of angry fingers. Fantastic, incredible, and sometimes frightening shapes, a world configurated by a mad god—and yet sometimes a world also of strange surrealist beauty.

And though you see fields and cultivated land everywhere, you seldom see houses. The peasants are tucked away in those loess hills also. Throughout the North-west, as has been the habit of centuries, men live in homes dug out of the hard, fudge-coloured cliffs—*yao fang*, or " cave houses," as the Chinese call them. But they are no caves in the Western sense. Cool in summer, warm in winter, they are easily built and easily cleaned. Even the wealthiest landlords often dig their homes in the hills. Some of them are many-roomed edifices gaily furnished and decorated, with stone floors and high-ceilinged chambers, lit through rice-paper windows opened in the walls of earth, and also in the stout, black-lacquered doors.

Once, not far from Lochuan, a young Tungpei officer, who rode beside me in the cavorting truck, pointed to such a *yao-fang-ts'un*—a cave village. It lay only a mile or so distant from the motor road, just across a deep ravine.

" They are Reds," he revealed. " One of our detachments was sent over there to buy millet a few weeks ago, and those villagers refused to sell us a catty of it. The stupid soldiers took some by force. As they retired the peasants shot at them." He swung his arms in an arc including everything on each side of the highway, so carefully guarded by dozens of *pao-lei*—hilltop machine-gun nests—manned by Kuomintang troops. "*Hung-fei*," he said, "everything out there is Red-bandit territory."

I gazed toward the spaces indicated with keener interest, for it was into that horizon of unknown hill and upland that I intended, within a few hours, to make my way.

On the road we passed part of the 105th Division, all Manchurians, moving back from Yenan to Lochuan. They were lean and sturdy youths, most of them taller than the average Chinese soldier. At a roadside inn we stopped to drink tea, and I sat down near several of them who were resting. They were just returning from Wa Ya Pao, in north Shensi, where there had been a skirmish with the Reds. I overheard scraps of conversation between them. They were talking about the Reds.

"They eat a lot better than we do," one argued.

"Yes—eat the flesh of the *lao-pai-hsing* !"[1] another replied.

"Never mind that—a few landlords—it's all to the good. Who thanked us for coming to Wa Ya Pao ? The landlords ! Isn't it a fact ? Why should we kill ourselves for these rich men ? "

"They say more than three thousand of our Tungpei men are with them now. . . ."

"Another thing on their side. Why should we fight our own people, when none of us want to fight anybody, unless it's a Japanese, eh ? "

An officer approached and this promising conversation came to an end. The officer ordered them to move on. They picked up their rifles and trudged off down the road. Soon afterwards we drove away.

Early in the afternoon of the second day we reached Yenan, where north Shensi's single road fit for wheeled traffic comes to an end—about 400 *li*,[2] more or less, south of the Great Wall. It is an historic town : through it, in centuries past, have come the nomadic raiders from the north, and through it swept the great Mongol cavalry of Genghis Khan, in its ride of conquest toward Sianfu.

Yenan is ideally suited for defence. Cradled in a bowl of high,

---

[1] *Lao-pai-hsing*, literally "old hundred names," is the colloquial Chinese expression for the country people.

[2] One Chinese *li* is about a third of an English mile.

rock-ribbed hills, its stout walls crawl up to the very tops, and corner in newly made fortifications, where machine guns bristled toward the Reds not far beyond. The road and its immediate environs were then held by Tungpei troops, but until recently Yenan had been completely cut off. The Reds had turned upon their enemy the blockade which the Generalissimo enforces against themselves, and hundreds of people had died of starvation.

Even aeroplanes had proved useless against the surrounding Reds. They mounted machine guns on the hilltops—lacking anti-aircraft guns—and used them so effectively that the Nanking pilots, forced to fly at high altitudes, had a long target for the bundles of provisions they attempted to drop inside the city walls. Most of them, in fact, landed in the arms of the Reds, who opened a market outside Yenan's gates, and sold the food back to the beleaguered inhabitants. Chang Hsueh-liang's own foreign pilots grew jittery from being shot at, and one American resigned. When I saw the Young Marshal's beautiful Boeing private plane in Sianfu, riddled with bullet-holes, I sympathized with the pilot.

The long Red siege of Yenan[1] had been lifted a few weeks before I arrived, but signs of it were still evident in the famished-looking inhabitants, and the empty shelves or barred doors of shops. Little food was available and prices were alpine. What could be bought at all had been secured as a result of a temporary truce with the Red partisans. In return for an agreement not to take the offensive against the Soviet districts on this front, the Soviet peasants now sold grain and vegetables to the hungry anti-Red troops.

I had my credentials for a visit to the front. My plan was to leave the city early next morning, and go toward the " White " lines, where the troops were merely holding their positions, without attempting any advance. Then I meant to branch off on one of the mountain lanes over which, I had been told, merchants smuggled their goods in and out of the Soviet regions.

To state precisely the manner in which, just as I had hoped, I

---

[1] Yenan was later occupied by the Red Army; is now (1937) the provisional Red capital.

did pass the last sentry and enter no-man's-land, might incur serious difficulties for the Kuomintang adherents who assisted me on my way. Suffice it to say that my experience proved once more that anything is possible in China, if it is done in the Chinese manner. For by seven o'clock next morning I had really left the last Kuomintang machine gun behind, and was walking through the thin strip of territory that divided Red from White.

With me was a single muleteer, whom I had hired in Yenan. He had agreed to carry my scant belongings—bedding-roll, a little food, two cameras and twenty-four rolls of film—to the first Red partisan outpost. I did not know whether he himself was a Red-bandit or a White-bandit—but bandit he certainly looked. All this territory having for several years alternately been controlled by armies of both colours, it was quite possible for him to have been either—or perhaps both. I decided it would be best not to ask impertinent questions, and merely docilely followed him, hoping for the best.

For four hours we followed a small winding stream and did not see any sign of human life. There was no road at all, but only the bed of the stream that rushed swiftly between high walls of rock, above which rose swift hills of loess. It was the perfect setting for the blotting-out of a too inquisitive foreign devil. A disturbing factor was the muleteer's frequently expressed admiration of my cowhide shoes.

" *Tao-la !* " he suddenly shouted around his ear, as the rock walls at last gave way and opened out into a narrow valley, green with young wheat. " We have arrived ! "

Relieved, I gazed beyond him and saw in the side of a hill a loess village, where blue smoke curled from the tall, clay chimneys that stood up like long fingers against the face of the cliff. In a few minutes we were there.

A young farmer wearing a turban of white towelling on his head, and a revolver strapped to his waist, came out and looked at me in astonishment. Who was I and what did I want ?

" I am an American journalist," I said. " I want to see the local chief of the Poor People's League."

He looked at me blankly and replied, " *Hai p'a !* "

Now *hai p'a* in any Chinese I had ever heard had only one meaning, " I'm afraid ! " If he is afraid, I thought to myself, what the devil am I supposed to feel ? But, anyway, his appearance belied his words: he looked completely self-assured. He turned to the *lofu*, and asked him who I was.

The muleteer repeated what I had said, adding a few flourishes of his own. With relief, I saw the young farmer's face soften and then I noticed that he was really a good-looking young man, with fine bronzed skin, and good white teeth. He did not seem to belong to the race of timid peasants of China elsewhere. There was a challenge in his sparkling merry eyes, and a certain bravado. He slowly moved his hand away from his revolver butt and smiled.

" I am that man," he said. " I am the chief. Come inside and drink some hot tea."

These Shensi hill people have a dialect of their own, full of slurred colloquialisms, but they understand *pai-hua*, or mandarin Chinese, and most of their own speech is quite comprehensible to an outlander. After a few more attempts at conversation with the chief, he began to show understanding, and we made good progress. Occasionally into our talk, however, would creep this *hai p'a* business, but for a while I was too disconcerted to ask him just *what* he feared. When I finally did probe into the matter, I discovered that *hai p'a* in the dialect of the Shensi hills is the equivalent of *pu chih-tao* in mandarin Chinese. It simply means " don't understand." My satisfaction at this discovery was considerable.

Seated on a felt-covered *k'ang* I told my host more about myself, and my plans. In a short time he seemed reassured. I wanted to go to An Tsai—the county seat—where I then believed Soviet Chairman Mao Tse-tung to be. Could he give me a guide and a muleteer ?

Certainly, certainly, he agreed, but I should not think of moving in the heat of day. The sun had already climbed to its zenith, it was really very hot, I looked tired, and, meanwhile, had I eaten ? Actually I was ravenous, and without any further ceremony I accepted this invitation to a first meal with a " Red-bandit." My muleteer was anxious to return to Yenan, and, paying him off, I bade him good-bye. It was a farewell to my last link with the White world for many weeks to come. I had crossed the Red Rubicon.

I was now at the mercy of Mr. Liu Lung-huo—Liu the Dragon Fire—as I learned the young peasant was called, and likewise at the mercy of his tough-looking comrades, who had begun to drift in from neighbouring *yao-fangs*. Similarly clad and armed, they all looked at me curiously and laughed at my preposterous accent.

Liu offered me tobacco, wine and tea, and plied me with numerous questions. He and his friends examined with close interest, interrupted by exclamations of approval, my camera, my shoes, my woollen stockings, the fabric of my cotton shorts, and (with lengthy admiration) the zipper on my khaki shirt. The general impression seemed to prevail that, however ridiculous it might look, the ensemble evidently served its purposes well enough. I did not know just what " Communism " might mean to these men, in practice, and I was prepared to see my belongings rapidly " Communized "—but of course nothing of the sort occurred. As nearly as I could ascertain, the object of the minute examination I underwent (and it was much pleasanter than the customs examination you submit to on other frontiers) was for the purpose of strengthening a previously held conviction that the foreign devil is incalculable.

In an hour a vast platter of scrambled eggs arrived, accompanied by steamed rolls, boiled millet, some cabbage, and a little roast pork. My host apologized for the simplicity of the fare, and I for an inordinate appetite. Which latter was quite beside the point, as I had to punt my chopsticks at a lively pace to keep up with the good fellows of the Poor People's League.

Dragon Fire assured me that An Tsai was " only a few steps," and though I was uneasy about it I could do nothing but wait, as he insisted. When finally a youthful guide appeared, accompanied by a muleteer, it was already past four in the afternoon. Before leaving, I ventured to pay Mr. Liu for his food, but he indignantly refused.

" You are a foreign guest," he explained, " and you have business with our Chairman, Mao. Moreover, your money is no good." Glancing at the bill I held out to him, he asked, " Haven't you any Soviet money ? " When I replied in the negative he counted out a dollar's worth of Soviet paper notes. " Here—you will need this on the road."

Mr. Liu accepted a Kuomintang dollar in exchange; I thanked him again, and climbed up the road behind my guide and muleteer.

" Well," I said to myself as I panted up the hill, " so far, so good." I had crashed the Red gates. How simple an operation it had been !

But ahead of me was a narrow escape and an incident which was later to nourish the rumour that I had been kidnapped and killed by bandits. And, as a matter of fact, bandits—not Red but White—were already trailing me behind those silent walls of loess.

PART TWO

THE ROAD TO THE RED CAPITAL

1

Chased by White-bandits

" Down with the landlords who eat our flesh ! "
" Down with the militarists who drink our blood ! "
" Down with the traitors who sell China to Japan ! "
" Welcome the United Front with all anti-Japanese armies ! "
" Long live the Chinese Revolution ! "
" Long live the Chinese Red Army ! "
It was under these somewhat disturbing exhortations, emblazoned in bold black characters, that I was destined to spend my first night in Red territory.

But it was not in An Tsai and not under the protection of any Red soldiers. For, as I had feared, we did not reach An Tsai that day, but by sunset had arrived only at a little village that lay nestled in the curve of a river, with hills brooding darkly on every side. Several layers of slate-roofed houses rose up from the lip of the stream, and it was on their mud walls that the slogans were chalked. Fifty or sixty peasants and staring children poured out to greet my caravan of one donkey.

My young guide—an emissary of the Poor People's League— decided to deposit me here. One of his cows had recently calved, he said; there were wolves in the neighbourhood, and he had to get back to his charges. An Tsai was still ten miles distant and we could not get there easily in the dark. He turned me over for safe-keeping to the chairman of the local branch of the Poor People's League. Both guide and muleteer refused any compensation for their services—either in White money or Red.

The chairman was a youth in his early twenties who wore a faded blue cotton jacket under a brown open face, and a pair of white trousers above a pair of leathery bare feet. He welcomed me and was very kind. He offered me a room in the village meeting-house, and had hot water brought to me, and a bowl of millet. But I declined the dark evil-smelling room, and petitioned for the use of two dismantled doors. Laying these on a couple of benches, I unrolled my blankets and made my bed in the open. It was a gorgeous night, with a clear sky spangled with northern stars, and the waters in a little falls below me murmured of peace and

tranquillity. Exhausted from the long walk I fell asleep immediately.

When I opened my eyes again dawn was just breaking. The
chairman was standing over me, shaking my shoulder. Of course
I was startled, and I sat up at once, fully awake.

" What is it ? " I demanded.

" You had better leave a little early. There are bandits near
here, and you ought to get to An Tsai quickly."

Bandits ? It was on my tongue to reply that I had in fact come
precisely to meet these so-called bandits, when I suddenly
realized what he meant. He was not talking about Reds, he
meant " White-bandits." I got up without further persuasion.
I did not want anything to happen to me so ridiculous as being
kidnapped by White-bandits in Soviet China.

The reader is entitled to some explanation. White-bandits were
in the Kuomintang's terminology called *min-t'uan,* or " people's
corps," just as Red-bandits were in Soviet terminology called
yu-chi-tui, or " Red partisans." In an effort to combat peasant
uprisings, these *min-t'uan* forces have increasingly been organized
by the Kuomintang. They function as an organic part of the *pao-
chia* system, an ancient method of controlling the peasantry
which is now being widely imposed both by the Kuomintang in
China and the Japanese in Manchukuo.

Pao-chia literally means " guaranteed armour." The system
thus known requires that every ten peasant families must have a
headman, through whom their respectability is established to the
satisfaction of the local magistrate. It is a mutual-guarantee
system, so that for any offence committed by one member of a
pao-chia the whole of any part of the group can be held responsible. This was also the way the Mongols and Manchus ruled
China as their empire.

As a measure for preventing the organization of peasant opposition it is almost unbeatable. Since headmen of the *pao-chia* are
nearly always rich farmers, landlords, pawnbrokers, or moneylenders—most zealous of subjects—it is natural that they are
not inclined to " guarantee " any tenant or debtor peasants of a
rebellious turn of mind. Yet not to be guaranteed is a serious
matter indeed. An unguaranteed man can be thrown in jail on
any pretext, as a " suspicious character."

This means in effect that the whole peasantry is placed at the mercy of the gentry, who at any time can ruin a man by refusing to guarantee him. Now, among the functions of the *pao-chia*, and a very important one, is the collection of taxes for the maintenance of the *min-t'uan*. The *min-t'uan* is selected, organized and commanded by the landlords and gentry. Its primary duties are to fight Communism, to help collect rents and share-crop debts, to collect loans and interest, and to support the local magistrates' efforts to gather in the ever-increasing taxes.

Hence it happened that, when the Red Army occupied a territory, its first as well as its last enemy was the *min-t'uan*. For the *min-t'uan* had no base except in the landlords who paid them, and of course they lost that base when the Reds came in. The real class-warfare of China was best seen in the struggles between *min-t'uan* and Red partisans, for here very often was a direct armed conflict between landlords and their former tenants and debtors. *Min-t'uan* mercenaries numbered hundreds of thousands and were most important auxiliaries of the some 2,000,000 nominally anti-Red troops of China.

Now, although there was a truce between the Red Army and the Kuomintang Army on this front, attacks by the *min-t'uan* on the Red partisan brigades continued intermittently. In Sian, Lochuan, and Yenan, I had heard that many landlords who had fled to these cities were now financing or personally leading the White-bandits to operate in the Soviet border districts. Taking advantage of the absence of the main Red forces, they made frequent raids into Red territory, burning and looting villages, and killing peasants. Leaders were carried off to the White districts, where generous rewards were given for such " Communist " captives by the landlords and White officers.

Interested primarily in *revanche* and quick cash returns on their adventures, the *min-t'uan* are credited with the most destructive work of the Red-White wars. I at any rate had no wish to test out the White-bandits' " foreign policy " on myself. Although my belongings were few, I felt certain that the little cash and clothing I had, together with my cameras, would prove prizes too tempting for them to overlook, if it only required the erasure of a lone foreign devil to possess them.

Hastily swallowing some hot tea and wheat cakes I set off with another guide and muleteer contributed by the chairman. For an hour we followed the bed of the stream, occasionally passing small cave-villages, where heavy-furred native dogs growled menacingly at me and child sentinels came out to demand our road pass. Then we reached a lovely pool of still water set in a natural basin hollowed from great rocks, and there I saw my first Red warrior.

He was alone except for a pretty white pony which stood grazing beside the stream, and wearing a vivid silky-blue saddle-blanket with a yellow star on it. The young man had been bathing, and at our approach he jumped up quickly, pulling on a sky-blue coat and a turban of white towelling, on which was fixed a red star. A mauser hung at his hip, with a red tassel dangling bravely from its wooden combination holster-stock. With his hand on his gun he waited for us to come up to him, and demanded our business from the guide. The latter having produced his road pass, and briefly explained how I had been cast upon him, the warrior looked at me curiously for further elucidation.

" I have come to interview Mao Tse-tung," I offered; " I understand he is at An Tsai. How much farther have we to go ? "

" Chairman Mao ? " he inquired slowly. " No, he is not at An Tsai." Then he peered behind us and asked if I were alone. Having convinced himself that I was, his reserve dropped from him, he smiled as if at some secret amusement, and said, " I am going to An Tsai. I'll just go along with you to the district Government."

He walked his pony beside me and I volunteered more details about myself, and ventured some inquiries about him. I learned that he was in the Political Defence Bureau (Gaypayoo), and was on patrol duty along this frontier. And the horse ? It was a " gift " from Young Marshal Chang Hsueh-liang. He told me that the Reds had captured over 1,000 horses from Chang's troops in recent battles in north Shensi. I learned further that he was called Yao, that he was twenty-two years old, and that he had been a Red for six years. Six years ! What tales he must have to tell !

I liked him. He was an honest-looking youth, rather well made, with a shock of glistening black hair under his red star. Meeting him in the lonely valley was reassuring. In fact I even neglected to question him about the bandits, for we were soon discussing the Red Army's spring march into Shansi. In return for my account of the effect it had produced in Peking, he told me of his own experiences in that astonishing " Anti-Japanese Expedition," in which the Red Army column had collected 15,000 new followers in a single month.

In a couple of hours we had reached An Tsai, which lay opposite the Fu Ho, a sub-tributary of the Yellow River. A big town on the map, An Tsai turned out to be little but the pretty shell of its wall. The streets were completely deserted and everything stood in crumbling ruins. My first thought was that these were the evidences of pillage and vandalism. But closer inspection showed no signs of burning and it was clear enough that the ruins were ancient and could not have been made by the Reds.

" The town was completely destroyed over a decade ago by a great flood," Yao explained. " The whole city went swimming."

An Tsai's inhabitants had not rebuilt the city, but lived now in the face of a great stone cliff, honey-combed with *yao-fang*, a little beyond the walls. Upon arrival we discovered, however, that the Red Army detachment stationed there had been dispatched to chase bandits, while members of the district Soviet had gone to Pai Chia P'ing, a near-by hamlet, to render a report to a provincial commissioner. Yao volunteered to escort me to Pai Chia P'ing—" Hundred Family Peace "—which we reached at dusk.

I had already been in Soviet territory a day and a half, yet I had seen no signs of war-time distress, had met but one Red soldier, and a populace that universally seemed to be pursuing its agrarian tasks in complete composure. Yet I was not to be misled by appearances. I remembered how, during the Sino-Japanese war at Shanghai in 1932, Chinese peasants had gone on tilling their fields in the very midst of battle, with apparent unconcern. So that when, just as we rounded a corner to enter " Hundred Family Peace," and I heard the most awful and blood-curdling yells directly above me, I was not entirely unprepared.

Looking toward the sound of the fierce battle-cries, I saw, standing on a ledge above the road, in front of a row of barrack-like houses, a dozen peasants brandishing spears, pikes and a few

rifles in the most uncompromising of attitudes. It seemed that
the question of my fate as a blockade-runner—whether I was to
be given the firing squad as an imperialist, or to be welcomed as
an honest inquirer—was about to be settled without further
delay.

I must have turned a comical face toward Yao, for he burst
into laughter. " *Pu p'a !* " he chuckled. " Don't be afraid. They
are only some partisans—*practising*. There is a Red partisan
school here. Don't be alarmed ! "

Later on I learned that the curriculum for partisans includes
this rehearsal of ancient Chinese war-cries, just as in the days of
feudal tourneys described in *All Men Are Brothers*. And having
experienced a certain frigidity of spine as an unwitting subject of
the technique, I can testify that it is still very effective in intimi-
dating an enemy. Shouted during a surprise attack in the dark,
when partisans prefer to act, these cries must be utterly terrifying.

I had just sat down and begun an interview with a Soviet
functionary to whom Yao had introduced me in Pai Chia P'ing,
when a young commander, wearing a Sam Browne belt, stumbled
up on a sweating horse, and plunged to the ground. He looked
curiously at me. And it was from him that I heard the full details
of my own adventure.

The new arrival was named Pien, and he was commandant of
the An Tsai Red Guard. He announced that he had just returned
from an encounter with a force of about a hundred *min-t'uan*. A
little peasant boy—a " Young Vanguard "—had run several
miles and arrived almost exhausted at An Tsai, to warn them
that *min-t'uan* had invaded the district. And that their leader
was a really *white* bandit !—a foreign devil—*myself* !

" I at once took a mounted detachment over a mountain
short-cut, and in an hour we sighted the bandits," Pien recounted. " They were following you "—he pointed at me—
" only about two *li*. But we surrounded them, attacked in a
valley, and captured some, including two of their leaders, and
several horses. The rest escaped toward the frontier." As he
concluded his brief report, some of his command filed into the
courtyard, leading several of the captured mounts.

I began to wonder if he really thought I *was* leading the *min-
t'uan*. Had I escaped from Whites—who, had they seized me in

no-man's-land, undoubtedly would have called me a Red—only to be captured by the Reds and accused of being a White ?

But presently a slender young officer appeared, ornamented with a heavy black beard. He came up and addressed me in a soft cultured voice. " Hello," he said, " are you looking for somebody ? "

He had spoken in *English* !

And in a moment I learned that he was Chou En-lai, the " notorious " Red commander, who had once been an honours student in a missionary school. Here at last my reception was decided.

2

The Insurrectionist

AFTER I had talked for a few minutes with Chou En-lai, and explained who I was, he arranged for me to spend the night in Pai Chia P'ing, and asked me to come next morning to his head-quarters, in a near-by village.

I sat down to dinner with a section of the Communications Department, which was stationed here, and I met a dozen young men who were billeted in Pai Chia P'ing. Some of them were teachers in the partisan school, one was a radio operator, and some were officers of the Red Army. Our meal consisted of boiled chicken, unleavened wholewheat bread, cabbage, millet, and potatoes, of which I ate heartily. But as usual there was nothing to drink but hot water and I could not touch it. I was famished with thirst.

The food was served—delivered is the word—by two nonchalant young lads wearing uniforms several sizes too large for them, and peaked Red caps with long peaks that kept flapping down over their eyes. They looked at me sourly at first, but after a few minutes I managed to provoke a friendly grin from one of them. Emboldened by this success, I called to him as he went past. " *Wei*," I demanded, " bring us some cold water."

The youth simply ignored me. In a few minutes I tried the other one, with no better result.

Then I saw that Li Ko-nung, head of the communications section, was laughing at me behind his thick-lensed goggles. He plucked my sleeve. " You can call him ' little devil,' " he advised, " or you can call him comrade—but you cannot call him *wei*! In here everybody is a comrade. These lads are Young Vanguards, and they are only here because they are revolutionaries and volunteer to help us. They are not servants. They are future Red warriors."

Just then the cold water did arrive.

" Thank you," I said apologetically, "—comrade ! "

The Young Vanguard looked at me boldly. " Never mind that," he said, " you don't thank a comrade for a thing like that ! "

But these lads were wonderful, I thought. I had never before seen so much personal dignity in any Chinese youngsters. This first encounter was only the beginning of a series of surprises that the Young Vanguards were to give me, for as I penetrated deeper into the Soviet districts I was to discover in these red-cheeked " little Red devils "—cheerful, gay, energetic and loyal—the living spirit of an astonishing crusade of youth.

It was one of those Sons of Lenin, in fact, who escorted me in the morning to Chou En-lai's headquarters. That turned out to be a bombproof hut, surrounded by many others exactly like it, in which farmers dwelt undismayed by the fact that they were in a battle area, and that in their midst was the Red commander of the Eastern Front. Was it the secret of the Red Army's alleged popularity with the peasantry, I wondered, that it was able to move into districts like this so unobtrusively ? The quartering of a few troops in the vicinity did not seem to have disturbed the rustic serenity at all.

Before the quarters of Chou En-lai, for whose head Chiang Kai-shek had offered $80,000, there was but one sentry.

Inside I saw that the room was clean but furnished in the barest fashion. A mosquito net hanging over the clay *k'ang* was the only " luxury " observable. A couple of iron dispatch-boxes stood at the foot of it, and a little wooden table served as desk. Chou was bending over this, reading radiograms, when the sentry announced my arrival.

" I have a report that you are a reliable journalist, friendly to the Chinese people, and that you can be trusted to tell the truth," said Chou. " This is all we want to know. It does not matter to us that you are not a Communist. We will welcome any journalist who comes to see the Soviet districts. It is not we, but the Kuomintang, who prevents it. You can write about anything you see and you will be given every help to investigate the Soviet districts."

I was a little surprised and a little sceptical of the sincerity of this *carte blanche*. I had expected, even if allowed to travel in the Soviet districts, that certain restrictions would be placed upon me concerning photography, or collecting notes, or holding conversations. It sounded too ideal; there must be a foil somewhere. . . .

Evidently the " report " about me had come from the Communists' secret headquarters in Sian. The Reds have radio communication with all important cities of China, including Shanghai, Hankow, Nanking and Tientsin. Despite frequent seizures of Red radio sets in the White cities, the Kuomintang has never succeeded in breaking communications with the Red areas for very long. According to Chou, the Kuomintang has never cracked the Red Army's codes since they first established a radio department, with equipment captured from the White troops.

Chou's radio station was erected only a short distance from his headquarters. Through it he was in touch with all important points in the Soviet areas, and with every front. He even had direct communication with Commander-in-Chief Chu Teh, whose forces were then stationed hundreds of miles to the south-west, on the Szechuan-Tibetan border. There was a Red radio school in Pao An, temporary Soviet capital in the North-west, where about ninety students were being trained as expert radio engineers. They picked up the daily broadcasts from Nanking, Shanghai and Tokyo, and furnished news to the Press of Soviet China.

Chou squatted before his little desk and put aside his radiograms—mostly reports from units stationed at various points along the Yellow River, opposite Shansi province, the Reds' " Eastern Front." He began working out a suggested itinerary for me. When he had finished he handed me a paper containing items covering a trip of ninety-two days.

" This is my recommendation," he said, " but whether you follow it is your own business. I think you will find it an interesting journey."

But ninety-two days ! And almost half of them to be spent merely in travel. What was there to be seen ? Were the Red districts so extensive as that ? I said nothing, but made mental reservations about the itinerary. Actually, I was to spend much longer than he had suggested, and in the end to leave with reluctance because I had seen so little.

Chou promised me the use of a horse to carry me to Pao An, three days distant, and arranged for me to leave the following morning, when I could accompany part of the communications corps that was returning to the provisional capital. I learned that Mao Tse-tung and other Soviet functionaries were there now, and Chou agreed to send a radio message to them, telling of my arrival.

During my conversation I had been studying Chou with deep interest, for in China, like many Red leaders, he was as much a legend as a man. He was of slender stature, of medium height, with a slight wiry frame, boyish in appearance despite his long black beard, and with large warm deep-set eyes. There was certainly a kind of magnetism about him that seemed to derive from a curious combination of shyness, personal charm and the complete assurance of command. His English was somewhat hesitant but fairly correct, and I was amazed when he told me he had not used it for five years.

I knew something about Chou from a former schoolmate, and from Kuomintang men who had worked with him in days of the Great Revolution of 1925–7, which is called the Chinese " Nationalist Revolution " by foreigners. From Chou En-lai I was to learn much more. He interested me especially for one reason. He was evidently that rarest of all creatures in China, a pure intellectual in whom action was perfectly co-ordinated with knowledge and conviction. He was a scholar turned insurrectionist.

Son of a great Mandarin family, grandfather a high official in the Manchu dynasty, father a brilliant teacher, mother extraordinary (a well-read woman who actually *liked* modern literature !), Chou En-lai himself seemed destined for a career as a scholar, for from early childhood he showed marked literary genius. But, like many others of his generation, educated in a period of national awakening, his interest in literature was deflected. When, after the First Revolution (1911), China's innocent " Literary Renaissance " began to germinate more serious growths, Chou En-lai was swept into the movement for social revolution which was to shake China to the depths of its soul.

He had learned English and got a " liberal " education in Nankai Middle School, and later in Nankai University, an American missionary-backed enterprise in Tientsin. Outstanding student of his class, during three of his years at Nankai he paid his way by scholarships. Then came Japan's " twenty-one

Demands," Yuan Shih-k'ai's attempt to restore the Empire, the beginning of revolt throughout China, the movement for democracy and social change, and the student rebellion of 1919. As a student leader, Chou was arrested and imprisoned for a year in Tientsin. Among other young patriots jailed with him, was a radical girl student of a Tientsin normal college—the woman who is now his wife and comrade.

Released, Chou went to France. Influenced by post-war Communism, he helped organize the Chinese Communist Party in Paris, became a founder of the organization simultaneously formed in China. Two years of study in Paris, a few months in England, to France again, and then a year of study in Germany. In 1924 he returned to China, already a well-known revolutionary organizer, and at once joined Sun Yat-sen at Canton, who was then preparing for the, Nationalist Revolution, in co-operation with the Chinese Communist Party and with Soviet Russia.

At twenty-six, Chou became a leading figure in the political life of Canton, was made secretary of famed Whampoa Academy, and confidant of General Bleucher, then Whampoa's No. 1 Russian adviser, now commander of the Soviet Union's Far Eastern Red Army. To Chiang Kai-shek, then president of Whampoa, the youthful Red was anathema. But Chiang was nevertheless obliged to appoint him chief of Whampoa Academy's political department, because of Chou's great influence with the radical cadets.

During 1925, 1926, and 1927, the Northern Expedition was under way, with Chiang Kai-shek as Commander-in-Chief, selected jointly by the Kuomintang and the Communists. Chou En-lai was ordered to prepare an insurrection and help the Nationalist Army seize Shanghai. A youth of twenty-eight, with no formal military training, little experience with the working class (from which, as son of a big bourgeois family, he had been isolated), with no guidebook to show him how to make an insurrection, and none to advise him (the chief Russian advisers being with Chiang Kai-shek), Chou arrived in Shanghai equipped only with a revolutionary determination and a strong theoretical knowledge of Marxism.

Within three months the Communist Party had organised

600,000 workers, and was able to call a general strike. The response was unanimous, and a terrifying experience to the smug populace of this greatest stronghold of foreign imperialism in China. But the insurrection failed to materialize. Unarmed and untrained, the workers did not know how to go about " seizing the city." They had to learn empirically the necessity of an armed nucleus of workers. And the militarists accommodated them.

Underestimating the significance of the first and then of a second strike, the old northern warlords merely cut off a number of heads, but failed to halt the labour movement. Chou En-lai and the famous Shanghai labour leaders, Chao Shi-yen, Ku Shun-chang, and Lo Yi-ming, now succeeded in organizing 50,000 pickets, and in the French concession secured premises where military training was secretly given to 2,000 cadres. With mausers smuggled into the city, an " iron band " of 300 marksmen was trained, and this was the only armed force these Shanghai workers had.

On March 21, 1927, the Communists called a general strike which closed all the industries of Shanghai, and put 600,000 workers, organized and militant for the first time in their lives, behind the barricades of revolution. They seized first the police stations, next the arsenal, then the garrison, and after that, victory. Five thousand workers were armed, six battalions of revolutionary troops created, and a " citizens' Government " was proclaimed.

It was the most remarkable *coup d'état* in modern Chinese history.

Thus it happened that Chiang Kai-shek, arriving a few days later at the outskirts of Shanghai, found his battle already won, and was able to enter the Chinese city[1] and accept power from a triumphant workers army. And thus it happened that when, about a month later, Chiang Kai-shek staged his own Right *coup d'état*, and the killing of radicals began, first on his list of condemned was this dangerous youth who had given him his victory—but who, the Generalissimo realized, might also take it away from him. And thus also began Chou En-lai's life as a

---

[1] The foreign concessions were not, of course, attacked, the Nationalists occupying only the Chinese parts of Shanghai.

fugitive from the Kuomintang, and as a leader of the Third Revoluton, the revolution that raised the Red banner in China.

Chao Shi-yen, Ku Shun-chang, Lo Yi-ming, and Ch'ên Yen-nien (son of Ch'ên Tu-hsiu, a founder of the Communist Party of China, and now imprisoned at Nanking), and dozens more of Chou En-lai's close co-workers in the Shanghai uprising, were seized and executed. The toll of the " Shanghai massacre " is estimated at 5,000 lives. Chou En-lai himself was captured by Chiang Kai-shek's 2nd Division, and General Pai Ch'ung-hsi (now ruler of Kuangsi) issued an order for his execution. But the brother of the division commander had been Chou's student at Whampoa, and he helped Chou to escape.

The Insurrectionist fled to Wuhan, then to Nanchang, where he helped organize the famous August First Uprising, the historical beginning of the Red Army of China. Next he went to Swatow, where Red workers seized the great seaport of South China, and under Chou En-lai held it for ten days against assaults from both foreign gunboats and the native troops of militarists ; and then on to Canton, and the organization of the famous Canton Commune.

With the failure and defeat of the Canton Commune, Chou was obliged to work underground—until 1931, when he succeeded in " running the blockade " and entered the Soviet districts of Kiangsi and Fukien. There he was made political commissar to Chu Teh, Commander-in-Chief of the Red Army. Later on he became vice-chairman of the revolutionary military council, an office he still held when I met him. There had been years of exhausting struggle in the South, with rifles, machine guns, and spades pitted against squadrons of bombers, against tanks and armoured cars, against all the wealth of the great cities behind their enemy, in a heroic effort to save the little Soviet republic, which lacked a seaport, which lacked even salt, and had to make up for it with the iron in men's wills; severe illness and narrow escapes from death; and then the Long March to the new Red base in the North-west.

Renunciation of the key-philosophy of ancient China, the philosophy of umbrella-truces and face-saving; matchless capacity for punishment and hardship; selfless adherence to an ideology, and a tenacity that did not know when it was beaten—

all these seemed implicit in this story of the Red Army and of one man who helped make it. Chou must be a fanatic, I told myself, and I looked for the fatal gleam of retina. But if it was there I failed to discern it. He talked on slowly, quietly, thoughtfully.

Chou left me, then, with an impression of a cool, logical, and empirical mind. His mildly uttered statements made a singular contrast against the background of nine years of defamation of the Communists by Kuomintang propaganda describing them as " ignorant bandits," " marauders," and by other choice epithets.

Somehow, as he walked with me back along the quiet country lane to Hundred Family Peace, through fields of sesame and ripe wheat and the nodding ears of corn, he did not seem to fit any of the well-worn descriptions of the Red-bandits. He seemed, on the contrary, genuinely light-hearted and as full of the love of life as the " little Red Devil " who trudged manfully beside him, and around whose shoulder he had thrown a fatherly arm. He seemed very much like that youth who used to take the feminine lead in the college plays at Nankai—because in those days Chou was handsome and had a figure willowy as a girl's.

3

Something about Ho Lung

NEXT morning at six I set out with a squad of about forty
youths of the communications corps, who were escorting a
caravan of goods to Pao An.

I found that only myself, Fu Chin-kuei, an emissary from the
Waichiaopu—the Reds' own " Foreign Office "—and Li Chiang-
lin, a Red commander, were mounted. It may not be precisely
the word: Fu had a privileged perch on a stout but already
heavily laden mule; Li Chiang-lin rode an equally over-burdened
ass; and I was vaguely astride the lone horse, which at times
I could not be quite sure was really there at all.

My animal had a quarter-moon back and a camel-gait. His
poor enfeebled legs wobbled dangerously, and I expected him
at any moment to buckle up and breathe his last. He was
especially disconcerting as we crept along the narrow trails
hewn from steep cliffs that rose up from the river bed we followed. It seemed to me that any sudden shift of my weight over
his sunken flanks would send us both hurtling to the rocky
gorge below.

Li Chiang-lin laughed down from his pyramid of luggage at
my discomfiture. " That's a fine saddle you are sitting, *t'ung-
chih*,[1] but what is that underneath it ? "

It was not my rôle to complain, for who was I to be riding,
anyway; but at this gibe I could not resist commenting: " Just
tell me this, Li Chiang-lin, how can you fight on dogs like these ?
Is this how you mount your Red cavalry ? "

" *Pu-shih !* No, you will see ! Is your steed *huai-la* ? Well, it's
just because we have bad ones like this at the rear that our
cavalry is unbeatable at the front ! If there is a horse that is fat
and can run, not even Mao Tse-tung can keep him from the
front ! Only the worn-out dogs we use in our rear. And that's
how it is with everything: guns, food, clothing, horses, mules,
camels, sheep—the best go to our Red fighters ! If it's a horse
you want, *t'ung-chih*, go to the front ! "

I determined to follow his advice as soon as I could.

[1] " Comrade."

" But Li Chiang-lin, how is it you yourself are not at the front ? Are you *huai-la* also ? "

" *Huai-la*, me ? Never ! But it's easier to spare a good man from the front than a good horse ! "

And truly Commander Li seemed to be a good man, a good Bolshevik and a good story-teller. He had been a Red for ten years, and was a veteran of the famous Nanchang Uprising of 1927, when Communism first became an independent force in China. As I rode, walked, panted and thirsted up and down the broken hills of Shensi beside Commander Li, he recounted incidents and anecdotes one after another, and sometimes, when pressed again and again, even stooped to talk about himself.

He was still a young man, about thirty-one or thirty-two, and yet as he gradually unfolded his story you might think that he had already lived and died a dozen times. With him I began to discover a peculiar quality that I was to encounter repeatedly in this strange iron brotherhood of Chinese revolutionaries. Something that makes every man's suffering and triumph the collective burden or joy of all, some force that levels out individuals, loses them, makes them really forget their own identity and yet find it somehow in the kind of fierce freedom and rigour and hardship they share with others.

Well, it is improbable, this thing, if you know China ! Yet it is a fact, and later on I shall try to explain why.

Li Chiang-lin was a Hunanese and he was a middle-school student when the Great Revolution began. He entered the Kuomintang, and remained in it until the *coup d'état* of '27, after which he joined the Reds. In Hongkong he worked as a labour organizer for a while, under Teng Fa. Later on he entered the Soviet districts in Kiangsi, and became a partisan leader. In 1925 he had been sent by the Kuomintang with a propaganda committee, on most responsible work. It was their duty to see the bandit leader, Ho Lung—now known in the Kuomintang Press as the " infamous " Ho Lung, but then a leader whose adherence was much valued. Li Chiang-lin was delegated with his committee to win Ho Lung to the Kuomintang Nationalist cause.

" Ho Lung's men were not bandits, even then," Li told me, as we sat resting one day beneath some trees that stood beside

Cc

a cool stream. " His father had been a leader in the Kê Lao Hui,[1] and Ho Lung inherited his prestige, so that he became famous throughout Hunan when still a young man. Many stories are told by the Hunanese of his bravery as a youth.

" His father was a military officer in the Ch'ing dynasty, and one day he was invited to a dinner by his fellow officers. He took his son, Ho Lung, with him. His father was boasting of Ho Lung's fearlessness, and one of the guests decided to test it out. He fired off a gun under the table. They say that Ho Lung did not even blink !

" When we met him he had already been commissioned in the provincial army. He then controlled a territory through which rich opium caravans had to pass from Yunnan to Hankow, and he lived by taxing them, and did not rob the people. His followers did not rape nor carouse, like the troops of many warlord armies, and he did not let them smoke opium. They kept their rifles clean. But it was the custom there to offer opium to guests. Ho Lung himself did not smoke, but when we arrived he had opium pipes and opium brought to the *k'ang*, and over these we talked about revolution !

" The head of our propaganda committee was Chou Yi-chung, a Communist, who had some family connection with Ho Lung. We talked to him for three weeks. Ho Lung had not had much education, except in military affairs, but he was not an ignorant man. He quickly understood the meaning of the revolution, but he carefully deliberated, and consulted with his troops, before he at last agreed to join the Kuomintang.

" We established a party training school in his army, with Chou Yi-sung—who was later killed—as leader. Although it was a Kuomintang Nationalist training school, most of the propagandists were Communists. Many students entered the school and later became political leaders. Besides Ho Lung's army, the school furnished political commissioners for the 3rd Division, under Yuan Tso-ming, who was then commander of the left-route army. Yuan Tso-ming was assassinated by agents of T'ang Sheng-chih, and the 3rd Division was given to Ho Lung. His enlarged command was called the 20th Army, which became

---

[1] The " Elder Brother Society," a big secret organization with branches throughout rural China.

part of the main 4th Group Army, under the Leftist Kuomintang general, Chang Fa-kuei."

Li Chiang-lin said that Ho Lung did not join the Communist
Party until after the August First Uprising at Nanchang in 1927.
Until a short time before that he had remained loyal to the
Wuhan (Kuomintang) Government of Wang Ching-wei. But
when T'ang Sheng-chih, Ho Chien and others suppressed the
anti-landlord movement and began the infamous " peasant
massacre," in which Kuomintang militarists executed, not only
Communists, but thousands of peasant union leaders, workers
and students, Ho Lung turned decisively Red. He was from a
lowly peasant family himself, his sympathies were entirely with
the poor, and the slaughter enraged him.

Ho Chien, who is now Nanking's governor of Hunan, was
" the most brutal and savage of all the counter-revolutionary
generals," according to Li. " I do not know how many people
he killed—certainly tens of thousands. I know that in my own
district, Liu-yang hsien in Hunan, he killed more than 20,000
peasants, students and workers between April and June 1927.
I was there. I know. He is said to have killed 15,000 in his own
hsien, Liling."

I wondered how Li himself had escaped, and I asked him.
He pulled off his blue cotton jacket—he wore nothing beneath
it—and pointed to a long, jagged scar. " You see I didn't—
not entirely," he laughed.

" What happened to Ho Lung after Nanchang ? "

" His forces were defeated. He and Chu Teh moved next to
Swatow. They were defeated again. The remnant of his army
went into the interior, but Ho Lung escaped to Hongkong.
Later he smuggled himself to Shanghai, and then, disguised, he
returned to Hunan.

" It is said of Ho Lung that he established a Soviet district
in Hunan with one knife. This was early in 1928. Ho Lung was
in hiding in a village, plotting with members of the Kê Lao Hui,
when some Kuomintang tax-collectors arrived. Leading a few
villagers, he attacked the tax-collectors and killed them with
his own knife, and then disarmed the tax-collectors' guard.
From this adventure he got enough revolvers and rifles to arm
his first peasants' army."

Ho Lung's fame in the " Elder Brother Society " extends over all China. The Reds say that he can go unarmed into any village of the country, announce himself to the Kê Lao Hui, and form an army. The society's special ritual and language are quite difficult to master, but Ho Lung has the highest degrees and is said to have more than once enlisted an entire Kê Lao Hui branch in the Red Army. His eloquence as a speaker is well known in the Kuomintang. Li said that when he spoke he could " raise the dead to fight."

When Ho Lung's 2nd Front Red Army finally withdrew from the Hunan Soviet districts, in 1935, its rifles were reported to number more than 40,000, and this army underwent even greater hardships in its own Long March to the North-west than the main forces from Kiangsi. Thousands died on the snow mountains, and thousands more starved to death or were killed by Nanking bombs. Yet so great was Ho Lung's personal magnetism, and his influence throughout rural China, that many of his men stayed with him and died on the road, rather than desert, and thousands of poor men along the route of march joined in to help fill up the dwindling ranks. In the end he reached eastern Tibet, where he finally connected with Chu Teh, with about 20,000 men—most of them barefoot, half-starved, and physically exhausted. After several months of recuperation, these troops were now on the march again, into Kansu, where they were expected to arrive in a few weeks.

" What does Ho Lung look like ? " I asked Li.

" He is a big man, and strong as a tiger. Although he is now over fifty, he is still in excellent health. He never gets tired. They say he carried many of his wounded men on the march. Even when he was a Kuomintang general he lived as simply as his men. He cares nothing about personal possessions—except horses. He loves horses. Once he had a beautiful horse that he liked very much. It was captured by some enemy troops. Ho Lung went to battle to recover that horse. He got it back !

" Although he is impetuous, Ho Lung is very humble. Since he joined the Communists he has been faithful to the Party, and has never broken Party discipline. He always asks for criticism and listens carefully to advice. His sister is much like him—a big woman, with large feet. She has led Red troops in battle herself—and carried wounded men on her back. So has Ho Lung's wife."

Ho Lung's hatred of the rich has become legendary in China— a record which seems to trace back chiefly to the days when his Red partisans were first forming, and the Hunan Soviets had not yet been placed under full control of the Communist Party. Many peasants who had lost friends or relatives during Ho Chien's "peasant massacre," or who had been beaten or oppressed by the landlords after the reaction had regained full power under Ho Chien, joined Ho Lung in a spirit of fierce vengeance. It is said that landlords and gentry used to flee without further ado, even from places well guarded by Nanking troops, if Ho Lung was reported as far away as 200 *li*—for he was famous for the swiftness of his movements.

Some time ago Ho Lung arrested a Swiss missionary named Bosshard, and a military court " sentenced " him to eighteen months imprisonment for alleged espionage—probably no more than passing on information about the Red movements to the Kuomintang authorities, a practice of many missionaries. The Rev. Bosshard's sentence had still not been completed when Ho Lung began the Long March, but he was ordered to move with the army. He was finally released during the march, when his sentence expired, and was given travelling expenses to Yunnanfu. Rather to most people's surprise, the Rev. Bosshard brought out few harsh words about Ho Lung. On the contrary, he is reported to have remarked, " If the peasants knew what the Communists were like, none of them would run away."[1]

It was the noon halt, and we decided to bathe in the cool, inviting stream. We got in and lay on a long flat rock, while the shallow water rippled over us in cool sheets. Some peasants went past, driving a big cloud of sheep before them; overhead the sky was clear and blue. There was nothing but peace and beauty here, and it was that odd midday moment when the world for centuries has been like this, with only peace, beauty and contentment.

[1] Related to me by Dr. Joseph F. Rock, who talked to the Rev. Bosshard when he arrived in Yunnanfu.

Suddenly I asked Li Chiang-lin if he was married.

" I was," he said slowly. " My wife was killed in the South, by the Kuomintang."

I began to understand a little bit why the Chinese Communists have fought so long, so uncompromisingly, so un-Chinese-like. And as I trudged on for many more miles I was to learn still more about that from other Red companions.

4

Red Companions

NORTH SHENSI was one of the poorest parts of China I had seen, not excluding western Yunnan. There was no real land scarcity, but there was in many places a serious scarcity of real land—at least real farming land. Here in Shensi a peasant may own as much as 100 *mou*[1] of land and yet be a poor man. A landlord in this country has to possess at least several hundred *mou* of land, and even on a Chinese scale he cannot be considered rich unless his holdings are part of the limited and fertile valley land, where rice and other valued crops can be grown.

The farms of Shensi may be described as slanting, and many of them also as slipping, for landslides are frequent. The fields are mostly patches laid on the serried landscape, between crevices and small streams. The land seems rich enough in many places, but the crops grown are strictly limited by the steep gradients, both in quantity and quality. There are few genuine mountains, only endless broken hills, hills as interminable as a sentence by James Joyce, and even more tiresome. Yet the effect is often strikingly like Picasso, the sharp-angled shadowing and colouring changing miraculously with the sun's wheel, and toward dusk it becomes a magnificent sea of purpled hilltops with dark velvety folds running down, like the pleats on a mandarin skirt, to ravines that seem bottomless.

After the first day I rode little, not so much out of pity for the languishing nag, but because everyone else marched. Li Chianglin was the oldest warrior of the company. Most of the others were lads in their teens, hardly more than children. One of these was nicknamed " Lao Kou," the Old Dog, and walking with him I asked why he had joined the Reds.

He was a southerner and had come all the way from the Fukien Soviet districts, on the Red Army's 6,000 mile expedition which foreign military experts refused to believe possible. Yet here was Old Dog, seventeen years old, and actually looking fourteen. He had made that march and thought nothing of it.

[1] One Chinese *mou* is about a sixth of an English acre.

He said that he was prepared to walk another 25,000 *li* if the Red Army did.

With him was a lad nicknamed Local Cousin, and he had walked, almost as far, from Kiangsi. Local Cousin was sixteen.

Did they like the Red Army ? I asked. They looked at me in genuine amazement. It had evidently never occurred to either of them that anyone could not like the Red Army.

" The Red Army has taught me to read and to write," said Old Dog. " Here I have learned to operate a radio, and how to aim a rifle straight. The Red Army helps the poor."

" Is that all ? "

" It is good to us and we are never beaten," added Local Cousin. " Here everybody is the same. It is not like the White districts, where poor people are slaves of the landlords and the Kuomintang. Here everybody fights to help the poor, and to save China. The Red Army fights the landlords and the White-bandits and the Red Army is anti-Japanese. Why should anyone not like such an army as this ? "

There was a peasant lad who had joined the Reds in Szechuan, and I asked him why he had done so. He told me that his parents were poor farmers, with only four *mou* of land (less than an acre), which wasn't enough to feed him and his two sisters. When the Reds came to his village, he said, all the peasants welcomed them, brought them hot tea and made sweets for them. The Red dramatists gave plays. It was a happy time. Only the landlords ran. When the land was re-distributed his parents received their share. So they were not sorry, but very glad, when he joined the poor people's army.

Another youth, about nineteen, had formerly been an iron-smith's apprentice in Hunan, and he was nicknamed " T'ieh Lao-hu," the Iron Tiger. The Reds arrived in his district, and he dropped bellows, pans and apprenticeship, and, clad only in a pair of sandals and trousers, he hurried off to enlist. Why ? Because he wanted to fight the masters who starved their apprentices, and to fight the landlords who robbed his parents. He was fighting for the revolution, which would free the poor. The Red Army was good to people and did not rob them and beat them like the White armies. He pulled up his trouser leg and displayed a long, white scar, his souvenir of battle.

There was another youth from Fukien, one from Chekiang, several more from Kiangsi and Szechuan, but the majority were natives of Shensi and Kansu. Some had " graduated " from the Young Vanguards, and (though they looked like infants) had already been Reds for years. Some had joined the Red Army to fight Japan, two had enlisted to escape from slavery, three had deserted from the Kuomintang troops, but most of them had joined " because the Red Army was a revolutionary army, fighting landlords and imperialism."

Then I talked to a squad commander, who was an " older " man, of twenty-four. He had been in the Red Army since 1931. In that year his father and mother were killed by a Nanking bomber, which also destroyed his house, in Kiangsi. When he had gone home from the fields and found both his parents dead he had at once thrown down his hoe, bade his wife good-bye, and enlisted with the Communists. One of his brothers, a Red partisan, was killed in Kiangsi in 1935.

They were a heterogeneous lot, but more truly " national " in composition than ordinary Chinese armies, usually carefully segregated according to provinces. Their different provincial backgrounds and dialects did not seem to divide them, but became the subject of constant good-natured raillery. I never saw a serious quarrel among them. In fact, during all my travel in the Red districts, I was not to see a single fist-fight between Red soldiers, and among young men I thought that remarkable.

Though tragedy had touched the lives of nearly all of them, they were perhaps too young for it to have depressed them much. They seemed to me fairly happy, and perhaps the first consciously happy group of Chinese proletarians I had seen. Passive contentment is the common phenomenon in China, but the higher emotion of happiness, which implies a feeling of positiveness about existence, is rare indeed.

They sang nearly all day on the road, and their supply of songs was endless. Their singing was not done at a command, but was spontaneous, and they sang well. Whenever the spirit moved him, or he thought of an appropriate song, one of them would suddenly burst forth, and commanders and men joined in. They sang at night, too, and learned new folk-tunes from the peasants, who brought out their Shensi guitars.

What discipline they had seemed almost entirely self-imposed. When we passed wild apricot-trees on the hills there was an abrupt dispersal until everyone had filled his pockets, and somebody always brought me back a handful. Then, leaving the trees looking as if a great wind had struck through them, they moved back into order and quick-timed to make up for the loss. But, when we passed private orchards, nobody touched the fruit in them, and the grain and vegetables we consumed in the village were paid for in full.

As far as I could see, the peasants bore no resentment toward my Red companions. Instead they seemed on close terms of friendship, and very loyal—a fact probably not unconnected with a recent redivision of land and the abolition of taxes. They freely offered for sale what edibles they had, and accepted Soviet money without hesitation. When we reached a village at noon or sunset the chairman of the local Soviet promptly provided quarters, and designated ovens for our use. I frequently saw peasant women or their daughters volunteer to pull the bellows of the fire of our ovens, and laugh and joke with the Red warriors; in a very emancipated way for Chinese women—especially Shensi women.

On the last day, we stopped for lunch at a village in a green valley, and here all the children came round to examine the first foreign devil many of them had seen. I decided to catechize them.

" What is a Communist ? " I asked.

" He is a citizen who helps the Red Army fight the White-bandits and the Japanese," one youngster of nine or ten piped up.

" What else ? "

" He helps fight the landlords and the capitalists ! "

" But what is a capitalist ? " That silenced one child, but another came forward: " A capitalist is a man who does not work, but makes others work for him." Over-simplification, perhaps, but I went on:

" Are there any landlords or capitalists here ? "

" No ! " they all shrieked together. " They've all run away ! "

" Run away ? From what ? "

" From our Red Army ! "

" Our " army, a peasant child talking about " his " army ? Well, obviously it wasn't China, but, if not, what was it ? I decided it was incredible. Who could have taught them all this ?

Later on I was to discover who it was, when I examined the textbooks of Red China, and met old Santa-Claus Hsu Teh-lih, once president of a normal college in Hunan, now Soviet Commissioner of Education.

I was to meet him, in fact, that very afternoon, when our little caravan stepped down the last mountainside into the provisional capital of Red China.

PART THREE

IN "DEFENDED PEACE"

1

Soviet Strong Man

SMALL villages are numerous in the North-west, but towns of any size are infrequent. Except for the industries begun by the Reds it is completely agrarian and in places a semi-pastoral country. Thus it was quite breath-taking to ride out suddenly on the brow of the wrinkled hills and see stretched out below me in a green valley the ancient walls of Pao An, which means " Defended Peace."[1]

Pao An was once a frontier stronghold, during the T'ang and Kin dynasties, against the nomadic invaders to the north. Remains of its fortifications, flame-struck in that afternoon sun, could be seen flanking the narrow pass through which once emptied into this valley the conquering legions of the Mongols. There is an inner city, still, where the garrisons were once quartered; and a high defensive masonry, lately improved by the Reds, embraces about a square mile in which the present town is located.

Here at last I found the Red leader whom Nanking had been fighting for ten years—Mao Tse-tung, chairman of the " Chinese People's Soviet Republic," to employ the official title which had recently been adopted. The old cognomen, " Chinese Workers' and Peasants' Soviet Republic " was dropped when the Reds began their new policy of struggle for a " United Front."

Chou En-lai's radiogram had been received, and I was expected. A room was provided for me in the " Foreign Office," and I became temporarily a guest of the Soviet State. My arrival resulted in a phenomenal increase of the foreign population of Pao An. The other Occidental resident was a German known as Li Teh T'ung-chih—the " Virtuous Comrade Li." Of Li Teh, a former high officer in the German Army, and the only foreign military adviser ever with the Red Army (to Herr Hitler's extreme vexation), more later.

I met Mao soon after my arrival: a gaunt, rather Lincolnesque

[1] In December 1936 the Reds occupied Yenan (Fushih), north Shensi, and the capital was transferred there.

figure, above average height for a Chinese, somewhat stooped, with a head of thick black hair grown very long, and with large, searching eyes, a high-bridged nose and prominent cheek-bones. My fleeting impression was of an intellectual face of great shrewdness, but I had no opportunity to verify this for several days. Next time I saw him, Mao was walking hatless along the street at dusk, talking with two young peasants, and gesticulating earnestly. I did not recognize him until he was pointed out to me—moving along unconcernedly with the rest of the strollers, despite the $250,000 which Nanking had hung over his head.

I could write a book about Mao Tse-tung alone. I talked with him many nights, on a wide range of subjects, and I heard dozens of stories about him from soldiers and Communists. My written interviews with him total about 20,000 words. He told me of his childhood and youth, how he became a leader in the Kuomintang and the Nationalist Revolution, why he became a Communist, and how the Red Army grew. He described the Long March to the North-west and wrote a classical poem about it for me. He told me stories of many other famous Reds, from Chu Teh down to the youth who carried on his shoulders for the whole March the two iron dispatch-boxes that held the archives of the Soviet Government.

How can I select, from all the wealth of unexploited, unknown material, a few hundred words to tell you about this peasant-born intellectual turned revolutionary? I do not propose to attempt any such condensation. The story of Mao's life is a rich cross-section of a whole generation, an important guide to understanding the sources of action in China, and further on I shall include that full exciting record of personal history, just as he told it to me. But here I want to try to convey some subjective impressions, and a few facts of interest about him.

Do not suppose, first of all, that Mao Tse-tung could be the " saviour " of China. Nonsense. There will never be any one " saviour " of China. Yet undeniably you feel a certain force of destiny in him. It is nothing quick or flashy, but a kind of solid elemental vitality. You feel that whatever extraordinary there is in this man grows out of the uncanny degree to which he synthesizes and expresses the urgent demands of millions of Chinese, and especially the peasantry—those impoverished, underfed, exploited, illiterate, but kind, generous, courageous and just now rather rebellious human beings who are the vast majority of the Chinese people. If these demands and the movement which is pressing them forward are the dynamics which can regenerate China, then in this deeply historical sense Mao Tse-tung may possibly become a very great man.

But I do not intend to pronounce the verdicts of history. Meanwhile, Mao is of interest as a personality, apart from his political life, because, although his name is as familiar to many Chinese as that of Chiang Kai-shek, very little was known about him, and all sorts of strange legends existed about him. I was the first foreign newspaperman ever to interview him.

Mao has the reputation of a charmed life. He has been repeatedly pronounced dead by Nanking, only to return to the news columns a few days later, as active as ever. The Kuomintang has also officially " killed " and buried Chu Teh many times, assisted by occasional corroborations from clairvoyant missionaries. Numerous deaths of the two famous men, nevertheless, did not prevent them from being involved in many spectacular exploits, including the Long March. Mao was indeed in one of his periods of newspaper demise when I visited Red China, but I found him quite substantially alive. There seems to be some basis for the legend of his charmed life, however, in the fact that, although he has been in scores of battles, was once captured by enemy troops and escaped, and has had the world's highest reward on his head, during all these years he has never once been wounded.

I happened to be in his house one evening when he was given a complete physical examination by a Red surgeon—a returned student from Europe who knew his business—and pronounced in excellent health. He has never had tuberculosis or any " incurable disease," as has been rumoured by some romantic travellers.[1] His lungs are completely sound, although, unlike most Red commanders, he is an inordinate cigarette-smoker. During the Long March, Mao and Li Teh (another heavy smoker) carried

[1] Mr. Peter Fleming, in *One's Company*, seems to have given widest currency to this falsehood.

on original botanical research by testing out various kinds of leaves as tobacco substitutes.

Ho Tze-nien, Mao's present wife, a former school-teacher and now a Communist organizer herself, has been less fortunate than her husband. She has more than a dozen wounds, caused by splinters from an air bomb, but all of them superficial. Just before I left Pao An the Maos were proud parents of a new baby girl. He has two other children by his former wife, Yang Kai-hui, the daughter of a noted Chinese professor. She was killed by Ho Chien several years ago.

Mao Tse-tung is now (1937) forty-four years old. He was elected chairman of the provisional Central Soviet Government at the Second All-China Soviet Congress, attended by delegates representing approximately 9,000,000 people then living under Red laws.[1] Here, incidentally, it may be inserted that Mao Tse-tung estimates the maximum population of the various districts under the direct control of the Soviet Central Government, in 1934, as follows: Kiangsi Soviet, 3,000,000; Hupeh-Anhui-Honan Soviet, 2,000,000; Hunan-Kiangsi-Hupeh Soviet, 1,000,000; Kiangsi-Hunan Soviet, 1,000,000; Chekiang-Fukien Soviet, 1,000,000; Hunan-Hupeh Soviet, 1,000,000; total, 9,000,000. Fantastic estimates ranging as high as ten times that figure were evidently achieved by adding up the entire population in every area in which the Red Army or Red partisans had been reported as operating. Mao laughed when I quoted him the figure of " 80,000,000 " people living under the Chinese Soviets, and said that when they had that big an area the revolution would be practically won. But of course there were many millions in areas held by Red partisans.

The influence of Mao Tse-tung throughout the Communist world of China to-day is probably greater than that of anyone else. He is a member of nearly everything—the revolutionary military committee, the political bureau of the Central Committee, the finance commission, the organization committee, the public health commission, and others. His real influence is

[1] Cf. *Fundamental Laws of the Chinese Soviet Republic* (Martin Lawrence, London, 1934). It contains the provisional constitution of the Soviets, and a statement of basic objectives during the " bourgeois-democratic " phase of the revolution. Cf. also, *Red China: Mao Tse-tung Reports on the Progress of the Chinese Soviet Republic* (London, 1934).

asserted through his domination of the political bureau, which has decisive power in the policies of the Party, the Government and the Army. Yet, while everyone knows and respects him, there is—as yet, at least—no ritual of hero-worship built up around him. I never met a Chinese Red who drivelled " our-great-leader " phrases, I did not hear Mao's name used as a synonym for the Chinese people, but still I never met one who did not like " the Chairman "—as everyone called him—and admire him. The rôle of his personality in the movement was clearly immense.

Mao seemed to me a very interesting and complex man. He had the simplicity and naturalness of the Chinese peasant, with a lively sense of humour and a love of rustic laughter. His laughter was even active on the subject of himself and the shortcomings of the Soviets—a boyish sort of laughter which never in the least shook his inner faith in his purpose. He is plain-speaking and plain-living, and some people might think him rather coarse and vulgar. Yet he combines curious qualities of *naïveté* with the most incisive wit and worldly sophistication.

I think my first impression—dominantly one of native shrewdness—was probably correct. And yet Mao is an accomplished scholar of Classical Chinese, an omnivorous reader, a deep student of philosophy and history, a good speaker, a man with an unusual memory and extraordinary powers of concentration, an able writer, careless in his personal habits and appearance but astonishingly meticulous about details of duty, a man of tireless energy, and a military and political strategist of considerable genius. It is an interesting fact that many Japanese regard him as the ablest Chinese strategist alive.

The Reds were putting up some new buildings in Pao An, but accommodations were very primitive while I was there. Mao lived with his wife in a two-roomed *yao-fang* with bare, poor, map-covered walls. He had known much worse, and as the son of a " rich " peasant in Hunan he had also known better. The chief luxury they boasted was a mosquito net. Otherwise Mao lived very much like the rank and file of the Red Army. After ten years of leadership of the Reds, after hundreds of confiscations of property of landlords, officials and tax-collectors, he owned only his blankets, and a few personal belongings, including two cotton uniforms. Although he is a Red Army commander as well as chairman, he wore on his coat collar only the two Red bars that are the insignia of the ordinary Red soldier.

I went with Mao several times to mass meetings of the villagers and the Red cadets, and to the Red theatre. He sat inconspicuously in the midst of the crowd and enjoyed himself hugely. I remember once, between acts at the Anti-Japanese Theatre, there was a general demand for a duet by Mao Tse-tung and Lin Piao, the twenty-eight-year-old president of the Red Academy, and formerly a famed young cadet on Chiang Kai-shek's staff. Lin blushed like a schoolboy, and got them out of the " command performance " by a graceful speech, calling upon the women Communists for a song instead.

Mao's food was the same as everybody's, but being a Hunanese he had the southerner's *ai-la*, or " love of pepper." He even had pepper cooked into his bread. Except for this passion, he scarcely seemed to notice what he ate. One night at dinner I heard him expand on a theory of pepper-loving peoples being revolutionaries. He first submitted his own province, Hunan, famous for the revolutionaries it has produced. Then he listed Spain, Mexico, Russia and France to support his contention, but laughingly had to admit defeat when somebody mentioned the well-known Italian love of red pepper and garlic, in refutation of his theory. One of the most amusing songs of the " bandits," incidentally, is a ditty called " The Hot Red Pepper." It tells of the disgust of the pepper with his pointless vegetable existence, waiting to be eaten, and how he ridicules the contentment of the cabbages, spinach and beans with their invertebrate careers. He ends up by leading a vegetable insurrection. " The Hot Red Pepper " was a great favourite with Chairman Mao.

He appears to be quite free from symptoms of megalomania, but he has a deep sense of personal dignity, and something about him suggests a power of ruthless decision when he deems it necessary. I never saw him angry, but I heard from others that on occasions he has been roused to an intense and withering fury. At such times his command of irony and invective is said to be classic and lethal.

I found him surprisingly well-informed on current world

politics. Even on the Long March, it seems, the Reds received
news broadcasts by radio, and in the North-west they publish
their own newspapers. Mao is exceptionally well read in world
history and has a realistic conception of European social and
political conditions. He was very interested in the Labour
Party of England, and questioned me intensely about its present
policies, soon exhausting all my information. It seemed to me
that he found it difficult fully to understand why, in a country
where workers are enfranchised, there is still no workers'
Government. I am afraid my answers did not satisfy him. He
expressed profound contempt for Ramsay MacDonald, whom
he designated as a *han-chien*—an arch-traitor of the British
people.

His opinion of President Roosevelt was rather interesting.
He believed him to be anti-Fascist, and thought China could
co-operate with such a man. He asked innumerable questions
about the New Deal, and Roosevelt's foreign policy. The questioning showed a remarkably clear conception of the objectives
of both. He regarded Mussolini and Hitler as mountebanks, but
considered Mussolini a much abler man, a real Machiavellian,
with a knowledge of history, while Hitler was a mere will-less
puppet of the capitalists.

Mao had read a number of books about India and had some
definite opinions on that country. Chief among these was that
Indian independence would never be realized without an
agrarian revolution. He questioned me about Gandhi, Jawarhalal
Nehru, Suhasini Chattopadhyay, and other Indian leaders I
had known. He knew something about the negro question in
America, and unfavourably compared the treatment of negroes
and American Indians with policies in the Soviet Union toward
national minorities. However, he was also interested when I
pointed out certain great differences in the historical and
psychological background of the negro in America and that of
the minor races of Russia. Interested—but he did not agree
with me.

Mao is an ardent student of philosophy. Once, when I was
having some nightly interviews with him on Communist history,
a visitor brought him several new books on philosophy, and Mao
asked me to postpone our engagements. He consumed these

books in three or four nights of intensive reading, during which he seemed oblivious to everything else. He had not confined his reading to Marxist philosophers, but had read something of the ancient Greeks, of Spinoza, Kant, Goethe, Hegel and Rousseau of course, and others.

I often wondered about Mao's own sense of responsibility over the question of force, violence and the " necessity of killing." He had had in his youth strongly liberal and humanistic tendencies, and the transition from idealism to realism could only have been made philosophically. Although he was peasant-born, he did not as a youth personally suffer much from oppression of the land-lords, as did many Reds, and, although Marxism is the core of his thought, I deduce that class hatred is for him probably fundamentally a mechanism in the bulwark of his philosophy, rather than a basic impulse to action.

There seemed to be nothing in him that might be called reli-gious feeling; his judgments were reached, I believe, on the basis of reason and necessity. Because of this I think he has probably on the whole been a moderating influence in the Communist movement where life and death are concerned. It seemed to me that he tried to make his philosophy, the dialectics of " the long view," his criterion in any large course of action, and in that range of thought the preciousness of human life is only relative. This is distinctly unusual among Chinese leaders, who historically have always placed expediency above ethics.

Mao works thirteen or fourteen hours a day, often until very late at night, frequently retiring at two or three. He seems to have an iron constitution. This he traces to a youth spent in hard work on his father's farm, and to an austere period in his schooldays when he formed a kind of Spartan club with some comrades. They used to fast, go on long hikes in the wooded hills of South China, swim in the coldest weather, walk shirtless in the rain and sleet—all this to toughen themselves. They in-tuitively knew that the years ahead in China would demand the capacity for withstanding great hardship and suffering.

Mao once spent a summer tramping all over Hunan, his native province. He earned his bread by working from farm to farm, and sometimes by begging. Another time, for days, he ate nothing but hard beans and water—again a process of " toughening " his stomach. The friendships he made on these country rambles in his early youth were of great value to him when, some ten years later, he began to organize thousands of farmers in Hunan into the famous peasant unions which became the first base of the Soviets, after the Kuomintang broke with the Communists in 1927.

Mao impressed me as a man of considerable depth of feeling. I remember that his eyes moistened once or twice when speaking of dead comrades, or recalling incidents in his youth, during the rice riots and famines of Hunan, when some starving peasants were beheaded in his province for demanding food from the yamen. One soldier told me of seeing Mao give his coat away to a wounded man at the front. They say that he refused to wear shoes when the Red warriors had none.

Yet I doubt very much if he would ever command great respect from the intellectual *élite* of China, perhaps not entirely because he has an extraordinary mind, but because he has the personal habits of a peasant. The Chinese disciples of Pareto might think him uncouth. I remember, when talking with Mao one day, seeing him absent-mindedly turn down the belt of his trousers and search for some guests—but then it is just possible that Pareto might do a little searching himself if he lived in similar circumstances. But I am sure that Pareto would never take off his trousers in the presence of the president of the Red Academy —as Mao did once when I was interviewing Lin Piao. It was extremely hot inside the little room. Mao lay down on the bed, pulled off his pants, and for twenty minutes carefully studied a military map on the wall—interrupted occasionally by Lin Piao, who asked for confirmation of dates and names, which Mao invariably knew. His nonchalant habits fitted with his complete indifference to personal appearance, although the means were at hand to fix himself up like a chocolate-box general or a politician's picture in *Who's Who in China*.

Except for a few weeks when he was ill, he walked most of the Long March, like the rank and file. At any time in recent years he could have achieved high office and riches by " betraying " to the Kuomintang, and this applies to most Red commanders. The tenacity with which these Communists for ten years clung to their principles cannot be fully evaluated unless you know the history of " silver bullets " in China, by means of which other rebels have customarily been bought off.

He seemed to me sincere, honest, and truthful in his statements. I was able to check up on many of his assertions, and usually found them to be correct. He subjected me to mild doses of political propaganda, but nothing compared to what I have received in non-bandit quarters, and he never imposed any censorship on me, either in my writing or photography, courtesies for which I was grateful. He did his best to see that I got facts to explain various aspects of Soviet life.

Because of their tremendous importance in the political scene of China to-day, his main declarations of Communist policies are worth serious consideration. For it is quite possible now—since the whole North-west and other large sections of the armed and unarmed Chinese people seem to be in sympathy with many of these policies—that they may become vital instruments of fundamental changes in the destiny of China.

2

Basic Communist Policies

WHAT are the fundamental policies of the Chinese Reds to-day ? I had a dozen or more talks on this subject with Mao Tse-tung and other leading Communists. But before we examine these policies it is necessary to have some conception of the nature of the long struggle between the Communists and Nanking. If we are to comprehend even the recent events in the Reddening North-west, we must first look at a few facts of history.

In the following paragraphs I paraphrase, in part, the comments of Lo Fu, the young American-educated secretary of the Communist Central Committee, whom I interviewed in Pao An. It is likely to be heavy going, but I believe it will prove worth while.

As is well known, the Chinese Communist Party began only in 1921. It grew very rapidly till 1923, when Dr. Sun Yat-sen, founder of the Kuomintang (Nationalist Party), made his famous *entente* with Soviet Russia. Neither the Kuomintang nor the Kungch'antang (Communist Party) had power, and both claimed to be struggling to establish democracy. It was easy to reach an understanding. In 1924 the Kuomintang was re-organized with the help of Russian advisers, along lines of the party of Lenin. An alliance was formed with the Chinese Communist Party, and Communists became very active in leading and organizing the Great Revolution of 1925-7, which finally overthrew the corrupt Peking dictatorship.

Now the basis of this co-operation, as far as the Communists were concerned, can be summarized as the acceptance by Dr. Sun Yat-sen and the Kuomintang of two major revolutionary principles. The first recognized the necessity of an anti-imperialist policy—the recovery of complete political, territorial and economic sovereignty by revolutionary action. The second demanded an internal policy of anti-feudalism and anti-militarism —the realization of a democratic revolution against the landlords and warlords, and the construction of new forms of social, economic and political life, which both the Communists and the Kuomintang agreed must be democratic in character.

The Communists, of course, regarded the successful fulfilment of the " bourgeois-democratic " revolution as a necessary preliminary for any Socialist society which might later be established, so their position was logical in supporting a " democratic national independence and liberation " movement.

Unfortunately, Dr. Sun Yat-sen died in 1925, before the revolution was completed. Co-operation between the Kuomintang and the Kungch'antang came to an end in 1927. From the Communist viewpoint, the Nationalist Revolution may also be said to have ended then. The Right wing of the Kuomintang, dominated by the new militarism, and supported by certain foreign powers, the treaty-port bankers, and the landlords, broke away from the legally-elected Government at Hankow. It formed a régime at Nanking under Chiang Kai-shek which the Communists and the majority of the Kuomintang at that time regarded as " counter-revolutionary "; that is, against the " bourgeois-democratic revolution " itself.

The Kuomintang soon reconciled itself to the Nanking *coup d'état*, but Communism became a crime punishable by death. What the Reds conceived to be the two main points of Nationalism—the anti-imperialist movement and the democratic revolution—were in practice abandoned. Militarists' civil wars and, later, intensive war against the rising agrarian revolution ensued. Many thousands of Communists and former peasant-union and labour leaders were killed. The unions were suppressed. An " enlightened dictatorship " made war on all forms of opposition. Even so, quite a number of Communists survived in the Army, and the Party held together throughout a period of great terrorism. In 1937, despite the expenditure of billions of dollars in civil war against them, the Red armies occupied in the Northwest the biggest single connected territory ever under their complete control.

Of course the Reds believe that the decade of history since 1927 has richly validated their thesis that national independence and democracy (which the Kuomintang also set as its objective) cannot be achieved in China without an anti-imperialist policy externally, and an agrarian revolution internally. Here it is not necessary fully to inspect their case. But if we are to see why Communism steadily increased its following, especially among patriotic youth, and why at the moment it still projects upon the screen of history the shadows of great upheaval and change in the Orient, we must note its main contentions. What are they ?

First of all, the Reds assert that, after Nanking split the living forces of the revolution, China rapidly lost much ground. Compromise followed compromise. The failure to realize agrarian revolution resulted in widespread discontent and open rebellion from the rural population in many parts of the country. General conditions of poverty and distress among the rural populace have seriously worsened during the past decade. No economist who has got beyond the discovery that China now has some passable motor-roads, an excellent fleet of aeroplanes, and a New Life movement, can fail to be depressed with the melancholy outlook for the future. Reports come in daily of catastrophes which in most countries would be considered colossal, but in China are more or less routine. Even as I write, for example, the Press brings this appalling news from Central and West China:

" Famine conditions continue to be reported in Honan, Anhui, Shensi, Kansu, Szechuan, and Kweichow. Quite evidently the country faces one of the most severe famines of many years, and thousands have already died. A recent survey by the Szechuan Famine Relief Commission discovered that 30,000,000 people are now in the famine belt of that province, where bark and ' Goddess-of-Mercy ' earth are being consumed by tens of thousands. There are said to be over 400,000 famine refugees in Shensi, over a million in Kansu, some 7,000,000 in Honan, and 3,000,000 in Kweichow. The famine in Kweichow is admitted by the official Central News to be the most serious in 100 years, affecting sixty districts of the province."[1]

Szechuan is one of the provinces where taxes have been collected sixty years or more in advance, and thousands of acres of land have been abandoned by farmers unable to pay rents and outrageous loan-interest. In my files are items, collected over a period of six years, showing comparable distress in many other provinces. There are few signs that the rate of frequency of these calamities is diminishing.

[1] *Democracy*, Peiping, May 15, 1937.

While the mass of the rural population is rapidly going bankrupt, concentration of land and wealth in the hands of a small number of landlords and landowning usurers is increasing in proportion to the general decline of independent farming.[1] Sir Frederick Leith-Ross is reported to have said that there is no middle class in China, but only the incredibly poor and the very rich; and, if this has not been true in the past, it may become so. Enormous taxes, the corrupt share-crop method, and the whole historical system of social, political and economic relationships described by Dr. Karlogus Wittfogel as the " Asiatic mode of production," contrive to leave the landless peasantry constantly heavily in debt, without reserves, and wholly unable to meet such crises as drought, famine and flood.

Mao Tse-tung, as secretary of the Peasants' Committee of the Kuomintang in 1926 (before the break with the Communists, when Mao was candidate to the Central Executive Committee of Kuomintang), supervized the collection of land statistics for areas in twenty-one provinces. He asserts that this investigation indicated that resident landlords, rich peasants, officials, absentee landlords and usurers, about 10 per cent of the whole rural population, together owned over 70 per cent of the cultivatable land in China. About 15 per cent was owned by middle peasants. But over 65 per cent of the rural population, made up of poor peasants, tenants and farm workers, owned only from 10 per cent to 15 per cent of the total arable land.

" These statistics were suppressed after the counter-revolution," according to Mao. " Now, ten years later, it is still impossible to get any statement from Nanking on land distribution in China."

The Communists think that rural bankruptcy has been accelerated by the disastrous consequences of abandoning the anti-imperialist struggle, which to most Chinese to-day means the " anti-Japanese struggle." As a result of Nanking's " no-war policy " against Japan, China has lost to Japanese invaders about a fifth of her national territory, over 40 per cent of her railway mileage, 85 per cent of her unsettled lands, a large part of her coal, 80 per cent of her iron deposits, 37 per cent of her

[1] The most brilliant recent work of research and analysis discussing this development is Ch'en Han-seng's *Landlord and Peasant in China* (New York, 1936).

finest forest lands, and about 40 per cent of her national export trade. Japan now controls over 75 per cent of the total pig iron and iron mining enterprises of what remains of China, and over half of the textile industry of China. The conquest of Manchuria also robbed China of its own best market as well as its most accessible raw materials. In 1931, Manchuria took over 27 per cent of its total imports from other Chinese provinces, but, in 1935, China could sell Manchukuo only 4 per cent of those imports. It presented Japan with the region of China best suited for industrial development—and enabled her to prevent that development, and shuttle the raw materials to her own industries. It gave to Japan the continental base from which she could inexorably continue her aggression in China. These are changes which, many feel, completely wiped out the benefits of any reforms that Nanking may be able to claim to its credit for generations in the future—even provided the rest of China remains intact.

And what was achieved by Nanking's nine years of war against the Reds? The North-west junta recently summarized these results in a manifesto opposing preparations for the sixth anti-Red " final-annihilation " drive. It reminded us that Manchuria had gone to Japan during one " final-annihilation " drive, Shanghai invaded during another, Jehol given up during the third, East Hopei lost during still another, and the sovereignty of Hopei and Chahar provinces badly impaired during the fifth " remnant-bandit extermination." Inevitably, so the North-west felt. Suiyuan would be lost during Chiang Kai-shek's newest anti-Red drive, which coincided with Japan's invasion of the northern regions of that province.

Of course Nanking could not stop civil war as long as the Reds continued to attempt to overthrow the Government by force. But as early as 1932 the Reds had proposed peace, and offered to unite with Nanking, on a common programme of resistance to Japan. Their proposals had been rejected. Now, once more, despite the great strategic advantages which the Red Army enjoyed in its developing position in the North-west, the Communist Party, in collaboration with anti-Japanese armies and patriotic associations throughout China, had renewed its offers to co-operate to end civil war and create a national " anti-Japanese front " against the aggressor. It promised to submit its Red

Army and its Soviet districts to the complete authority of the Central Government provided that Nanking would agree to establish democratic representative government, resist Japan, enfranchise the people, and guarantee civil liberties to the masses. In other words, the Reds were ready to " remarry " the Kuomintang if it would return to the " bourgeois-nationalist " programme of anti-imperialism and anti-feudalism. But of these two basic aims they realized that the fight for national survival was paramount, and must be conducted even at the expense of abandoning the internal struggle over the land question; that class antagonisms might have to be sublimated in, certainly could not be satisfied without, the successful solution of the external antagonism with Japan.

To quote Mao Tse-tung, in his interview with me:

" The fundamental issue before the Chinese people to-day is the struggle against Japanese imperialism. Our Soviet policy is decisively conditioned by this struggle. Japan's warlords hope to subjugate the whole of China and make of the Chinese people their colonial slaves. The fight against the Japanese invasion, the fight against Japanese economic and military conquest—these are the main tasks that must be remembered in analysing Soviet policies.

" Japanese imperialism is not only the enemy of China, but also of all people of the world who desire peace. Especially it is the enemy of those peoples with interests on the Pacific Ocean; namely, the American, British, French and Soviet Russian nations. The Japanese continental policy, as well as naval policy, is directed, not only against China, but also against those countries. . . .

" What do we expect from the foreign powers ? We expect at least that friendly nations will not help Japanese imperialism, and will adopt a neutral position. We hope that they will actively help China to resist invasion and conquest."

In using the word " imperialism," the Communists now sharply distinguish between Japan, who is actively aggressive and invading China to-day, and democratic capitalist powers who are friendly and non-aggressive at present. Mao Tse-tung explained:

" Concerning the question of imperialism in general we observe that among the great powers some express unwillingness to engage in a new world war, some are not ready to see Japan occupy China: countries such as America, Great Britain, France, Holland and Belgium. Then there are countries permanently under the menace of the aggressive powers, such as Siam, the Philippines, Central American countries, Canada, India, Australia, the Dutch Indies, etc.—all more or less under the threat of Japan. We consider them our friends and invite their cooperation. . . .

" So, except for Japan and those countries which help Japanese imperialism [meaning Italy and Germany, as indicated by Mao elsewhere], the categories mentioned above can be organized into anti-war, anti-aggression, anti-Fascist world alliances. . . . In the past, Nanking has received much help from America, England and other countries. Most of these funds and supplies have been used in civil war. For every Red soldier killed, Nanking has slain many peasants and workers. According to a recent article by the banker, Chang Nai-ch'i, it has cost the Chinese people about $80,000 for every Red soldier killed by Nanking.[1] Such ' help,' therefore, does not seem to us to have been rendered to the Chinese people.

" Only when Nanking determines to cease civil war and to fight against Japanese imperialism, and unites with the people's revolution to organize a democratic national defence Government—only then can such help be of real benefit to the Chinese nation."

I asked Mao whether the Soviets were in favour of cancelling unequal treaties. He pointed out that many of these unequal treaties have, in effect, already been destroyed by the Japanese, especially in the case of Manchuria. But as for the future attitude of a representative Government in China, he declared:

" Those powers that help or do not oppose China in her war of independence and liberation should be invited to enjoy close friendly relations with China. Those powers which actively assist Japan should naturally not be given the same treatment: for example, Germany and Italy, which have already established

---

[1] Far more civilians and " partisans " were killed than regular Red soldiers. Mr. Chang's estimate included costs of lost labour, lost crops, ruined villages and towns, ruined farmlands, etc., as well as actual military expenses.

special relations with Manchukuo, and cannot be regarded as powers friendly to the Chinese people.

" With friendly powers, China will peacefully negotiate treaties of mutual advantage. With other powers China is prepared to maintain co-operation on a much broader scale. . . . So far as Japan is concerned, China must by the act of war of liberation cancel all unequal treaties, confiscate all Japanese imperialist holdings, and annul Japan's special privileges, concessions, and influence in this country. Concerning our relations with other powers, we Communists do not advocate any measure that may place at disadvantage the world position of China in her struggle against Japanese imperialism.

" When China really wins her independence, then legitimate foreign trading interests will enjoy more opportunities than ever before. The power of production and consumption of 450,000,000 people is not a matter that can remain the exclusive interest of the Chinese, but one that must engage the many nations. Our millions of people, once really emancipated, with their great latent productive possibilities freed for creative activity in every field, can help improve the economy as well as raise the cultural level of the whole world. But the productive power of the Chinese people has in the past scarcely been touched; on the contrary, it has been suppressed—both by native militarists and Japanese imperialism."

Finally I asked, " Is it possible for China to make anti-imperialist alliances with democratic capitalist powers ? "

" Anti-imperialist, anti-Fascist alliances," replied Mao, " are in the nature of peace alliances, and for mutual defence against war-making nations. A Chinese anti-Fascist pact with capitalist democracies is perfectly possible and desirable. It is to the interest of such countries to join the anti-Fascist front in self-defence. . . .

" If China should become completely colonized it would mean the beginning of a long series of terrible and senseless wars. A choice must be made. For itself, the Chinese people will take the road of struggle against its oppressors, and we hope also that the statesmen and people of foreign nations will march with us on this road, and not follow the dark paths laid down by the bloody history of imperialism. . . .

" To oppose Japan successfully, China must also seek assistance from other powers. *This does not mean, however, that China is incapable of fighting Japan without foreign help !* The Chinese Communist Party, the Soviet Government, the Red Army, and the Chinese people, are ready to unite with any power to shorten the duration of this war. But if none join us we are determined to carry on alone ! "

But how absurd ! Do the Reds really imagine that China can defeat Japan's mighty war-machine ? I believe they do. What is the peculiar shape of logic on which they base their assumption of triumph ? It was one of dozens of questions I put to Mao Tse-tung. And his answer, which follows, is a stimulating and perhaps a prophetic thing indeed, even though the orthodox military mind may find it technically fallacious.

Dc

3

On War with Japan

On July 16, 1936, I sat on a square, backless stool inside Mao Tse-tung's residence. It was after nine at night, " Taps " had been sounded and nearly all lights were out. The walls and ceiling of Mao's home were of solid rock; beneath was a flooring of bricks. Cotton gauze extended half-way up windows also hollowed from stone, and candles sputtered on the square, unpainted table before us, spread with a clean red-felt cloth. Mrs. Mao was in an adjoining room making *compote* from wild peaches purchased that day from a fruit merchant. Mao sat with his legs crossed, in a deep shelf hewn from the solid rock, and smoked a Chien Men cigarette.

Seated next to me was Wu Liang-p'ing, a young Soviet " functionary " who acted as interpreter in my " formal " interviews with Mao Tse-tung. I wrote down in full in English Mao Tse-tung's answers to my questions, and these were then translated into Chinese and corrected by Mao, who is noted for his insistence upon accuracy of detail. With the assistance of Mr. Wu, the interviews were re-translated into English, and because of such precautions I believe these pages to contain few errors of reporting.

Wu Liang-p'ing, to whom I am indebted for much assistance in gathering material, is the son of a rich landlord in Fenghua, Chiang Kai-shek's native district in Chekiang. He fled from there some years ago when his father, apparently an ambitious burgher, wished to betroth him to a relative of the Generalissimo. Wu is a graduate of Ta Hsia University, in Shanghai—where Pat Givens once arrested him and had him sentenced to two years in the Ward Road jail. He had studied in France, England and Russia, was twenty-six years old, and for his energetic labours as a Communist received his uniform, room and food—the latter consisting chiefly of millet and noodles.

Mao began to answer my first question, about Communist policy toward Japan, which was this: " If Japan is defeated and driven from China, do you think that the major problem of ' foreign imperialism ' will in general have been solved here ? "

" Yes. If other imperialist countries do not act as Japan, and if China defeats Japan, it will mean that the Chinese masses have awakened, have mobilized, and have established their independence. Therefore the main problem of imperialism will have been solved."

" Under what conditions do you think the Chinese people can defeat and exhaust the forces of Japan ? " I asked.

He replied: " Three conditions will guarantee our success: first, the achievement of the National United Front against Japanese imperialism in China; second, the formation of a World Anti-Japanese United Front; third, revolutionary action by the oppressed peoples at present suffering under Japanese imperialism. Of these, the central necessity is the union of the Chinese people themselves."

My question: " How long do you think such a war would last ? "

Mao's answer: " That depends on the strength of the Chinese People's Front, many conditioning factors in China and Japan, and the degree of international help given to China, as well as the rate of revolutionary development in Japan. If the Chinese People's Front is powerfully homogeneous, if it is effectively organized horizontally and vertically, if the international aid to China is considerable from those Governments which recognize the menace of Japanese imperialism to their own interests, if revolution come quickly in Japan, the war[1] will be short and victory speedily won. If these conditions are not realized, however, the war will be very long, but in the end, just the same, Japan will be defeated, only the sacrifices will be extensive and it will be a painful period for the whole world."

Question: " What is your opinion of the probable course of development of such a war, politically and military ? "

Answer: " Two questions are involved here—the policy of the foreign powers, and the strategy of China's armies.

" Now, the Japanese continental policy is already fixed and it is well known. Those who imagine that by further sacrifices of Chinese sovereignty, by making economic, political or territorial

---

[1] The Communists are " officially " at war with Japan, the Soviet Government having declared such war in a proclamation issued in Kiangsi, early in 1932. Publication of the proclamation was suppressed by the Kuomintang. Cf. *Red China: President Mao Tse-tung Reports*, etc., p. 6 (London, 1934).

compromises and concessions, they can halt the advance of Japan, are only indulging in Utopian fancy. Nanking has in the past adopted erroneous policies based on this strategy, and we have only to look at the map of East Asia to see the results of it.

" But we know well enough that, not only North China, but the Lower Yangtze Valley and our southern seaports are already included in the Japanese continental programme. Moreover, it is just as clear that the Japanese Navy aspires to blockade the China seas and to seize the Philippines, Siam, Indo-China, Malaya, and the Dutch East Indies. In the event of war, Japan will try to make them her strategic bases, cutting off Great Britain, France and America from China, and monopolizing the seas of the southern Pacific. These moves are included in Japan's plans of naval strategy, copies of which we have seen. And such naval strategy will be co-ordinated with the land strategy of Japan.

" Many people think it would be impossible for China to continue her fight against Japan, once the latter had seized certain strategic points on the coast and enforced a blockade. This is nonsense. To refute it we have only to refer to the history of the Red Army. In certain periods our forces have been exceeded numerically some ten or twenty times by the Kuomintang troops, which were also superior to us in equipment. Their economic resources many times surpassed ours, and they received material assistance from the outside. Why, then, has the Red Army scored success after success against the White troops and not only survived till to-day, but increased its power ?

" The explanation is that the Red Army and the Soviet Government had created among all people within their areas a rock-like solidarity, because everyone in the Soviets was ready to fight for their Government against its oppressors, because every person was voluntarily and consciously fighting for his own interests and what he believed to be right. Secondly, in the struggle of the Soviets the people were led by men of ability, strength and determination, equipped with deep understanding of the strategic, political, economic and military needs of their position. The Red Army won its many victories—beginning with only a few dozen rifles in the hands of determined revolutionaries—because its solid base in the people attracted friends even among the White troops, among the civilian populace as well as among the troops. The enemy was infinitely our superior militarily, but politically it was immobilized.

" In the anti-Japanese war the Chinese people would have on their side greater advantages then those the Red Army has utilized in its struggle with the Kuomintang. China is a very big nation, and it cannot be said to be conquered until every inch of it is under the sword of the invader. If Japan should succeed in occupying even a large section of China, getting possession of an area with as many as 100 or even 200 million people, we would still be far from defeated. We would still have left a great force to fight against Japan's warlords, who would also have to fight a heavy and constant rear-guard action throughout the entire war.

" As for munitions, the Japanese cannot seize our arsenals in the interior, which are sufficient to equip Chinese armies for many years, nor can they prevent us from capturing great amounts of arms and ammunition from their own hands. By the latter method the Red Army has equipped its present forces from the Kuomintang: for nine years they have been our ' ammunition-carriers.' What infinitely greater possibilities would open up for the utilization of such tactics as won our arms for us if the whole Chinese people were united against Japan !

" Economically, of course, China is not unified. But the uneven development of China's economy also presents advantages in a war against the highly centralized and highly concentrated economy of Japan. For example, to sever Shanghai from the rest of China is not as disastrous to the country as would be, for instance, the severance of New York from the rest of America. Moreover, it is impossible for Japan to isolate all of China: China's North-west, South-west and West cannot be blockaded by Japan, who continentally is still a sea power.

" Thus, once more the central point of the problem becomes the mobilization and unification of the entire Chinese people and the building up of a United Front, such as has been advocated by the Communist Party ever since 1932."

Question: " In the event of a Sino-Japanese war, do you think there will be a revolution in Japan ? "

Answer: " The Japanese revolution is not only a possibility

but a certainty. It is inevitable and will begin to occur promptly after the first severe defeats suffered by the Japanese Army."

Question: " Do you think Soviet Russia and Outer Mongolia would become involved in this war, and would come to the assistance of China ? Under what circumstances is that likely ? "

Answer: " Of course the Soviet Union is also not an isolated country. It cannot ignore events in the Far East. It cannot remain passive. Will it complacently watch Japan conquer all China and make of it a strategic base from which to attack the U.S.S.R. ? Or will it help the Chinese people to oppose their Japanese oppressors, win their independence, and establish friendly relations with the Russian people ? We think Russia will choose the latter course.

" We believe that once the Chinese people have their own government and begin this war of resistance and want to establish friendly alliances with the U.S.S.R., as well as other friendly powers, the Soviet Union will be in the vanguard to shake hands with us. The struggle against Japanese imperialism is a world task and the Soviet Union, as part of that world, can no more remain neutral than can England or America."

Question: " Is it the immediate task of the Chinese people to regain all the territories lost to Japanese imperialism, or only to drive Japan from North China, and all Chinese territory above the Great Wall ? "

Answer: " It is the immediate task of China to regain all our lost territories, not merely to defend our sovereignty below the Great Wall. This means that Manchuria must be regained. We do not, however, include Korea, formerly a Chinese colony, but when we have re-established the independence of the lost territories of China, and if the Koreans wish to break away from the chains of Japanese imperialism, we will extend them our enthusiastic help in their struggle for independence. The same thing applies for Formosa. As for Inner Mongolia,[1] which is

[1] In answer to a later question, in another interview, Mao Tse-tung made the following statement concerning Outer Mongolia:
" The relationship between Outer Mongolia and the Soviet Union, now and in the past, has always been based on the principle of complete equality. When the people's revolution has been victorious in China the Outer Mongolian republic will automatically become a part of the Chinese federation, at their own will. The Mohammedan and Tibetan peoples, likewise, will form autonomous republics attached to the China federation."

populated by both Chinese and Mongolians, we will struggle to drive Japan from there and help Inner Mongolia to establish an autonomous State."

Question: " In actual practice, how could the Soviet Government and the Red Army co-operate with the Kuomintang armies in a war against Japan ? In a foreign war it would be necessary for all Chinese armies to be placed under a centralized command: Would the Red Army agree, if allowed representation on a supreme war council, to submit to its decisions both militarily and politically ? "

Answer: " Yes. Our Government will whole-heartedly submit to the decisions of such a council, provided it really resists Japan."

Question : " Would the Red Army agree not to move its troops into or against any areas occupied by Kuomintang armies, except with the consent or at the order of the supreme war council ? "

Answer: " Yes. Certainly we will not move our troops into any areas occupied by anti-Japanese armies—nor have we done so for some time past. The Red Army would not utilize any war-time situation in an opportunist way."

Question: " What demands would the Communist Party make in return for such co-operation ? "

Answer: " It would insist upon waging war, decisively and finally, against Japanese aggression. In addition it would request the observance of the points advanced in the calls for a democratic republic and the establishment of a national defence Government."[1]

Question: " How can the people best be armed, organized and trained to participate in such a war ? "

Answer: " The people *must* be given the right to organize and to arm themselves. This is a freedom which Chiang Kai-shek has in the past denied to them. The suppression has not, however, been entirely successful—as, for example, in the case of the Red Army. Also, despite severe repression in Peiping, in Shanghai and other places, the students have begun to organize themselves and have already prepared themselves politically. But still the

[1] Discussed in several proclamations issued in 1935 and 1936, by the Soviet Government and the Red Army, to the Kuomintang.

students and the revolutionary anti-Japanese masses have not yet got their freedom, cannot be mobilized, cannot be trained and armed. When the contrary is true, when the masses are given economic, social and political freedom, their strength will be intensified hundreds of times, and the true power of the nation will be revealed.

" The Red Army through its own struggle has won its freedom from the militarists to become an unconquerable power. The anti-Japanese volunteers have won their freedom of action from the Japanese oppressors and have armed themselves in a similar way. If the Chinese people are trained, armed and organized they can likewise become an invincible force."

Question: " What, in your opinion, should be the main strategy and tactics to be followed in this ' war of liberation ' ? "

Answer: " The strategy should be that of a war of manœuvre, over an extended, shifting and indefinite front: a strategy depending for success on a high degree of mobility in difficult terrain, and featured by swift attack and withdrawal, swift concentration and dispersal. It will be a large-scale war of manœuvre rather than the simple positional war of extensive trench-work, deep-massed lines and heavy fortifications. Our strategy and tactics must be conditioned by the theatre in which the war will take place, and this dictates a war of manœuvre.

" This does not mean the abandonment of vital strategic points, which can be defended in positional warfare as long as profitable. But the pivotal strategy must be a war of manœuvre, and important reliance must be placed on guerilla and partisan tactics. Fortified warfare must be utilized, but it will be of auxiliary and secondary strategic importance."

Here it may be inserted that this sort of strategy in general seems to be rather widely supported also among non-Communist Chinese military leaders. Nanking's wholly imported air force provides an impressive if costly internal police machine, but few experts have any illusions about its long-range value in a foreign war. Both the air force and such mechanization as has taken place in the central army are looked upon by many as costly toys certain to be of surprise value and auxiliary defence service in the early stages of the war, but quite incapable of retaining a rôle of initiative after the first few weeks, since China is almost utterly lacking in the basic war industries necessary to maintain and replenish either an air force or any other highly technical branch of modern warfare.

Pai Chung-hsi, Li Tsung-jen, Han Fu-chu, Hu Tsung-nan, Chen Ch'eng, Chang Hsueh-liang, Feng Yü-hsiang and Ts'ai T''ing-k'ai are among those who seem to have this belief: that China's sole hope of victory over Japan must rest ultimately on superior manœuvring of great masses of troops, divided into mobile units, and the ability to maintain a protracted defence over immense partisan areas, thus gradually breaking Japan economically first, and then militarily. Such, at least, is the theory.

Mao Tse-tung continued:

" Geographically the theatre of the war is so vast that it is possible for us to pursue mobile warfare with the utmost efficiency and with a telling effect on a slow-moving war-machine like Japan's, cautiously feeling its way in front of fierce rearguard actions. Deep-line concentration and the exhausting defence of a vital position or two on a narrow front would be to throw away all the tactical advantages of our geography and economic organization, and to repeat the mistake of the Abyssinians. Our strategy and tactics must aim to avoid great decisive battles in the early stages of the war, and gradually to break the morale, the fighting spirit and the military efficiency of the living forces of the enemy.

" The mistake of the Abyssinians, quite aside from the internal political weaknesses of their position, was that they attempted to hold a deep front, enabling the Fascists to bombard, gas and strike with their technically stronger military machines at heavy immobile concentrations, exposing themselves to vital organic injury.

" Besides the regular Chinese troops we should create, direct, and politically and militarily equip great numbers of partisan and guerilla detachments among the peasantry. What has been accomplished by the anti-Japanese volunteer units of this type in Manchuria is only a very minor demonstration of the latent power of resistance that can be mobilized from the revolutionary peasantry of all China. Properly led and organized, such units can keep the Japanese busy twenty-four hours a day and worry them to death.

" It must be remembered that the war will be fought in China. This means that the Japanese will be entirely surrounded by a hostile Chinese people. The Japanese will be forced to move in all their provisions and guard them, maintaining troops along all lines of communications, and heavily garrisoning their bases in Manchuria and Japan as well.

" The process of the war will present to China the possibility of capturing many Japanese prisoners, arms, ammunition, war-machines, and so forth. A point will be reached where it will become more and more possible to engage Japan's armies on a basis of positional warfare, using fortifications and deep en-trenchment, for, as the war progresses, the technical equipment of the anti-Japanese forces will greatly improve, and will be reinforced by important foreign help. Japan's economy will crack under the strain of a long, expensive occupation of China and the morale of her forces will break under the trial of a war of innumerable but indecisive battles. The great reservoirs of human material in the revolutionary Chinese people will still be pouring men ready to fight for their freedom into our front lines long after the tidal flood of Japanese imperialism has wrecked itself on the hidden reefs of Chinese resistance !

" All these and other factors will condition the war and will enable us to make the final and decisive attacks on Japan's fortifications and strategic bases and to drive Japan's army of occupation from China.

" Japanese officers and soldiers captured and disarmed by us will be welcomed and will be well treated. They will not be killed. They will be treated in a brotherly way. Every method will be adopted to make the Japanese proletarian soldiers, with whom we have no quarrel, stand up and oppose their own Fascist oppressors. Our slogan will be: ' Unite and oppose the common oppressors, the Fascist leaders.' Anti-Fascist Japanese troops are our friends, and there is no conflict in our aims."

It was past two o'clock in the morning and I was exhausted, but I could see no signs of fatigue on Mao's pale, somewhat jaundiced-looking face. He alternately walked up and down between the two little rooms, sat down, lay down, leaned on the table, and read from a sheaf of reports in the intervals when Wu translated and I wrote. Mrs. Mao also was still awake. Suddenly both of them bent over and gave an exclamation of delight at a moth that had languished beside the candle. It was a really lovely thing, with wings shaded a delicate apple-green and fringed in a soft rainbow of saffron and rose. Mao opened a book and pressed this gossamer of colour between its leaves.

Could such people really be thinking seriously of war?

I suddenly remembered that I had a date next morning at eight, to visit the Hung-Chün Ta-Hsueh, or Red Army Academy —which is perhaps as good a place as any to study the " sincerity " of the anti-Japanese feelings of Chinese Communists.

4

$2,000,000 *in Heads*

THERE were many things unique about the Hung-Chün Ta-Hsueh.

Its president was a twenty-eight-year-old army commander who was said to have never lost a battle. It boasted, in one class of undergraduates, veteran warriors whose average age was twenty-seven, with an average of eight years of fighting experience and three wounds each. Was there any other school where " paper shortage " made it necessary to use the blank side of enemy propaganda leaflets for classroom notebooks ? Or where the cost of educating each cadet, including food, clothing, all institutional expenses, was less than $15 silver per month ? Or where the aggregate value of rewards, offered for the heads of various notorious cadets, exceeded $2,000,000 ?

Such was the Red Academy.

Finally, it was probably the world's only seat of " higher learning " whose classrooms were caves, with chairs and desks of stone and brick, whose blackboards were walls of limestone and clay, and whose buildings were completely bomb-proof.

This latter happened because in Shensi and Kansu, besides ordinary houses, there are great cave dwellings, temple grottoes and castled battlements, hundreds of years old. Wealthy officials and landlords built these queer edifices, a thousand years ago, to guard against flood and invasion and famine, and here hoarded the grain and treasure to see them through sieges of each. Many-vaulted chambers, cut deeply into the loess or solid rock, some with rooms that will hold several hundred people, these cliff-dwellings made perfect bomb-proof shelters against the new Nanking bombers which the Chinese people presented to Chiang Kai-shek to fight Japan. In such archaic manors the Red Army Academy found strange but safe accommodation.

Lin Piao, the Academy president, was introduced to me soon after my arrival, and he invited me to speak one day to his cadets. He suggested the topic: " British and American policies toward China." I demurred. I know too little about both. Besides, I was incompetent to explain either in Marxist terminology. But Lin insisted. He said they could supply the Marxist terminology for themselves. When he arranged a " noodle dinner " for the occasion it was too much for me, and I succumbed.

Lin Piao is the son of a factory owner in Hupeh province, and was born in 1908. His father was ruined by extortionate taxation, but Lin managed to get through prep. school, and became a cadet in the Whampoa Academy at Canton. There he made a brilliant record. He received intensive political and military training, under Chiang Kai-shek and Chiang's chief adviser, the Russian General Bleucher. Soon after his graduation the Nationalist Expedition began, and Lin Piao was promoted to a captaincy. By 1927, at the age of twenty, he was a colonel in the noted 4th Kuomintang Army, under Chang Fa-kuei. And in August of that year, after the Right *coup d'état* at Nanking, he led his regiment to join the 20th Army under Ho Lung and Yeh Ting in the Nanchang Uprising, which began the Communist opposition in China.

With Mao Tse-tung, Lin Piao shared the distinction of being one of the few Red commanders never wounded. Engaged on the front in more than a hundred battles, in field command for more than ten years, exposed to every hardship that his men have known, with a reward of $100,000 on his head, he miraculously remained unhurt and in good health.

In 1932, Lin Piao was given command of the 1st Red Army Corps, which then numbered about 20,000 rifles. It became the most dreaded section of the Red Army. Chiefly due to Lin's extraordinary talent as a tactician, it destroyed, defeated or outmanœuvred every Government force sent against it and was never broken in battle. The mere discovery that they were fighting the 1st Red Army Corps is said to have at times put a Nanking army to rout. But of these famed " iron troops " more later, when I have reached the front.

Like many able Red commanders, Lin has never been outside China, speaks and reads no language but Chinese. Before the age of thirty, however, he has already won recognition beyond Red circles. His articles in the Chinese Reds' military magazines, *Struggle* and *War and Revolution*, have been republished, studied and criticized in Nanking military journals, and also in Japan and Soviet Russia. He is noted as the originator of the " short-attack "—a manœuvre on which General Feng Yu-hsiang has critically commented. To the Reds' skilful mastery of the " short-attack " many victories of the 1st Army Corps are said to be traceable.

With Commander Lin and his faculty I journeyed one morning a short distance beyond the walls of Pao An to the Red Army Academy. We arrived at recreation hour. Some of the cadets were playing basket-ball on the two courts set up; others were playing tennis on a court laid down on the turf beside a tributary of the Yellow River, which skirts Pao An. Still other cadets were playing table tennis, writing, reading new books and magazines, or studying in their primitive " clubrooms."

This was the First Section of the Academy, in which there were some 200 students. Altogether, Hung Ta, as the school was known in the Soviet districts, had four sections, with over 800 students. There were also, near Pao An, and under the administrative control of the education commissioner, radio, cavalry, agricultural and medical-training schools. There was a Communist Party training school and a mass-education training centre.

Over 200 cadets assembled to hear me explain " British and American policies." I made a crude summary of Anglo-American attitudes, and agreed to answer questions. It was a great mistake, I soon realized, and the noodle dinner hardly compensated for my embarrassment. The questions put to me would defy the erudition and ingenuity of Mr. H. G. Wells. Consider, for example, how you would answer the following interrogations that confronted me:

" What is the attitude of the British Government toward the formation of the pro-Japanese Hopei-Chahar Council, and the garrisoning of North China by Japanese troops ! "

" What are the results of the N.R.A. policy in America, and how has it benefited the working classes ? "

" Will Germany and Italy help Japan if a war breaks out with China ? "

" How long do you think Japan can carry on a major war against China, if she is not helped by other powers ? "

" Why has the League of Nations failed ? "

" Why is it that, although the Communist Party is legal in both Great Britain and America, there is no workers' Government in either country ? "

" What progress is being made in the formation of an ·anti-Fascist front in England ? In America ? "

" What is the future of the international student movement, which has its centre in Paris ? "

" In your opinion, can Leith-Ross's visit to Japan result in Anglo-Japanese agreement on policies toward China ? "

" When China begins to resist Japan, will America and Great Britain assist China or Japan ? "

" Please tell us why America and Great Britain keep their fleets and armed forces in China, if they are friends of the Chinese people ? "

" What do the American and British workers think of the U.S.S.R. ? "

No small territory, you may agree, to cover in a two-hour question-period ! And indeed it was not confined to two hours. Beginning at ten in the morning it continued till late in the afternoon. In the end it proved inconclusive, and disrupted work for the day.

Afterward I toured the various classrooms, and talked with Lin Piao and his faculty. They told me something of the conditions of enrolment in their school, and showed me printed announcements of its courses, thousands of copies of which had been secretly distributed throughout China. Four sections of the academy invited " all who are determined to fight Japanese imperialism and to offer themselves for the national revolutionary cause, regardless of class, social or political differences." The age limit was sixteen to twenty-eight, " regardless of sex." " The applicants must be physically strong, free from epidemic diseases," and also—which seems quite sweeping—" free from all bad habits."

In practice, I discovered, most of the cadets in the First Section were battalion, regimental or division commanders or political commissars of the Red Army, receiving advanced military and political training. The course offered here lasted four months. According to Red Army regulations, every active commander or commissar is supposed to spend at least that period in the Red Academy during every two years of active service.

Second and Third Sections included platoon, company and squad commanders, experienced fighters in the Red Army, as well as new recruits selected from " graduates of middle schools or the equivalent, unemployed teachers or officers, cadres of anti-Japanese volunteer corps, and anti-Japanese partisan leaders, and workers who have engaged in organizing and leading labour movements." Over sixty middle-school graduates from Shansi had joined the Reds during their expedition to that province.

Classes in the Second and Third Sections lasted six months. The Fourth Section was devoted chiefly to " training engineers, cavalry cadres, and artillery units." Here I met some former machinists and apprentices. Later on, as I was leaving Red China, I was to meet, entering by truck, eight new recruits for the Red Academy, arriving from Shanghai and Peiping. Lin Piao told me that they had a waiting list of over 2,000 student applicants from all parts of China, the chief problem (at that time) being one of transportation, as every cadet had to be " smuggled " in.

The curriculum varied in different sections of Hung Ta, but the diet of cadets in the First Section may be taken as sample fare. Political lectures included these courses: Political Knowledge, Problems of the Chinese Revolution, Political Economy, Party Construction, Tactical Problems of the Republic, Leninism and Historical Foundations of Democracy, and Political and Social Forces in Japan. Military courses included: Problems of Strategy in the War with Japan, Manœuvring Warfare (against Japan), and the Development of Partisan Warfare in the Anti-Japanese War.

Special textbooks had been prepared for some of these courses. Some were carried clear from the Soviet publishing house in Kiangsi, where (I was told) more than 800 printers were employed in the main plant. In other courses the materials used were lectures by Red Army commanders and party leaders, dealing with historical experiences of the Russian and the Chinese revolutions, or utilizing material from captured Government files, documents and statistics.

These courses of Hung Ta perhaps suggest a reply to the question, " Do the Reds really intend to fight Japan ? " It suffices to show how the Reds foresee and actively plan for China's " war of independence " against Japan—a war which they regard as inevitable unless, by some miracle, Japan withdraws from the vast areas of China now under the wheels of Nippon's military juggernaut.

It is not a pleasant prospect. Some foreign capitalists in China consider it a mad prospect. But others frankly admit that they do not blame the Chinese, when millions of their people are already the conquered subjects of Japan, if they now prepare to die rather than yield without struggle any more of their freedom.

That the Reds, at least, are fully determined to fight, and believe that the opening of war will find them first on the front, was indicated, not only in the impassioned utterances of their leaders, in grim practical schooling in the Army, and in their proposals for a " United Front " with their ten-year enemy, the Kuomintang, but also by the intensive propagandizing you saw throughout the Soviet districts.

Playing a leading part in this educative mission were the many companies of youths, known as the Jen-Min K'ang-Erh Chü-Shê, or People's Anti-Japanese Dramatic Society, who travelled ceaselessly back and forth in the Red districts, spreading the gospel of resistance, and awakening the slumbering nationalism of the peasantry.

It was to one of the performances of this astonishing children's theatre that I went soon after my first visit to the Red Academy.

5

Red Theatre

PEOPLE were already moving down toward the open-air stage, improvised from an old temple, when I set out with the young official who had invited me to the Red Theatre. It was Saturday, two or three hours before sunset, and all Pao An seemed to be going.

Cadets, muleteers, women and girl workers from the uniform and shoe factory, clerks from the co-operatives and from the Soviet Post Office, soldiers, carpenters, villagers followed by their infants, all began streaming toward the big grassy plain beside the river, where the players were performing. It would be hard to imagine a more democratic gathering. Even some goats were grazing on the tennis-court not far beyond.

No tickets were sold, there was no " dress circle," and there were no preferred seats. I noticed Lo Fu, secretary of the Central Committee, Lin Piao, president of the Red Academy, Lin Pai-chu, the commissioner of finance, Mao Tse-tung, chairman of the Government, and other officials and their wives, scattered through the crowd, seated on the springy turf, like the rest. No one paid much attention to them, once the performance had begun.

Across the stage was a big pink curtain of silk, with the words, " People's Anti-Japanese Dramatic Society," in Chinese characters, as well as Latinized Chinese, which the Reds were promoting to hasten mass education. The programme was to last three hours. It proved to be a combination of playlets, dancing, singing, and pantomime—a kind of variety show, or vaudeville, given unity chiefly by two central themes: anti-Nipponism and the revolution. It was full of overt propaganda, wholly unsophisticated, and the " props " were primitive. But it had the advantage of being emancipated from cymbal-crashing and falsetto-singing, and of dealing with living material rather than with meaningless historical intrigues that are the concern of the decadent Chinese opera.

Finally, what it lacked in subtlety and refinement it partly made up by its robust vitality, its sparkling humour, and a sort

of participation between actors and audience. Guests at the
Red Theatre seemed actually to *listen* to what was said: a
really astonishing thing in contrast with the bored opera
audience, for in China opera-goers chiefly spend their time eating
fruit and melon seeds, gossiping, tossing hot towels back and
forth, visiting from one box to another, and only occasionally
looking at the stage.

The first playlet here was called *Invasion*. It opens in a Manchurian village, in 1931, with the Japanese arriving and driving
out the " non-resisting " Chinese soldiers. In the second scene,
Japanese officers banquet in a peasant's home, using Chinese
men for chairs, and drunkenly making love to their wives.
Another scene shows Japanese dope pedlars selling morphine
and heroin and forcing every peasant to buy a quantity. A
youth who refuses to buy is singled out for questioning.

" You don't buy morphine, you don't obey Manchukuo health
rules, you don't love your ' divine ' Emperor P'u Yi," charge
his tormentors. " You are no good, you are an *anti-Japanese*
bandit ! " And the youth is promptly executed.

A scene in the village market-place shows small merchants
peacefully selling their wares. Suddenly Japanese soldiers arrive,
searching for more " anti-Japanese bandits." Instantly they
demand passports, and those who have forgotten them are shot.
Then two Japanese officers gorge themselves on a pedlar's pork.
When he asks for payment they look at him in astonishment.
" *You* ask for payment ? Why, Chiang Kai-shek gave us Manchuria, Jehol, Chahar, the Tangku Truce, the Ho-Umetsu
Agreement, and the Hopei-Chahar Council, without asking a
single copper ! And *you* want us to pay for a little pork ! "
Whereupon, they impale him as a " bandit."

In the end, of course, all this proves too much for the villagers.
Merchants turn over their stands and umbrellas, farmers rush
forth with their spears, women and children come with their
knives, and all swear to " fight to the death " against the
Jih-pen-kuei—the " Japanese devils."

The little play was sprinkled with humour and local idiom.
Bursts of laughter alternated with oaths of disgust and hatred
for the Japanese. The audience got quite agitated. It was not
just political propaganda to them, nor slapstick melodrama, but

the poignant truth itself. The fact that the players were mostly youths in their teens and natives of Shensi and Shansi seemed entirely forgotten in the onlookers' absorption with the *ideas* presented.

The substratum of bitter reality behind this portrayal, done as a sort of farce, was not obscured by its wit and humour for at least one young soldier there. He stood up, at the end, and in a voice shaking with emotion cried out: " Death to the Japanese bandits ! Down with the murderers of our Chinese people ! Fight back to our homes ! " The whole assembly echoed his slogans mightily. I learned that this lad was a Manchurian whose parents had been killed by the Japanese.

Comic relief was provided at this moment by the meandering goats. They were discovered nonchalantly consuming the tennis-net, which someone had forgotten to take down. A wave of laughter swept the audience while some cadets gave chase to the culprits and salvaged this important property of the recreation department.

Second number on the programme was a harvest dance, exquisitely done by a dozen girls of the Dramatic Society. Bare-footed, clad in peasant trousers and coats and fancy vests, with silk bandannas on their heads, they performed with good unison and grace. Two of these girls, I learned, had walked clear from Kiangsi, where they had learned to dance in the Reds' dramatic school at Juichin. They had genuine talent.

Another unique and amusing number was called the " United Front Dance," which interpreted the mobilization of China to resist Japan. By what legerdemain they produced their costumes I do not know, but suddenly there were groups of youths wearing sailor's white jumpers and caps, and shorts—first appearing as cavalry formations, next as aviation corps, then as foot soldiers, and finally as the Navy. Their pantomime and gesture, at which Chinese are born artists, very realistically conveyed the spirit of the dance. Then there was something called the " Dance of the Red Machines." By sound and gesture, by an interplay and inter-locking of arms, legs and heads, the little dancers ingenuously imitated the thrust and drive of pistons, the turn of cogs and wheels, the hum of dynamos—and visions of a machine-age China of the future.

Between acts, shouts arose for extemporaneous singing by people in the audience. Half a dozen native Shensi girls—workers in the factories—were by popular demand required to sing an old folk-song of the province, accompaniment being furnished by a Shensi farmer with his home-made guitar. Another " command " performance was given by a cadet who played the harmonica, and one was called upon to sing a favourite song of the Southland. Then, to my utter consternation, a demand began that the *wai-kuo hsin-wen chi-chê*—the " foreign newspaperman "—strain his lungs in a solo of his own !

They refused to excuse me. Alas, I could think of nothing but fox-trots, waltzes, *La Bohème*, and "Ave Maria," which all seemed inappropriate for this martial audience. I could not even remember the " Marseillaise." The demand persisted. In extreme embarrassment I at last rendered "The Man on the Flying Trapeze"! They were very polite about it. No encore was requested.

With infinite relief I saw the curtain go up on the next act, which turned out to be a social play with a revolutionary theme —an accountant who fell in love with his landlord's wife. Then there was more dancing, a " Living Newspaper " dealing with some late news from the South-west, and a chorus of children singing the " Internationale." Here the flags of several nations were hung on streamers from a central illuminated column, around which reclined the young dancers. They rose slowly, as the words unfolded, to stand erect, clenched fists upraised, as the song ended.

The theatre was over, but my curiosity remained. And thus, next day, I went to interview Miss Wei Kung-chih, director of the People's Anti-Japanese Red Dramatic Society.

Miss Wei was born in Honan in 1907 and had been a Red for ten years. She originally joined a propaganda corps of the Kuominchun, " Christian General " Feng Yü-hsiang's army, but when Feng reconciled himself to the Nanking *coup d'état* in 1927 she deserted, along with many young students, and became a Communist in Hankow. In 1929 she was sent to Europe by the Communist Party, and studied for a while in France, and then in Moscow. A year later she returned to China, successfully ran the Kuomintang blockade around Red China, and began to work at Juichin.

She told me something of the history of the Red Theatre. Dramatic groups were first organized in Kiangsi, it seems, in 1931. There, at the famous Gorky School in Juichin, with over 1,000 students recruited from the Soviet districts, the Reds trained about sixty theatrical troupes, according to Miss Wei. They travelled through the villages and at the front. Every troupe had long waiting lists of requests from village Soviets. The peasants, always grateful for any diversion in their culture-starved lives, voluntarily arranged all transport, food and housing for these visits.

In the South, Miss Wei was an assistant director, but in the North-west she had taken charge of the whole organization of dramatics. She made the Long March from Kiangsi, one of several scores of Soviet women who lived through it. Theatrical troupes were created in Soviet Shensi before the southern army reached the North-west, but with the arrival of new talent from Kiangsi the dramatic art apparently acquired new life. There were over thirty such travelling theatrical troupes there now, Miss Wei told me, and others in Kansu. I was to meet many later on in my travels.

" Every army has its own dramatic group," Miss Wei continued, " as well as nearly every district. The actors are nearly all locally recruited. Most of our experienced players from the South have now become instructors."

I met several Young Vanguards, veterans of the Long March, still in their early teens, who had charge of organizing and training childrens' dramatic societies in various villages.

" Peasants come from long distances to our Red dramatics," Miss Wei proudly informed me. " Sometimes, when we are near the White borders, Kuomintang soldiers secretly send messages to ask our players to come to some market-town in the border districts. When we do this, both Red soldiers and White leave their arms behind and go to this market-place to watch our performance. But the higher officers of the Kuomintang never permit this, if they know about it, because once they have seen our players many of the Kuomintang soldiers will no longer fight our Red Army ! "

What surprised me about these dramatic clubs, however, was not that they offered anything of artistic importance to the world, which obviously they did not, but that, equipped with so little, they were able to meet a genuine social need. They had the scantiest properties and costumes, yet with these primitive materials they managed to produce the authentic illusion of drama. The players received only their food and clothing and small living allowances, but they studied every day, like all Communists, and they believed themselves to be working for China and the Chinese people. They slept anywhere, cheerfully ate what was provided for them, walked long distances from village to village. From the standpoint of material comforts they were unquestionably the most miserably rewarded thespians on earth, yet I don't seem to have seen any who were happier. '

The Reds write nearly all their own plays and songs. Some are contributed by versatile officials, but most of them are prepared by story-writers and artists in the propaganda department. Several Red dramatic skits have been written by Chen Fang-wu, the great literary critic who joined the Reds three years ago, and others, more recently, by Ting Ling, China's most famous woman author, who is now with the Red Army.

There is no more powerful weapon of propaganda in the Communist movement than the Reds' dramatic troupes, and none more subtly manipulated. By constant shifts of programme, by almost daily changes of the " Living Newspaper " scenes, new military, political, economic and social problems become the material of drama, and doubts and questionings are answered in a humorous, understandable way for the sceptical peasantry. When the Reds occupy new areas, too, it is the Red Theatre which calms the fears of the people, gives them rudimentary ideas of the Red programme, dispenses great quantities of revolutionary ideas, and counter-propaganda, to win the people's confidence. During the Reds' recent Shansi expedition, for example, hundreds of peasants heard about the Red players with the army, and flocked to see them, willing subjects for any propaganda dispensed in the pleasant form of drama.

The whole thing is " propaganda in art " carried to the ultimate degree, and plenty of people would say, " Why drag art into it ? " Yet in its broadest meaning it is art, for it conveys for its spectators the illusions of life, and if it is a naïve art it is because the living material with which it is made and the living men to whom it appeals are in their approach to life's problems also naïve. For the masses of China there is no fine partition between art and propaganda. There is only a distinction between what is understandable in human experience and what is not.

You know in one sense you can think of the whole history of the Communist movement in China as a grand propaganda tour, and the defence, not so much of the absolute right of certain ideas, perhaps, as of their right to exist. I'm not sure that it may not prove to have been the most permanent service of the Reds, even if they are in the end defeated and broken. For millions of young peasants who have heard the Marxist gospel preached by those beardless youths, thousands of whom are now dead, the old exorcisms of Chinese culture will never again be quite as effective. Wherever in their incredible migrations destiny has moved these Reds, they have vigorously demanded deep social changes—of which the peasants could have learned in no other way—and have brought new faith in action to the poor and the oppressed.

However badly they have erred at times, however tragic have been their excesses, however exaggerated has been the emphasis here or the stress there, it has been their sincere and sharply felt propagandist aim to shake, to arouse, the millions of rural China to their responsibilities in society; to awaken them to a belief in human rights, to combat the timidity, passiveness and static faiths of Taoism and Confucianism, to educate, to persuade and, I have no doubt, at times to beleaguer and coerce them to fight for " the reign of the people "—a new vision in rural China—to fight for a life of justice, equality, freedom and human dignity, as the Communists see it. Far more than all the pious but meaningless resolutions passed at Nanking, this growing pressure now from a peasantry gradually standing erect in a state of consciousness, after two millenniums of sleep, may force the realization of a vast mutation over the land.

What this " Communism " has amounted to in a way is that, for the first time in history, thousands of educated youths, stirred to great dreams themselves by a universe of scientific knowledge to which they have suddenly been given access, have " returned to the people," turned back to the deep soil-base of their country, to " reveal " some of their new-won learning to the intellectually sterile countryside, the dark-living peasantry, and have sought to enlist its alliance in building this " more abundant life." Fired by the belief that a better world can be made, and that only they can make it, they have carried their formula—the ideal of the commune—back to the people for sanction and support. And to a startling degree they have won it. They have brought to millions, by propaganda and by action, a new conception of the State, society and the individual.

I often had a queer feeling among the Reds that I was in the midst of a host of schoolboys, engaged in a life of violence because some strange design of history had made this seem infinitely more important to them than football games, textbooks, love, or the main concerns of youth in other countries. At times I could scarcely believe that it had been only this determined aggregation of youth, equipped with an Idea, that had directed a mass struggle for ten years against all the armies of Nanking. How had the incredible brotherhood arisen, banded together, held together, and whence came its strength? And why had it perhaps, after all, failed to mature, why did it still seem fundamentally like a mighty demonstration, like a crusade, of youth?

This can be answered only when you understand the remarkable gestation through which Chinese history has gone during the past quarter of a century—a gestation the legitimate offspring of which clearly is this Red Army. For hundreds of years the literate men of China have striven to rise above the people, win access to the little bureaucracy which from a distant height ruled the masses—by closely guarding its hieroglyphics and its knowledge, trifling as it was, and using these as weapons with which to control the darkness of the countryside, but never to enlighten it. But the new gestation produced a phenomenon— a child that wanted to share its knowledge with the " dark masses " and even idealize them.

I used to wonder, while I was in Pao An, how I could possibly explain this profound natural disturbance that has shaken the womb of China. How could I describe the slow fertilization, the quickening of the womb, the pain of birth, and the result? I could list the bare historic facts; but the human anguish of it I could not describe. Then Mao Tse-tung began to tell me something about his personal history, and as I wrote it down, night after night, I realized that this was not only his story, but a record also of how Communism grew—a variety of it real and indigenous to China, and no mere orphan adopted from abroad, as some writers naïvely suppose—and why it won the adherence and support of thousands of young men and women. It was a story that I was to hear later on, with rich variations, in the autobiographies of many other Red leaders. It was a story people would want to read, I thought. And here it is.

Part Four

GENESIS OF A COMMUNIST

1

Childhood

I HAD given to Mao a long list of questions to answer about himself, and I felt almost as embarrassed for my inquisitiveness as a Japanese immigration official ought to feel for his impertinence, but doesn't. On the five or six sets of questions I had submitted on different matters, Mao had talked for a dozen nights, hardly ever referring to himself or his own rôle in some of the events described. I was beginning to think it was hopeless to expect him to give me such details: he obviously considered the individual of very little importance. Like other Reds I met he tended to talk only about committees, organizations, armies, resolutions, battles, tactics, " measures " and so on, but seldom in terms of personal experience.

For a while I thought this reluctance to expand on subjective matters, or even the exploits of their comrades as individuals, might derive from modesty, or a fear or suspicion of me, or a consciousness of the price so many of these men had on their heads. Later on I discovered that this was not so much the case as was the fact that most of them actually did not remember these personal details. As I began collecting biographies I found repeatedly that the Communist would be able to tell everything that had happened in his early youth, but once he had become identified with the Red Army he lost himself somewhere, and without repeated questioning you could hear nothing more about *him*, but only stories of the Army, or the Soviets, or the Party—capitalized. They could talk indefinitely about dates and circumstances of battles, and movements to and from a thousand unheard-of places, but those events seemed to have had significance for them only collectively, not because they as individuals had made history there, but because the Red Army had been there, and behind it the whole organic force of an ideology for which they were fighting. It was an interesting discovery, but it made difficult reporting.

One night when all other questions had been satisfied, Mao turned to this list I had headed " Personal History." He smiled at a question, " How many times have you been married ? "

—and the rumour later spread that I had asked Mao, a mono-gamist if nothing else, how many wives he had. He was sceptical, anyway, about the necessity for supplying an autobiography. But I argued that in a way this was more important than in-formation on other matters. " People want to know what sort of man you are," I said, " when they read what you say. Then you ought also to correct some of the false rumours circulated."

I reminded him of various reports of his death, how some people believed he spoke fluent French, while others said he was an ignorant peasant, how one report described him as a half-dead tubercular, while others maintained that he was a mad fanatic. He was mildly surprised that people should spend their time speculating about him. He agreed that such reports ought to be corrected. Then he looked over the items again, as I had written them down.

" Suppose," he said at last, " that I just disregard your questions, and instead give you a general sketch of my life ? I think it will be more understandable, and in the end all of your questions will be answered just the same."

" But that's exactly what I want ! " I exclaimed.

During the several nightly interviews that followed—we were like conspirators indeed, huddled in that cave over that red-covered table, with sputtering candles between us—I wrote until I was ready to fall asleep. Wu Liang-p'ing sat next to me and inter-preted Mao's soft southern dialect, in which a chicken, instead of being a good substantial northern *chi* became a romantic *ghii*, and *Hunan* became *Funan*, and a bowl of *ch'a* turned into *ts'a*, and many much stranger variations occurred. Mao related everything from memory, and I put it down as he talked. It was, as I have said, re-translated and corrected, and this is the result, with no attempt to give it literary excellence, beyond some necessary corrections in the syntax of the patient Mr. Wu:

" I was born in the village of Shao Shan, in Hsiang T'an Hsien, Hunan province, in 1893. My father's name was Mao Jen-shêng, and my mother's maiden name was Wen Ch'i-mei.

" My father was a poor peasant and while still young was obliged to join the Army because of heavy debts. He was a soldier for many years. Later on he returned to the village where

I was born, and by saving carefully and gathering together a little money through small trading and other enterprise he managed to buy back his land.

"As middle peasants then my family owned fifteen *mou* of land. On this they could raise sixty *tan*[1] of rice a year. The five members of the family consumed a total of thirty-five *tan*— that is, about seven each—which left an annual surplus of twenty-five *tan*. Using this surplus, my father accumulated a little capital and in time purchased seven more *mou*, which gave the family the status of 'rich' peasants. We could then raise eighty-four *tan* of rice a year.

"When I was ten years of age and the family owned only fifteen *mou* of land, the five members of the family consisted of my father, mother, grandfather, younger brother and myself. After we had acquired the additional seven *mou*, my grandfather died, but there came another younger brother. However, we still had a surplus of forty-nine *tan* of rice each year, and on this my father steadily prospered.

"At the time my father was a middle peasant he began to deal in grain transport and selling, by which he made a little money. After be became a 'rich' peasant, he devoted most of his time to that business. He hired a full-time farm labourer, and put his children to work on the farm, as well as his wife. I began to work at farming tasks when I was six years old. My father had no shop for his business. He simply purchased grain from the poor farmers and then transported it to the city merchants, where he got a higher price. In the winter, when the rice was being ground, he hired an extra labourer to work on the farm, so that at that time there were seven mouths to feed. My family ate frugally, but had enough always.

"I began studying in a local primary school when I was eight and remained there until I was thirteen years old. In the early morning and at night I worked on the farm. During the day I read the Confucian Analects and the Four Classics. My Chinese teacher belonged to the stern-treatment school. He was harsh and severe, frequently beating his students. Because of this I ran away from the school when I was ten. I was afraid to return home, for fear of receiving a beating there, and set

[1] One *tan* is a *picul*, or 133⅓ lb.

out in the general direction of the city, which I believed to be in a valley somewhere. I wandered for three days before I was finally found by my family. Then I learned that I had circled around and around in my travels, and in all my walking had got only about eight *li* from my home.

" After my return to the family, however, to my surprise, conditions somewhat improved. My father was slightly more considerate and the teacher was more inclined to moderation. The result of my act of protest impressed me very much. It was a successful ' strike.'

" My father wanted me to begin keeping the family books as soon as I had learned a few characters. He wanted me to learn to use the abacus. As my father insisted upon this I began to work at those accounts at night. He was a severe taskmaster. He hated to see me idle, and if there were no books to be kept he put me to work at farm tasks. He was a hot-tempered man and frequently beat both me and my brothers. He gave us no money whatever, and the most meagre food. On the 15th of every month he made a concession to his labourers and gave them eggs with their rice, but never meat. To me he gave neither eggs nor meat.

" My mother was a kind woman, generous and sympathetic, and ever ready to share what she had. She pitied the poor and often gave them rice when they came to ask for it during famines. But she could not do so when my father was present. He disapproved of charity. We had many quarrels in my home over this question.

" There were two ' parties ' in the family. One was my father, the Ruling Power. The Opposition was made up of myself, my mother, my brother and sometimes even the labourer. In the ' United Front ' of the Opposition, however, there was a difference of opinion. My mother advocated a policy of indirect attack. She criticized any overt display of emotion and attempts at open rebellion against the Ruling Power. She said it was not the Chinese way.

" But when I was thirteen I discovered a powerful argument of my own for debating with my father on his own ground, by quoting the Classics. My father's favourite accusations against me were of unfilial conduct and laziness. I quoted, in exchange, passages from the Classics saying that the elder must be kind and affectionate. Against his charge that I was lazy, I used the rebuttal that older people should do more work than younger, that my father was over three times as old as myself, and therefore should do more work. And I declared that when I was his age I would be much more energetic.

" The old man continued to ' amass wealth,' or what was considered to be a great fortune in that little village. He did not buy more land himself, but he bought many mortgages on other people's land. His capital grew to $2,000 or $3,000.

" My dissatisfaction increased. The dialectical struggle in our family was constantly developing.[1] One incident I especially remember. When I was about thirteen my father invited many guests to his home, and while they were present a dispute arose between the two of us. My father denounced me before the whole group, calling me lazy and useless. This infuriated me. I cursed him and left the house. My mother ran after me and tried to persuade me to return. My father also pursued me, cursing at the same time that he demanded me to come back. I reached the edge of a pond and threatened to jump in if he came any nearer. In this situation demands and counter-demands were presented for cessation of the civil war. My father insisted that I apologize and *k'ou-t'ou* as a sign of submission. I agreed to give a one-knee *k'ou-t'ou* if he would promise not to beat me. Thus the war ended, and from it I learned that when I defended my rights by open rebellion my father relented, but when I remained meek and submissive he only cursed and beat me the more.

" Reflecting on this, I think that in the end the strictness of my father defeated him. I learned to hate him, and we created a real United Front against him. At the same time it probably benefited me. It made me most diligent in my work; it made me keep my books carefully, so that he should have no basis for criticizing me.

" My father had had two years of schooling and he could read enough to keep books. My mother was wholly illiterate. Both were from peasant families. I was the family ' scholar.' I knew the Classics, but disliked them. What I enjoyed were the romances of old China, and especially stories of rebellions. I read the *Yo Fei Chuan (Chin Chung Chuan), Shui Hu Chuan, Fan*

---

[1] Mao used all these political terms humorously in his explanations, laughing as he recalled such incidents.

Ec

T"ang, San Kuo, and *Hsi Yu Chi,* while still very young, and despite the vigilance of my old teacher, who hated these outlawed books and called them wicked. I used to read them in school, covering them up with a Classic when the teacher walked past. So also did most of my schoolmates. We learned many of the stories almost by heart, and discussed and re-discussed them many times. We knew more of them than the old men of the village, who also loved them and used to exchange stories with us. I believe that perhaps I was much influenced by such books, read at an impressionable age.

" I finally left the primary school when I was thirteen and began to work long hours on the farm, helping the hired labourer, doing the full labour of a man during the day and at night keeping books for my father. Nevertheless, I succeeded in continuing my reading, devouring everything I could find except the Classics. This annoyed my father, who wanted me to master the Classics, especially after he was defeated in a lawsuit due to an apt Classical quotation used by his adversary in the Chinese court. I used to cover up the window of my room late at night so that my father would not see the light. In this way I read a book called *Words of Warning (Shen Shih Wei-yen),* which I liked very much. The authors, a number of old reformist scholars, thought that the weakness of China lay in her lack of Western appliances—railways, telephones, telegraphs, and steamships—and wanted to have them introduced into the country. My father considered such books a waste of time. He wanted me to read something practical like the Classics, which could help him in winning lawsuits.

" I continued to read the old romances and tales of Chinese literature. It occurred to me one day that there was one thing peculiar about these stories, and that was the absence of peasants who tilled the land. All the characters were warriors, officials or scholars; there was never a peasant hero. I wondered about this for two years, and then I analysed the content of the stories. I found that they all glorified men of arms, rulers of the people, who did not have to work the land, because they owned and controlled it and evidently made the peasants work it for them.

" My father, Mao Jen-shêng, was in his early days, and in middle age, a sceptic, but my mother devoutly worshipped

Buddha. She gave her children religious instruction, and we were all saddened that our father was an unbeliever. When I was nine years old I seriously discussed the problem of my father's lack of piety with my mother. We made many attempts then and later on to convert him, but without success. He only cursed us, and, overwhelmed by his attacks, we withdrew to devise new plans. But he would have nothing to do with the gods.

" My reading gradually began to influence me, however; I myself became more and more sceptical. My mother became concerned about me, and scolded me for my indifference to the requirements of the faith, but my father made no comment. Then one day he went out on the road to collect some money, and on his way he met a tiger. The tiger was surprised at the encounter and fled at once, but my father was even more astonished and afterwards reflected a good deal on his miraculous escape. He began to wonder if he had not offended the gods. From then on he showed more respect to Buddhism and burned incense now and then. Yet, when my own backsliding grew worse, the old man did not interfere. He only prayed to the gods when he was in difficulties.

" *Words of Warning* stimulated in me a desire to resume my studies. I had also become disgusted with my labour on the farm. My father naturally opposed this. We quarrelled about it, and finally I ran away from home. I went to the home of an unemployed law student, and there I studied for half a year. After that I studied more of the Classics under an old Chinese scholar, and also read many contemporary articles and a few books.

" At this time an incident occurred in Hunan which influenced my whole life. Outside the little Chinese school where I was studying, we students noticed many bean merchants, coming back from Changsha. We asked them why they were all leaving. They told us about a big uprising in the city.

" There had been a severe famine that year, and in Changsha thousands were without food. The starving sent a delegation to the civil governor, to beg for relief, but he replied to them haughtily, ' Why haven't you food ? There is plenty in the city. I always have enough.' When the people were told the governor's reply, they became very angry. They held mass meetings and organized a demonstration. They attacked the Manchu yamen,

cut down the flagpole, the symbol of office, and drove out the
governor. Following this, the Commissioner of Internal Affairs,
a man named Chang, came out on his horse and told the people
that the Government would take measures to help them.
Chang was evidently sincere in his promise, but the Emperor
disliked him and accused him of having intimate connections
with ' the mob.' He was removed. A new governor arrived, and
at once ordered the arrest of the leaders of the uprising. Many
of them were beheaded and their heads displayed on poles as a
warning to future ' rebels.'

" This incident was discussed in my school for many days. It
made a deep impression on me. Most of the other students
sympathized with the ' insurrectionists,' but only from an
observer's point of view. They did not understand that it had
any relation to their own lives. They were merely interested in
it as an exciting incident. I never forgot it. I felt that there
with the rebels were ordinary people like my own family and I
deeply resented the injustice of the treatment given to them.

" Not long afterward, in Shao Shan, there was a conflict
between members of the Kê Lao Hui,[1] a secret society, and a
local landlord. He sued them in court, and as he was a powerful
landlord he easily bought a decision favourable to himself.
The Kê Lao Hui members were defeated. But, instead of sub-
mitting, they rebelled against the landlord and the Government
and withdrew to a local mountain called Liu Shan, where they
built a stronghold. Troops were sent against them and the
landlord spread a story that they had sacrificed a child when
they raised the banner of revolt. The leader of the rebels was
called P'ang the Millstone-maker. They were finally suppressed
and P'ang was forced to flee. He was eventually captured and
beheaded. In the eyes of the students, however, he was a hero,
for all sympathized with the revolt.

" Next year, when the new rice was not yet harvested and the
winter rice was exhausted, there was a food shortage in our
district. The poor demanded help from the rich farmers and
they began a movement called ' Eat Rice Without Charge.'
My father was a rice merchant and was exporting much grain
to the city from our district, despite the shortage. One of his

---

[1] The same society to which Ho Lung belonged.

consignments was seized by the poor villagers and his wrath was boundless. I did not sympathize with him. At the same time I thought the villagers' method was wrong also.

" Another influence on me at this time was the presence in a local primary school of a ' radical ' teacher. He was ' radical ' because he was opposed to Buddhism, and wanted to get rid of the gods. He urged people to convert their temples into schools. He was a widely discussed personality. I admired him and agreed with his views.

" These incidents, occurring close together, made lasting impressions on my young mind, already rebellious. In this period also I began to have a certain amount of political consciousness, especially after I read a pamphlet telling of the dismemberment of China. I remember even now that this pamphlet opened with the sentence: ' Alas, China will be subjugated ! ' It told of Japan's occupation of Korea and Formosa, of the loss of suzerainty in Indo-China, Burma and elsewhere. After I read this I felt depressed about the future of my country and began to realize that it was the duty of all the people to help save it.

" My father had decided to apprentice me to a rice shop in Hsiang T'an, with which he had connections. I was not opposed to it at first, thinking it might be interesting. But about this time I heard of an unusual new school and made up my mind to go there, despite my father's opposition. This school was in Hsiang Hsiang *hsien* (county), where my mother's family lived. A cousin of mine was a student there and he told me of the new school and of the changing conditions in ' modern education.' There was less emphasis on the Classics, and more was taught of the ' new knowledge ' of the West. The educational methods, also, were quite ' radical.'

" I went to the school with my cousin and registered. I claimed to be a Hsiang Hsiang man, because I understood that the school was open only to natives of Hsiang Hsiang. Later on I took my true status as a Hsiang T'an native when I discovered that the place was open to all. I paid 1,400 coppers here for five months' board, lodging, and all materials necessary for study. My father finally agreed to let me enter, after friends had argued to him that this ' advanced ' education would increase my earning powers. This was the first time I had been as far away from home as fifty *li*. I was sixteen years old.

" In the new school I could study natural science and new subjects of Western learning. Another notable thing was that one of the teachers was a returned student from Japan, and he wore a false queue. It was quite easy to tell that his queue was false. Everyone laughed at him and called him the ' False Foreign Devil.'

" I had never before seen so many children together. Most of them were sons of landlords, wearing expensive clothes; very few peasants could afford to send their children to such a school. I was more poorly dressed than the others. I owned only one decent coat-and-trousers suit. Gowns were not worn by students, but only by the teachers, and none but ' foreign devils ' wore foreign clothes. Many of the richer students despised me because usually I was wearing my ragged coat and trousers. However, among them I had friends, and two especially were my good comrades. One of those is now a writer, living in Soviet Russia.

" I was also disliked because I was not a native of Hsiang Hsiang. It was very important to be a native of Hsiang Hsiang and also important to be from a certain district of Hsiang Hsiang. There was an upper, lower and middle district, and lower and upper were continually fighting, purely on a regional basis. Neither could become reconciled to the existence of the other. I took a neutral position in this war, because I was not a native at all. Consequently all three factions despised me. I felt spiritually very depressed.

" I made good progress at this school. The teachers liked me, especially those who taught the Classics, because I wrote good essays in the Classical manner. But my mind was not on the Classics. I was reading two books sent to me by my cousin, telling of the Reform movement of K'ang Yu-wei. One was called the *Journal of the New People* (*Hsin Min Chung Pao*), and was edited by Liang Ch'i-ch'ao.[1] I read and re-read these until I knew them by heart. I worshipped K'ang Yu-wei and

[1] Liang Ch'i-ch'ao, a talented essayist at the end of the Manchu dynasty, was the leader of a reform movement which resulted in his exile. K'ang Yu-wei and he were the " intellectual godfathers " of the first revolution, in 1911. Lin Yü-t'ang calls Liang Ch'i-ch'ao " the greatest personality in the history of Chinese journalism."

Liang Ch'i-ch'ao, and was very grateful to my cousin, whom I then thought very progressive, but who later became a counter-revolutionary, a member of the gentry, and joined the reactionaries in the period of the Great Revolution of 1925–7.

" Many of the students disliked the ' False Foreign Devil ' because of his inhuman queue, but I liked hearing him talk about Japan. He taught music and English. One of his songs was Japanese and was called ' The Battle on the Yellow Sea.' I still remember some charming words from it:

> *The sparrow sings,*
> *The nightingale dances,*
> *And the green fields are lovely in the spring.*
> *The pomegranate flowers crimson,*
> *The willows are green-leaved,*
> *And there is a new picture.*

At that time I knew and felt the beauty of Japan, and felt something of her pride and might, in this song of her victory over Russia.[1] I did not think there was also a barbarous Japan —the Japan we know to-day.

" This is all I learned from the ' False Foreign Devil.'

" I recall also that at this time I first heard that the Emperor and Tzu Hsi, the Empress Dowager, were both dead, although the new Emperor, Hsuan T'ung [the present P'u Yi], had already been ruling for two years. I was not yet an anti-monarchist, indeed, I considered the Emperor as well as most officials to be honest, good and clever men. They only needed the help of K'ang Yu-wei's reforms. I was fascinated by accounts of the rulers of ancient China: Yao, Shun, Ch'in Shih Huang-ti, and Han Wu-ti, and read many books about them. I also learned something of foreign history at this time, and of geography. I had first heard of America in an article which told of the American Revolution and contained a sentence like this: ' After eight years of difficult war, Washington won victory and built up his nation.' In a book called *Great Heroes of the World*, I read also of Napoleon, Catherine of Russia, Peter the Great, Wellington, Gladstone, Rousseau, Montesquieu and Lincoln.''

[1] The poem evidently referred to the spring festival and tremendous rejoicing in Japan following the Treaty of Portsmouth and the end of the Russo-Japanese War.

2

Days in Changsha

MAO TSE-TUNG continued:

" I began to long to go to Changsha, the great city, the capital of the province, which was 120 *li* from my home. It was said that this city was very big, contained many, many people, numerous schools, and the yamen of the governor. It was a magnificent place altogether ! I wanted very much to go there at this time, and enter the middle school for Hsiang Hsiang people. That winter I asked one of my teachers in the higher primary school to introduce me there. The teacher agreed, and I walked to Changsha, exceedingly excited, half-fearing that I would be refused entrance, hardly daring to hope that I could actually become a student in this great school. To my astonishment, I was admitted without difficulty. But political events were moving rapidly and I was to remain there only half a year.

" In Changsha I read my first newspaper, the *People's Strength* (*Min Li Pao*), a nationalist revolutionary journal which told of the Canton Uprising against the Manchu dynasty and the death of the Seventy-two Heroes, under the leadership of a Hunanese, named Wang Hsing. I was most impressed with this story and found the *Min Li Pao* full of stimulating material. It was edited by Yü Yu-jen, who later became a famous leader of the Kuomintang. I learned also of Sun Yat-sen at this time, and of the programme of the T'ung Meng Hui. The country was on the eve of the First Revolution. I was agitated so much that I wrote an article, which I posted on the school wall. It was my first expression of a political opinion, and it was somewhat muddled. I had not yet given up my admiration of K'ang Yu-wei and Liang Ch'i-ch'ao. I did not clearly understand the differences between them. Therefore in my article I advocated that Sun Yat-sen must be called back from Japan to become President of a new Government, that K'ang Yu-wei be made Premier, and Liang Ch'i-ch'ao Minister of Foreign Affairs !

" The anti-foreign capital movement began in connection with the building of the Szechuan–Hankow railway and a popular demand for a parliament became widespread. In reply to it the

Emperor decreed merely that an Advisory Council be created.
The students in my school became more and more agitated. They
demonstrated their anti-Manchu sentiments by a rebellion
against the pigtail. One friend and I clipped off our pigtails, but
others, who had promised to do so, afterward failed to keep their
word. My friend and I therefore assaulted them in secret and
forcibly removed their queues, a total of more than ten falling
victim to our shears. Thus in a short space of time I had pro-
gressed from ridiculing the False Foreign Devil's imitation
queue to demanding the general abolition of queues. How a political idea can change a point of view !

" I got into a dispute with a friend in a law school over the
pigtail episode, and we each advanced opposing theories on the
subject. The law student held that the body, skin, hair and nails
are heritages from one's parents and must not be destroyed,
quoting the Classics to clinch his argument. But I myself and the
anti-pigtailers developed a counter-theory, on an anti-Manchu
political basis, and thoroughly silenced him.

" After the Wuhan Uprising occurred, led by Li Yuan-hung,
martial law was declared in Hunan. The political scene rapidly
altered. One day a revolutionary appeared in the middle school
and made a stirring speech, with the permission of the principal.
Seven or eight students arose in the assembly and supported him
with vigorous denunciations of the Manchus, and calls for action
to establish the Republic. Everyone listened with complete
attention. Not a sound was heard as the orator of the revolution,
one of the officials of Li Yuan-hung, spoke before the excited
students.

" Four or five days after hearing this speech, I determined to
join the revolutionary army of Li Yuan-hung. I decided to go to
Hankow with several other friends, and we collected some money
from our classmates. Having heard that the streets of Hankow
were very wet, and that it was necessary to wear rain-shoes, I
went to borrow some from a friend in the army, who was quartered outside the city. I was stopped by the garrison guards. The
place had become very active, the soldiers had for the first time
been furnished with bullets, and they were pouring into the
streets.

" Rebels were approaching the city along the Canton–Hankow

railway, and fighting had begun. A big battle occurred outside
the city walls of Changsha. There was at the same time an insurrection within the city, and the gates were stormed and taken
by Chinese labourers. Through one of them I re-entered the city.
Then I stood on a high place and watched the battle, until at
last I saw the *Han*[1] flag raised over the yamen. It was a white
banner with the character *Han* in it. I returned to my school,
to find it under military guard.

" On the following day, a *tutuh*[2] Government was organized.
Two prominent members of the Kê Lao Hui were made *tutuh*
and vice-*tutuh*. These were Chao Ta-feng and Chen Tso-hsing,
respectively. The new Government was established in the former
buildings of the Provincial Advisory Council, chief of which was
T'an Yen-k'ai, who was dismissed. The Council itself was
abolished. Among the Manchu documents found by the revolutionaries were some copies of a petition begging for the opening of
parliament. The original had been written in blood by Hsu
Teh-lih, who is now Commissioner of Education in the Soviet
Government. Hsu had cut off the end of his finger, as a demonstration of sincerity and determination, and his petition began,
' Begging that parliament be opened, I bid farewell [to the provincial delegates to Peking] by cutting my finger.'

" The new *tutuh* and vice-*tutuh* did not last long. They were
not bad men, and had some revolutionary intentions, but they
were poor and represented the interests of the oppressed. The
landlords and merchants were dissatisfied with them. Not many
days later, when I went to call on a friend, I saw their corpses
lying in the street. T'an Yen-k'ai had organized a revolt against
them, as representative of the Hunan landlords and militarists.

" Many students were now joining the army. A student army
had been organized and among these students was T'ang Sheng-
chih.[3] I did not like the student army; I considered the basis of
it too confused. I decided to join the regular army instead, and
help complete the revolution. The Ch'ing Emperor had not yet
abdicated, and there was a period of struggle.

---

[1] *Han*, i.e. Chinese.

[2] A *tutuh* was a military governor.

[3] T'ang Sheng-chih later became commander of the Nationalist armies of the
Wuhan Government of Wang Ching-wei, in 1927. He betrayed both Wang and the
Reds and began the " peasant massacre " of Hunan.

" My salary was seven dollars a month—which is more than I get in the Red Army now, however—and of this I spent two dollars a month on food. I also had to buy water. The soldiers had to carry water in from outside the city, but I, being a student, could not condescend to carrying, and bought it from the water-pedlars. The rest of my wages were spent on newspapers, of which I became an avid reader. Among journals then dealing with the revolution was the *Hsiang Kiang Daily News* (*Hsiang Kiang Erh Pao*). Socialism was discussed in it, and in these columns I first learned the term. I also discussed Socialism, really social-reformism, with other students and soldiers. I read some pamphlets written by Kiang K'ang-hu about Socialism and its principles. I wrote enthusiastically to several of my classmates on this subject, but only one of them responded in agreement.

" There was a Hunan miner in my squad, and an ironsmith, whom I liked very much. The rest were mediocre, and one was a rascal. I persuaded two more students to join the army, and became on friendly terms with the platoon commander and most of the soldiers. I could write, I knew something about books, and they respected my ' Great Learning.' I could help by writing letters for them or in other such ways.

" The outcome of the revolution was not yet decided. The Ch'ing had not wholly given up the power, and there was a struggle within the Kuomintang concerning the leadership. It was said in Hunan that further war was inevitable. Several armies were organized against the Manchus and against Yuan Shih-k'ai.[1] Among these was the Hunan army. But just as the Hunanese were preparing to move into action, Sun Yat-sen and Yuan Shih-k'ai came to an agreement, the scheduled war was called off, North and South were ' unified,' and the Nanking Government was dissolved. Thinking the revolution was over, I resigned from the army and decided to return to my books. I had been a soldier for half a year.

" I began to read advertisements in the papers. Many schools were then being opened and used this medium to attract new students. I had no special standard for judging schools; I did not know exactly what I wanted to do. An advertisement for a

[1] Yuan later became " President " of China, and in 1915 attempted to become Emperor.

police school caught my eye and I registered for entrance to it. Before I was examined, however, I read an advertisement of a soap-making 'school.' No tuition was required, board was furnished and a small salary was promised. It was an attractive and inspiring advertisement. It told of the great social benefits of soap-making, how it would enrich the country and enrich the people. I changed my mind about the police school and decided to become a soap-maker. I paid my dollar registration fee here also.

" Meanwhile, a friend of mine had become a law student and he urged me to enter his school. I also read an alluring advertisement of this law school, which promised many wonderful things. It promised to teach students all about law in three years and guaranteed that at the end of this period they would instantly become mandarins. My friend kept praising the school to me, until finally I wrote to my family, repeated all the promises of the advertisement, and asked them to send me tuition money. I painted a bright picture for them of my future as a jurist and mandarin. Then I paid a dollar to register in the law school and waited to hear from my parents.

" Fate again intervened in the form of an advertisement for a commercial school. Another friend counselled me that the country was in economic war, and that what was most needed were economists who could build up the nation's economy. His argument prevailed and I spent another dollar to register in this commercial middle school. I actually enrolled there and was accepted. Meanwhile, however, I continued to read advertisements, and one day I read one describing the charms of a higher commercial public school. It was operated by the Government, it offered a wide curriculum, and I heard that its instructors were very able men. I decided it would be better to become a commercial expert there, paid my dollar and registered, then wrote to my father of my decision. He was pleased. My father readily appreciated the advantages of commercial cleverness. I entered this school and remained—for one month.

" The trouble with my new school, I discovered, was that most of the courses were taught in English, and, in common with other students, I knew little English; indeed, scarcely more than the alphabet. An additional handicap was that the school provided no English teacher. Disgusted with this situation, I withdrew from the institution at the end of the month and continued my perusal of the advertisements.

" My next scholastic adventure was in the First Provincial Middle School. I registered for a dollar, took the entrance examination, and passed at the head of the list of candidates. It was a big school, with many students, and its graduates were numerous. A Chinese teacher there helped me very much; he was attracted to me because of my literary tendency. This teacher loaned me a book called the *Chronicles with Imperial Commentaries* (*Yü P'i T'ung Chien*), which contained imperial edicts and critiques by Ch'ien Lung.

" About this time a Government magazine exploded in Changsha. There was a huge fire, and we students found it very interesting. Tons of bullets and shells exploded, and gunpowder made an intense blaze. It was better than fire-crackers. About a month later T'an Yen-k'ai was driven out by Yuan Shih-k'ai, who now had control of the political machinery of the Republic. T'ang Hsiang-ming replaced T'an Yen-k'ai and he set about making arrangements for Yuan's enthronement.

" I did not like the First Middle School. Its curriculum was limited and its regulations were objectionable. After reading *Chronicles with Imperial Commentaries*, I had also come to the conclusion that it would be better for me to read and study alone. After six months I left the school, and arranged a schedule of education of my own, which consisted of reading every day in the Hunan Provincial Library. I was very regular and conscientious about it, and the half-year I spent in this way I consider to have been extremely valuable to me. I went to the library in the morning when it opened. At noon I paused only long enough to buy and consume two rice cakes, which were my daily lunch. I stayed in the library every day reading until it closed.

" During this period of self-education I read many books, studied world geography and world history. There for the first time I saw and studied with great interest a map of the world. I read Adam Smith's *The Wealth of Nations*, and Darwin's *Origin of Species*, and a book on ethics by John Stuart Mill. I read the works of Rousseau, Spencer's *Logic*, and a book on law written by Montesquieu. I mixed poetry and romances, and the tales of ancient Greece, with serious study of history and geography of Russia, America, England, France and other countries.

" I was then living in a guild house for natives of Hsiang Hsiang district. Many soldiers were there also—'retired' or disbanded men from the district, who had no work to do and little money. Students and soldiers were always quarrelling in the guild house, and one night this hostility between them broke out in physical violence. The soldiers attacked and tried to kill the students. I escaped by fleeing to the toilet, where I hid until the fight was over.

" I had no money then, my family refusing to support me unless I entered school, and since I could no longer live in the guild house I began looking for a new place to lodge. Meanwhile, I had been thinking seriously of my ' career ' and had about decided that I was best suited for teaching. I had begun reading advertisements again. An attractive announcement of the Hunan Normal School now came to my attention, and I read with interest of its advantages: no tuition required, and cheap board and cheap lodging. Two of my friends were also urging me to enter. They wanted my help in preparing entrance essays. I wrote of my intention to my family and received their consent. I composed essays for my two friends, and wrote one of my own. All were accepted—in reality, therefore, I was accepted three times. I did not then think my act of substituting for my friends an immoral one; it was merely a matter of friendship.

" I was a student in the Normal School for five years, and managed to resist the appeals of all future advertising. Finally I actually got my degree. Incidents in my life here, in the Hunan Provincial First Normal School, were many, and during this period my political ideas began to take shape. Here also I acquired my first experiences in social action.

" There were many regulations in the new school and I agreed with very few of them. For one thing, I was opposed to the required courses in natural science. I wanted to specialize in social sciences. Natural sciences did not especially interest me, and I did not study them, so I got poor marks in most of these courses. Most of all I hated a compulsory course in still-life drawing. I thought it extremely stupid. I used to think of the simplest subjects possible to draw, finish up quickly and leave the class. I remember once drawing a picture of the ' half-sun, half-rock,'[1] which I represented by a straight line with a semi-circle over it. Another time during an examination in drawing I contented myself with making an oval. I called it an egg. I got 40 in drawing, and failed. Fortunately my marks in social sciences were all excellent, and they balanced my poor grades in these other classes.

" A Chinese teacher here, whom the students nicknamed ' Yuan the Big Beard,' ridiculed my writing and called it the work of a journalist. He despised Liang Ch'i-ch'ao, who had been my model, and considered him half-literate. I was obliged to alter my style. I studied the writings of Han Yü, and mastered the old Classical phraseology. Thanks to Yuan the Big Beard, therefore, I can to-day still turn out a passable Classical essay if required.

" The teacher who made the strongest impression on me was Yang Chen-ch'i, a returned student from England, with whose life I was later to become intimately related. He taught ethics, he was an idealist, and a man of high moral character. He believed in his ethics very strongly and tried to imbue his students with the desire to become just, moral, virtuous men, useful in society. Under his influence, I read a book on ethics translated by Ts'ai Yuan-p'ei and was inspired to write an essay which I entitled ' The Energy of the Mind.' I was then an idealist and my essay was highly praised by Professor Yang Chen-ch'i, from his idealist viewpoint. He gave me a mark of 100 for it.

" A teacher named T'ang used to give me old copies of the *People's Paper* (*Min Pao*), and I read them with keen interest. I learned from them about the activities and programme of the T'ung Meng Hui.[2] One day I read a copy of the *Min Pao* containing a story about two Chinese students who were travelling across China and had reached Tatsienlu, on the edge of Tibet. This inspired me very much. I wanted to follow their example;

---

[1] The reference is to a line in a famous poem by Li T'ai-po.

[2] The T'ung Meng Hui, a revolutionary secret society, was founded by Dr. Sun Yat-sen, and was forerunner of the Kuomintang, which now has power in Nanking. Most of its members were exiles in Japan, where they carried on a vigorous "brush-war" against Liang Ch'i-ch'ao and K'ang Yu-wei, leaders of the " reformed monarchist " party.

but I had no money, and thought I should first try out travelling in Hunan.

" The next summer I set out across the province by foot, and journeyed through five counties. I was accompanied by a student named Hsiao Yü. We walked through these five counties without using a single copper. The peasants fed us and gave us a place to sleep; wherever we went we were kindly treated and welcomed. This fellow, Hsiao Yü, with whom I travelled, later became a Kuomintang official in Nanking, under Yi Pei-chi, who was then president of Hunan Normal College. Yi Pei-chi became a high official at Nanking and got Hsiao Yü appointed to the office of custodian of the Peking Palace Museum. Hsiao sold some of the most valuable treasures in the museum and absconded with the funds in 1934.

" Feeling expansive and the need for a few intimate companions, I one day inserted an advertisement in a Changsha paper, inviting young men interested in patriotic work to make a contact with me. I specified youths who were hardened and determined, and ready to make sacrifices for their country. To this advertisement I received three and one-half replies. One was from Liu Chiang-lung, who later was to join the Communist Party and afterward to betray it. Two others were from young men who later were to become ultra-reactionaries. The ' half ' reply came from a non-committal youth named Li Li-san.[1] Li listened to all I had to say, and then went away without making any definite proposals himself, and our friendship never developed.

" But gradually I did build up a group of students around myself, and the nucleus was formed of what later was to become a society[2] that was to have a widespread influence on the affairs and destiny of China. It was a serious-minded little group of men and they had no time to discuss trivialities. Everything they did or said must have a purpose. They had no time for love or ' romance ' and considered the times too critical and the need for knowledge too urgent to discuss women or personal matters. I was not interested in women. My parents had married me when

[1] Li Li-san later became responsible for the famous " Li Li-san line," which Mao Tse-tung bitterly opposed. Further on Mao tells of Li's struggle with the Red Army, and of its results.
[2] The Hsin Min Hsüeh Hui.

I was fourteen to a girl of twenty, but I had never lived with her —and never subsequently did. I did not consider her my wife and at this time gave little thought to her. Quite aside from the discussions of feminine charm, which usually play an important rôle in the lives of young men of this age, my companions even rejected talk of ordinary matters of daily life. I remember once being in the house of a youth who began to talk to me about buying some meat, and in my presence called in his servant and discussed the matter with him, then ordering him to buy a piece. I was annoyed and did not see this fellow again. My friends and I preferred to talk only of large matters—the nature of men, of human society, of China, the world, and the universe !

" We also became ardent physical culturists. In the winter holidays we tramped through the fields, up and down mountains, along city walls, and across the streams and rivers. If it rained we took off our shirts and called it a rain bath. When the sun was hot we also doffed shirts and called it a sun-bath. In the spring winds we shouted that this was a new sport called ' wind bathing.' We slept in the open when frost was already falling and even in November swam in the cold rivers. All this went on under the title of ' body-training.' Perhaps it helped much to build the physique which I was to need so badly later on in my many marches back and forth across South China, and on the Long March from Kiangsi to the North-west.

" I built up a wide correspondence with many students and friends in other towns and cities. Gradually I began to realize the necessity for a more closely knit organization. In 1917, with some other friends, I helped to found the Hsin Min Hsüeh Hui (' New People's Study Society '). It had from seventy to eighty members, and of these many were later to become famous names in Chinese Communism, and in the history of the Chinese Revolution. Among the better-known Communists who were in the Hsin Min Hsüeh Hui were: Lo Man, now secretary of the Party Organization Committee; Hsia Hsi, now in the 2nd Front Red Army; Ho Hsien-hôn, who became high judge of the Supreme Court in the Central Soviet regions and was later killed by Chiang Kai-shek; Kuo Liang, a famous labour-organizer, killed by General Ho Chien in 1930; Hsiao Chu-chang, a writer now in Soviet Russia; Ts'ai Ho-shêng, a member of the Central

Committee of the Communist Party, killed by Chiang Kai-shek
in 1927; Yeh Li-yün, who became a member of the Central Committee, and later ' betrayed ' to' the Kuomintang, and became a
capitalist trade-union organizer; and Hsiao Chen, a prominent
Party leader, one of the six signers of the original agreement for
the formation of the Party, but who died not long ago from illness. The majority of the members of the Hsin Min Hsüeh Hui
were killed in the counter-revolution of 1927.

" Another society that was formed about that time, and
resembled the Hsin Min Hsüeh Hui, was the ' Social Welfare
Society ' of Hupeh. Many of its members also later became
Communists. Among them was Wen Teh-ying, its leader, who
was killed during the counter-revolution by Chiang Kai-shek.
Lin Piao, now president of the Red Army Academy, was a
member. So was Chang Hao, now in charge of work among
White troops. In Peiping there was a society called Fu Hsieh,
some of whose members later became Reds. Elsewhere in China,
notably in Shanghai, Hangchow, Hankow and Tientsin,[1] radical
societies were organized by the militant youth then beginning to
assert an influence on Chinese politics.

" Most of these societies were organized more or less under the
influence of *New Youth (Hsin Ch'ing Nien)*, the famous magazine
of the Literary Renaissance, edited by Ch'ên Tu-hsiu. I began to
read this magazine while I was a student in the normal college
and admired the articles of Hu Shih and Ch'ên Tu-hsiu very
much. They became for a while my models, replacing Liang
Ch'i-ch'ao and K'ang Yu-wei, whom I had already discarded.

" At this time my mind was a curious mixture of ideas of
liberalism, democratic reformism, and Utopian Socialism. I had
somewhat vague passions about ' nineteenth-century democracy,' Utopianism and old-fashioned liberalism, and I was
definitely anti-militarist and anti-imperialist.

" I had entered the normal college in 1912. I graduated in
1918."

[1] In Tientsin it was the Chou-Wu Hsüeh Hui, or " Awakening Society," which
led in organization of radical youth. Chou En-lai was one of the founders. Others
included: Miss Teng Ying-ch'ao (now Mrs. Chou En-lai); Ma Chun, who was
executed in Peking in 1927; and Sun Hsiao-ch'ing, now secretary of the Canton
Committee of the Kuomintang.

3

Prelude to Revolution

DURING Mao's recollections of his past I noticed that an auditor at least as interested as myself was Ho Tze-nien—his wife. Many of the facts he told about himself and the Communist movement she had evidently never heard before, and this was true of most of Mao's comrades in Pao An. Later on, when I gathered biographical notes from other Red leaders, their colleagues often crowded around interestedly to listen to the stories for the first time. Although they had all fought together for years, very often they knew nothing of each other's pre-Communist days, which they had tended to regard as a kind of Dark Ages period, one's real life beginning only when one became a Communist.

It was another night, and Mao sat cross-legged, leaning against two dispatch-boxes. He lit a cigarette, and took up the thread of the story where he had left off the day before:

" During my years in normal school in Changsha I had spent, altogether, only $160—including my numerous registration fees ! Of this amount I must have used a third for newspapers, because regular subscriptions cost me about a dollar a month, and I often bought books and journals on the news-stands. My father cursed me for this extravagance. He called it wasted money on wasted paper. But I had acquired the newspaper-reading habit,[1] and from 1911 to 1927, when I climbed up Chingkanshan, I never stopped reading the daily papers of Peiping, Shanghai and Hunan.

" In my last year in school my mother died, and more than ever I lost interest in returning home. I decided, that summer, to go to Peiping—then Peking. Many students from Hunan were planning trips to France, to study under the ' work and learn ' scheme, which France used to recruit young Chinese in her cause during the World War. Before leaving China these students planned to study French in Peiping. I helped organize the movement, and in the groups who went abroad were many students

[1] Modern newspapers were then still a novelty in China, and many people, particularly officials, looked upon them with extreme repugnance, as indeed they do to-day !

from the Hunan Normal School, most of whom were later to become famous radicals. Hsu Teh-lih was influenced by the movement also, and when he was over forty he left his professorship at Hunan Normal College and went to France. He did not become a Communist, however, till 1927.

" I accompanied some of the Hunanese students to Peking. However, although I had helped organize the movement, and it had the support of the Hsin Min Hsüeh Hui, I did not want to go to Europe. I felt that I did not know enough about my own country, and that my time could be more profitably spent in China. Those students who had decided to go to France studied French then from Li Shih-ts'un, who is now president of the Chung-fa (Sino-French) University, but I did not. I had other plans.

" Peiping seemed very expensive to me. I had reached the capital by borrowing from friends, and when I arrived I had to look for work at once. Yang Chen-ch'i, my former ethics teacher at the normal school, had become a professor at Peking National University. I appealed to him for help in finding a job, and he introduced me to the university librarian. This was Li Ta-chao, who later became a founder of the Communist Party of China, and was afterwards executed by Chang Tso-lin. Li Ta-chao gave me work, as assistant librarian, for which I was paid the generous sum of eight dollars a month.

" My office was so low that people avoided me. One of my tasks was to register the names of people who came to read newspapers, but to most of them I didn't exist as a human being. Among those who came to read I recognized the names of famous leaders of the renaissance movement, men like Fu Ssu-nien, Lo Chia-lung, and others, in whom I was intensely interested. I tried to begin conversations with them on political and cultural subjects, but they were very busy men. They had no time to listen to an assistant librarian speaking southern dialect.

" But I wasn't discouraged. I joined the Society of Philosophy, and the Journalism Society, in order to be able to attend classes in the university. In the Journalism Society I met fellow-students like Chen Kung-po, who is now a high official at Nanking; T'an P'ing-shan, who later became a Communist and still later a member of the so-called ' Third Party '; and Shao P'iao-p'ing. Shao, especially, helped me very much. He was a lecturer in the Journalism Society, a liberal, and a man of fervent idealism and fine character. He was killed by Chang Tso-lin in 1926.

" While I was working in the library I also met Chang Kuo-t'ao, now vice-chairman of the Soviet Government; K'ang P'ei-ch'en, who later joined the Ku Klux Klan in California [! ! !—E. S.]; and Tuan Hsi-p'en, now Vice-Minister of Education in Nanking. And here also I met and fell in love with Yang K'ai-hui. She was the daughter of my former ethics teacher, Yang Chen-ch'i, who had made a great impression on me in my youth, and who afterwards was a genuine friend in Peking.

" My interest in politics continued to increase, and my mind turned more and more radical. I have told you of the background for this. But just now I was still confused, looking for a road, as we say. I read some pamphlets on anarchy, and was much influenced by them. With a student named Chu Hsun-pei, who used to visit me, I often discussed anarchism and its possibilities in China. At that time I favoured many of its proposals.

" My own living conditions in Peking were quite miserable, and in contrast the beauty of the old capital was a vivid and living compensation. I stayed in a place called ' Three-Eyes Well ' (San Yen-ching), in a little room which held seven other people. When we were all packed fast on the *k'ang* there was scarcely room enough for any of us to breathe. I used to have to warn people on each side of me when I wanted to turn over. But in the parks and the old palace grounds I saw the early northern spring, I saw the white plum blossoms flower while the ice still held solid over the North Sea. I saw the willows over Pei Hai with the ice crystals hanging from them and remembered the description of the scene by the T'ang poet Chen Chang, who wrote about Pei Hai's winter-jewelled trees, looking ' like 10,000 peach-trees blossoming.' The innumerable trees of Peking aroused my wonder and admiration.

" Early in 1919 I went to Shanghai, with the students bound for France. I had a ticket only to Tientsin, and I did not know how I was to get any farther. But, as the Chinese proverb says, ' Heaven will not delay a traveller,' and a fortunate loan of $10 from a fellow-student, who had got some money from the

Compte School in Peiping, enabled me to buy a ticket as far as P'u-k'ou. *En route* to Nanking I stopped at Ch'u Fou and visited Confucius's grave. I saw the small stream where Confucius's disciples bathed their feet and the little town where the sage lived as a child. He is supposed to have planted a famous tree near the historic temple dedicated to him, and I saw that. I also stopped by the river where Yen Hui, one of Confucius's famous disciples, had once lived, and I saw the birthplace of Mencius. On this trip I climbed T'ai Shan, the sacred mountain of Shantung, where General Feng Yu-hsiang retired and wrote his patriotic scrolls.

" But when I reached P'u-k'ou I was again without a copper, and without a ticket. Nobody had any money to lend me; I did not know how I was to get out of town. But the worst of the tragedy happened when a thief stole my only pair of shoes ! Ai-ya ! What was I to do ? But again, ' Heaven will not delay a traveller,' and I had a very good piece of luck. Outside the railway station I met an old friend from Hunan, and he proved to be my ' good angel.' He lent me money for a pair of shoes, and enough to buy a ticket to Shanghai. Thus I safely completed my journey—keeping an eye on my new shoes. At Shanghai I found that a good sum had been raised to help send the students to France, and an allowance had been provided to help me return to Hunan. I saw my friends off on the steamer and then set off for Changsha.

" High marks of my first trip to the North, as I remember it, were these excursions:

" I walked on the ice of the Gulf of Pei Hai. I walked around the lake of T'ung T'ing, and I circled the wall of Paotingfu. I walked around the wall of Hsuchou, famous in the *Three Kingdoms* (*San Kuo*), and around Nanking's wall, also famous in history. Finally, I climbed T'ai Shan and visited Confucius's grave. These seemed to me then achievements worth adding to my adventures and walking tours in Hunan.

" When I returned to Changsha I took a more direct rôle in politics. After the May Fourth Movement I had devoted most of my time to student political activities, and I was editor of the *Hsiang Chiang Review*, the Hunan student's paper, which had a great influence on the student movement in South China.

In Changsha I helped found the Wen-hua Shu Hui (Cultural Book Society), an association for study of modern cultural and political tendencies. This society, and more especially the Hsin Min Hsüeh Hui, were violently opposed to Chang Ching-yao, then *tuchun* of Hunan, and a vicious character. We led a general student-strike against Chang, demanding his removal, and sent delegations to Peiping and the South-west, where Sun Yat-sen was then active, to agitate against him. In retaliation to the students' opposition, Chang Ching-yao suppressed the *Hsiang Chiang Review*.

" After this I went to Peking, to represent the Hsin Min Hsüeh Hui, and organize an anti-militarist movement there. The Hsin Min Hsüeh Hui broadened its fight against Chang Ching-yao into a general anti-militarist agitation, and I became head of a news agency, to promote this work. In Hunan the movement was rewarded with some success. Chang Ching-yao was overthrown by T'an Yen-k'ai, and a new régime was established in Changsha. About this time the Hsin Min Hsüeh Hui began to divide into two groups, a Right and Left wing—the Left wing insisting on a programme of far-reaching social and economic and political changes.

" I went to Shanghai for the second time in 1919. There once more I saw Ch'ên Tu-hsiu.[1] I had first met him in Peking, when I was at Peking National University, and he had influenced me perhaps more than anyone else. I also met Hu Shih at that time, having called on him to try to win his support for the Hunanese students' struggle. In Shanghai I discussed with Ch'ên Tu-hsiu our plans for a League for Reconstruction of Hunan. Then I returned to Changsha, and began to organize it. I took a place as a teacher there, meanwhile continuing my activity in the Hsin Min Hsüeh Hui. The society had a programme then for the ' independence ' of Hunan, meaning, really, autonomy.

---

[1] Ch'ên Tu-hsiu was born in Anhui, in 1879, became a noted scholar and essayist and for years headed the department of literature at Peking National University —" cradle of the Literary Renaissance "—of which Ch'ên was the leader. His *Hsin Ch'ing-Nien (New Youth)* magazine began the movement for adoption of the *pai-hua* or vernacular Chinese as the national language to replace the " dead " *wen-yen* or Classical language. He was founder and chief promoter of the Communist Party in China, later became a member of the Central Executive Committee of the Kuomintang. He was arrested in Shanghai in 1933 by the Kuomintang authorities, given a farcical " trial," and is now serving a long sentence at Nanking. With Lu Hsun he ranks as a most important literary figure of his time.

Disgusted with the Northern Government, and believing that Hunan could modernize more rapidly if freed from connections with Peking, our group agitated for separation. I was then a strong supporter of America's Monroe Doctrine and the Open Door.

" T'an Yen-k'ai was driven out of Hunan by a militarist called Chao Hêng-t'i, who utilized the ' Hunan independence ' movement for his own ends. He pretended to support it, advocating the idea of a United Autonomous States of China, but as soon as he got power he suppressed the democratic movement with great energy. Our group had demanded equal rights for men and women, and representative government, and in general approved of a platform for a bourgeois democracy. We openly advocated these reforms in our paper, the *New Hunan*. We led an attack on the provincial parliament, the majority of whose members were landlords and gentry appointed by the militarists. This struggle ended up in our pulling down the scrolls and banners, which were full of nonsensical and extravagant phrases.

" The attack on the parliament was considered a big incident in Hunan, and frightened the rulers. However, when Chao Hêng-t'i seized control he betrayed all the ideas he had supported, and especially he violently suppressed all demands for democracy. Our society therefore turned the struggle against him. I remember an episode in 1920, when the Hsin Min Hsüeh Hui organized a demonstration to celebrate the third anniversary of the Russian October Revolution. It was suppressed by the police. Some of the demonstrators had attempted to raise the Red Flag at that meeting, but were prohibited from doing so by the police. They then pointed out that, according to Article 12 of the (then) Constitution, the people had the right to assemble, organize, and speak, but the police were not impressed. They replied that they were not there to be taught the Constitution, but to carry out the orders of the governor, Chao Hêng-t'i. From this time on I became more and more convinced that only mass political power, secured through mass action, could guarantee the realization of dynamic reforms.

" In the winter of 1920, I organized workers politically, for the first time, and began to be guided in this by the influence of Marxist theory and the history of the Russian Revolution.

During my second visit to Peking I had read much about the events in Russia, and had eagerly sought out what little Communist literature was then available in Chinese. Three books especially deeply carved my mind, and built up in me a faith in Marxism, from which, once I had accepted it as the correct interpretation of history, I did not afterwards waver. These books were the *Communist Manifesto*, translated by Chen Wang-tao, and the first Marxist book ever published in Chinese; *Class Struggle*, by Kautsky; and a *History of Socialism*, by Kirkupp. By the summer of 1920 I had become, in theory and to some extent in action, a Marxist, and from this time on I considered myself a Marxist. In the same year I married Yang K'ai-hui."[1]

[1] Mao made no further reference to his life with Yang K'ai-hui. She was from all accounts a brilliant woman, a student of Peking National University, later a leader of youth during the Great Revolution, and one of the most active women Communists. Their marriage was celebrated as an " ideal romance " among radical youths in Hunan. It seems to have begun as a trial marriage; and they were evidently very devoted. She was killed by Ho Chien—in 1930, I believe.

4

The Nationalist Period

MAO was now a Marxist, but not a Communist—simply because as yet there did not exist in China such an organization as the Communist Party. Ch'ên Tu-hsiu had established contact with the Comintern as early as 1919. In 1920, M. Marlin, an energetic and persuasive representative of the Third International— the Ti San Kuo Chi, as the Chinese call it—came to Shanghai and arranged for connections to be made with a Chinese Party. Shortly afterwards Ch'ên summoned a conference in Shanghai, while almost simultaneously a group of Chinese students conferred in Paris and proposed to form a Communist organization there.

When one remembers that the Chinese Communist Party is still an adolescent of sixteen years, its achievements may be regarded as not inconsiderable. It is the strongest Communist Party in the world, outside of Russia, and the only one, with the same exception, that can boast a mighty army of its own.

Another night, and Mao carried on his narrative:

" In May of 1921, I went to Shanghai to attend the foundation meeting of the Communist Party. In its organization the leading rôles were played by Ch'ên Tu-hsiu and Li Ta-chao, both of whom were among the most brilliant intellectual leaders of China. Under Li Ta-chao, as assistant librarian at Peking National University, I had rapidly developed towards Marxism, and Ch'ên Tu-hsiu had been instrumental in my interests in that direction too. I had discussed with Ch'ên, on my second visit to Shanghai, the Marxist books that I had read, and Ch'ên's own assertions of belief had deeply impressed me at what was probably a critical period in my life.

" There was only one other Hunanese at the historic first meeting in Shanghai. Others present were Chang Kuo-t'ao, Pao Hui-aheng and Chou Hu-hai. Altogether there were twelve of us. The following October the first provincial branch of the Communist Party was organised in Hunan, and I became a member of it. Organizations were also established then in other provinces and cities. In Shanghai the Central Party Committee included Ch'ên Tu-hsiu, Chang Kuo-t'ao (now with the 4th Front Red Army), Chen Kung-po (now a Kuomintang official), Shih Tseng-tung (now a Nanking official), Sun Yuan-lu, Li Han-tsen (killed in Wuhan in 1927), Li Ta (later executed), and Li Sun. Members in Hupeh included Teng Pi-wu (now chairman of the Communist Party School in Pao An), Hsu Pei-hao, and Ssu Yang. In the Shansi party were Kao Chung-yu and some famous student leaders. In Peiping were Li Ta-chao (later executed), Teng Sung-hsia, Chang Kuo-t'ao (now vice-chairman of the Red military council), Lo Chang-lun, Lu Jen-ching (now a Trotskyite), and others. In Canton were Lin Pai-ch'u (now Commissioner of Finance in the Soviet Government) and P'eng Pai (executed in 1927). Wang Chin-mei and Teng En-ming were among the founders of the Shantung branch.

" Meanwhile, in France, a Chinese Communist Party had been organized by many of the worker-students there, and its founding was almost simultaneous with the beginning of the organization in China. Among the founders of the Party there were Chou En-lai, Li Li-san, and Shang Chen-yu, the wife of Tsai Ho-sheng, and the only Chinese woman among the founders. Lo Man and Tsai Ho-sheng were also founders of the French branch. A Chinese Party was organized in Germany, but this was somewhat later: among its members were Kao Yu-han, Chu Teh (now Commander-in-Chief of the Red Army), and Chang Sheng-fu (now a professor at Tsinghua University). In Moscow the founders of the branch were Ch'ü Ch'iu-pai and others, and in Japan there was Chou Fu-hai.

" In May 1922 the Hunan Party, of which I was then secretary, had already organized more than twenty trade unions, among miners, railway workers, municipal employees, printers, and workers in the Government Mint. A vigorous labour movement began that winter. The work of the Communist Party was then concentrated mainly on students and workers, and very little was done among the peasants. Most of the big mines were organized and virtually all the students. There were numerous struggles on both the students' and workers' fronts. In the winter of 1922, Chao Hêng-t'i, civil governor of Hunan, ordered the execution of two Hunanese workers, Huang Ai and Pang Yuan-ch'ing, and as a result a widespread agitation began against him. Huang Ai, one of the two workers killed, was a leader of the Right wing labour movement, which had its base in the industrial school students and was opposed to us, but we supported them in this case, and in many other struggles. Anarchists were also influential in the trade unions, which were then organized into an All-Hunan Labour Syndicate. But we compromised with them, and through negotiation prevented many hasty and useless actions by them.

" I was sent to Shanghai to help organize the movement against Chao Hêng-t'i. The Second Congress of the Party was convened in Shanghai that winter (1922), and I intended to attend. However, I forgot the name of the place where it was to be held, could not find any comrades, and missed it. I returned to Hunan and vigorously pushed the work among the labour unions. That spring there were many strikes for better wages and better treatment and recognition of the labour unions. Most of these were successful. On May 1 a general strike was called in Hunan, and this marked the achievement of unprecedented strength in the labour movement of China.

" The Third Congress of the Communist Party was held in Canton in 1923 and the historic decision was reached to enter the Kuomintang, co-operate with it, and create a United Front against the northern militarists. I went to Shanghai and worked in the Central Committee of the Party. Next spring (1924) I went to Canton and attended the First National Congress of the Kuomintang. In March I returned to Shanghai and combined my work in the executive bureau of the Communist Party with membership in the executive bureau of the Kuomintang of Shanghai. The other members of this bureau then were Wang Ching-wei (later Premier at Nanking), and Hu Han-min, with whom I worked in co-ordinating the measures of the Communist Party and the Kuomintang. That summer the Whampoa Military Academy was set up. Galen became its adviser, other Soviet advisers arrived from Russia, and the Kuomintang-Communist Party *entente* began to assume the proportions of a nation-wide revolutionary movement. The following winter I returned to Hunan for a rest. I had become ill in Shanghai, but while in Hunan I organized the nucleus of the great peasant movement of that province.

" Formerly I had not fully realized the degree of class struggle among the peasantry, but after the May 30 Incident (1925), and during the great wave of political activity which followed it, the Hunanese peasantry became very militant. I left my home, where I had been resting, and began a rural organizational campaign. In a few months we had formed more than twenty peasant unions, and had aroused the wrath of the landlords, who demanded my arrest. Chao Hêng-t'i sent troops after me, and I fled to Canton! I reached there just at the time the Whampoa students had defeated Yang Hsi-ming, the Yünnan militarist, and Lu Tsung-wai, the Kwangsi militarist, and an air of great optimism pervaded the city and the Kuomintang. Chiang Kai-shek had been made commander of the 1st Army and Wang Ching-wei chairman of the Government, following the death of Sun Yat-sen in Peking.

" I became editor of the *Political Weekly,* a publication of the political department of the Kuomintang. It later played a very active rôle in attacking and discrediting the Right wing of the Kuomintang, led by Tai Chi-t'ao. I was also put in charge of training organizers for the peasant movement, and established a course for this purpose which was attended by representatives from twenty-one different provinces, and included students from Inner Mongolia. Not long after my arrival in Canton I became chief of the Agitprop department of the Kuomintang, and candidate for the Central Committee. Lin Pai-ch'u was then chief of the peasant department of the Kuomintang, and T'an P'ing-shan, another Communist, was chief of the workers' department.

" I was writing more and more, and assuming special responsibilities in peasant work in the Communist Party. On the basis of my study and of my work in organizing the Hunan peasants, I wrote two pamphlets, one called *An Analysis of the Different Classes of Chinese Society,* and the other called *The Class Basis of Chao Hêng-t'i, and the Tasks Before Us.* Ch'ên Tu-hsiu opposed the opinions expressed in the first one, which advocated a radical land policy and vigorous organization of the peasantry, under the Communist Party, and he refused it publication in the Communist central organs. It was later published in the *Peasant Monthly,* of Canton, and in the magazine *Chung Kuo Ch'ing-mien (Chinese Youth).* The second thesis was published as a pamphlet in Hunan. I began to disagree with Ch'ên's Right opportunist policy about this time, and we gradually drew further apart, although the struggle between us did not come to a climax until 1927.

" I continued to work in the Kuomintang in Canton until about the time Chiang Kai-shek attempted his first *coup d'état* there in March 1926. After the reconciliation of Left and Right wing Kuomintang and the reaffirmation of the Kuomintang-Communist solidarity, I went to Shanghai, in the spring of 1926. The Second Congress of the Kuomintang was held in May of that year, under the leadership of Chiang Kai-shek. In Shanghai I directed the peasant department of the Communist Party, and from there was sent to Hunan, as inspector of the peasant movement. Meanwhile, under the United Front of the Kuomintang and the Communist Party, the historic Northern Expedition began in the autumn of 1926.

" In Hunan I inspected peasant organization and political conditions in five *hsien*—Changsha, Li Ling, Hsiang T'an, Hung Shan and Hsiang Hsiang—and made my report to the Central Committee, urging the adoption of a new line in the peasant movement. Early next spring, when I reached Wuhan, an inter-provincial meeting of peasants was held, and I attended it and discussed the proposals of my thesis, which carried recommendations for a widespread redistribution of land. At this meeting were P'eng Pai, Fang Chih-min and two Russian Communists, York and Volen, among others. A resolution was passed adopting my proposal for submission to the Fifth Conference of the Communist Party. The Central Committee, however, rejected it.

" When the Fifth Conference was convened in Wuhan in May 1927 the Party was still under the domination of Ch'ên Tu-hsiu. Although Chiang Kai-shek had already led the counter-revolution and begun his attacks on the Communist Party in Shanghai and Nanking, Ch'ên was still for moderation and concessions to the Wuhan Kuomintang. Overriding all opposition, he followed a Right opportunist petty-bourgeois policy. I was very dissatisfied with the Party policy then, especially toward the peasant movement. I think to-day that if the peasant movement had been more thoroughly organized and armed for a class struggle against the landlords, the Soviets would have had an earlier and far more powerful development throughout the whole country.

" But Ch'ên Tu-hsiu violently disagreed. He did not understand the rôle of the peasantry in the revolution and greatly underestimated its possibilities at this time. Consequently, the Fifth Conference, held on the eve of the crisis of the Great Revolution, failed to pass an adequate land programme. My opinions, which called for rapid intensification of the agrarian struggle, were not even discussed, for the Central Committee, also dominated by Ch'ên Tu-hsiu, refused to bring them up for consideration. The Conference dismissed the land problem by defining a landlord as ' a peasant who owned over 500 *mou* of land '—a wholly inadequate and unpractical basis on which to develop the class struggle, and quite without consideration of the special character of land economy in China. Following the Conference, however, an All-China Peasants' Union was organized and I became first president of it.

" By the spring of 1927 the peasant movement in Hupeh, Kiangsi and Fukien, and especially in Hunan, had developed a startling militancy, despite the lukewarm attitude of the Communist Party to it, and the definite alarm of the Kuomintang. High officials and army commanders began to demand its suppression, describing the Peasants' Union as a ' vagabond union,' and its actions and demands as excessive. Ch'ên Tu-hsiu had withdrawn me from Hunan, holding me responsible for certain happenings there, and violently opposing my ideas.

" In April the counter-revolutionary movement had begun in Nanking and Shanghai, and a general massacre of organized workers had taken place under Chiang Kai-shek. The same measures were carried out in Canton. On May 21 the Hsu Ko-hsiang Uprising occurred in Hunan. Scores of peasants and workers were killed by the reactionaries. Shortly afterward the ' Left ' Kuomintang at Wuhan annulled its agreement with the Communists and ' expelled ' them from the Kuomintang and from a Government which quickly ceased to exist.

" Many Communist leaders were now ordered by the Party to leave the country, go to Russia or Shanghai or places of safety. I was ordered to go to Szechuan. I persuaded Ch'ên

Tu-hsiu to send me to Hunan instead, as secretary of the Provincial Committee, but after ten days he ordered me hastily to return, accusing me of organizing an uprising against T'ang Sheng-chih, then in command at Wuhan. The affairs of the Party were now in a chaotic state. Nearly everyone was opposed to Ch'ên Tu-hsiu's leadership and his opportunist line. The collapse of the *entente* at Wuhan soon afterward brought about his downfall."

5

The Soviet Movement

A CONVERSATION I had with Mao Tse-tung concerning the much disputed events of the spring of 1927 seems to me of sufficient interest to mention here. It was not part of his autobiography, as he told it to me; but, as a personal reflection on what was a turning-point experience in the life of every Chinese Communist, it is important to note.

I asked Mao whom he considered most responsible for the failure of the Communist Party in 1927, the defeat of the Wuhan Coalition Government, and the whole triumph of the Nanking dictatorship. Mao placed the greatest blame on Ch'ên Tu-hsiu, whose " wavering opportunism deprived the Party of decisive leadership and a direct line of its own at a moment when further compromise clearly meant catastrophe."

After Ch'ên, the man most responsible for the defeat was Borodin, chief Russian political adviser. Mao explained that Borodin had completely reversed his position, favouring a radical land redistribution in 1926, but strongly opposing it in 1927, without any logical support for his vacillations. " Borodin stood just a little to the right of Ch'ên Tu-hsiu," Mao said, " and was ready to do everything to please the bourgeoisie, even to the disarming of the workers, which he finally ordered." Roy, the Indian delegate of the Comintern, " stood a little to the left of both Ch'ên and Borodin, but he only stood." He " could talk," according to Mao, " and he talked too much, without offering any method of realization." Mao thought that, objectively, Roy had been a fool, Borodin a blunderer, and Ch'ên an unconscious traitor.

" Ch'ên was really frightened of the workers and especially of the armed peasants. Confronted at last with the reality of armed insurrection he completely lost his senses. He could no longer see clearly what was happening, and his petty-bourgeois instincts betrayed him into panic and defeat."

Ch'ên was at that time complete dictator of the Chinese Party, and took vital decisions without even consulting the Central Committee. " He did not show other Party leaders the orders of

Fc

the Comintern, nor even discuss them with us." But in the end
it was Roy who forced the break with the Kuomintang. The
Comintern sent a message to Borodin, ordering the Party to begin
confiscation of the landlords' land. Roy got hold of a copy of it,
and promptly showed it to Wang Ching-wei, then chairman of
the Leftist Wuhan Government. The result of this caprice[1] is well
known. The Communists were expelled from the Kuomintang by
the Wuhan régime, its strength collapsed, and soon afterwards
Chiang Kai-shek destroyed Wuhan itself.

It appears that in 1927 the Comintern was not giving
" advice," but flat orders, to the Chinese Communist Party,
which was apparently not even empowered to reject them.
The fiasco of Wuhan became, of course, a pivot of the struggle in
Russia over the nature of the world revolution. It was following
this period that the Opposition in Russia was crushed, Trotsky's
theory of " permanent revolution " was discredited, and the
Soviet Union set out in earnest to " build Socialism in one
country "—from which point it has now arrived at the position
of bulwark of world peace.

Mao does not think that the counter-revolution would have
been defeated in 1927, however, even if the Communist Party
had carried out a more aggressive policy, and created Communist
armies from the workers and peasants before the split with the
Kuomintang. " But the Soviets could have got an immense start
in the South, and a base in which, afterwards, they would never
have been destroyed. . . ."

In his narrative of himself Mao had now reached the beginning
of the Soviets, which arose from the wreckage of the revolution
and struggled with bare hands even yet to build a new victory
out of defeat. He continued:

" On August 1, 1927, the 20th Army, under Ho Lung and Yeh
T'ing, and in co-operation with Chu Teh, led the historic Nanchang Uprising, and the beginning of what was to become the
Red Army was organized. A week later, on August 7, an extraordinary meeting of the Central Committee of the Party deposed

---

[1] An interesting account of this incident, and the whole period, from the Left
Kuomintang point of view, is given in *The Inner History of the Chinese Revolution*,
by T'ang Leang-li (London, 1930).

Ch'ên Tu-hsiu as secretary. I had been a member of the political bureau of the Party since the Third Conference at Canton in 1924, and was active in this decision, and among the ten other members present at the meeting were: Ts'ai Ho-shêng, P'eng Kung-t'a and Ch'ü Ch'iu-pai. A new line was adopted by the Party, and all hope of co-operation with the Kuomintang was given up for the present, as it had already become hopelessly the tool of imperialism and could not carry out the responsibilities of a democratic revolution. The long open struggle for power now began.

" I was sent to Changsha to organize the movement which later became known as the Autumn Crop Uprising. My programme there called for the realization of five points: (1) complete severance of the Provincial Party from the Kuomintang, (2) organization of a peasant-worker revolutionary army, (3) confiscation of the property of small and middle, as well as great, landlords, (4) setting up the power of the Communist Party in Hunan, independent of the Kuomintang, and (5) organization of Soviets. The fifth point at that time was opposed by the Comintern, and not till later did it advance it as a slogan.

" In September we had already succeeded in organizing a widespread uprising, through the peasant unions of Hunan, and the first units of a peasant-worker army were formed. Recruits were drawn from three principal sources—the peasantry itself, the Hanyang miners, and the insurrectionist troops of the Kuomintang. This early military force of the revolution was called the ' 1st Division of the 1st Peasants' and Workers' Army.' The first regiment was formed from the Hanyang miners. A second was created among the peasant guards in P'ing Kiang, Liu Yang, Li Ling and two other *hsien* of Hunan, and a third from part of the garrison forces of Wuhan, which had revolted against Wang Ching-wei. This army was organized with the sanction of the Hunan Provincial Committee, but the general programme of the Hunan Committee and of our army was opposed by the Central Committee of the Party, which seemed, however, to have adopted a policy of wait-and-see rather than of active opposition.

" While I was organizing the army and travelling between the Hanyang miners and the peasant guards, I was captured by

some *min-t'uan*, working with the Kuomintang. The Kuomintang
terror was then at its height and hundreds of suspected Reds
were being shot. I was ordered to be taken to the *min-t'uan*
headquarters, where I was to be killed. Borrowing several tens
of dollars from a comrade, however, I attempted to bribe the
escort to free me. The ordinary soldiers were mercenaries, with
no special interest in seeing me killed, and they agreed to release
me, but the subaltern in charge refused to permit it. I therefore
decided to attempt to escape, but had no opportunity to do so
until I was within about two hundred yards of the *min-t'uan*
headquarters. At that point I broke loose and ran into the fields.

" I reached a high place, above a pond, with some tall grass
surrounding it, and there I hid until sunset. The soldiers pursued
me, and forced some peasants to help them search for me. Many
times they came very near, once or twice so close that I could
almost have touched them, but somehow I escaped discovery,
although half a dozen times I gave up hope, feeling certain I
would be recaptured. At last, when it was dusk, they abandoned
the search. At once I set off across the mountains, travelling all
night. I had no shoes and my feet were badly bruised. On the
road I met a peasant who befriended me, gave me shelter and
later guided me to the next district. I had seven dollars with
me, and used this to buy some shoes, an umbrella and food.
When at last I reached the peasant guards safely, I had only two
coppers in my pocket.

" With the establishment of the new division, I became chairman of its Party Front Committee, and Yü Sha-t'ou, a commander of the garrison troops at Wuhan, became commander of
the 1st Army. Yü, however, had been more or less forced to take
the position by the attitude of his men; soon afterwards he
deserted and joined the Kuomintang. He is now working for
Chiang Kai-shek at Nanking.

" The little army, leading the peasant uprising, moved southward through Hunan. It had to break its way through thousands
of Kuomintang troops and fought many battles, with many
reverses. Discipline was poor, political training was at a low level,
and many wavering elements were among the men and officers.
There were many desertions. After Yü Sha-t'ou fled, the army
was reorganized when it reached Ning K'ou. Cheng Hao was

made commander of the remaining troops, about one regiment; he, too, later on ' betrayed.' But many in that first group remained loyal to the end, and are to-day still in the Red Army—men such as Lo Yun-hui, political commissar of the 1st Army Corps, and Yang Lo-sou, now an army commander. When the little band finally climbed up Chingkanshan[1] they numbered in all only about one thousand.

" Because the programme of the Autumn Crop Uprising had not been sanctioned by the Central Committee, because also the 1st Army had suffered some severe losses, and from the angle of the cities the movement appeared doomed to failure, the Central Committee now definitely repudiated me. I was dismissed from the Politbureau, and also from the Party Front Committee. The Hunan Provincial Committee also attacked us, calling us ' the rifle movement.' We nevertheless held our army together at Chingkanshan, feeling certain that we were following the correct line, and subsequent events were to vindicate us fully. New recruits were added and the division filled out again. I became its commander.

" From the winter of 1927 to the autumn of 1928, the 1st Division held its base at Chingkanshan. In November 1927 the first Soviet was set up in Ch'alin, on the Hunan border, and the first Soviet Government was elected. Its chairman was Tou Tsung-ping. In this Soviet, and subsequently, we promoted a democratic programme, with a moderate policy, based on slow but regular development. This earned Chingkanshan the recriminations of putschists in the Party, who were demanding a terrorist policy of raiding, and burning and killing of landlords, in order to destroy their morale. The 1st Army Front Committee refused to adopt such tactics, and were therefore branded by the hotheads as ' reformists.' I was bitterly attacked by them for not carrying out a more ' radical ' policy.

" Two former bandit leaders near Chingkanshan, named Wang Tso and Yuan Wen-tsai, joined the Red Army in the winter of 1927. This increased the strength to about three regiments. Wang and Yuan were each made regimental commanders and I

---

[1] Chingkanshan was a nearly impregnable mountain stronghold, formerly held by bandits, on the Hunan–Kiangsi border. An account of the Communists' seizure of this mountain, and their subsequent experiences there, will be found in *China's Red Army Marches*, by Agnes Smedley (New York, 1933).

was army commander. These two men, although former bandits, had thrown in their forces with the Nationalist Revolution, and were now ready to fight against the reaction. While I remained on Chingkanshan they were faithful Communists, and carried out the orders of the Party. Later on, when they were left alone at Chingkanshan, they returned to their bandit habits. Subsequently they were killed by the peasants, by then organized and Sovietized and able to defend themselves.

" In May of 1928, Chu Teh arrived at Chingkanshan, and our forces were combined. Together we drew up a plan to establish a six-*hsien* Soviet area, to stabilize and consolidate gradually the Communist power in the Hunan–Kiangsi–Kwangtung border districts, and, with that as a base, to expand over greater areas. This strategy was in opposition to recommendations of the Party, which had grandiose ideas of rapid expansion. In the army itself Chu Teh and I had to fight against two tendencies: first, a desire to advance on Changsha at once, which we considered adventurism; secondly, a desire to withdraw to the south of the Kwangtung border, which we regarded as 'retreatism.' Our main tasks, as we saw them then, were two: to divide the land, and to establish Soviets. We wanted to arm the masses to hasten those processes. Our policy called for free trade, generous treatment of captured enemy troops, and, in general, democratic moderation.

" A representative meeting was called at Chingkanshan in the autumn of 1928, and was attended by delegates from Soviet districts north of Chingkanshan. Some division of opinion still existed among Party men in the Soviet districts concerning the points mentioned above, and at this meeting differences were thoroughly aired. A minority argued that our future on this basis was narrowly limited, but the majority had faith in the policy, and, when a resolution was proposed, declaring that the Soviet movement would be victorious, it was easily passed. The Party Central Committee, however, had not yet given the movement its sanction. This was not received till the winter of 1928, when the report of proceedings at the Sixth Congress of the Communist Party, held in Moscow, reached Chingkanshan.

" With the new line adopted at that Congress, Chu Teh and I were in complete agreement. From that time on, the differences between the leaders of the Party and the leaders of the Soviet movement in the agrarian districts disappeared. Party harmony was re-established.

" Resolutions at the Sixth Conference summarized the experience of the 1925-7 revolution, the Nanchang, Canton and Autumn Crop Uprisings, and concluded with approval of the emphasis on the agrarian movement. About this time Red armies began to appear elsewhere in China. Uprisings had occurred in western and eastern Hupeh, in the winter of 1927, and these furnished the basis for new Soviet districts. Ho Lung in the west and Hsu Hai-tung in the east began to form their own worker-peasant armies. The latter's area of operations became the nucleus of the Oyüwan Soviet, to which, later on, went Hsu Hsiang-ch'ien and Chang Kuo-t'ao. Fang Chih-min and Hsiao Shih-ping had also begun a movement along the north-eastern frontier of Kiangsi, adjacent to Fukien, in the winter of 1927, and out of this later developed a powerful Soviet base. After the failure of the Canton Uprising, P'eng Pai had led part of the loyal troops to Hailofeng, and there formed a Soviet, which, following a policy of putschism, was soon destroyed. Part of the army, however, emerged from the district under the command of Ku Ta-chen, and made connections with Chu Teh and myself, later on becoming the nucleus of the 11th Red Army.

" In the spring of 1928, partisans became active in Hsingku and Tungku in Kiangsi, led by Li Wen-lung and Li Sao-chu. This movement had its base around Kian, and these partisans later became the core of the 3rd Army, while the district itself became the base of the Central Soviet Government. In western Fukien Soviets were established by Chang Ting-chen, Teng Tzu-hui (later killed), and Hu Pei-tseh, who afterward became a Social-Democrat.

" During the ' struggle v. adventurism ' period at Chingkan-shan, the 1st Army had defeated two attempts by White troops to retake the mountain. Chingkanshan proved to be an excellent base for a mobile army such as we were building. It had good natural defences, and grew enough crops to supply a small army. It had a circuit of five hundred *li* and was about eighty *li* in diameter. Locally it was known otherwise, as Ta Hsiao Wu Chin (the real Chingkanshan being a near-by mountain, long deserted), and got its name from five main wells on its sides—*ta, hsiao, shang, hsia*, and *chung*, or big, small, upper, lower, and middle wells. The five villages on the mountain were named after these wells.

" After the forces of our army combined at Chingkanshan there was a reorganization, the famous 4th Red Army was created, and Chu Teh was made commander, while I became political commissar. More troops arrived at Chingkanshan, after uprisings and mutinies in Ho Chien's army, in the winter of 1928, and out of these emerged the 5th Red Army, commander of which was P'eng Teh-huai. In addition to P'eng there were Teng P'ing (killed at Tsun-yi, Kweichow, during the Long March), Huang Kuo-nu (killed in Kwangsi in 1931), and T'ien Teh-yuan.

" Conditions on the mountain, with the arrival of so many troops, were becoming very bad. The troops had no winter uniforms, and food was extremely scarce. For months we lived practically on squash. The soldiers shouted a slogan of their own: ' Down with capitalism, and eat squash ! '—for to them capitalism meant landlords and the landlords' squash. Leaving P'eng Teh-huai at Chingkanshan, Chu Teh broke through the blockade established by the White troops, and in January 1929 our first sojourn on the embattled mountain ended.

" The 4th Army now began a campaign through the south of Kiangsi which rapidly developed successfully. We established a Soviet in Tungku, and there met and united with local Red troops. Dividing forces, we continued into Yungting, Shangheng and Lung Yeh, and established Soviets in all those counties. The existence of militant mass movements prior to the arrival of the Red Army assured our success, and helped to consolidate Soviet power on a stable basis very quickly. The influence of the Red Army now extended, through the agrarian mass movement and partisans, to several other *hsien*, but the Communists did not fully take power there until later on.

" Conditions in the Red Army began to improve, both materially and politically, but there were still many bad tendencies. ' Partisanism,' for example, was a weakness reflected in lack of discipline, exaggerated ideas of democracy, and looseness of organization. Another tendency that had to be fought was ' vagabondage '—a disinclination to settle down to the serious tasks of government, a love of movement, change, new experience and incident. There were also remnants of militarism, with some of the commanders maltreating or even beating the men, and discriminating against those they disliked personally, while showing favouritism to others.

" Many of these weaknesses were overcome after the convening of the Ninth Party Conference of the 4th Red Army, held in west Fukien in December 1929. Ideas for improvements were discussed, many misunderstandings levelled out, and new plans were adopted, which laid the foundations for a high type of ideological leadership in the Red Army. Prior to this the tendencies already described were very serious, and were utilized by a Trotskyist faction in the Party and military leadership to undermine the strength of the movement. A vigorous struggle was now begun against them, and several were deprived of their Party positions and army command. Of these Liu En-kung, an army commander, was typical. It was found that they intended to destroy the Red Army by leading it into difficult positions in battles with the enemy, and after several unsuccessful encounters their plans became quite evident. They bitterly attacked our programme and everything we advocated. Experience having shown their errors, they were eliminated from responsible positions and after the Fukien Conference lost their influence.

" This conference prepared the way for the establishment of the Soviet power in Kiangsi. The following year was marked with some brilliant successes. Nearly the whole of southern Kiangsi fell to the Red Army. The base of the Central Soviet regions had been established.

" On February 7, 1930, an important local Party conference was called in south Kiangsi, to discuss the future programme of the Soviets. It was attended by local representatives from the Party, the Army and the Government. Here the question of the land policy was argued at great length, and the struggle against ' opportunism,' led by those opposed to redistribution, was overcome. It was resolved to carry out land redistribution and quicken the formation of Soviets. Until then the Red Army had formed only local and district Soviets. At this conference it was decided to establish the Kiangsi Provincial Soviet Government. To the new programme the peasants responded with a warm, enthusiastic support which helped, in the months ahead, to defeat the extermination campaigns of the Kuomintang armies."

6

Growth of the Red Army

MAO TSE-TUNG's account had begun to pass out of the category of " personal history," and to sublimate itself somehow intangibly in the career of a great movement in which, though he retained a dominant rôle, you could not see him clearly as a personality. It was no longer " I " but " we "; no longer Mao Tse-tung, but the Red Army; no longer a subjective impression of the experiences of a single life, but an objective record by a bystander concerned with the mutations of collective human destiny as the material of history.

As his story drew to a close it became more and more necessary for me to interrogate him about himself. What was *he* doing at that time ? What office did *he* hold then ? What was *his* attitude in this or that situation ? And my questioning, generally, evoked such references as there are to himself in this last chapter of the narrative:

" Gradually the Red Army's work with the masses improved, discipline strengthened, and a new technique in organization developed. The peasantry everywhere began to volunteer to help the revolution. As early as Chingkanshan the Red Army had imposed three simple rules of discipline upon its fighters, and these were: prompt obedience to orders; no confiscations whatever from the poor peasantry; and prompt delivery directly to the Government, for its disposal, of all goods confiscated from the landlords. After the 1928 Conference emphatic efforts to enlist the support of the peasantry were made, and eight rules were added to the three listed above. These were as follows:

" 1. Replace all doors when you leave a house;[1]
" 2. Return and roll up the straw matting on which you sleep;
" 3. Be courteous and polite to the people and help them when you can;
" 4. Return all borrowed articles;

---

[1] This order is not so enigmatic as it sounds. The wooden doors of a Chinese house are easily detachable, and are often taken down at night, put across wooden blocks and used for an improvised bed.

" 5. Replace all damaged articles;

" 6. Be honest in all transactions with the peasants;

" 7. Pay for all articles purchased;

" 8. Be sanitary, and especially establish latrines a safe distance from people's houses.

" The last two rules were added by Lin Piao. These eight points were enforced with better and better success, and to-day are still the code of the Red soldier, are memorized and frequently repeated by him.[1] Three other duties were taught to the Red Army as its primary purpose: first, to struggle to the death against the enemy; second, to arm the masses; third, to raise money to support the struggle.

" Early in 1929 several groups of partisans under Li Wen-lung and Li Sao-chu were reorganized into the 3rd Red Army, commanded by Huang Kung-lu, and with Chu Yi as political commissar. During the same period, part of Chu Pei-teh's *min-t'uan* mutinied and joined the Red Army. They were led to the Communist camp by a Kuomintang commander, Lo Ping-hui, who was disillusioned about the Kuomintang and wanted to join the Red Army. He is now commander of the 32nd Red Army of the 2nd Front Army. From the Fukien partisans and nucleus of regular Red troops the 12th Red Army was created under the command of Wu Chung-hao, with T'ai Tsung-ling as political commissar. Wu was later killed in battle and replaced by Lo Ping-hui.

" It was at this time that the 1st Army Corps was organized, with Chu Teh as commander and I as political commissar. It was composed of the 3rd Army, the 4th Army commanded by Lin Piao, and the 12th Army, under Lo Ping-hui. Party leadership was vested in a Front Committee, of which I was chairman. There were already more than 10,000 men in the 1st Army Corps then, organized into ten divisions. Besides this main force, there were many local and independent regiments, Red guards and partisans.

" Red tactics, apart from the political basis of the movement, explained much of the successful military development. At Chingkanshan four slogans had been adopted, and these give the

[1] Also sung daily in a Red Army song.

clue to the methods of partisan warfare used, out of which the Red Army grew. The slogans were:

" 1. When the enemy advances, we retreat !
" 2. When the enemy halts and encamps, we trouble them !
" 3. When the enemy seeks to avoid a battle, we attack !
" 4. When the enemy retreats, we pursue !

" These slogans [of four characters each in Chinese] were at first opposed by many experienced military men, who did not agree with the type of tactics advocated. But much experience proved that the tactics were correct. Whenever the Red Army departed from them, in general, it did not succeed. Our forces were small, exceeded from ten to twenty times by the enemy; our resources and fighting materials were limited, and only by skilfully combining the tactics of manœuvring and guerilla warfare could we hope to succeed in our struggle against the Kuomintang, fighting from vastly richer and superior bases.

" The most important single tactic of the Red Army was, and remains, in its ability to concentrate its main forces in the attack, and swiftly divide and separate them afterwards. This implied that positional warfare was to be avoided, and every effort made to meet the living forces of the enemy while in movement, and destroy them. On the basis of these tactics the wonderful mobility and the swift powerful ' short attack ' of the Red Army was developed.

" In expanding Soviet areas in general the programme of the Red Army favoured a wave-like or tidal development, rather than an uneven advance, gained by ' leaps ' or ' jumps,' and without deep consolidation in the territories gained. The policy was pragmatical, just as were the tactics already described, and grew out of many years of collective military and political experience. These tactics were severely criticized by Li Li-san, who advocated the concentration of all weapons in the hands of the Red Army, and the absorption of all partisan groups. He wanted attacks rather than consolidation; advances without securing the rear; sensational assaults on big cities, accompanied by uprisings and extremism. The Li Li-san line dominated the Party then, outside Soviet areas, and was sufficiently influential to force acceptance, to some extent, in the Red Army, against the judgment of its field command. One result of it was the attack on Changsha and another was the advance on Nanchang. But the Red Army refused to immobilize its partisan groups and open up its rear to the enemy during these adventures.

" In the autumn of 1929 the Red Army moved into northern Kiangsi, attacking and occupying many cities, and inflicting numerous defeats on Kuomintang armies. When within striking distance of Nanchang the 1st Army Corps turned sharply west and moved on Changsha. In this drive it met and joined forces with P'eng Teh-huai, who had already occupied Changsha once, but had been forced to withdraw to avoid being surrounded by vastly superior enemy troops. P'eng had been obliged to leave Chingkanshan in April 1929, and had carried out operations in southern Kiangsi, resulting in greatly increasing his troops. He rejoined Chu Teh and the main forces of the Red Army at Juichin in April 1930, and after a conference it was decided that P'eng's 3rd Army should operate on the Kiangsi–Hunan border, while Chu Teh and I moved into Fukien. It was in June 1930 that the 3rd Army and the 1st Army Corps re-established a junction and began the second attack on Changsha. The 1st and 3rd Army Corps were combined into the 1st Front Army, with Chu Teh as Commander-in-Chief and myself as political commissar. Under this leadership we arrived outside the walls of Changsha.

" The Chinese Workers' and Peasants' Revolutionary Committee was organized about this time, and I was elected chairman. The Red Army's influence in Hunan was widespread, almost as much so as in Kiangsi. My name was known among the Hunanese peasants, for big rewards were offered for my capture, dead or alive, as well as for Chu Teh and other Reds. My land[1] in Hsiang T'an was confiscated by the Kuomintang. My wife and my sister, as well as the wives of my two brothers, Mao Tse-hung and Mao Tse-tan, and my own son, were all arrested by Ho Chien. My wife and younger sister were executed. The others were later released. The prestige of the Red Army even extended to my own village, Hsiang T'an, for I heard the tale that the local peasants believed that I would be soon

[1] The rent from which Mao used during the Great Revolution for the peasant movement in Hunan.

returning to my native home. When one day an aeroplane passed overhead, they decided it was I. They warned the man who was then tilling my land that I had come back to look over my old farm, to see whether or not any trees had been cut. If so, I would surely demand compensation from Chiang Kai-shek, they said.

" But the second attack on Changsha proved to be a failure. Great reinforcements had been sent to the city, and it was heavily garrisoned; besides, new troops were pouring into Hunan in September to attack the Red Army. Only one important battle occurred during the siege, and in it the Red Army eliminated two brigades of enemy troops. It could not, however, take the city of Changsha, and after a few weeks withdrew to Kiangsi.

" This failure helped to destroy the Li Li-san line, and saved the Red Army from what would probably have been a catastrophic attack on Wuhan, which Li was demanding. The main tasks of the Red Army then were the recruiting of new troops, the Sovietization of new rural areas, and, above all, the consolidation under thorough Soviet power of such areas as already had fallen to the Red Army. For such a programme the attacks on Changsha were not necessary and had an element of adventure in them. Had the first occupation been undertaken as a temporary action, however, and not with the idea of attempting to hold the city and set up a State power there, its effects might have been considered beneficial, for the reaction produced on the national revolutionary movement was very great. The error was a strategic and tactical one, in attempting to make a base of Changsha while the Soviet power was still not consolidated behind it."

If it is permissible rudely to interrupt Mao's narrative for a moment, further interesting comment may be offered about Li Li-san. A Hunanese and a returned student from France, he divided his time in Shanghai and Hankow, where the Communist Party had " underground " headquarters—only after 1931 transferring the Central Committee to the Soviet districts. Li was one of the most brilliant (if also erratic) of Chinese Communists, and perhaps the nearest to a Trotsky that China produced. He dominated the Party from 1929 to 1931, when he was removed from the Politburo and sent to Moscow for " study," where he still remains. Like Ch'ên Tu-hsiu, Li Li-san lacked faith in the rural Soviets, and urged that strong aggressive tactics be adopted against strategic big capitals like Changsha, Wuhan, and Nanchang. He wanted a " terror " in the villages to demoralize the gentry, a " mighty offensive " by the workers, risings and strikes to paralyse the enemy in his bases, and " flank attacks " in the north, from Outer Mongolia and Man-churia, backed by the U.S.S.R. Perhaps his greatest " sin," in Moscow's eyes, was that in 1930 he held China to be the " centre " of the world revolution, thus denying that rôle to the Soviet Union.

To continue:

" But Li Li-san over-estimated both the military strength of the Red Army at that time and the revolutionary factors in the national political scene. He believed that the revolution was nearing success and would shortly have power over the entire country. This belief was encouraged by the long and exhausting civil war then proceeding between Feng Yü-hsiang and Chiang Kai-shek, which made the outlook seem highly favourable to Li Li-san. But in the opinion of the Red Army the enemy was making preparations for a great drive against the Soviets as soon as the civil war was concluded, and it was no time for possibly disastrous putschism and adventures. This estimate proved to be entirely correct.

" With the events in Hunan, the Red Army's return to Kiangsi, and especially after the capture of Kian, ' Lilisanism ' was overcome in the army; and Li himself, proved to have been in error, soon lost his influence in the Party. There was, however, a critical period in the army before ' Lilisanism ' was definitely buried. Part of the 3rd Corps favoured following out Li's line, and demanded the separation of the 3rd Corps from the rest of the army. P'eng Teh-huai fought vigorously against this ten-dency, however, and succeeded in maintaining the unity of the forces under his command and their loyalty to the high com-mand. But the 20th Army, led by Liu Ti-tsao, rose in open revolt, arrested the chairman of the Kiangsi Soviet, arrested many officers and officials, and attacked us politically, on the basis of the Li Li-san line. This occurred at Fu Tien and is known as the Fu Tien Incident. Fu Tien being near Kian, then the heart of the Soviet districts, the events produced a sensation, and to many it must have seemed that the fate of the revolution depended on the outcome of this struggle. However, the revolt was quickly suppressed, due to the loyalty of the 3rd Army, to the general solidarity of the Party and the Red troops, and to the support of the peasantry. Liu Ti-tsao was arrested, and other rebels disarmed and liquidated. Our line was re-affirmed, ' Lilisanism ' was definitely suppressed, and as a result the Soviet movement subsequently scored great gains.

" But Nanking was now thoroughly aroused to the revolutionary potentialities of the Soviets in Kiangsi, and at the end of 1930 began its First Extermination Campaign[1] against the Red Army. Enemy forces totalling over 100,000 men began an encirclement of the Red areas, penetrating by five routes, under the chief command of Lu Ti-p'ing. Against these troops the Red Army was then able to mobilize a total of about 40,000 men. By skilful use of manœuvring warfare we met and overcame this First Campaign, with great victories. Following out the tactics of swift concentration and swift dispersal, we attacked each unit separately, using our main forces. Admitting the enemy troops deeply into Soviet territory, we staged sudden concentrated attacks, in superior numbers, on isolated units of the Kuomintang troops, achieving positions of manœuvre in which, momentarily, we could encircle them, thus reversing the general strategic advantage enjoyed by a numerically greatly superior enemy.

" By January 1931 this First Campaign had been completely defeated. I believe that this would not have been possible except for three conditions achieved by the Red Army just before its commencement. First, the consolidation of the 1st and 3rd Army Corps under a centralized command; second, the liquidation of the Li Li-san line; and, third, the triumph of the Party over the anti-Bolshevik (Liu Ti-tsao) faction and other active

[1] This campaign is described in interesting detail in *The Communist Situation in China* by Yang Chien (Nanking, 1931).

counter-revolutionaries within the Red Army and in the Soviet districts.

" After a respite of only four months, Nanking launched its Second Campaign, under the supreme command of Ho Ying-ching, now Minister of War. His forces exceeded 200,000 men, who moved into the Red areas by seven routes. The situation for the Red Army was then thought to be very critical. The area of Soviet power was very small, resources were limited, equipment scanty, and enemy material strength vastly exceeded that of the Red Army in every respect. To meet this offensive, however, the Red Army still clung to the same tactics that had thus far won success. Admitting the enemy columns well into Red territory, our main forces suddenly concentrated 'against the second route of the enemy, defeated several regiments, and destroyed their offensive power. Immediately afterwards we attacked in quick succession the third route, the sixth and the seventh, defeating each of them in turn. The fourth route retreated without giving battle, and the fifth route was partly destroyed. Within fourteen days the Red Army had fought six battles, and marched eight days, ending with a decisive victory. With the break-up or retreat of the other six routes, the first route army, commanded by Chiang Kuang-nai and Ts'ai T'ing-k'ai, withdrew without any serious fighting.

" One month later, Chiang Kai-shek took command of an army of 300,000 men ' for the final extermination of the " Red-bandits." ' He was assisted by his ablest commanders: Ch'ên Ming-shu, Ho Ying-ch'ing and Chu Shao-liang, each of whom had charge of a main route of advance. Chiang hoped to take the Red areas by storm—a rapid ' wiping-up ' of the ' Red-bandits.' He began by moving his armies 80 *li* a day into the heart of Soviet territory. This supplied the very conditions under which the Red Army fights best, and it soon proved the serious mistake of Chiang's tactics. With a main force of only 30,000 men, by a series of brilliant manœuvres, our army attacked five different columns in five days. In the first battle the Red Army captured many enemy troops, and large amounts of ammunition, guns and equipment. By September the Third Campaign had been admitted to be a failure and Chiang Kai-shek in October withdrew his troops.

" The Red Army now entered a period of comparative peace and growth. Expansion was very rapid. The First Soviet Congress was called on December 11, 1931, and the Central Soviet Government was established, with myself as chairman. Chu Teh was elected Commander-in-Chief of the Red Army. In the same month there occurred the great Ningtu Uprising, when over 20,000 troops of the 28th Route Army of the Kuomintang revolted and joined the Red Army. They were led by Teng Ch'ing-tan and Tsao Pu-shen. Tsao was later killed in battle in Kiangsi, but Teng is to-day still commander of the 5th Red Army—the 5th Army Corps having been created out of the troops taken in from the Ningtu Uprising.

" The Red Army now began offensives of its own. In 1932 it fought a great battle at Changchow, in Fukien, and captured the city. In the South it attacked Ch'ên Chi-t'ang at Nan Hsiang, and on Chiang Kai-shek's front it stormed Lo An, Li Chuan, Chien Ning and T'an Ning. It attacked but did not occupy Kanchow. From October 1932 onward, and until the beginning of the Long March to the North-west, I myself devoted my time almost exclusively to work with the Soviet Government, leaving the military command to Chu Teh and others.

" In April 1933 began the Fourth, and, for Nanking, perhaps the most disastrous, of its Extermination Campaigns.[1] In the first battle of this period two divisions were disarmed and two divisional commanders were captured. The 59th Division was partly destroyed and the 52nd was completely destroyed. Thirteen thousand men were captured in this one battle at Ta Lung P'ing and Chiao Hui in Lo An Hsien. The Kuomintang's

[1] There is considerable confusion, in many accounts written of the anti-Red wars, concerning the number of major expeditions sent against the Soviet districts. Some writers have totalled up as many as eight different " annihilation drives," but several of these big mobilizations by Nanking were purely defensive. Red Army commanders speak of only five main anti-Red campaigns. These are, with the approximate number of Nanking troops directly involved in each, as follows: First, December 1930 to January 1931, 100,000; Second, May to June 1931, 200,000; Third, July to October 1931, 300,000; Fourth, April to October 1933, 250,000; Fifth, October 1933 to October 1934, 400,000 (over 900,000 troops were *mobilized* against the three main Soviet districts). No major expedition was launched by Nanking during 1932, when Chiang Kai-shek was using approximately 500,000 troops in defensive positions around the Red districts. It was, on the contrary, a year of big Red offensives. Evidently Nanking's defensive operations in 1932, which were, of course, propagandized as " anti-Red campaigns," were misunderstood by many writers as major expeditions. The Reds do not so discuss them, nor Chiang Kai-shek.

11th Division, then Chiang Kai-shek's best, was next eliminated, being almost totally disarmed, and its commander seriously wounded. These engagements proved decisive turning-points and the Fourth Campaign soon afterwards ended. Chiang Kai-shek at this time wrote to Ch'ên Ch'êng, his field commander, that he considered this defeat ' the greatest humiliation ' in his life. Ch'ên Ch'êng did not favour pushing the campaign. He told people then that in his opinion fighting the Reds was a ' lifetime job ' and a ' life sentence.' Reports of this coming to Chiang Kai-shek, he removed Ch'ên Ch'êng from the high command.

" For his Fifth and Last Campaign, Chiang Kai-shek mobilized nearly one million men and adopted new tactics and strategy. Already, in the Fourth Campaign, Chiang had, on the recommendation of his German advisers, begun the use of the blockhouse and fortifications system. In the Fifth Campaign he placed his entire reliance upon it.

" In this period we made two important errors. The first was the failure to unite with Ts'ai T'ing-k'ai's army in 1933 during the Fukien Rebellion. The second was the adoption of the erroneous strategy of simple defence, abandoning our former tactics of manœuvre. It was a serious mistake to meet the vastly superior Nanking forces in positional warfare, at which the Red Army was neither technically nor spiritually at its best.

" As a result of these mistakes, and the new tactics and strategy of China's campaign, combined with the overwhelming numerical and technical superiority of the Kuomintang forces, the Red Army was obliged, in 1934, to seek to change the conditions of its existence in Kiangsi, which were rapidly becoming more unfavourable. Secondly, the national political situation influenced the decision to move the scene of main operations to the North-west. Following Japan's invasion of Manchuria and Shanghai, the Soviet Government had, as early as February 1932, formally declared war on Japan. This declaration, which could not, of course, be made effective, owing to the blockade and encirclement of Soviet China by the Kuomintang troops, had been followed by the issuance of a manifesto calling for a United Front of all armed forces in China to resist Japanese imperialism.

Early in 1933 the Soviet Government announced that it would co-operate with any White army on the basis of cessation of civil war and attacks on the Soviets and the Red Army, guarantee of civil liberties and democratic rights to the masses, and arming of the people for an anti-Japanese war.

" The Fifth Extermination Campaign began in October 1933. In January 1934 the Second All-China Soviet Congress of Soviets was convened in Juichin, the Soviet capital, and a survey of the achievements of the Revolution took place. Here I gave a long report, and here the Central Soviet Government, as its personnel exists to-day, was elected. Preparations soon afterwards were made for the Long March. It was begun in October 1934, just a year after Chiang Kai-shek launched his last Campaign—a year of almost constant fighting, struggle and enormous losses on both sides.

" By January 1935 the main forces of the Red Army reached Tsun Yi, in Kweichow. For the next four months the army was almost constantly moving and the most energetic combat and fighting took place. Through many, many difficulties, across the longest and deepest and most dangerous rivers of China, across some of its highest and most hazardous mountain passes, through the country of fierce aborigines, through the empty grasslands, through cold and through intense heat, through wind and snow and rainstorm, pursued by half the White armies of China, through all these natural barriers, and fighting its way past the local troops of Kwangtung, Hunan, Kwangsi, Kweichow, Yunnan, Sikong, Szechuan, Kansu and Shensi, the Red Army at last reached northern Shensi in October 1935, and enlarged the present base in China's great North-west.

" The victorious march of the Red Army, and its triumphant arrival in Kansu and Shensi with its living forces still intact, was due first to the correct leadership of the Communist Party, and secondly to the great skill, courage, determination and almost superhuman endurance and revolutionary ardour of the basic cadres of our Soviet people. The Communist Party of China was, is, and will ever be, faithful to Marxist-Leninism, and it will continue its struggles against every opportunist tendency. In this determination lies one explanation of its invincibility and the certainty of its final victory."

PART FIVE

THE LONG MARCH

1

The Fifth Campaign

HERE I cannot even outline the absorbing and as yet only fragmentarily written history of the six years of the Soviets of South China—a period that was destined to be a prelude to the epic of the Long March. Mao Tse-tung has told briefly of the organic development of the Soviets, and of the birth of the Red Army. He has told how the Communists built up, from a few hundred ragged and half-starved but young and determined revolutionaries, an army of several tens of thousands of workers and peasants, until by 1930 they had become such serious contenders for power that Nanking had to hurl its first large-scale offensive against them. The initial " annihilation drive," and then a second, a third and a fourth, were not defeats. In each of those campaigns the Reds destroyed many brigades and whole divisions of Kuomintang troops, replenished their supplies of arms and ammunition, enlisted new warriors, and expanded their territory.

Meanwhile, what sort of life went on beyond the impenetrable lines of the Red irregulars ? It is one of the amazing facts of our age that during the entire history of the Soviets in South China not a single " outside " foreign observer entered Red territory —the only Communist-ruled nation in the world besides the U.S.S.R. Everything that has been written about the southern Soviets by foreigners is therefore secondary material. But a few salient points are now confirmable from accounts both friendly and inimical, and these clearly indicate the basis of the Red Army's support. Land was redistributed and taxes were lightened. Collective enterprise was established on a wide scale; by 1933 there were more than 1,000 Soviet co-operatives in Kiangsi alone. Unemployment, opium, prostitution, child slavery, and compulsory marriage were eliminated, and the living conditions of the workers and poor peasants in the peaceful areas were greatly improved. Mass education made much progress in the stabilized Soviets. In some counties the Reds attained a higher degree of literacy among the populace in three or four years than had been achieved anywhere else in rural China after

centuries. This did not exclude even the Rockefeller-backed
de luxe mass education experiment at Ting Hsien, run by
" Jimonic " Yen. In Hsin Kuo, the Communists' model *hsien*,
there was a populace nearly 80 per cent literate—much higher
than in the famous Rockefeller county.

That much at least has now been established by a wealth of
independent testimony. But while documentary material is
becoming abundantly available on other phases of the little
Soviet Republic, it is impossible to discuss them except in
terms of polemics which are not within the shape of this book.
What might have been accomplished by the Reds had they held
their bases in the South and strengthened them ? Here at once
one enters a realm of sheer prophecy, where the subjective
factor naturally conditions the conclusions reached.

Speculation on the southern Soviets in any case is now a
matter chiefly of academic interest. For, late in October 1933,
Nanking mobilized for the fifth and the greatest of its anti-
Red wars, and one year later the Reds were finally forced to
carry out a general retreat. Nearly everyone then supposed it
was the end, the Red Army's funeral march. How badly mistaken they were was not to become manifest for almost two
years, when a remarkable come-back, seldom equalled in history,
was to reach a climax with events that put into the hands of
the Communists the life of the Generalissimo who for a while
really had believed his own boast—that he had " exterminated
the menace of Communism."

It was not until the seventh year of the fighting against the
Reds that any notable success crowned the attempts to destroy
them. The Reds then had actual administrative control over a
great part of Kiangsi, and large areas of Fukien and Hunan.
There were other Soviet districts, not physically connected with
the Kiangsi territory, located in the provinces of Hunan, Hupeh,
Honan, Anhui, Szechuan, and Shensi.

Against the Reds, in the Fifth Campaign, Chiang Kai-shek
mobilized about 900,000 troops, of whom perhaps 400,000—some
360 regiments—actively took part in the warfare in the Kiangsi–
Fukien area, and against the Red Army in the Anhui–Honan–
Hupeh (Oyüwan) area. But Kiangsi was the pivot of the whole
campaign. Here the regular Red Army was able to mobilize a

combined strength of 180,000 men, including all reserve divisions, and it had perhaps 200,000 partisan and Red Guards, but altogether could muster a firing power of somewhat less than 100,000 rifles, no heavy artillery, and a very limited supply of grenades, shells, and ammunition, all of which were now being made in the Red arsenal at Juichin.

Chiang adopted a new strategy to make the fullest use of his greatest assets—superior resources, technical equipment, access to unlimited supplies from the outside world (to which the Reds had no outlet), mechanized warfare, and a modern air force that had come to comprise nearly 400 navigable war planes. The Reds had captured a few of Chiang's aeroplanes, and they had three or four pilots, but they lacked petrol, bombs, and mechanics. Instead of an invasion of the Red districts and an attempt to take them by storm of superior force, which had in the past proved disastrous, Chiang now used the majority of his troops to surround the " bandits " and impose on them a strict economic blockade. It was, therefore, primarily a war of exhaustion.

And it was very costly. Chiang Kai-shek built hundreds of miles of military roads and thousands of small fortifications, which were made connectable by machine-gun or artillery fire. His defensive-offensive strategy and tactics tended to diminish the Reds' superiority in manœuvring, and emphasized the disadvantages of their smaller numbers and lack of resources. In effect, in his famous Fifth Campaign, the Generalissimo built a kind of Great Wall around the Soviet districts, which gradually moved inward. Its ultimate aim was to encompass and crush the Red Army in a stone vice.

Chiang wisely avoided exposing any large body of troops beyond the fringes of his network of roads and fortifications. They advanced only when very well covered by heavy artillery, armoured cars, tanks, and heavy air bombardment, and rarely moved more than a few hundred yards ahead of the noose of forts, which stretched through the provinces of Kiangsi, Fukien, Hunan, Kwantung, and Kwangsi. Deprived of opportunities to decoy, ambush, or outmanœuvre their enemy in open battle, the Reds were obliged to plan a new strategy. They began to place their main reliance on positional warfare—and the error

of this decision, and the reasons for it, will be alluded to farther
on.

The Fifth Campaign is said to have been planned largely by
Chiang Kai-shek's German advisers, notably the late General
Von Seeckt, former chief-of-staff of the Nazi army, and for a
while the Generalissimo's chief adviser. The new tactics were
thorough, but they were also very slow and expensive. Operations dragged on for months and still Nanking had not struck
a decisive blow at the main forces of its enemy. The effect of the
blockade, however, was seriously felt in the Red districts, and
especially the total absence of salt. The little Red base was
becoming inadequate to repel the combined military and
economic pressure being applied against it. The Reds deny it,
but I suspect that considerable exploitation of the peasantry
must have been necessary to maintain the astonishing year of
resistance which was put up during this campaign. At the same
time, it must be remembered that their fighters were mostly
enfranchised peasants and proud owners of newly acquired
land. For land alone, most peasants in China will fight to the
death. The Kiangsi people knew that return of the Kuomintang
meant return of the landlords.

Nanking believed that its efforts at annihilation were about to
succeed. The enemy was caged and could not escape. Tens of
thousands of peasants had been killed in the daily bombing
and machine-gunning from the air, as well as by " purgations "
in districts re-occupied by the Kuomintang. The Red Army itself,
according to Chou En-lai, suffered over 60,000 casualties in this
one siege, and sacrifice of life among the civilian population was
terrific. Whole areas were depopulated, sometimes by forced
mass migrations, sometimes by the simpler expedient of mass
executions. The Kuomintang itself admits that about 1,000,000
people were killed or starved to death in the process of recovering
Soviet Kiangsi.

Nevertheless, the Fifth Campaign proved inconclusive. It
failed in its objective, which was to destroy the living forces of
the Red Army. A Red military conference was called at Juichin,
and it was decided to withdraw, transferring the main Red
strength to a new base. The plans for this great expedition,
which was to last a whole year, were complete and efficient.

They perhaps revealed a certain military genius that the Reds had not shown during their periods of offensive. For it is one thing to command a victorious advancing army, and quite another to carry through to success a plan calling for retreat under such handicaps as those which lay ahead in the now famous Long March to the North-west.

The retreat from Kiangsi evidently was so swiftly and secretly managed that the main forces of the Red troops, estimated at about 90,000 men, had already been marching for several days before the enemy headquarters became aware of what was taking place. They had mobilized in southern Kiangsi, withdrawing most of their regular troops from the northern front, and replacing them with partisans. Those movements occurred always at night. When practically the whole Red Army was concentrated near Yütu, in southern Kiangsi, the order was given for the Great March, which began on October 16, 1934.

For three nights the Reds pressed in two columns to the west and to the south. On the fourth they advanced, totally unexpectedly, almost simultaneously attacking the Hunan and Kwangtung lines of fortifications. They took these by assault, put their astonished enemy on the run, and never stopped until they had occupied the ribbon of blockading forts and entrenchments on the southern front. This gave them roads to the south and to the west, along which their vanguard began its sensational trek.

Besides the main strength of the army, thousands of Red peasants began this march—old and young, men, women, children, Communists and non-Communists. The arsenal was stripped, all the factories were dismantled, all machinery was loaded on to mules and donkeys—everything that was portable and of value went with this strange cavalcade. As the march lengthened out, much of this burden had to be discarded, and the Reds tell you to-day that thousands of rifles and machine guns, much machinery, much ammunition, even much silver, lies buried on their long trail from the south. Some day in the future, they say, Red peasants, now surrounded by thousands of policing troops, will dig it up again and re-establish their Soviets. They await only the signal—and the threatening war with Japan may prove to be that beacon.

After the main forces of the Red Army evacuated Kiangsi, it

was still many weeks before Nanking troops succeeded in occupying the chief Red cities. Thousands of peasant guards and partisans, held together and led by a few Red regulars, put up a stiff resistance till the end. The heroism of many of these Red leaders, who volunteered to stay behind for self-immolation, is memorialized in many ways by the Reds to-day. They provided the rearguard action which enabled the main forces to get well under way before Nanking could mobilize sufficient forces to surround and annihilate them on the march. Even in 1937 there were regions in Kiangsi, Fukien, and Kweichow held by these fragments of the Red Army, and only recently the Government announced the beginning of another anti-Red campaign for a " final clean-up " in Fukien.

2

A Nation Emigrates

HAVING successfully broken through the first line of fortifications, the Red Army set out on its epochal year-long trek to the west and to the north, a vari-coloured and many-storied expedition that can be described here only in briefest outline. The Communists are now writing a collective account of the Long March, with contributions from dozens who made it, which already totals over 300,000 words, and is still incomplete. Adventure, exploration, discovery, human courage and cowardice, ecstasy and triumph, suffering, sacrifice, and loyalty, and then through it all, like a flame, this undimmed ardour and undying hope and amazing revolutionary optimism of those thousands of youths who would not admit defeat either by man or nature or god or death—all this and more are wrapped up in the history of an Odyssey unequalled in modern times.

The Reds themselves generally speak of it as the " 25,000-*li* March," and with all its twists, turns and counter-marches, from the farthest point in Fukien to the end of the road in far northwest Shensi, some sections of the marchers undoubtedly did that much or more. An accurate stage-by-stage itinerary prepared by the 1st Army Corps[1] shows that its route covered a total of 18,088 *li*, or 6,000 miles—about twice the width of the American continent—and this figure may be accepted as a minimum for the march of the main forces. It must be remembered that the whole journey was covered on foot, across some of the world's most impassable trails, most of them unfit for wheeled traffic, across some of the highest mountains and the greatest rivers of Asia. It was one long battle from beginning to end.

Four main lines of defence works, supported by strings of concrete machine-gun nests and blockhouses, surrounded the Soviet districts in South-west China, and the Reds had to shatter those before they could reach the unblockaded areas to the west. The first line, in Kiangsi, was broken on October 21, 1934; the second, in Hunan, was occupied on November 3, and a week later the third, also in Hunan, fell to the Reds after bloody

[1] *An Account of the Long March*, 1st Army Corps, Yuwang Pao, August 1936.

fighting. The Kwangsi and Hunan troops gave up the fourth and last line on November 29, and the Reds swung northward into Hunan, to begin trekking in a straight line for Szechuan, where they planned to enter the Soviet districts and combine with the Fourth Front Army there, under Hsu Hsiang-chien. Between the dates mentioned above, nine battles were fought. In all, a combination of 110 regiments had been mobilized in their path by Nanking and by the provincial warlords, Chen Chi-tang, Ho Chien, and Pai Ch'ung-hsi.

During the march through Kiangsi, Kwangtung, Kwangsi, and Hunan, the Reds suffered very heavy losses. Their numbers were reduced by about one-third by the time they reached the border of Kweichow province. This was due first to the impediment of a vast amount of transport, 5,000 men being engaged in that task alone. The vanguard was very much retarded, and in many cases the enemy was given time to prepare elaborate obstructions in the line of march. Secondly, from Kiangsi an undeviating north-westerly route was maintained, which enabled Nanking to anticipate most of the Red Army's movements.

Serious losses as a result of these errors caused the Reds to adopt new tactics in Kweichow. Instead of an arrow-like advance, they began a series of distracting manœuvres, so that it became more and more difficult for Nanking planes to identify the day-by-day objective of the main forces. Two columns, and sometimes as many as four columns, engaged in a baffling series of manœuvres on the flanks of the central column, and the vanguard developed a pincer-like front. Only the barest and lightest essentials of equipment were retained, and night marches for the greatly reduced transport corps—a daily target for the air bombing—became routine.

Anticipating an attempt to cross the Yangtze River into Szechuan, Chiang Kai-shek withdrew thousands of troops from Hupeh, Anhui, and Kiangsi, and shipped them hurriedly westward, to cut off (from the north) the Red Army's route of advance. All crossings were heavily fortified; all ferries were drawn to the north bank of the river; all roads were blocked; great areas were denuded of grain. Other thousands of Nanking troops poured into Kweichow to reinforce the opium-soaked provincials of Warlord Wang Chia-lieh, whose army in the end was practically immobilized by the Reds. Still others were dispatched to the Yunnan border, to set up obstacles there. In Kweichow, therefore, the Reds found a reception committee of a couple of hundred thousand troops, and obstructions thrown up everywhere in their path. This necessitated two great counter-marches—across the province, and a wide circular movement around the capital.

Manœuvres in Kweichow occupied the Reds for four months, during which they destroyed five enemy divisions, captured the headquarters of Governor Wang, and occupied his foreign-style palace in Tsunyi, recruited about 20,000 men, and visited most of the villages and towns of the province, calling mass meetings and organizing Communist cadres among the youth. Their losses were negligible, but they still faced the problem of crossing the Yangtze. By his swift concentration on the Kweichow-Szechuan border, Chiang Kai-shek had skilfully blocked the short, direct roads that led to the great river. He now placed his main hope of exterminating the Reds on the prevention of this crossing at any point, hoping to push them far into the south-west, or into the wastelands of Tibet. To his various commanders and the provincial warlords he telegraphed that " the fate of the nation and the party " depended on bottling up the Reds south of the Yangtze.

Suddenly, early in May 1935, the Reds turned southward and entered Yunnan, where China's frontier meets Burma and Indo-China. A spectacular march in four days brought them within ten miles of the capital, Yunnanfu, and Warlord Lung Yun (Dragon Cloud) frantically mobilized all available troops for defence. Chiang's reinforcements meanwhile moved in from Kweichow in hot pursuit. Chiang himself and Mme Chiang, who had been staying in Yunnanfu, hastily repaired down the French railway. A big squadron of Nanking bombers kept up their daily egg-laying over the Reds, but on they came. Presently the panic ended. It was discovered that the drive on Yunnanfu had been only a distraction carried out by a few troops. The main Red forces were moving westward, obviously with the intention of crossing the river at Lengkai, one of the few navigable points of the upper Yangtze.

Through the wild mountainous country of Yunnan, the

Yangtze River flows deeply and swiftly between immense gorges, great peaks in places rising in defiles of a mile or more, with steep walls of rock lifting almost perpendicularly on either side. The few crossings had all been occupied long ago by Government troops. Chiang was well pleased. He now ordered all boats drawn to the north bank of the river to be *burned*. Then he started his own troops, and Lung Yun's, in an enveloping movement around the Red Army, hoping to finish it off for ever on the banks of this historic and treacherous stream.

Seemingly unaware of their fate, the Reds continued to march rapidly westward in three columns toward Lengkai. The boats had been burned there, and Nanking pilots reported that a Red vanguard had begun building a bamboo bridge. Chiang became more confident; this bridge-building would take weeks. But one evening, quite unobtrusively, a Red battalion suddenly reversed its direction. On a phenomenal forced march it covered eighty-five miles in one night and day, and in late afternoon descended upon the only other possible ferry-crossing in the vicinity, at Chou P'ing Fort. Dressed in captured Nanking uniforms, the battalion entered the town at dusk without arousing comment, and quietly disarmed the garrison.

Boats had been withdrawn to the north bank—but they had not been destroyed! (Why spoil boats, when the Reds were hundreds of *li* distant, and not coming there anyway? So the Government troops had reasoned.) But how to get one over to the south bank? After dark the Reds escorted the village official to the river, and forced him to call out to the guards on the opposite side that some Government troops had arrived, and wanted a boat. Unsuspectingly, one was sent across. Into it piled a detachment of these " Nanking " soldiers, who soon disembarked on the north shore—in Szechuan at last. Calmly entering the garrison quarters, they found the troops peacefully playing mah-jong, their guns resting safely on the walls. In open-mouthed amazement they stared as the Reds ordered " Hands up ! " and pocketed their weapons. They did not for some time comprehend that they were prisoners of the " bandits " whom they had believed to be at least three days' distant.

Meanwhile the main forces of the Red Army had executed a wide counter-march, and by noon of the next day the vanguard reached the fort. Crossing was now a simple matter. Six big boats worked constantly for nine days. The entire army was transported into Szechuan without a life lost. Having concluded the operation, the Reds promptly destroyed the vessels and lay down to sleep. When Chiang's forces reached the river, two days later, the rearguard of their enemy called cheerily to them from the north bank to come on over; the swimming was fine. The Government troops were obliged to make a detour of over 200 miles to the nearest crossing, and the Reds thus shook them from their trail. Infuriated, the Generalissimo now flew to Szechuan, where he mobilized new forces in the path of the oncoming horde, hoping to cut them off at one more strategic river—the great Tatu.

Gc

3

The Heroes of Tatu

THE crossing of the Tatu River was the most critical single incident of the Long March. Had the Red Army failed there, quite possibly it would have been exterminated. The historic precedent for such a fate already existed. On the banks of the remote Tatu the heroes of the *Three Kingdoms* and many warriors since then had met defeat, and in these same gorges the last of the T'aiping rebels, an army of 100,000 led by Prince Shih Ta-k'ai, was in the nineteenth century surrounded and completely destroyed by the Manchu forces under the famous Tseng Kuo-fan. To Warlords Liu Hsiang and Liu Wen-hui, his allies in Szechuan, and to his own generals in command of the Government pursuit, Generalissimo Chiang now wired an exhortation to repeat the history of the T'aipings. Here, inevitably, the Reds would perish.

But the Reds also knew about Shih Ta-k'ai, and that the main cause of his defeat had been a costly delay. Arriving at the banks of the Tatu, Prince Shih had paused for three days to honour the birth of his son—an imperial prince. Those days of rest had given his enemy the chance to concentrate against him, and to make the swift marches in his rear that blocked his line of retreat. Realizing his mistake too late, Prince Shih had tried to break the enemy encirclement, but it was impossible to manœuvre in the narrow terrain of the defiles, and he was erased from the map.

The Reds determined not to repeat his error. Moving rapidly northward from the Gold Sand River (as the Yangtze there is known) into Szechuan, they soon entered the tribal country of warlike aborigines, the White and Black Lolos of Independent Lololand. Never conquered, never absorbed by the Chinese who dwell all around them, the turbulent Lolos have for centuries occupied that densely forested and mountainous spur of Szechuan whose borders are marked by the great southward arc described by the Yangtze just east of Tibet. Chiang Kai-shek confidently counted on a long delay and weakening of the Reds here which would enable him to concentrate north of the Tatu. Lolo hatred of the Chinese is traditional, and rarely has any

Chinese army crossed their borders without heavy losses or extermination.

But the Reds had a method. They had already safely passed through the tribal districts of the Miao and the Shan peoples, aborigines of Kweichow and Yunnan, and had won their friendship and even enlisted some tribesmen in their army. Now they sent envoys ahead to parley with the Lolos. *En route*, they captured several towns on the borders of Independent Lololand, where they found a number of Lolo chieftains who had been imprisoned as hostages by the Chinese militarists. Freed and sent back to their people, these men naturally praised the Reds.

In the vanguard of the Red Army was Commander Liu Pei-ch'eng, who had once been an officer in a warlord army of Szechuan. Liu knew the tribal people, and their inner feuds and discontent. Especially he knew their hatred of Chinese, and he could speak something of the Lolo tongue. Assigned the task of negotiating a friendly alliance, he entered their territory and went into conference with the chieftains. The Lolos, he said, opposed Warlords Liu Hsiang and Liu Wen-hui and the Kuomintang; so did the Reds. The Lolos wanted to preserve their independence; Red policies favoured autonomy for all the national minorities of China. The Lolos hated the Chinese because they had been oppressed by them; but there were " White Chinese " and " Red Chinese," just as there were White Lolos and Black Lolos, and it was the White Chinese who had always slain and oppressed the Lolos. Should not the Red Chinese and the Black Lolos unite against their common enemies, the White Chinese ? The Lolos listened interestedly. Slyly they asked for arms and bullets to guard their independence and help Red Chinese fight the Whites. To their astonishment, the Reds gave them both.

And so it happened that not only a speedy but a safe and pleasant passage was accomplished. Hundreds of Lolos enlisted with the " Red Chinese " to march to the Tatu River and fight the common enemy. Some of those Lolos were to trek clear to the North-west. Liu Pei-ch'eng drank the blood of a newly killed chicken before the high chieftain of the Lolos, who drank also, and they swore blood brotherhood in the tribal manner. By this vow the Reds declared that whosoever should violate the terms of their alliance would be even as weak and cowardly as the fowl that they had killed.

Thus a vanguard division of the 1st Army Corps, led by Lin Piao, reached the Tatu Ho. On the last day of the march they emerged from the forests of Lololand (in the thick foliage of which Nanking pilots had completely lost track of them), to descend suddenly on the river town of An Jen Ch'ang—just as unheralded as they had come into Chou P'ing Fort. Guided over narrow mountain trails by the Lolos, the vanguard crept quietly up to the little town, and from the heights looked down to the river-bank, and saw with amazement and delight one of the three ferry-boats made fast on the *south* bank of the river ! Once more an act of fate had befriended them.

How did it happen ? Now, on the opposite shore, there was only one regiment of the troops of General Liu Wen-hui, the co-dictator of Szechuan province. Other Szechuan troops, as well as reinforcements from Nanking, were leisurely proceeding toward the Tatu, but the single regiment meanwhile was enough. A squad should have been ample, indeed, with all boats moored to the north. But the commander of that regiment was a native of the district; he knew the country the Reds must pass through, and how long it would take them to penetrate to the river. They would be many days yet, he told his men. And his wife, you see, had been a native of An Jen Ch'ang, so he must cross to the south bank to visit his relatives and his friends and to feast with them. Thus it happened that the Reds, taking the town by surprise, captured the commander, his boat, and their passage to the north.

Sixteen men from each of five companies volunteered to cross in the first boat and bring back the others, while on the south bank the Reds set up machine guns on the mountain-sides and over the river spread a screen of protective fire concentrated on the enemy's exposed positions. It was May. Floods poured down the mountains, and the river was swift and even wider than the Yangtze. Starting far upstream, the ferry took two hours to cross and land just opposite the town. From the south bank the villagers of An Jen Ch'ang watched breathlessly. They would be wiped out ! But wait. They saw the voyagers land almost beneath the guns of the enemy. Now, surely, they would be finished. And yet . . . From the south bank the Red machine guns barked on. The onlookers saw the little party climb ashore, hurriedly take cover, then slowly work their way up a steep cliff overhanging the enemy's positions. There they set up their own light machine guns, and sent a downpour of lead and hand grenades into the enemy redoubts along the river.

Suddenly the White troops ceased firing, broke from their redoubts, and fled to a second and then a third line of defence. A great murmur went up from the south bank, and shouts of " *Hao !* " drifted across the river to the little band who had captured the ferry landing. Meanwhile the first boat returned, towing two others, and on the second trip each carried eighty men. The enemy had entirely fled. That day and night, and the next, and the next, those three ferries of An Jen Ch'ang worked back and forth, until at last nearly a division had been transferred to the northern bank.

But the river flowed faster and faster. The crossing became more and more difficult. On the third day it took four hours to shift a boatload of men from shore to shore ! At this rate it would be weeks before the whole army and its animals and supplies could be moved. Long before the operation was completed they would be encircled. The 1st Army Corps had now crowded into An Jen Ch'ang, and behind were the flanking columns, and the transport and rearguard. Chiang Kai-shek's aeroplanes had found the spot, and heavily bombarded it. Enemy troops were racing up from the south-east; others approached from the north. A hurried military conference was summoned by Lin Piao. Chu Teh, Mao Tse-tung, Chou En-lai, and Peng Teh-huai had by now reached the river. They took a decision, and began to carry it out at once.

Some 400 *li* to the west of An Jen Ch'ang, where the gorges rise very high and the river flows narrow, deep, and swift, there is a famous iron-chain suspension bridge called the Liu Ting Chiao—the Bridge Fixed by Liu. It is the last possible crossing of the Tatu east of Tibet. Toward this the barefoot Reds now set out along a trail that wound through the gorges, at times climbing several thousand feet, again dropping low to the level of the swollen stream itself, and wallowing through waist-deep mud. If they captured the Liu Ting Chiao the whole army could enter central Szechuan. And if they failed ? If they failed they would have to retrace their steps through Lololand, re-enter Yunnan, and fight their way westward toward Likiang, on the Tibetan border—a detour of more than a thousand miles, which few might hope to survive.

As their main forces pushed westward along the southern bank, the Red division already on the northern bank moved also. Sometimes the gorges between them closed so narrowly that the two lines of Reds could shout to each other across the stream; sometimes that gulf between them measured their fear that the Tatu might separate them for ever, and they stepped more swiftly. As they wound in long dragon files along the cliffs at night their 10,000 torches sent arrows of light slanting down the dark, inscrutable face of the imprisoning river. Day and night these vanguards moved at double-quick, pausing only for brief ten-minute rests and meals, when the soldiers listened to lectures by their weary political workers, who over and over again explained the importance of this one action, exhorting each to give his last breath, his last urgent strength, for victory in the test ahead of them. There could be no slackening of pace, no half-heartedness, no fatigue. Victory was life; defeat, certain death.

On the second day the vanguard on the right bank fell behind. Szechuan troops had set up positions in the road, and skirmishes took place. Those on the southern bank pressed on more grimly. Presently new troops appeared on the opposite bank, and through their field-glasses the Reds saw that they were White reinforcements, hurrying to the Bridge Fixed by Liu ! For a whole day these troops raced each other along the stream, but gradually the Red vanguard, the pick of all the Red Army, pulled away from the enemy's tired soldiers, whose rests were longer and more frequent, whose energy seemed more spent, and who after all were none too anxious to die over a bridge.

The Bridge Fixed by Liu was built centuries ago, and in the manner of all bridges of the deep rivers of Western China. Sixteen heavy iron chains, with a span of some 100 yards or more, were stretched across the river, their ends imbedded on each side under great piles of cemented rock, beneath the stone bridge-heads. Thick boards lashed over the chains made the road of the bridge, but upon their arrival the Reds found that half this wooden flooring had been removed, and before them only the bare iron chains swung to a point midway in the stream. At the northern bridgehead an enemy machine-gun nest faced them, and behind it were positions held by a division of White troops. Now that bridge should, of course, have been destroyed. But the Szechuanese are sentimental about their few bridges; it is not easy to rebuild them, and they are costly. Of Liu Ting it was said that " the wealth of the eighteen provinces contributed to build it." And, anyway, who should have thought the Reds would insanely try to cross on the chains alone ? But that is just what they did.

No time was to be lost. The bridge must be captured before enemy reinforcements arrived. Once more volunteers were called for. One by one Red soldiers stepped forward to risk their lives, and, of those who offered themselves, thirty were chosen. Hand grenades and mausers were strapped to their backs, and soon they were swinging out above the boiling river, moving hand over hand, clinging to the iron chains. Red machine guns barked at the enemy redoubts and spattered the bridgehead with bullets. The enemy replied with machine-gunning of its own, and snipers shot at the Reds tossing high above the water, working slowly toward them. The first warrior was hit, and dropped into the current below; a second fell, and then a third. But, as they drew nearer the chains, the bridge flooring somewhat protected these dare-to-dies, and most of the enemy bullets glanced off, or ended in the cliffs on the opposite bank.

Never before had the Szechuanese seen Chinese fighters like these—men for whom soldiering was not just a rice-bowl, but youths ready to commit suicide to win ! Were they human beings or madmen or gods ? wondered the superstitious Szechuanese. Their own morale was affected; perhaps they did not shoot to kill; perhaps some of them secretly prayed that they would succeed in their attempt ! At last one Red crawled up over the bridge flooring, uncapped a grenade, and tossed it with perfect aim into the enemy redoubt. Desperate, the officers ordered the rest of the planking to be torn up. It was already too late. More Reds were crawling into sight. Paraffin was thrown on the planking, and it began to burn. By then about twenty

Reds were moving forward on their hands and knees, tossing grenade after grenade into the enemy machine-gun nest.

Suddenly, on the southern shore, their comrades began to scream with joy. " Long live the Red Army ! Long live the Revolution ! Long live the thirty heroes of Tatu Ho ! " For the Whites were withdrawing, were in pell-mell flight ! Running full speed over the remaining planks of the bridge, right through the flames licking towards them, the assailants nimbly hopped into the enemy's redoubt and turned the abandoned machine gun against the shore.

More Reds now swarmed over the chains, and arrived to help put out the fire and replace the boards. And soon afterwards the Red division that had crossed at An Jen Ch'ang came into sight, opening a flank attack on the remaining enemy positions, so that in a little while the White troops were wholly in flight —either in flight, that is, or with the Reds, for about a hundred Szechuan soldiers here threw down their rifles and turned to join their pursuers. In an hour or two the whole army was joyously tramping and singing its way across the River Tatu into Szechuan. Far overhead angrily and impotently roared the planes of Chiang Kai-shek, and the Reds cried out in delirious challenge to them. As the Communist troops poured over the river, these planes tried to hit the bridge, but their torpedoes only made pretty splashes in the river.

For their distinguished bravery the heroes of An Jen Ch'ang and Liu Ting Chiao were awarded the Gold Star, highest decoration in the Red Army of China. Later on I was to meet some of them in Ninghsia, and to be amazed at their youth, for they were all under twenty-five.

4

Across the Great Grasslands

SAFELY across the Tatu, the Reds struck off into the comparative freedom of western Szechuan, where the blockhouse system had not been completed, and where the initiative rested largely in their own hands. But hardships between battles were not over. Another 2,000 miles of marching, studded by seven great mountain ranges, still lay ahead of them.

North of the Tatu River the Reds climbed 16,000 feet over the Great Snowy Mountain, and in the rarefied air of its crest looked to the west and saw a sea of snow peaks—Tibet. It was already June, and in the lowlands very warm, but as they crossed the Ta Hsueh Shan many of those poorly clad, thin-blooded southerners, unused to the high altitudes, perished from exposure. Harder yet to ascend was the desolate Paotung Kang Mountain, up which they literally built their own road, felling long bamboos and laying them down for a track through a tortuous treacle of waist-deep mud. " On this peak," Mao Tse-tung told me, " one army corps lost two-thirds of its transport animals. Hundreds fell down and never got up."

They climbed on. The Chung Lai range next, and more lost men and animals. Then they straddled the lovely Dream Pen Mountain, and after it the Big Drum, and these also took their toll of life. Finally, on July 20, 1935, they entered the rich Maoerhkai area, in north-west Szechuan, and connected with the Fourth Front Army and the Soviet regions of the Sungpan. Here at last they paused for a long rest, took assessment of their losses, and re-formed their ranks.

The 1st, 3rd, 5th, 8th, and 9th Army Corps, that had begun the journey in Kiangsi nine months earlier with about 90,000 armed men, could now muster beneath their hammer-and-sickle banners but 45,000. Not all had been lost, strayed or captured. Behind the line of march in Hunan, Kweichow, and Yunnan the Red Army had, as part of its tactics of defence, left small cadres of regular troops to organize partisan groups among the peasantry, and create disturbances and diversionist activity on the enemy's flanks. Hundreds of captured rifles had been distributed along the route, and stretching clear from Kiangsi to Szechuan were new zones of trouble for Nanking. Ho Lung still held his little Soviet area in northern Hunan, and had been joined there by the army of Hsiao K'eh. The numerous newly-created partisan detachments began working slowly toward that region. Nanking was not to dislodge Ho Lung for a whole year, and then only after he had been ordered by Red Army headquarters to move into Szechuan, an operation which he would complete—via Tibet!—against amazing obstacles.

The journey of the Kiangsi Reds thus far had provided them with much food for reflection. They had won many new friends—and made many bitter enemies. Along their route they had provisioned themselves by " confiscating " the supplies of the rich—the landlords, officials, bureaucrats, and big gentry. The poor they had protected. Seizures were systematically carried out according to Soviet laws, and only the confiscation department of the finance commission was empowered to distribute the goods that were taken. It husbanded the army's resources, was informed by radio of all confiscations made, and assigned quantities of provisions for each section of the marchers, who often made a solid serpentine of fifty miles or more curling over the hills.

There were big " surpluses "—more than the Reds could carry—and these were distributed among the local poor. In Yunnan the Reds seized thousands of hams from rich packers there, and peasants came from miles around to receive their free portions—a new incident in the history of the ham industry. Tons of salt were likewise distributed. In Kweichow many duck farms were seized from the landlords and officials, and the Reds ate duck until, in the words of one of them, they were " simply disgusted with duck." From Kiangsi they had carried big quantities of Nanking notes, and silver dollars and bullion from their State bank, and in poor districts in their path they used this money to pay for their needs. Land deeds were destroyed, taxes abolished, and the poor peasantry armed.

Except for their experiences in western Szechuan, the Reds told me they were welcomed everywhere by the mass of the peasantry. Their fame spread ahead of them, and often the oppressed peasantry sent groups to urge them to detour and

" liberate " their districts. They had little conception of the Red Army's political programme, of course; they only knew that it was " a poor man's army." That was enough. Mao Tse-tung told me laughingly of one such delegation which arrived to welcome " Su Wei-ai Hsien-shêng "—Mr. Soviet ![1] These rustics were no more ignorant, however, than the Fukien militarist, Lu Hsing-pong, who once posted a notice throughout his fiefdom offering a reward for the " capture, dead or alive, of Su Wei-ai." Lu announced that this fellow had been doing a lot of damage everywhere, and must be exterminated !

In Maoerhkai and Mokung the southern armies rested for three weeks, while the revolutionary military council, and representatives of the Party and the Soviet Government, discussed plans for the future. It may be recalled that the Fourth Front Red Army, which had made its base in Szechuan as early as 1933, had originally been formed in the Honan–Hupeh–Anhui Soviet districts. Its march across Honan to Szechuan had been led by Hsu Hsiang-ch'ien and Chang Kuo-t'ao, two veteran Reds, of whom something more shall be said later on. Remarkable successes—and tragic excesses—had marked their campaigns in Szechuan, the whole northern half of which had once been under their sway. At the time of its junction in Maoerhkai with the southern Bolsheviks, Hsu Hsiang-ch'ien's army numbered about 50,000 men, so that the combined Red force concentrated in western Szechuan in July 1935 was nearly 100,000.

Here the two armies divided, part of the southerners continuing northward while the rest remained with the Fourth Front Army in Szechuan. There was disagreement about the correct course to pursue. Chang Kuo-t'ao and Hsu Hsiang-ch'ien favoured remaining in Szechuan and attempting to reassert Communist influence south of the Yangtze. Mao Tse-tung, Chu Teh, and the majority of the Cheka were determined to continue into the North-west. The period of indecision was ended by two factors. First was the rapid completion of an enveloping movement by Chiang Kai-shek's troops, moving into Szechuan from

[1] *Su*, the first Chinese character used in transliterating the word " Soviet," is a common family name, and *wei-ai*, when suffixed to it, might easily seem like a given name.

the east and from the north, which succeeded in driving a wedge between two sections of the Red Army. Second was the rapid rise of one of the hurried rivers of Szechuan, which then physically divided the forces, and which suddenly became impassable. There were other factors of intra-Party struggle involved which here need not be discussed.

In August, with the 1st Army Corps as vanguard, the main forces from Kiangsi continued the northward march, leaving Chu Teh in command in Szechuan, with Hsu Hsiang-ch'ien and Chang Kuo-t'ao. The Fourth Front Army was to remain there and in Tibet for another year, and be joined by Ho Lung's Second Front Army, before making a sensational march into Kansu, which I shall describe farther on. At the head of the Red cavalcade that in August 1935 moved toward the Great Grasslands, on the border of Szechuan and Tibet, were Commanders Lin Piao, Peng Teh-huai, Tso Chuan, Ch'en Keng, Chou En-lai, and Mao Tse-tung, most of the officials from the Kiangsi Central Government, and a majority of the members of the Central Committee of the Party. They began this last phase of the march with about 30,000 men.

The most dangerous and exciting travel lay before them, for the route they chose led through wild country inhabited by the independent Mantzu tribesmen, and the nomadic Hsifan, a warring people of eastern Tibet. Passing into the Mantzu and Tibetan territories, the Reds for the first time faced a populace united in its hostility to them, and their sufferings on this part of the trek exceeded anything of the past. They had money, but could buy no food. They had guns, but their enemies were invisible. As they marched into the thick forests and jungles and across the headwaters of a dozen great rivers, the tribesmen withdrew from the vicinity of the march. They stripped their houses bare, carried off all edibles, drove their cattle and fowl to the plateaus, and simply disinhabited the whole area.

A few hundred yards on either side of the road, however, it was quite unsafe. Many a Red who ventured to forage for a sheep never returned. The mountaineers hid in the thick bush and sniped at the marching " invaders." They climbed the mountains, and when the Reds filed through the deep, narrow, rock passes, where sometimes only one or two could pass abreast, the Mantzu rolled huge boulders down to crush them and their animals. Here were no chances to explain " Red policy toward national minorities," no opportunities for friendly alliance! The Mantzu Queen had an implacable traditional hatred for Chinese of any variety, and recognized no distinctions between Red and White. She threatened to boil alive anyone who helped the travellers.

Unable to get food except by capturing it, the Reds were obliged to make war for a few cattle. They had a saying then that " to buy one sheep costs the life of one man." But from the Mantzu fields they harvested green Tibetan wheat, and vegetables such as beets and turnips—the latter of an enormous size that would " feed fifteen men," according to Mao Tse-tung. On such meagre supplies they equipped themselves to cross the Great Grasslands. " This is our only foreign debt," Mao said to me humorously, " and some day we must pay the Mantzu and the Tibetans for the provisions we were obliged to take from them." Only by capturing tribesmen could they find guides through the country. But of these guides they made friends, and after the Mantzu frontier was crossed they continued the journey. Some of them are now students in the Communist Party School in Shensi, and will one day return to their land to tell the people the difference between " Red Chinese " and White.

In the Grasslands there was no human habitation for ten days. Almost perpetual rain falls over this swampland, and it is possible to cross its centre only by a maze of narrow footholds known to the native mountaineers who led the Reds. More animals were lost, and more men. Many foundered in the weird sea of wet grass, and dropped from sight into the depth of the swamp, beyond reach of their comrades. There was no firewood; they were obliged to eat their green wheat and vegetables raw. There were even no trees for shelter, and the lightly equipped Reds carried no tents. At night they huddled under bushes tied together, which gave but scant protection against the rain. But from this trial, too, they emerged triumphant—more so, at least, than the White troops, who pursued them, lost their way, and turned back, with only a fraction of their number intact.

The Red Army now reached the Kansu border. Several battles still lay ahead, the loss of any one of which might have meant decisive defeat. More Nanking, Tungpei, and Moslem troops had been mobilized in southern Kansu to stop their march, but they managed to break through all these blockades, and in the process annexed hundreds of horses from the Moslem cavalry which people had confidently predicted would finish them once and for all. Footsore, weary, and at the limit of human endurance, they finally entered northern Shensi, just below the Great Wall, and on October 20, 1935, a year after its departure from Kiangsi, the vanguard of the First Front Army connected with the 25th, 26th, and 27th Red Armies, which had already established a small base of Soviet power in Shensi in 1933. Numbering less than 20,000 survivors now, they sat down to realize the significance of their achievement.

The statistical recapitulation[1] of the Long March is impressive. It shows that there was an average of almost a skirmish a day, somewhere on the line, while altogether fifteen whole days were devoted to major pitched battles. Out of a total of 368 days *en route*, 235 were consumed in marches by day, and 18 in marches by night. Of the 100 days of halts—many of which were devoted to skirmishes—56 days were spent in north-western Szechuan, leaving only 44 days of rest over a distance of about 5,000 miles, or an average of one halt for every 114 miles of marching. The mean daily stage covered was 71 *li*, or nearly 24 miles—a phenomenal pace for a great army and its transport to *average* over some of the most hazardous terrain on earth.

Altogether the Reds crossed 18 mountain ranges, 5 of which were perennially snow-capped, and they crossed 24 rivers. They passed through 12 different provinces, occupied 62 cities, and broke through enveloping armies of 10 different provincial warlords, besides defeating, eluding, or outmanœuvring the various forces of Central Government troops sent against them. They entered and successfully crossed 6 different aboriginal districts, and penetrated areas through which no Chinese army had gone for scores of years.

However one may feel about the Reds and what they represent

[1] *An Account of the Long March*, op. cit.

politically (and here is plenty of room for argument!), it is impossible to deny recognition of their Long March—the Ch'ang Cheng, as they call it—as one of the great exploits of military history. In Asia only the Mongols have surpassed it, and in the last three centuries there has been no similar armed *migration of a nation* with the exception, perhaps, of the amazing Flight of the Torgut, of which Sven Hedin tells in his *Jehol, City of Emperors*. Hannibal's march over the Alps looks like a holiday excursion beside it. A more interesting comparison is Napoleon's retreat from Moscow, when the Grand Army was utterly broken and demoralized.

While the Red Army's March to the North-west was unquestionably a strategic retreat, it can hardly be called a rout, for the Reds finally reached their objective with their nucleus still intact, and their morale and political will evidently as strong as ever. The Reds themselves declared, and apparently believed, that they were advancing toward the anti-Japanese front, and this was a psychological factor of great importance. It helped them turn what might have been a demoralized retreat into a spirited march of victory. History has subsequently shown that they were right in emphasizing what was undoubtedly the second fundamental reason for their migration: an advance to the strategic North-west, a region which they correctly foresaw was to play a determining rôle in the immediate destinies of China, Japan, and Soviet Russia. This skilful propagandive manœuvre must be noted as a piece of brilliant political strategy. It was to a large extent responsible for the successful conclusion of the heroic trek.

In one sense this mass migration was the biggest armed propaganda tour in history. The Reds passed through provinces populated by more than 200,000,000 people. Between battles and skirmishes, in every town occupied, they called great mass meetings, gave theatrical performances, heavily " taxed " the rich, freed many slaves (some of whom joined the Red Army), preached " liberty, equality, democracy," confiscated the property of the " traitors " (officials, big landlords, and tax-collectors) and distributed their goods among the poor. Millions of peasants have now seen the Red Army and heard it speak, and are no longer afraid of it. The Reds explained the aims of agrarian revolution and their anti-Japanese policy. They armed thousands of peasants, and left cadres behind to train the Red partisans, who have kept Nanking's troops busy ever since. Many thousands dropped out on the long and heart-breaking march, but thousands of others—farmers, apprentices, slaves, deserters from the Kuomintang ranks, workers, all the disinherited—joined in and filled the ranks.

Some day someone will write the full epic of this exciting expedition. Meanwhile I must get on with my story, for we have now brought the Reds together in the North-west. As epilogue, I offer a free translation of a classical poem about this 6,000-mile excursion, done by Chairman Mao Tse-tung—a rebel who can write verse as well as lead a crusade:

The Red Army, never fearing the challenging Long March,
Looked lightly on the many peaks and rivers.
Wu Liang's Range rose, lowered, rippled,
And green-tiered were the rounded steps of Wu Meng.
Warm-beating the Gold-Sand River's waves against the rocks,
And cold the iron-chain spans of Tatu's bridge.
A thousand joyous li of freshening snow on Min Shan,
And then, the last pass vanquished, Three Armies smiled!

PART SIX

RED STAR IN THE NORTH-WEST

1

The Shensi Soviets: Beginnings

WHILE the Communists in Kiangsi, Fukien, and Hunan were gradually building a base for their opposition to Nanking, Red Armies appeared in other widely scattered parts of China. Of these, the biggest single area was the Honan–Anhui–Hupeh Soviet, which covered a good part of those three rich provinces of the central Yangtze valley, and embraced a population of more than 2,000,000 people. The Red Army there began under the command of Hsu Hai-tung, and later on, to lead it, came Hsu Hsiang-ch'ien, a graduate of the first class of Whampoa Academy, a former colonel in the Kuomintang Army, and a veteran of the Canton Commune.

Far in the mountains to the north-west of them, another Whampoa cadet, Liu Tzu-tan, was laying the foundations for the present Soviet areas in Shensi, Kansu, and Ninghsia. A modern Robin Hood, with the mountaineer's hatred of rich men, Liu Tzu-tan's name was becoming among the poor a promise, and among landlords and moneylenders the scourge of the gods.

This chaotic warrior was born in the hill-cradled town of Pao An, north Shensi, the son of middle-class peasants. He went to high school in Yulin, which stands under the shadow of the Great Wall, and is the seat of Shensi's prosperous trade with the caravans of Mongolia. Leaving Yulin, Liu Tzu-tan secured an appointment to the Whampoa Academy in Canton, completed his course there in 1926, and became a Communist and a young officer in the Kuomintang. With the Nationalist Expedition as far as Hankow, he was there when the split occurred in the Kuomintang-Communist alliance.

In 1927, following the Nanking *coup d'état*, he fled from the " purgation," and worked secretly for the Communist Party in Shanghai. Returning to his native province in 1928, he re-established connections with some of his former comrades, then in the Kuominchun, the " People's Army " of General Feng Yü-hsiang. Next year he led a peasant uprising in south Shensi. This broke out near Hua Hsien—where in the recent North-west revolt Nanking bombers attacked a vanguard of Tungpei troops, and did much damage. Although Liu's uprising was sanguinarily suppressed, out of it grew the nucleus of the first guerilla bands of Shensi.

Liu Tzu-tan's career from 1929 till 1932 was a kaleidoscope of defeats, failures, discouragements, escapades, adventure, and remarkable escapes from death, interspersed by periods of respectability as a reinstated officer. Several small armies under him were completely destroyed. Once he was made head of the *min-t'uan* at Pao An, and he used his office to arrest and execute several landlords and moneylenders. Strange caprice, for a *min-t'uan* leader ! The magistrate of Pao An was dismissed, and Liu fled, with but three followers, to a neighbouring *hsien*. There one of General Feng Yü-hsiang's officers invited them to a banquet, in the midst of which Liu and his friends disarmed their hosts, seized twenty guns, and made off to the hills, where he soon collected a following of about 300 men.

This little army was surrounded, however, and Liu sued for peace. His offer was accepted, and he became a colonel in the Kuomintang Army, with a garrison post in west Shensi. Again he began an anti-landlord movement, and again he was outlawed, this time arrested. Owing chiefly to his influence in the Shensi Kê Lao Hui he was pardoned once more, but his troops were reorganized into a transportation brigade, of which he was made commander. And now the incredible happened: for the third time Liu Tzu-tan repeated the error of his ways. Some landlords in his district, long accustomed to tax-exemption (a more or less " hereditary right " of landlords in Shensi), refused to pay taxes. Liu promptly arrested a number of them, with the result that the gentry rose up in arms, and demanded that Sian remove and punish him. His troops were surrounded and disarmed.

Finally he was driven back to Pao An with a price on his head—but followed by many young Communist officers and men from his own brigade. Here at last he set about organizing an independent army under a Red flag in 1931, took possession of Pao An and Chung Yang counties, and rapidly pushed operations in north Shensi. Government troops sent against him very often turned over to the Reds in battle; deserters even drifted across the Yellow River from Shansi to join this outlaw whose dare-deviltry, courage, and impetuousness soon won him fame throughout the North-west and created the usual legend that he was " invulnerable to bullets."

From all independent testimony I could get, there seems no

doubt that in the first year or two of struggle in Shensi the killing of officials, tax-collectors, and landlords was excessive. Unleashing long-hushed fury, the armed peasants raided, plundered, carried off captives, whom they held for ransom in their fortified areas, and conducted themselves much like ordinary bandits. But by 1932 Liu Tzu-tan's followers had occupied eleven counties in the loess hills of northern Shensi, and the Communist Party had organized a political department at Yulin, to direct Liu's troops. Early in 1933 the first Shensi Soviet and a regular administration were established, and a programme was attempted similar to that in Kiangsi.

In 1934 and 1935 these Shensi Reds expanded considerably, improved their armies, and somewhat stabilized conditions in their districts. A Shensi provincial Soviet Government was set up, a Party training school established, and military headquarters were located at An Ting. The Soviets opened their own bank and post office and began to issue crude money and stamps. In the completely Sovietized areas a Soviet economy was begun, landlords' land was confiscated and redistributed, all sur-taxes were abolished, co-operatives were opened, and a call was sent out by the Party to furnish teachers for primary schools.

Meanwhile Liu Tzu-tan moved well south of the Red base toward the capital. He occupied Lin T'ung, just outside Sianfu, and besieged the city for some days, without success. A column of Reds pushed down to southern Shensi, and established Soviets in several counties there. They had some bad defeats and reverses in battles with General Yang Hu-ch'eng (later to become the Red's ally), and they had some victories. As discipline increased in the army, and bandit elements were eliminated, support for the Reds deepened among the peasantry. By the middle of 1935 the Soviets controlled twenty-two counties in Shensi and Kansu. The 26th and 27th Red Armies, with a total of over 5,000 men, were now under Liu Tzu-tan's command, and could establish contact by radio with the main forces of the Red Army in the south and in the west. As the southern Reds began to withdraw from their Kiangsi–Fukien base, these hillmen of Shensi greatly strengthened themselves, until in 1935 Chiang Kai-shek was forced to send his vice-commander-in-chief, Marshal Chang Hsueh-liang, to lead a big army against them.

Late in 1934 the 25th Red Army, under Hsu Hai-tung, left Honan with some 8,000 men. By October it had reached south Shensi and connected with about 1,000 Red partisans in that area who had been armed by Liu Tzu-tan. Hsu encamped for the winter there, helped the partisans to build a regular army, fought several successful battles with General Yang Hu-ch'eng's troops, and armed the peasants in five counties of south Shensi. A provisional Soviet Government was established, with Cheng Wei-shan, a twenty-three-year-old member of the Cheka of Shenski province, as chairman, and Li Lung-kuei and Chêng Shan-jui as commanders of two independent Red brigades. Leaving them to defend this area, Hsu Hai-tung then moved into Kansu with his 25th Army, and fought his way into the Soviet districts through thousands of Government troops, capturing five county capitals *en route* and disarming two regiments of Mohammedan troops, under General Ma Hung-ping.

On July 25, 1935, the 25th, 26th, and 27th Armies united near Yung Ch'ang, north Shensi. Their troops were reorganized into the 15th Red Army Corps, with Hsu Hai-tung as commander and Liu Tzu-tan as vice-commander, and chairman of the Shensi-Kansu-Shansi Revolutionary Military Committee. In August 1935 this army corps met and defeated two divisions of Tungpei troops, under General Wang Yi-che. New recruits were added, and much-needed guns and ammunition.

And now happened a curious thing. In August there came to north Shensi a delegate of the Central Committee of the Communist Party, a stout young gentleman named Chang Ching-fu. According to my informant, who was then a staff officer under Liu Tzu-tan, this Mr. Chang (nicknamed Chang the Corpulent) was empowered to " reorganize " the Party and the Army. He was a kind of super-inspector.

Chang the Corpulent proceeded to collect evidence to prove that Liu Tzu-tan had not followed the " Party line." He " tried " Liu, and demanded his resignation from all posts. Now it is either ridiculous or miraculous, or perhaps both, but in any case it is a striking example of " Party discipline " that Liu Tzu-tan did not put Mr. Chang against a wall as an interloper for presuming to criticize him, but he quietly accepted his sentence, retired from all active command, and went, Achilles-like, to sulk in his cave in Pao An ! Mr. Chang also ordered the arrest and imprisonment of more than 100 other " reactionaries " in the Party and the Army and quietly sat back well satisfied with himself.

It was into this queer scene that the vanguard of the southern Reds the 1st Army Corps, headed by Lin Piao, Chou En-lai, Peng Teh-huai, and Mao Tse-tung, entered in October 1935. Shocked at the amazing situation, they called for a re-examination of evidence, found most of it baseless, discovered that Chang Ching-fu had exceeded his orders and been misled by " reactionaries " himself. They promptly reinstated Liu and all his confederates. Chang the Corpulent was himself arrested, tried, imprisoned for a term, and later given menial tasks to perform.

Thus it happened that when, early in 1936, the combined Red Armies attempted their famous " anti-Japanese " expedition, crossed the river, and invaded neighbouring Shansi, Liu Tzu-tan was again in command. He distinguished himself in that remarkable campaign during which the Reds occupied over eighteen counties of the so-called " model province " in two months. But the reports of his death on that expedition—unlike many others—were no mere wish-fancies of the Kuomintang Press. He was fatally wounded in March 1936, when he led a raiding-party against an enemy fortification, the capture of which enabled the Red Army to cross the Yellow River. He was carried back to Shensi. Liu Tzu-tan died gazing upon the hills he had roamed and loved as a boy, and among the mountain people he had led along the road he believed in, the road of revolutionary struggle. He was buried at Wa Ya Pao, and the Soviets renamed a county of their Red China after him—Tzu-tan *hsien*.

In Pao An I met his widow and his child, a beautiful little boy of six. The Reds had tailored him a special uniform; he wore an officer's belt, and a red star on his cap. He was the idol of everybody there. Young Liu carried himself like a field marshal and he was mightily proud of his " bandit " father.

But, although Liu Tzu-tan was the personality around which these Soviets of the North-west grew up, it was not Liu, but the conditions of life itself, which produced this convulsive movement of his people. And to understand whatever success they have had it is necessary not so much just now to look at what these men fought for, as to examine what they fought against.

Death and Taxes

DURING the great North-west famine, which lasted roughly for three years, and affected four huge provinces, I visited some of the drought-stricken areas in Suiyuan, on the edge of Mongolia, in June 1929. How many people starved to death in those years I do not accurately know, and probably no one will ever know; it is forgotten now. A conservative semi-official figure of 3,000,000 is often accepted, but I am not inclined to doubt other estimates ranging as high as 6,000,000.

This catastrophe passed hardly noticed in the Western world, or even in the coastal cities of China, but a few courageous men of the China International Famine Relief Commission—many Chinese and some foreigners like Edwards and O. J. Todd and wonderful old Dr. Ingram—risked their skins in those typhus-infested districts to try to salvage a little of the human wreckage. I spent some days with them, passing through cities of death, across a once fertile countryside turned into desert wasteland, through a land of naked horror.

I was twenty-three. I had come to the East looking for the " glamour of the Orient," I suppose. I believe I fancied myself an adventurer, and this excursion to Suiyuan had begun as something like that. But here for the first time in my life I came abruptly upon men who were dying because they had nothing to eat. In those hours of nightmare I spent in Suiyuan I saw thousands of men, women, and children starving to death before my eyes.

Have you ever seen a man—a good honest man who has worked hard, a " law-abiding citizen," doing no serious harm to anyone—when he has had no food for more than a month ? It is a most agonizing sight. His dying flesh hangs from him in wrinkled folds; you can clearly see every bone in his body; his eyes stare out unseeing, and even if he is a youth of twenty he moves like an ancient crone, dragging himself from spot to spot. If he has been lucky he has long ago sold his wife and daughters. He has also sold everything he owns—the timbers of his house itself, and most of his clothes. Sometimes he has, indeed, even sold the

last rag of decency, and he sways there in the scorching sun, his
testicles dangling from him like withered olive-seeds—the last
grim jest to remind you that this was once a man !

Children are even more pitiable, with their little skeletons
bent over and misshapen, their crooked bones, their little arms
like twigs, and their purpling bellies, filled with bark and saw-
dust, protruding like tumours. Women lie slumped in corners,
waiting for death, their black blade-like buttocks protruding,
their breasts hanging like collapsed sacks. But there are, after all,
not many women and girls. Most of them have died or been sold.

I don't mean to dramatize horror. These are things I saw myself and shall never forget. Millions of people died that way in
famine, and thousands more still die in China to-day like that. I
saw fresh corpses on the streets of Saratsi, and in the villages I
saw shallow graves where victims of famine and disease were laid
by the dozens. But these were not the most shocking things after
all. The shocking thing was that in many of those towns there
were still rich men, rice-hoarders, wheat-hoarders, moneylenders, and landlords, with armed guards to defend them, while
they profiteered enormously. The shocking thing was that in the
cities—where officials danced or played with sing-song girls—
there was grain and food, and had been for months; that in
Peking and Tientsin and elsewhere were thousands of tons of
wheat and millet, collected (mostly by contributions from
abroad) by the Famine Commission, but which could not be
shipped to the starving. Why not ? Because in the North-west
there were some militarists who wanted to hold all of their
rolling-stock and would release none of it toward the east, while
in the east there were other Kuomintang generals who would
send no rolling-stock westward—even to starving people—
because they feared it would be seized by their rivals.

While this famine raged the Commission decided to build a big
canal (with American funds) to help flood some of the lands
baked by drought. The officials gave them every co-operation—
and promptly began to buy for a few cents an acre all the lands
to be irrigated. A flock of vultures descended upon this benighted
country, and purchased from the starving farmers thousands of
acres for the taxes in arrears, or for a few coppers, and held it to
await tenants and rainy days.

Yet the great majority of those people who died did so without any act of protest !

" Why don't they revolt ? " I asked myself. " Why don't they march in a great army and attack the scoundrels who can tax them but cannot feed them, who can seize their lands but cannot repair an irrigation canal ? Or why don't they sweep into the great cities, and plunder the wealth of the rascals who buy their daughters and wives, the men who continue to gorge themselves on elaborate thirty-six-course banquets while honest men starve ? Why not ? "

I was profoundly puzzled by their passivity. For a while I thought nothing would make a Chinese fight.

I was mistaken. The Chinese peasant is not passive; he is not a coward. He will fight when he is given a method, an organization, leadership, a workable programme, hope—*and arms*. The development of Communism in China has proved that. Against the above background, therefore, it should not surprise us to see Communism especially popular in the North-west, for conditions there have enjoyed no more fundamental improvement for the mass of the peasantry than elsewhere in China.

Evidence to this effect has been vividly documented in a quarter where you might least expect it. Here I refer to the brilliant report[1] prepared by Dr. A. Stampar, the distinguished health expert sent by the League of Nations as adviser to the Nanking Government. It is the best thing available on the subject. Dr. Stampar recently toured the Kuomintang areas of Shensi and Kansu, and his reports are based on his own observations as well as official data opened for him.

He points out that " in the year 240 B.C. an engineer called Cheng Kuo is said to have constructed a system for irrigating nearly a million acres " in the historic Wei valley of Shensi, cradle of the Chinese race, but that " this system was neglected; the dams collapsed, and, though new works were from time to time carried out, the amount of territory irrigated at the end of the Manchu Dynasty (1912) was less than 20,000 *mou* "—about

[1] *The North-western Provinces and their Possibilities of Development*, by Dr. A. Stampar (Nanking, July 1934, published privately by the National Economic Council). Unfortunately, like many of the illuminating reports of Dr. Stampar and other League experts on parts of South and Central China, this volume is not available to the public.

3,300 acres ! Figures he obtained showed that during the great famine 62 per cent of the population died outright in one county of Shensi; in another, 75 per cent; and so on. He quotes official estimates revealing that 2,000,000 people starved in Kansu alone —about 20 per cent of the population. And many of these deaths could have been prevented had officials prohibited grain-hoarding, and had not rival militarists interfered with shipments of famine-relief supplies.

To quote from this Geneva investigator *ad lib.* on conditions in the North-west before the Reds arrived:

" In the famine of 1930 twenty acres of land could be pur-chased for three days' food-supply. Making use of this oppor-tunity, the wealthy classes of the province [Shensi] built up large estates, and the number of owner-cultivators diminished. The following extract from the report for 1930 of Mr. Findlay Andrew of the China International Famine Relief Commission conveys a good impression of the situation in that year:

" ' . . . The external appearances of the province have much improved on those of last year. Why ? Because in this par-ticular section of Kansu with which our work deals, death from starvation, pestilence, and sword have doomed during the past two years such large numbers of the population that the very demand for food has considerably lessened.' "

Much land has become waste, much has been concentrated in the hands of landlords and officials. Kansu especially has "sur-prisingly large " areas of cultivable but uncultivated land. " Land during the famine of 1928–30 was bought at extremely cheap rates by landowners who, since that period, have realized fortunes by the execution of the Wei Pei Irrigation project."

" In Shensi it is considered a mark of honour to pay no land tax, and wealthy landowners are therefore as a rule exempted. . . . A practice which is particularly undesirable is to claim arrears of taxes, for the period during which they were absent, from the farmers who abandoned their land during famines, the farmers being forbidden to resume possession until their arrears are paid."

Dr. Stampar finds that Shensi farmers (evidently excluding the landlords, who are " as a rule exempted ") have to pay land taxes and sur-taxes amounting to about 45 per cent of their income, while other taxes " represent a further 20 per cent "; and " not only is taxation thus fantastically heavy, but its assessment appears to be haphazard and its manner of collection wasteful, brutal, and in many cases corrupt."

As for Kansu, Dr. Stampar says:

" The revenues of Kansu have during the last five years averaged over eight millions . . . heavier taxation than in Chekiang, one of the richest and most heavily taxed provinces in China. It will be seen also that this revenue, especially in Kansu, is not drawn from one or two major sources, but from a multitude of taxes each yielding a small sum, scarcely any commodity or productive or commercial activity going untaxed. The amount which the population pays is even higher than is shown by the published figures. In the first place, the tax-collectors are able to retain a share—in some cases a very large share—of the amounts collected. In the second place, to the taxes levied by the provincial or *hsien* governments must be added those imposed by military leaders, which in Kansu province are officially estimated at more than ten millions.[1]

" A further cause of expense to the population is the local militia [*min-t'uan*], which, formed originally for defence against the bandits, has in many instances degenerated into a gang living at the cost of the countryside." Dr. Stampar quotes figures showing that the cost of supporting the *min-t'uan* ranges from 30 per cent to 40 per cent of the total local government budget—this quite in addition, of course, to the burden of maintaining the big regular armies. These latter, according to Dr. Stampar, have absorbed over 60 per cent of the provincial revenues in both Kansu and Shensi.

A foreign missionary I met in Shensi told me that he had once personally followed a pig from owner to the consumer, and in the process saw six different taxes being paid. Another missionary, of Kansu, described seeing peasants knock down the

---

[1] This is a very conservative estimate indeed, since it includes no mention of the chief illegal military taxation in both Kansu and Shensi, which has for many years been the opium revenue. Figures given to me in Sianfu indicate that when General Feng Yü-hsiang was in control of this region he realized about $80,000,000 a year from this source. This income has doubtlessly considerably diminished since then, owing to competition from Nanking's State opium monopoly, but it still brings in many millions annually.

wooden walls of their houses (wood being expensive in the North-west) and cart it to market to sell in order to pay tax-collectors. He said that the attitude of even some of the " rich " peasants, while not friendly when the Reds first arrived, was one of indifference, and a belief that " no Government could be worse than the old."

And yet the North-west is by no means a hopeless country economically. It is not over-populated; much of its land is very rich; it can easily produce far more than it can consume, and with an improved irrigation system parts of it might become a " Chinese Ukraine." Shensi and Kansu have abundant coal deposits. Shensi has a little oil. Dr. Stampar thinks that " Shensi, especially the plain in the neighbourhood of Sian, may itself become an industrial centre of an importance second only to the Yangtze valley, and needing for its service its own coal-fields." Mineral deposits of Kansu, Chinghai, and Sinkiang, said to be very rich, are scarcely touched. In gold alone, says Stampar, " the region may turn out to be a second Klondyke."

Here, surely, were conditions which seem over-ripe for change. Here, surely, were things for men to fight against, even if they had nothing to fight *for* ! And no wonder, when the Red Star appeared in the North-west, thousands of men arose to welcome it as a symbol of hope and freedom.

But did the Reds, after all, prove any better ?

3

Soviet Society

WHATEVER it may have been in the South, Chinese Communism as I found it in the North-west might more accurately be called rural equalitarianism than anything Marx would have found agreeable as a model child of his own. This was manifestly true economically, and although in the social, political, and cultural life of the organized Soviets there was a crude Marxist guidance, limitations of material conditions were everywhere obvious.

It has already been emphasized that there is no machine industry of any importance in the North-west. The region is far less influenced by industrialism than the eastern parts of China; it is farming and grazing country primarily, the culture of which has been for centuries in stagnation, though many of the economic abuses prevalent no doubt reflect the changing economy in the semi-industrialized cities. Yet the Red Army itself was an outstanding product of the impact of " industrialization " on China, and the shock of the ideas it brought into the fossilized culture here was in a true sense revolutionary.

Objective conditions, however, denied the Reds the possibility of organizing much more than the political framework for the beginnings of Socialist economy, of which naturally they could think only in terms of a future which might give them power in the great cities, where they could take over the industrial bases from the foreign concessions and thus lay the foundations for a true Socialist society. Meanwhile, in the rural areas, their activity centred chiefly on the solution of the immediate problems of the peasants—land and taxes. This may sound like the reactionary programme of the old Narodniks of Russia, but the great difference lies in the fact that Chinese Communists never regarded land distribution as anything more than a phase in the building of a mass base, a tactic enabling them to develop the revolutionary struggle toward the conquest of power and the ultimate realization of thoroughgoing Socialist changes—in which collectivization would be inevitable. In *Fundamental Laws of the Chinese Soviet Republic*[1] the First All-China Soviet Congress

[1] Martin Lawrence, London, op. cit.

in 1931 set forth in detail the " maximum programme " of the Communist Party of China—and reference to it shows clearly that the ultimate aim of Chinese Communists is a true and complete Socialist State of the Marx-Leninist conception. Meanwhile, however, it has to be remembered that the social, political, and economic organization of the Red districts has all along been only a very provisional affair. Even in Kiangsi it was little more than that. Because the Soviets have had to fight for an existence ever since they began, their main task has always been to build a military and political base for the extension of the revolution on a wider and deeper scale, rather than to " try out Communism in China," which is what some people think the Reds have been attempting in their little blockaded areas.

The immediate basis of support for the Reds in the North-west was obviously not so much the idea of " from each according to his ability, to each according to his need " as it was something like the promise of Dr. Sun Yat-sen: " Land to those who till it." Among economic reforms which the Reds could claim to their credit these four evidently counted most to the peasantry: redistribution of land, abolition of usury, abolition of tax-extortion, and elimination of privileged groups.

While theoretically the Soviets were a " workers' and peasants' " Government, in actual practice the whole constituency was overwhelmingly peasant in character and occupation, and the régime had to shape itself accordingly. An attempt was made to balance peasant influence, and offset it, by classifying the rural population into these categories: great landlords, middle and small landlords, rich peasants, middle peasants, poor peasants, tenant peasants, rural workers, handicraft workers, *lumpen* proletariat, and a division called *tzu-yo chih-yeh chieh*, or professional workers—which included teachers, doctors, and technicians, the " rural intelligentsia." These divisions were political as well as economic, and in the election of the Soviets the tenant peasants, rural workers, handicraft workers, and so on, were given a very much greater representation than the other categories—the aim apparently being to create some kind of democratic dictatorship of the " rural proletariat." However, it was hard to see that there was any important basic class division operative in these categories, as they were all directly attached to agrarian economy.

Within these limitations the Soviets seemed to work very well in areas where the régime was stabilized. The structure of representative government was built up from the village Soviet, as the smallest unit: above it were the district Soviet, the county Soviet, and the provincial and central Soviets. Each village elected its delegates to the higher Soviets clear up to the delegates elected for the Soviet Congress. Suffrage was universal over the age of sixteen, but it was not equal, for reasons mentioned above.

Various committees were established under each of the district Soviets. An all-powerful committee, usually elected in a mass meeting shortly after the occupation of a district by the Red Army, and preceded by an intensified propaganda campaign, was the revolutionary committee. It called for elections or re-elections, and closely co-operated with the Communist Party. Under the district Soviet, and appointed by it, were committees for education, co-operatives, military training, political training, land, public health, partisan training, revolutionary defence, enlargement of the Red Army, agrarian mutual aid, Red Army land-tilling, and others. Such committees were found in every branch organ of the Soviets, right up to the Central Government, where policies were co-ordinated and State decisions made.

Organization did not stop with the Government itself. The Communist Party had an extensive membership among farmers and workers, in the towns and in the villages. In addition there were the Young Communists, and under them two organizations which embraced in their membership most of the youth. These were called the Shao-Nien Hsien-Feng Tui and the Erh-T'ung T'uan—the Young Vanguards and the Children's Brigades. The Communist Party organized the women also into Young Communist Leagues, anti-Japanese societies, nursing schools, weaving schools, and tilling brigades. Adult farmers were organized into the P'in-Min Hui, or Poor People's Society, and into anti-Japanese societies. Even the Elder Brother Society, an ancient secret organization, was brought into Soviet life and given open and legal work to do. The Nung-min Tui, or Peasant Guards, and the Yu Chi Tui, or Partisan (Roving) Brigades, were

I   MAO TSE-TUNG

(Full description of this and the following photographs on pages 457–9)

HARVEST DANCE BY A WORKERS' THEATRICAL TROUPE

(*Photo, Edgar Snow*)

2

3 " UNITED FRONT " DANCE BY YOUNG VANGUARDS OF RED CHINA

(Photo, Edgar Snow)

DANCE OF RED MACHINES

(*Photo, Edgar Snow*)

4

RED CHORUS GIRLS

(Photo, Nym Wales)

5

6   RED SCHOOLBOY BELONGING TO " CHILDREN'S BRIGADE "

(Photo, Nym Wales)

CHINESE SOVIET WORKERS' CLUB-ROOM

(Photo, " Daily Herald ")

8 CLASSROOM AND LENIN CORNER OF A RED ARMY DETACHMENT IN NORTH SHENSI

(Photo, Nym Wales)

POSTERS WITH REVOLUTIONARY SLOGANS

(*Photo, Edgar Snow*)

9

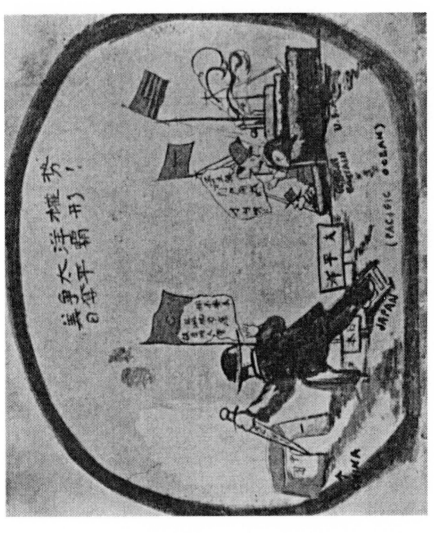

ANTI-JAPANESE WALL DRAWING

10

WALL NEWSPAPER

(Photo, Edgar Snow)

11

YOUNG VANGUARDS IN SOVIET FACTORIES

(*Photo, " Daily Herald "*)

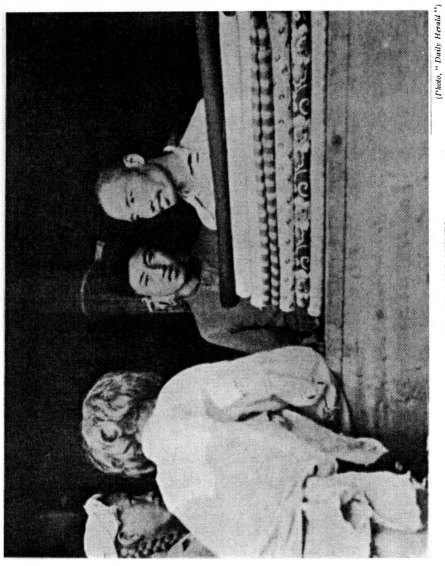

RED CO-OPERATIVES

(*Photo, " Daily Herald "*)

13

LIBRARY TABLE IN THE SOVIET DISTRICTS

(*Photo, Edgar Snow*)

14

(*Photo, Edgar Snow*)

CHINESE REDS SALUTE THE SPANISH REPUBLICANS

(*Photo, Nym Wales*)

RED FLAG AND KUOMINTANG FLAG CROSSED IN UNION

16

also part of the intensely organized rural political and social structure.

The work of all these organizations and their various committees was co-ordinated by the Central Soviet Government, the Communist Party, and the Red Army. Here I shall not enter into statistical detail, or tiresome tables and charts, to explain the organic connections of these groups, but it can be said in general that they were all skilfully interwoven, and each directly under the guidance of some Communist, though decisions of organization, membership, and work seemed to be carried out in a democratic way by the peasants themselves. The aim of Soviet organization obviously was to make every man, woman, or child a member of something, with definite work assigned to him to perform.

Rather typical of the intensity of Soviet efforts were the methods used to increase production and utilize great areas of wasteland. I have copies of many orders, quite astonishing in their scope and common-sense practicality, issued by the land commission to its various branches to guide them in organizing and propagandizing the peasants in the tasks of cultivation. To illustrate: in one of these orders that I picked up in a branch land office, instructions were given concerning spring cultivation, the commission urging its workers to " make widespread propaganda to induce the masses to participate voluntarily, without involving any form of compulsory command." Detailed advice was offered on how to achieve the four main demands of this planting period, which the previous winter had been recognized by the Soviets to be: more extensive utilization of wasteland, and expansion of Red Army land; increased crop yields; greater diversity of crops, with special emphasis on new varieties of melons and vegetables; and expansion of cotton acreage.

Among the devices recommended by this order[1] to expand labour power, and especially to bring women directly into agricultural production (particularly in districts where the male population had declined as a result of enlistments in the Red Army), the following amusing and ingenious instruction suggests the efficiency with which the Reds went about utilizing their available materials:

[1] *Order of Instruction*, Land Commission, January 28, 1936 (Wayapao).

Hc

" To mobilize women, boys, and old men to participate in spring planting and cultivation, each according to his ability to carry on either a principal or an auxiliary task in the labour processes of production. For example, ' large feet ' (natural feet) and young women should be mobilized to organize production-teaching corps, with tasks varying from land-clearance up to the main tasks of agricultural production itself. ' Small feet ' (bound feet), young boys, and old men must be mobilized to help in weed-pulling, collecting dung, and for other auxiliary tasks."

But how did the peasants feel about this ? The Chinese peasant is supposed to hate organization, discipline, and any social activity beyond his own family. Well, the Reds simply laugh at you when you tell them that. They say that no Chinese peasant dislikes organization or social activity if he is working for himself and not the *min-t'uan*—the landlord or the tax-collector. And I must admit that most of the peasants to whom I talked seemed to support the Soviets and the Red Army. Many of them were very free in their criticisms and complaints, but, when asked whether they preferred it to the old days, the answer was nearly always an emphatic yes. I noticed also that most of them talked about the Soviets as *womenti chengfu*—" our government "—and this struck me as something new in rural China.

One thing which suggested that the Reds have their base in the mass of the population was that in all the older Soviet districts the policing and guarding was done almost entirely by the peasant organizations alone. There were few actual Red Army garrisons in the Soviet districts, all the fighting strength of the army being kept at the front. Local defence was shared by the village revolutionary defence corps, peasant guards, and partisans. This fact may explain some of the popularity of the Red Army with the peasantry, for it was rarely planted down on them as an instrument of oppression and exploitation, like other armies, but was generally at the front, fighting for its food there, and engaged in meeting enemy attacks. On the other hand, the intensive organization of the peasantry created a rearguard and base which freed the Red Army to operate with the extreme mobility for which it has been noted.

But really to understand the peasant support for the Communist movement it is necessary to keep in mind its economic basis. I have already described the burden borne by the peasantry in the North-west under the former régime. Now, wherever the Reds went there is no doubt they radically changed the situation for the tenant farmer, the poor farmer, the middle farmer, and all the " have-not " elements. *All* forms of taxation were abolished in the new districts for the first year, to give the farmers a breathing-space, and in the old districts only a progressive single tax on land was collected, and a small single tax (from 5 to 10 per cent) on business. Secondly, they gave land to the land-hungry peasants, and began the reclamation of great areas of " wasteland "—mostly the land of absentee or fleeing landlords. Thirdly, they took land and livestock from the wealthy classes and redistributed among the poor.

Redistribution of land was a fundamental of Red policy. How was it carried out? Later on, for reasons of national political manœuvre, there was to be a drastic retreat in the Soviet land policy, but when I travelled in the North-west the land laws in force (promulgated by the North-west Soviet Government in December 1935) provided for the confiscation of all landlords' land and the confiscation of all land of rich peasants that was not cultivated by the owners themselves. However, both the landlord and the rich peasant were allowed as much land as they could till with their own labour. In districts where there was no land scarcity—and there were many such districts in the North-west—the lands of resident landlords and rich peasants were in practice not confiscated at all, but the wasteland and land of absentee owners was distributed, and sometimes there was a re-division of best quality land, poor peasants being given better soil, and landlords being allotted the same amount of poorer land.

What was a landlord? According to the Communists' definition (greatly simplified), any farmer who collected the greater part of his income from land rented out to others, and not from his own labour, was a landlord. By this definition the usurers and *t'u-hao*[1] were put in about the same category as landlords,

[1] *T'u-hao*, which actually means " local rascals," is the Reds' term for landowners who also derive a big part of their income from lending money and buying mortgages.

and similarly treated. Usury rates, according to Dr. Stampar, formerly ranged as high as 60 per cent in the North-west, or very much higher in times of stress. Although land is very cheap in many parts of Kansu, Shensi, and Ninghsia, it is practically impossible for a farm worker or tenant with no capital to accumulate enough to buy sufficient land for his family. I met farmers in the Red districts who formerly had never been able to own any land, although rates in some places were as low as two or three dollars an acre.

Classes other than those mentioned above were not subject to confiscatory action, so a big percentage of the farmers stood to benefit immediately by the redistribution. The poorest farmers, tenants, and farm labourers were all provided with land enough for a livelihood. There did not seem to be an attempt to " equalize " land-ownership. The primary purpose of the Soviet land laws, as explained to me by Wang Kuan-lan (the twenty-nine-year-old Russian-returned student who was land commissioner for the three Red provinces of the North-west), was to provide for every person sufficient land to guarantee him and his family a decent livelihood—which was claimed to be the most urgent demand of the peasantry.

The land problem—confiscation and redistribution—was greatly simplified in the North-west by the fact that big estates were formerly owned by officials, tax-collectors, and absentee landlords. With the confiscation of these, in many cases the immediate demands of the poor peasantry were satisfied, without much interference with either the resident small landlords or the rich peasants. Thus the Reds not only created the economic base for support in the poor and landless peasantry by giving them farms, but in some cases won the gratitude of middle peasants by abolishing tax-exploitation, and in a few instances enlisted the aid of small landlords on the same basis or on the patriotic appeals of the anti-Japanese movement. There were several prominent Shensi Communists from landlord families.

Additional help was given to the poor farmers in the form of loans at very low rates of interest or no interest at all. Usury was entirely abolished, but private lending, at rates fixed at a maximum of 10 per cent annually, was permitted. The ordinary Government lending rate was 5 per cent. Several thousand agricultural implements made in the Red arsenals, and thousands of pounds of seed-grain, were supplied to landless peasants breaking wasteland. A primitive agricultural school had been established, and I was told it was planned to open an animal husbandry school as soon as an expert in this field, expected from Shanghai, had arrived.

The co-operative movement was being vigorously pushed. These activities extended beyond production and distribution co-operatives, branching out to include co-operation in such (for China) novel forms as the collective use of farm animals and implements—especially in tilling public lands and Red Army lands—and in the organization of labour mutual-aid societies. By the latter device great areas could be quickly planted and harvested collectively, and periods of idleness by individual farmers eliminated. The Reds saw to it that a man earned his new land ! In busy periods the system of " Saturday Brigades " was used, when not only all the children's organizations, but every Soviet official, Red partisan, Red guard, women's organization, and any Red Army detachment that happened to be near by, were mobilized to work at least one day a week at farming tasks. Even Mao Tse-tung took part in this work.

Here the Reds were introducing the germs of the drastically revolutionary idea of collective effort—and doing primary education work for some future period when collectivization might become practicable. At the same time, into the dark recesses of peasant mentality there was slowly penetrating the concept of a broader realm of social life. For the organizations created among the peasantry were what the Reds called three-in-one: economic, political, and cultural in their utility.

What cultural progress the Reds had made among these people was, by any advanced Western standards, negligible indeed. But certain outstanding evils common in most parts of China had definitely been eliminated in the score of long-Sovietized counties in north Shensi, and a crusade of propaganda was being conducted among inhabitants of newer areas to spread the same elementary reforms there. As an outstanding achievement, opium had been completely eliminated in north Shensi, and in fact I did not see any sign of poppies after I entered the Soviet districts. Official corruption was almost unheard-of.

Beggary and unemployment did seem to have been, as the Reds claimed, " liquidated." I did not see a beggar during all my travels in the Red areas. Foot-binding and infanticide were criminal offences, child slavery and prostitution had disappeared, and polyandry and polygamy were prohibited.

The myths of " communized wives " or " nationalization of women " are too patently absurd to be denied, but changes in marriage, divorce, and inheritance were in themselves extremely radical against the background of semi-feudal law and practice elsewhere in China. Marriage regulations[1] included interesting provisions against mother-in-law tyranny, the buying and selling of women as wives and concubines, and the custom of " arranged matches." Marriage was by mutual consent, the legal age had been moved up sharply to twenty for men and eighteen for women; dowries were prohibited, and any couple registering as man and wife before a county, municipal, or village Soviet was given a marriage certificate without cost. Men and women actually cohabiting were considered legally married, whether registered or not—which seems to rule out " free love "—and their offspring were legitimate. No illegitimacy of children was recognized.

Divorce could also be secured from the registration bureau of the Soviet, free of charge, on the " insistent demand " of either party to the marriage contract, but wives of Red Army men were required to have their husband's consent before a divorce was granted. Property was divided equally between the divorcees, and both were legally obliged to care for their children, but responsibility for debts was shouldered by the man alone (!), who was also obliged to supply two-thirds of the children's living expenses.

Education, in theory, was " free and universal," but parents had of course to supply their children with food and clothing. In practice, nothing like " free and universal " education had yet been achieved, although old Hsu Teh-lih, the Commissioner of Education, boasted to me that if they were given a few years of peace in the North-west they would astound the rest of China with the educational progress they would make. Farther on I shall

[1] *The Marriage Law of the Chinese Soviet Republic* (Reprinted) (Pao An, July 1936).

discuss more in detail what the Communists had done and hoped to do to liquidate the appalling illiteracy of this region, but first it is interesting to know how the Government was financing not only the educational programme, such as it was, but this whole seemingly simple and yet in its way vastly complex organism which I have called Soviet society.

Anatomy of Money

It was imperative for Soviet economy to fulfil at least two elementary functions: to feed and equip the Red Army, and to bring immediate relief to the poor peasantry. Failing in either, the Soviet base would soon collapse. To guarantee success at these tasks it was necessary for the Reds, even from earliest days, to begin some kind of economic construction.

Soviet economy in the North-west was a curious mixture of private capitalism, State capitalism, and primitive Socialism. Private enterprise and industry were permitted and encouraged, and private transaction in the land and its products was allowed, with restrictions. At the same time the State owned and exploited enterprises such as oil-wells, salt-wells, and coal-mines, and it traded in cattle, hides, salt, wool, cotton, paper, and other raw materials. But it did not establish a monopoly in these articles, and in all of them private enterprises could, and to some extent did, compete.

A third kind of economy was created by the establishment of co-operatives, in which the Government and the masses participated as partners, competing not only with private capitalism, but also with State capitalism ! But remember that it was all conducted on a very small and primitive scale. Thus, although the fundamental antagonisms in such an arrangement were obvious, and in an economically more highly developed area would have been ruinous, here in the Red regions they somehow supplemented each other.

Clearly the tendency of the Soviet co-operative movement was Socialistic. The Reds defined the co-operative " as an instrument to resist private capitalism and develop a new economic system," and they listed its five main functions as follows: " to combat the exploitation of the masses by the merchants; to combat the enemy's blockade; to develop the national economy of the Soviet districts; to raise the economic-political level of the masses; and to prepare the conditions for Socialist construction " —a period in which " the democratic revolution of the Chinese bourgeoisie, under the leadership of the proletariat, may create energetic conditions enabling the transition of this revolution into Socialism."[1]

The first two of those high-sounding functions, as a matter of fact, meant simply that the co-operative could help the masses organize their own blockade-running corps, as auxiliaries to the blockade-running activity of the Government. Trade between Red and White districts was prohibited by Nanking, but by using small mountain roads, and by oiling the palms of border guards, the Reds at times managed to carry on a fairly lively export business. Taking out raw materials from the Soviet districts, the transport corps in the service of the State Trade Bureau, or the co-operatives, exchanged them for Kuomintang money and needed manufactures.

Consumption, sales, production, and credit co-operatives were organized in the village, district, county, and province. Above them was a central bureau of co-operatives, under the Finance Commissioner and a department of national economy. These co-operatives were really constructed to encourage the participation of the lowest strata of society. Shares entitling the purchaser to membership were priced as low as fifty cents, or even twenty cents, and organizational duties were so extensive as to bring nearly every shareholder into the economic or political life of the co-operative. While there was no restriction on the number of shares an individual member could buy, each member was entitled to but one vote, regardless of how many shares he held. Co-operatives elected their own managing committees and supervisory committees, with the assistance of the central bureau, which also furnished trained workers and organizers. Each co-operative had departments for business, propaganda, organization, survey, and statistics.

Various prizes were offered for efficient management, and widespread propaganda stimulated and educated the peasants concerning the usefulness of the movement. Financial as well as technical help was furnished by the Government, which participated in the enterprises on a profit-sharing basis, like the members. Some $70,000 in non-interest-bearing loans had been

[1] *Outline for Co-operative Development*, Department of National Economy (November 1935, Wayapao, Shensi), p. 4.

invested by the Government in the co-operatives of Shensi and Kansu.

Only Soviet paper was in use, except in the border counties, where White paper was also accepted. In their Soviets in Kiangsi, Anhui, and Szechuan the Reds minted silver dollars, and subsidiary coins in copper, and some also in silver, and much of this metal was transported to the North-west. But after the decree of November 1935, when Nanking began the confiscation of all silver in China, and its price soared, the Reds withdrew their silver, and held it as reserve for their note issue. To-day they have one of the few caches of silver in the country not yet in the hands of the Kuomintang.

Paper currency in the South, bearing the signature of the " Chinese Workers' and Peasants' Soviet Government State Bank," was excellently printed, on good bank paper. In the North-west, technical deficiencies resulted in a much cruder issue on poor paper, and sometimes on cloth. Their slogans appeared on all money. Notes issued in Shensi bore such exhortations as these: " Stop civil war ! " " Unite to resist Japan ! " " Long live the Chinese revolution ! "

Soviet money was accepted nearly everywhere in the stabilized Soviets, and had full buying power, prices being generally slightly lower than in the White districts. What held it up? I did not know what reserve the Reds had on their notes, nor what the latter totalled, but obviously it was no promise of redemption that made the peasants use it. Compulsory acceptance may have been enforced in some places; personally I saw no instances of it. On the borders the peasants often refused Soviet money, but the Reds paid them in Kuomintang paper, with which the army was supplied. Elsewhere, however, Soviet currency seemed to get its status on the basis of popular confidence in the Government, and the fact that it had some real purchasing value in the market. Of course, that is about all that holds up the Kuomintang dollar also.

But how could merchants sell articles imported from the White regions for currency which had no exchange value outside the Soviet districts ? This difficulty was met by the State treasury, which had fixed an exchange rate of Soviet $1·21 to Kuomintang $1. Regulations provided that " all goods imported

from the White districts, and sold directly to the State Trade
Bureau, will be paid for in foreign (Kuomintang) currency;
imports of necessities, when not sold directly to the State Trade
Bureau, but through co-operatives or by private merchants,
shall first be registered with the State Trade Bureau, and
proceeds of their sale for Soviet currency may be exchanged for
White paper; other exchange will be given when its necessity is
established."[1] In practice this of course meant that all " foreign "
imports had to be paid for in " foreign " exchange. But as the
value of imported manufactures (meagre enough) greatly ·
exceeded the value of Soviet exports (which were chiefly raw
materials, and were all sold in a depressed market as smuggled
goods), there was always a tendency toward a heavy unfavourable balance of payments. In other words, bankruptcy. How was
it overcome ?

It was not, entirely. But as far as I could discover, the problem
was met principally by the ingenuity of Lin Pai-chu, the dignified
white-haired Commissioner of Finance, whose task was to make
Red ends meet. This interesting old custodian of the exchequer
had once been treasurer of the Kuomintang, and behind him lay
an amazing story, which I can only outline here.

Son of a Hunanese schoolteacher, Lin Pai-chu was born in
1882, educated in the Classics, attended normal college at
Changtehfu, and later studied in Tokyo. While in Japan he met
Sun Yat-sen, then exiled from China by the Manchus, and joined
his secret revolutionary society, the T'ung Meng Hui. When Sun
merged his T'ung Meng Hui with other revolutionary groups to
found the Kuomintang, Lin Pai-chu became a charter member.
Later on he met Ch'ên Tu-hsiu, was much influenced by him,
and in 1922 joined the Communist Party. He continued to work
closely with Dr. Sun Yat-sen, however, who admitted Communists to his party, and Lin was in turn treasurer and chairman
of the General Affairs Department of the Kuomintang. He was
with Sun Yat-sen when he died.

At the beginning of the Nationalist Revolution, Lin Pai-chu
was one of the several elders in the Central Executive Committee of the Kuomintang who had precedence over Chiang

[1] " Concerning Soviet Monetary Policy," *Tangti Kungtso* (*Party Work*), No. 12
(Pao An, 1936).

Kai-shek. In Canton he was chairman of the Peasant Ministry
and during the Northern Expedition he became political
commissar of the 6th Army, commanded by General Ch'eng
Ch'ien—the late chief-of-staff at Nanking. When Chiang Kai-
shek began the extermination of the Communists in 1927, Lin
denounced him, fled to Hongkong, and then to Soviet Russia,
where he studied for four years in the Communist Academy.
On his return to China he took passage on the " underground
railway " and safely reached Kiangsi. There he was appointed
· Commissioner of Finance. Now a widower, Lin has not seen his
grown-up daughter and son since 1927. At the age of forty-five
he abandoned the comfortable assets of his position and staked
his destiny with the young Communists.

Into my room in the Foreign Office one morning came this
fifty-five-year-old veteran of the Long March, wearing a cheerful
smile, a faded uniform, a Red-starred cap with a broken peak,
and in front of his kindly eyes a pair of spectacles one side of
which was trussed up over his ear with a piece of string. The
Commissioner of Finance ! He sat down on the edge of the k'ang
and we began to talk about sources of revenue. The Government, I understood, collected practically no taxes; its industrial
income must be negligible; then where, I wanted to know, did it
get its money ?

Lin began to explain: " We say we do not tax the masses, and
this is true. But we do heavily tax the exploiting classes, confiscating their surplus cash and goods. Thus, all our taxation is
direct. This is just the opposite of the Kuomintang practice,
under which ultimately the workers and the poor peasants have
to carry most of the tax burden. Here we tax less than 10 per
cent of the population—the landlords and usurers. We also levy
a small tax on a few big merchants, but none on small merchants.
Later on we may impose a small progressive tax on the peasantry, but at the present moment all mass taxes have been
completely abolished.

" Another source of income is from voluntary contributions of
the people. Revolutionary patriotic feeling runs very high where
war is on, and the people realize that they may lose their
Soviets. They make big voluntary contributions of food, money,
and clothing to the Red Army. We derive some income also from

State trade, from Red Army lands, from our own industries, from the co-operatives, and from bank loans. But of course our biggest revenue is from confiscations."

" By confiscation," I interrupted, " you mean what is commonly described as loot ? "

Lin laughed shortly. " The Kuomintang calls it loot. Well, if taxation of the exploiters of the masses is loot, so is the Kuomintang's taxation of the masses. But the Red Army does no looting in the sense that White armies loot. Confiscations are made only by authorized persons, under the direction of the Finance Commission. Every item must be reported by inventory to the Government, and is utilized only for the general benefit of society. Private looting is heavily punished. Just ask the people if Red soldiers take anything without paying for it."

Well, you are quite right. The answer to that naturally would depend on whether you asked a landlord or a peasant.

" If we did not have to conduct incessant war," Lin continued, " we could easily build a self-supporting economy here. Our budget is carefully made, and every possible economy is practised. Because every Soviet official is also a patriot and a revolutionary, we demand no wages, and we can exist on little but food. It will probably surprise you to know how small our budget is. For this whole area[1] our present expenditure is only about $320,000 per month. This represents goods value as well as money value. Of this sum, from 40 to 50 per cent comes from confiscations, and 15 or 20 per cent comes from voluntary contributions, including cash raised by the Party among our supporters in the White districts. The rest of our revenue is derived from trade, economic construction, Red Army lands, and bank loans to the Government."

The Reds claimed to have devised a squeeze-proof machinery of budgeting, of receipts and disbursements. I have read part of Lin Pai-chu's *Outline for Budget Compilation*, which gives a detailed description of the system and all its safeguards. Its integrity seemed to be based primarily on collective control of receipts and disbursements. From the highest organ down to the village the treasurer was accountable, both for payments and collections, to a supervising committee, so that juggling of figures

[1] Then about the size of Austria.

for individual profit was extremely difficult. Commissioner Lin was very proud of his system, and asserted that under it any kind of squeeze was effectively impossible. It may have been true. Anyway, it was obvious that in the Red districts the real problem as yet was not one of squeeze, in the traditional sense, but of squeezing through ! Despite Lin's cheerful optimism, this is what I wrote in my diary after that interview:

" Whatever Lin's figures may mean exactly, it is simply a Chinese miracle, when one remembers that partisans have been fighting back and forth across this territory for five years, that the economy maintains itself at all, that there is no famine, and that the peasants on the whole seem to accept Soviet currency with faith in it. In fact this cannot be explained in terms of finance alone, but is only understandable on a social and political basis.

" Nevertheless, it is perfectly clear that the situation is extremely grave, even for an organization that exists on such shoe-strings as the Reds feed upon, and one of three changes must shortly occur in Soviet economy: (1) some form of machine industrialization, to supply the market with needed manufactures; (2) the establishment of a good connection with some modern economic base in the outside world, or the capture of some economic base on a higher level than the present one (Sian or Lanchow, for example); or (3) the actual coalition of such a base, now under White control, with the Red districts."

The Reds agreed, but did not share my pessimism. " A way out was sure to be found." And in a few months it was ! The " way out " appeared in the form of an " actual coalition."

Lin Pai-chu didn't seem to be " getting ahead " financially very fast himself, by the way. His " allowance " as Commissioner of Finance was five dollars a month—Red money.

5

Life Begins at Fifty!

I CALL him " Old Hsu " because that is what everyone in the Soviet districts called him—*Lao Hsu,* the Educator—for, although sixty-one is only just an average age for most high Government officials elsewhere in the Orient, in Red China he seemed a sort of hoary grandfather by contrast with others. Yet he was no specimen of decrepitude. Like his sexagenarian crony, Hsieh Chüeh-tsai (and you could often see this pair of white-haired bandits walking along arm-in-arm like middle-school lads), he had an erect and vigorous step, bright and merry eyes, and a pair of muscular legs that had carried him across the greatest rivers and mountain ranges of China on the Long March.

Hsu Teh-lih was a highly respected professor until at the age of fifty he amazingly gave up his home, four children, and the presidency of a normal school in Changsha to stake his future with the Communists. Born in 1876 near Changsha, not far from Peng Teh-huai's birthplace, he was the fourth son in a poor peasant family. By various sacrifices his parents gave him six years of Classical schooling, at the end of which he became a schoolteacher under the Manchu régime. There he remained till he was twenty-nine, when he entered the Changsha Normal College, graduated, and became an instructor in mathematics.

Mao Tse-tung was one of his students in the normal college (Hsu says he was terrible in maths !), and so were many youths who later became Reds. Hsu himself had a rôle in politics long before Mao knew a republican from a monarchist. He still bears that mark of combat from feudal politics in days of the empire, when he cut off the tip of his little finger to demonstrate his sincerity in begging by petition that a parliament be granted the people. After the first revolution, when for a while Hunan had a provincial parliament, old Hsu was a member of it.

He accompanied the Hunanese delegation of " worker-students " to France after the war, and he studied a year at Lyons, where he paid his way by odd-time work in a metal factory. Later he was a student for three years in Paris University, earning his tuition then by tutoring Chinese students in mathematics. Returning to Hunan in 1923, he established two modern normal schools in the capital, and for four years enjoyed some prosperity. Not till 1927 did he become a Communist and an outcast from bourgeois society.

During the Nationalist Revolution, Hsu Teh-lih was active in the provincial Kuomintang, but he sympathized with the Communists. He openly preached Marxism to his students. When the " purgation " period began he was a marked man; he had to do the disappearing act, and, having no connection with the Communist Party, he had to find a haven on his own. " I wanted to be a Communist," he told me rather wistfully, " but nobody ever asked me to join. I was already fifty, and I concluded that the Communists considered me too old." But one day a Communist sought out Hsu in his hiding-place and asked him to enter the Party. He was overjoyed, the old rascal, and he told me he wept then to think that he was still of some use in building a new world.

The Party sent him to Russia, where he studied for two years. On his return he ran the blockade to Kiangsi; soon afterwards he became Assistant Commissioner of Education, under Ch'ü Ch'iu-pai, and, after Ch'ü was killed, the Executive Committee appointed Hsu in his place. Since then he has been *Lao Hsu*, the Educator. And surely his varied experience—life and teaching under monarchist, capitalist, and Communist forms of society ! —would seem to qualify him for the tasks that faced him. He certainly needed all that experience, and more, for those tasks were so great that any Western educator would stagger at the scene in despair. But Old Hsu was too young to be discouraged.'

One day when we were talking he began humorously to enumerate some of his difficulties. " As nearly as we can estimate," he asserted, " virtually nobody but a few landlords, officials, and merchants could read in the North-west before we arrived. The illiteracy seemed to be about 95 per cent. This is culturally one of the darkest places on earth. Do you know the people in north Shensi and Kansu believe that water is harmful to them ? The average man here has a bath all over only twice in his life—once when he is born, the second time when he is married ! They hate to wash their feet, hands, or faces, or cut their nails or their hair. There are more pigtails in this part of China than anywhere else.

" But all this and many other prejudices are due to ignorance, and it's my job to change their mentality. Such a population, compared with Kiangsi, is very backward indeed. There the illiteracy was about 90 per cent, but the cultural level was very much higher, we had better material conditions to work in, and many more trained teachers. In our model *hsien*, Hsing Kuo, we had over 300 primary schools and about 800 school-teachers—which is as many as we have of both in all the Red districts here. When we finally withdrew from Hsing Kuo, illiteracy had been reduced to less than 20 per cent of the population !

" Here the work is very much slower. We have to start everything from the beginning. Our material resources are very limited. Even our printing machinery has been destroyed, and now we have to print everything by mimeograph and stone-block lithograph. The blockade prevents us from importing enough paper, and, although we have begun to make paper of our own, the quality is terrible. But never mind these difficulties. We have already been able to accomplish something. If we are given time we can do things here that will astonish the rest of China. We are training scores of teachers from the masses now, and the Party is training others, many of whom will become voluntary teachers for the mass educational schools. Our results show that the peasants here are eager to learn when given the chance.

" And they are not stupid. They learn very quickly, and they change their habits when they are given good reasons for doing so. In the older Soviet districts here you won't see any girl children with bound feet, and you will see many young women with bobbed hair. The men are gradually cutting off their queues now, and a lot of them are learning to read and write from the Young Communists and the Vanguards."

It should be explained that under the emergency Soviet educational system there were three sections: institutional, military, and social. The first was run more or less by the Soviets, the second by the Red Army, the third by Communist organizations. Emphasis in all of them was primarily political—even the littlest children learning their first characters in the shape of simple revolutionary slogans, and then working forward into stories of conflict between the Reds and the Kuomintang, landlords and peasants, capitalists and workers, and so on, with plenty of heroics about the Young Communists and the Red Army, and promises of an earthly paradise of the Soviet future.

Under institutional education the Reds already claimed to have established about 200 primary schools, and they had one normal school for primary teachers, one agricultural school, a textile school, a trade union school of five grades, and a Party school, with some 400 students. Courses in all these lasted only about six months.

Greatest emphasis naturally was on military education, and here very much had been achieved in two years, despite all the handicaps of the little beleaguered State. There were the Red Army Academy, and the cavalry and infantry schools, already described. There was a radio school, and a medical school, which was really for training nurses. There was an engineering school, where the students actually got the rudimentary training of apprentices. Like the whole Soviet organization itself, everything was very provisional and designed primarily as a kind of rear-line activity to strengthen the Red Army and provide it with new cadres. Many of the teachers were not even middle-school graduates. What was interesting was the collective use of whatever knowledge they had. These schools were really Communist not only in ideology, but in the utilization of every scrap of technical experience they could mobilize, to " raise the cultural level."

Even in social education the Soviet aims were primarily political. There was no time or occasion to be teaching farmers literature or flower arrangement. The Reds were practical people. To the Lenin Clubs, the Young Communist Leagues, the Partisans, and the village Soviets they sent simple, crudely illustrated *Shih-tzu,* or " Know Characters," texts, and helped mass organizations form self-study groups of their own, with some Communist or literate among them as a leader. When the youths, or sometimes even aged peasants, began droning off the short sentences, they found themselves absorbing ideas along with their ideographs. Thus, entering one of these little " social education centres " in the mountains, you might hear these people catechizing themselves aloud:

" What is this ? "

" This is the Red Flag."

" What is this ? "

" This is a poor man."

" What is the Red Flag ? "

" The Red Flag is the flag of the Red Army."

" What is the Red Army ? "

" The Red Army is the Army of the poor men ! "

And so on, right up to the point where, if he knew the whole 500 or 600 characters before anyone else, the youth could collect the red tassel or pencil or whatever was promised. Crude propaganda, of course. But when the farmers and farmers' sons and daughters finished the book they could not only read for the first time in their lives, but they knew who had taught them, and why. They had grasped the basic fighting ideas of Chinese Communism.

And, anyway, I should think it was a lot more amusing than teaching people to read via the this-is-a-cat, that-is-a-mouse, and the what-is-the-cat-doing, the-cat-is-eating-the-mouse method. Why teach to realists in allegories ?

In an effort to find a quicker medium for bringing literacy to the masses the Communists had begun a limited use of Latinized Chinese. They had worked out an alphabet of twenty-eight letters by which they claimed to be able to reproduce nearly all Chinese phonetics, and had written and published a little pocket dictionary with the commonest phrases of Chinese rendered into polysyllabic, easily readable words. Part of the paper *Hung Ssu Chung Hua (Red China)* was published in *Latin-hua*, and Old Hsu was experimenting with it on a class of youngsters he had picked up in Pao An. He believed that the complicated Chinese character would eventually have to be abandoned in education on a mass scale, and he had many arguments in favour of his system, on which he had been working for years.

But so far he wasn't boasting about results, either with his

Latin-hua or his other educational efforts. " The cultural level was so low here it couldn't be made worse, so naturally we've made some progress," he said. As for the future, he only wanted time. Meanwhile he urged me to concentrate on studying educational methods in the Red Army, where he claimed real revolutionary teaching could be seen. It sounded strange. " Learn while you fight " is a novel slogan for any army, but in China it strains your credulity. The Reds promised me that if I went to the front I could see how it was done. And soon afterwards they had actually talked me on to a horse and sent me on my way—but not primarily to study education.

PART SEVEN

EN ROUTE TO THE FRONT

1

Conversation with Red Peasants

As I travelled beyond Pao An, toward the Kansu border and the front, I stayed in the rude huts of peasants, slept on their mud *k'angs* (when the luxury of wooden doors was not available), ate their food, and enjoyed their talk. They were all poor people, kind and hospitable. Some of them refused any money from me when they heard I was a " foreign guest." I remember one old bound-footed peasant woman, with five or six youngsters to feed, who insisted upon killing one of her half-dozen chickens for me.

" We can't have a foreign devil telling people in the outer world that we Reds don't know etiquette ! " I overheard her say to one of my companions. I am sure she did not mean to be impolite. She simply knew no other words but foreign devil to describe the situation.

I was travelling then with Fu Chin-kuei, a young Communist who had been delegated by the Red Foreign Office to accompany me to the front. Like all the Reds in the rear, Fu was delighted at the prospect of a chance to be with the army, and he looked upon me as a godsend. At the same time he regarded me frankly as an imperialist, and viewed my whole trip with open scepticism. He was unfailingly helpful in every way, however, and before the trip was over we were to become very good friends.

One night at Chou Chia, a village of north Shensi near the Kansu border, Fu and I found quarters in a compound where five or six peasant families lived. A farmer of about forty-five, responsible for six of the fifteen little children who scampered back and forth incessantly, agreed to accommodate us, with ready courtesy. He gave us a clean room with new felt on the *k'ang*, and provided our animals with corn and straw. He sold us a chicken for twenty cents, and some eggs, but for the room would take nothing. He had been to Yenan and he had seen foreigners before, but none of the other men, women or children had seen one, and they all now came round diffidently to have a peek. One of the young children burst into frightened tears at the astonishing sight.

After dinner a number of the peasants came into our room, offered me tobacco, and began to talk. They wanted to know what we grew in my country, whether we had corn and millet, horses and cows, and whether we used goat-dung for fertilizer. (One peasant asked whether we had chickens, and at this our host sniffed contemptuously. " Where there are men, there must be chickens ! " he observed.) Were there rich and poor in my country ? Was there a Communist Party and a Red Army ? I'm afraid my explanation of why there was a Communist Party but no Red Army quite baffled them.

In return for answering their numerous questions, I asked a few of my own. What did they think of the Red Army ? They promptly began to complain about the excessive eating habits of the cavalry's horses. It seemed that when the Red Army Academy had recently moved its cavalry school it paused in this village for several days, with the result that a big depression had been made in the corn and straw reserves.

" Didn't they pay you for what they bought ? " demanded Fu Chin-kuei.

" Yes, yes, they paid all right; that isn't the question. We haven't a great amount you know, only so many *tan* of corn and millet and straw. We have only enough for ourselves and maybe a little more, and we have the winter ahead of us. Will the co-operatives sell us grain next January ? That's what we wonder. What can we buy with Soviet money ? We can't even buy opium ! "

This came from a ragged old man who still wore a queue and looked sourly down his wrinkled nose and along the two-foot stem of his bamboo pipe. The younger men grinned when he spoke. Fu admitted they couldn't buy opium, but he said they could buy in the co-operatives anything else they needed.

" Can we now ? " demanded our host. " Can we buy a bowl like this one, eh ? " And he picked up the cheap red celluloid bowl (Japanese-made, I suspect) which I had brought with me from Sian. Fu confessed the co-operatives had no red bowls, but said they had plenty of grain, cloth, paraffin, candles, needles, matches, salt—what did they want ?

" I hear you can't get more than six feet of cloth per man; now, isn't it so ? " demanded one farmer.

Fu wasn't sure; he thought there was plenty of cloth. He resorted to the anti-Japanese argument. " Life is as bitter for us as for you," he said. " The Red Army is fighting for you, the farmers and workers, to protect you from the Japanese and the Kuomintang. Suppose you can't always buy all the cloth you want, and you can't get opium, it's a fact you don't pay taxes, isn't it ? You don't go in debt to the landlords and lose your house and land, do you ? Well, old brother, do you like the White Army better than us, or not ?—just answer that question. What does the White Army give you for your crops, eh ? "

At this, all complaints appeared to melt away, and opinion was unanimous. " Certainly not, old Fu, certainly not ! " nodded our host. " If we have to choose, we take the Red Army. A son of mine is in the Red Army, and I sent him there. Does anyone deny that ? "

I asked why they preferred the Red Army.

In answer the old man who had sneered at the co-operatives for having no opium gave a heated discourse.

" What happens when the Whites come ? " he asked. " They demand such and such amounts of food, and never a word about payment. If we refuse, we are arrested as Communist. If we give it to them we cannot pay the taxes. *In any case*, we cannot pay the taxes ! What happens then ? They take our animals to sell. Last year, when the Red Army was not here and the Whites returned, they took my two mules and my four pigs. These mules were worth $30 each, and the pigs were full grown, worth $2 each. What did they give me ?

" *Ai-ya, ai-ya !* They said I owed $80 in taxes and rent, and they allowed me $40 for my stock. They demanded $40 more. Could I get it ? I had nothing else for them to steal. They wanted me to sell my daughter; it's a fact ! Some of us here had to do that. Those who had no cattle and no daughters went to jail in Pao An, and plenty died from the cold. . . ."

I asked this old man how much land he had.

" Land ? " he croaked. " There is my land," and he pointed to a hilltop patched with corn and millet and vegetables. It lay just across the stream from our courtyard.

" How much it is worth ? "

" Land here isn't worth anything unless it's valley land," he said. " We can buy a mountain like that for $25. What costs money are mules, goats, pigs, chickens, houses and tools."

" Well, how much is your farm worth, for example ? "

He still refused to count his land worth anything at all. " You can have the house, my animals and tools for $100—with the mountain thrown in," he finally estimated.

" And on that you had to pay how much in taxes and rent ? "

" Forty dollars a year ! "

" That was before the Red Army came ? "

" Yes. Now we pay no taxes. But who knows about next year ? When the Reds leave, the Whites come back. One year Red, the next White. When the Whites come they call us Red-bandits. When the Reds come they look for counter-revolutionaries."

" But there is this difference," a young farmer interposed. " If our neighbours say we have not helped the Whites that satisfies the Reds. But if we have a hundred names of honest men, but no landlord's name, we are still Red-bandits to the Whites ! Isn't that a fact ? "

The old man nodded his head. He said that the last time the White Army was here it had killed a whole family of poor farmers in a village just over the hill. Why ? Because the Whites had asked where the Reds were hiding, and this family refused to tell them. " After that we all fled from here, and took our cattle with us. We came back with the Reds."

" Will you leave next time, if the Whites return ? "

" *Ai-ya !* " exclaimed an elder with long hair but fine teeth. " This time we will leave, certainly ! They will kill us ! "

He began to tell of the villagers' crimes. They had joined the Poor People's League, they had voted for the district Soviets, they had given information to the Red Army about the White Army's movements, two had sons in the Red Army, and another had two daughters in a nursing school. Were these crimes or not ? They could be shot for any one of them, I was assured.

But now a barefooted youth in his teens stepped up, engrossed in the discussion, and forgetful of the foreign devil. " You call these things crimes, grandfather ? These are patriotic acts ! Why do we do them ? Isn't it because our Red Army is a poor people's army and fights for our rights ? "

He continued enthusiastically: " Did we have a free school in Chou Chia before ? Did we ever get news of the world before the Reds brought us wireless electricity ? Who told us what the world is like ? You say the co-operative has no cloth, but did we ever even have a co-operative before ? And how about your farm, wasn't there a big mortgage on it to landlord Wang ? My sister starved to death three years ago, but haven't we had plenty to eat since the Reds came ? You say it's bitter, but it isn't bitter for us young people if we can learn to read ! It isn't bitter for us Young Vanguards when we learn to use a rifle and fight the traitors and Japan ! "

This constant reference to Japan and the " traitors " may sound improbable to people who know the ignorance (not indifference) of the mass of the ordinary Chinese peasants concerning Japanese invasions. But I found it constantly recurring, not only in the speech of the Communists, but among peasants like these. Red propaganda has made a wide impression until many of these backward mountaineers believe themselves in imminent danger of being enslaved by the " Japanese dwarfs " —a specimen of which most of them have yet to see outside Red posters and cartoons.

The youth subsided, out of breath. I looked at Fu Chin-kuei and saw a pleased smirk on his face. Several others present called out in approval, and most of them smiled.

The dialogue went on till nearly nine o'clock, long past bedtime. It interested me chiefly because it took place before Fu Chin-kuei, whom the farmers appeared to hold in no awe as a Red " official." They seemed to look upon him as one of themselves—and indeed, as a peasant's son, he was.

The last one to leave us was the old man with the queue and most of the complaints. As he went out the door he leaned over and whispered once more to Fu, " Old comrade," he implored, " is there any opium at Pao An; now, is there any ? "

When he had left, Fu turned to me in disgust. " Would you believe it ? " he demanded. " That old defile-mother is chairman of the Poor People's Society here, and still he wants opium ! This village needs more educational work."

2

Soviet Industries

A few days north-west of Pao An, on my way to the front, I stopped to visit Wu Ch'i Chen, a Soviet " industrial centre " of Shensi. Wu Ch'i Chen was remarkable, not for any achievements in industrial science of which Detriot or Manchester need take note—as the reader will soon see—but because it was there at all.

For hundreds of miles around there is only semi-pastoral country, the people live in cave-houses exactly as did their ancestors millenniums ago, many of the farmers still wear queues braided round their heads, and the horse, the ass and the camel are the last thing in communications. Rape-oil is used for lighting here, candles are a luxury, electricity is unknown, and foreigners are as rare as Eskimos in Africa.

In this medieval world it was astonishing suddenly to come upon Soviet factories, and find machines turning, and a colony of workers busily producing the goods and tools of a Red China.

I knew that in Kiangsi the Communists had, despite the enormous handicaps of lacking a seaport and suffering an enemy blockade which cut them off from contact with any big modern industrial base, built up several prosperous industries. They operated China's richest tungsten mines, for example, annually turning out over one million pounds of this precious ore—secretly selling it to General Ch'en Chi-t'ang's Kuangtung tungsten monopoly. In the central Soviet printing plant at Kian, with its 800 workers, many books, magazines, and a big " national " paper—the *Red China Daily News*—were published.

In Kiangsi also were weaving plants, textile mills and machine-shops. Small industries produced sufficient manufactured goods to supply their simple needs. The Reds claim to have had a " foreign export trade " of over $12,000,000 in 1933, most of which was carried on through adventurous southern merchants, who made enormous profits by running the Kuomintang blockade. The bulk of manufacturing, however, was by handicraft and home industry, the products of which were sold through production co-operatives.

According to Mao Tse-tung, in September 1933 the Soviets had 1,423 " production and distribution " co-operatives in Kiangsi, all owned and run by the people.[1] Testimony by League of Nations investigators leaves little doubt that the Reds were succeeding with this type of collective enterprise—even while they were still fighting for their existence. The Kuomintang itself is in fact attempting to copy the Red system in parts of the South, but results thus far suggest that it is extremely difficult, if not impossible, to operate such co-operatives under a strictly *laissez-faire* capitalism.

But in the North-west I had not expected to find any industry at all. Much greater handicaps faced the Reds here than in the South, for even a small machine industry was almost entirely absent before the Soviets were set up. In the whole North-west, in Shensi, Kansu, Chinghai, Ninghsia and Suiyuan, provinces in area nearly the size of all Europe excluding Russia, the combined machine-industry investment certainly must be considerably less than the plant of one big assembly branch of, for instance, the Ford Motor Company.

Sian and Lanchow have a few small modern factories, but for the most part are dependent upon the bigger industrial centres farther east. Any major development of the tremendous industrial possibilities of the North-west can only take place by borrowing technique and machinery from the outside. And if this is true in Sian and Lanchow, the two great cities of the region, the difficulties confronting the Reds, occupying the even more backward areas of Kansu, Shensi and Ningshia, should be manifest.

The blockade, of course, cut off the Soviet Government from importing machinery, and from " importing " technicians. Of the latter, however, the Reds said their supply was at present ample. Machinery and raw materials were more serious problems. Battles have been fought by the Red Army just to get a few lathes, weaving machines, engines or scrap iron. Nearly everything they had in the category of machinery while I was there had been " captured " ! During their expedition to Shansi

[1] *Red China: President Mao Tse-tung Reports on Progress*, etc., p. 26.

province last year, for example, they seized machines, tools and raw materials, which were carried by mule all the way across the interminable mountains of Shensi, to their fantastic cliff-dwelling factories.

The southern Reds, when they came up to the North-west, spurred on an "industrial boom." They brought with them (6,000 miles, over some of the world's most difficult routes) many lathes, turning machines, stampers, dies, etc. They brought dozens of Singer sewing machines, which now equip their clothing factories; they brought silver and gold from the Red mines in Szechuan; and they brought lithographing blocks and light printing machines. Small wonder that the Reds have respect and affection for ponies and mules, especially those plucky animals that carried their burdens up from the southland !

Soviet industries, when I visited Red China, included clothing, uniform, shoe, and paper factories at Pao An, and Holienwan (Kansu), rug factories at Tingpien (on the Great Wall), mines at Yung P'ing which produce the cheapest coal[1] in China, and woollen and cotton spinning factories in several *hsien*—all of which had plans to produce enough goods to stock the 400 co-operatives in Red Shensi and Kansu. The aim of the present " industrial programme," according to Mao Tse-ming, Commissioner of People's Economy, was to make Red China " economically self-sufficient " — strong enough to survive despite the Kuomintang blockade—if Nanking refused to accept the Communists' offers for a " United Front " and a cessation of civil war.

Biggest and most important of the Soviet State enterprises were the salt-refining plants at Yen Ch'ih, the great salt lakes on the Ninghsia border, along the Great Wall; and the oil wells at Yung P'ing and Yen Ch'ang, which produce petrol, paraffin, and vaseline, wax, candles and other by-products. Salt deposits at Yen Ch'ih are the finest in China, producing beautiful rock-crystal salt in large quantities. Consequently salt was cheaper and more plentiful in the Soviet districts than in

[1] The price quoted in the Red districts was 800 *catties*—about half a ton—for $1 silver. Cf. " Economic Construction in the Kansu and Shensi Soviet Districts," by Mao Tse-ming, *Tou Tsung (Struggle)*, April 24, 1936 (Pao An, Shensi).

Kuomintung China, where it is made a principal source of
Government income, to the distress of the farmer. After the
capture of Yen Ch'ih the Reds won the sympathy of the Mongols
north of the Wall by agreeing to turn over part of the production
to them, revoking the Kuomintang's practice of monopolising
the entire output.

North Shensi's oil wells are the only ones in China, and their
output was formerly sold to an American company, which had
leases on other reserves in the district. After they had seized
Yung P'ing the Reds sank two new wells, and claimed increased
production, by about 40 per cent over any previous period,
when Yung P'ing and Yen Ch'ang were in " non-bandit " hands.
This included increases of " 2,000 *catties* of petrol, 25,000 *catties*
of first-class oil, and 13,500 *catties* of second-class oil " during a
three-month era reported upon.[1]

Efforts were being made to develop cotton-growing in areas
cleared of poppies, and the Reds had established a spinning-
school at An Ting, with 100 women students. The workers were
given three hours' general education daily and five hours instruction in spinning and weaving. Upon completion of their course,
after three months, students were sent to various districts to
open textile factories. " It is expected that in two years north
Shensi will be able to produce its entire supply of cloth."[2]

But Wu Ch'i Chen had the largest concentration of factory
workers in the Red districts, and was important also as the
location of the Reds' main arsenal. It commanded an important
trade route leading to Kansu, and the ruins of two ancient forts
near by testified to its former strategic importance. The present
town is built high up on the steep clay banks of a rapid stream,
and is made up half of *yang-fang*, or " foreign houses "—as the
Shensi natives still call anything that has four sides and a roof
—and half of *yao-fang*, or cave-dwellings.

I arrived late at night and I was very tired. The head of the
supply commissariat for the front armies had received word of
my coming, and he rode out to meet me. He " put me up " at a
workers' Lenin Club—an earthen-floored *yao-fang* with clean
whitewashed walls strung with festoons of coloured paper
chains encircling a portrait of the immortal Ilyitch.

[1] op. cit.   [2] op. cit.

Hot water, clean towels—stamped with New Life slogans !— and soap soon appeared. They were followed by an ample dinner, with good *baked* bread. I began to feel better. I unrolled my bedding on the table-tennis court and lit a cigarette. But man is a difficult animal to satisfy. All this luxury and attention only made me yearn for my favourite beverage.

And then, of all things, this commissar suddenly produced, from heaven knows where, some rich brown coffee and sugar ! Wu Ch'i Chen had won my heart.

" Products of our five-year plan ! " the commissar laughed.

" Products of your confiscation department, you mean," I amended. I think it must have been stolen fruit at that, for it had all the charms of the illicit.

3

" *They Sing Too Much* "

I STAYED three days at Wu Ch'i Chen, visiting workers in the factories, " inspecting " their working conditions, attending their theatre and their political meetings, reading their wall newspapers and their character-books, talking—and getting athletic. For I took part in a basketball game on one of Wu Ch'i's three courts. We made up a scratch team composed of the Foreign Office emissary, Fu Chin-kuei, a young English-speaking college student working in the political department, a Red doctor, a soldier, and myself. The arsenal basketball team accepted our challenge and beat us to a pulp. Quite literally, in my own case.

Those arsenal workers could make guns, too, as well as toss goals. I spent a day in their unusual factory and had lunch in their Lenin Club.

The arsenal, like the Red Academy, was housed in a big series of vaulted rooms built into a mountain-side. They were cool, well ventilated, and lighted by a series of shafts sunk at angles in the walls, and had the major advantage of being completely bomb-proof. Here I found over a hundred workers making hand-grenades, trench-mortars, gunpowder, pistols, small shells and bullets, and a few farming tools. A repair department was engaged in rehabilitating stacks of broken rifles, machine guns, automatic rifles, and sub-machine guns. But the arsenal's output was crude work, and most of its products equipped the Red partisans, the regular Red forces being supplied almost entirely with guns and munitions captured from enemy troops !

Ho Hsi-yang, director of the arsenal, took me through its various chambers, introduced his workers, and told me something about them and himself. He was thirty-six, unmarried, and had formerly been a technician in the famous Mukden arsenal, before the Japanese invasion. After September 18, 1931, he went to Shanghai, and there he joined the Communist Party, later on making his way to the North-west, and into Red areas. Most of the machinists here were also " outside " men. Many

Ic

had been employed at Hanyang, China's greatest iron works (Japanese-owned), and a few had worked in Kuomintang arsenals. I met two young Shanghai master mechanics, and an expert fitter, who showed me excellent letters of recommendation from the noted British and American firms of Jardine, Matheson & Co., Anderson Meyer & Co., and the Shanghai Power Company. Another had been foreman in a Shanghai machine-shop. There were also machinists from Tientsin, Canton and Peiping, and some had made the Long March with the Red Army.

I learned that of the 114 arsenal machinists and apprentices only 20 were married. These had their wives with them in Wu Ch'i Chen, either as factory workers or as party functionaries. In the arsenal trade union, which represented the most highly skilled labour in the Red districts, there was a big percentage of Party membership. Over 80 per cent belonged to the Communist Party or to the Communist Youth League.

Besides the arsenal in Wu Ch'i Chen there were cloth and uniform factories, a shoe factory, a stocking factory, and a pharmacy and drug dispensary, with a doctor in attendance. He was a youth just out of a medical training school of Shansi, and his young and pretty wife was with him working as a nurse. Both of them had joined the Reds during the Shansi expedition last winter. Near by also was a hospital, with three army doctors in attendance, and taken up mostly with wounded soldiers, and there was a radio station, a crude laboratory, a co-operative, and the army supply base.

Except in the arsenal, and uniform factory, most of the workers were young women from eighteen up to twenty-five or thirty. Some of them were married to Red soldiers then at the front; nearly all were Kansu, Shensi or Shansi women; and all had bobbed hair. " Equal pay for equal labour " is a slogan of the Chinese Soviets, and there is supposed to be no wage-discrimination against women. Labour appears to get preferential financial treatment over everybody else in the Soviet districts. This includes Red commanders, who receive no regular salary, but only a small living allowance, which varies according to the weight of the treasury.

Wu Ch'i Chen was headquarters of pretty Miss Liu Ch'ünhsien, aged twenty-nine; a former mill-worker of Wusih and Shanghai, and a former friend of Rhena Prohm, she was a returned student from Moscow's Chung Shan University, and now director of the women's department of the Red trade unions. Miss Liu described working conditions to me. Factory workers got from $10 to $15 monthly, with board and room furnished by the State. Workers were guaranteed free medical attention, and compensation for injuries. Women were given four months of rest with pay during and after pregnancy, and there was a crude " nursery " for workers' children—but most of them seemed to run wild as soon as they could walk. Mothers could collect part of their " social insurance." This latter is provided from a fund created by deducting 10 per cent of the workers' salaries, to which the Government adds an equal amount. The Government also contributes the equivalent of 2 per cent of the entire wage output for workers' education and recreation, these funds being managed jointly by the trade unions and the workers' factory committees. There was an eight-hour day and a six-day week. When I visited them the factories were running twenty-four hours a day, with three shifts working—probably the busiest plants in China !

All this sounds very progressive, though perhaps far from a Communistic Utopia. The fact that these conditions were actually being realized, in the midst of the Soviets' struggle for life, is really interesting. How *primitively* they were being realized is quite another matter ! They had clubs, schools, ample dormitories—all these, certainly—but in cave-houses with earthen floors, no shower baths, no movies, no electricity. They were furnished food; but meals consisted of millet, vegetables and sometimes mutton, with no delicacies whatever. They collected their wages and social insurance all right, in Soviet currency, but the articles they could buy were strictly limited to necessities—and none too much of those !

" Unbearable ! " the average American or English worker would say. But obviously it wasn't to these people. You have to contrast their life with the system elsewhere in China to understand why. I remembered, for example, the hundreds of factories where little boy and girl slave-workers sit or stand at their tasks twelve or thirteen hours a day, and then drop, in exhausted sleep, to the dirty cotton quilt, their bed, directly beneath their machine. I remembered little girls in silk filatures, and the pale young women in cotton factories—all of them, like most factory contract labour in Shanghai, literally sold into these jobs as virtual slaves for four or five years, unable to leave the heavily guarded, high-walled premises, day or night, without special permission. And I remembered that during 1935 more than 29,000 bodies were picked up from the streets and rivers and canals of Shanghai—bodies of the destitute poor, and the starved or drowned babies or children they could not feed.

But, for these workers in Wu Ch'i Chen, however primitive it might be, here was a life at least of good health, exercise, clean mountain air, freedom, dignity and hope, in which there was room for growth. They knew that nobody was making money out of them, I think they felt they were working for themselves and for China, and they said they were *revolutionaries* ! In this way I understood why they took so seriously their two hours of daily reading and writing, their political lectures, and their dramatic groups, and why they keenly contested for the miserable prizes offered in competitions between groups and individuals in sport, literacy, public health, wall newspapers, and " factory efficiency." All these things were *real* to them, things they had never known before, could never possibly know in any other factory of China, and they seemed grateful for the doors of life opened up for them.

Well, it is all hard for any old-China hand like myself to believe, and I am still confused about its ultimate significance, but I cannot deny the evidence I saw. Here space prevents me from presenting that evidence in detail. I should have to tell a dozen stories of workers to whom I talked; quote to you from their essays and criticisms in the wall newspapers—written in the childish scrawl of the newly literate—many of which I translated, with the aid of the college student; tell you of the political meetings I attended; and of the plays created and dramatized by these workers; and of the many little things that go to make up that intangible, an " impression."

But I just happen to remember one of those " little things " as I write. I met an electrical engineer there, a brilliant but very serious-minded Communist named Chu Tso-chih. He knew

English and German very well, he was a power expert, and he had written an engineering textbook widely used in China. He had once been with the Shanghai Power Company, and later with Anderson Meyer & Co. Until recently he had had a practice of $10,000 a year in South China, where he was a consulting engineer and efficiency man, and had given it up and left his family to come up to these wild dark hills of Shensi and offer his services to the Reds for nothing. Incredible ! The background to this phenomenon was to be traced to a beloved grandfather, a famous philanthropist of Ningpo, whose death-bed injunction to young Chu had been to " devote his life to raising the cultural standard of the masses." And Chu had decided the quickest method was the Communist one.

I think Chu had come into the thing somewhat melodramatically, in the spirit of the martyr and zealot. It was a solemn thing for him; he thought it meant an early death, and he expected everyone else to feel that way. I believe he was a little shocked when he found so much that he considered horse-play going on, and everybody apparently happy. When I asked him how he liked it, he replied gravely that he had but one serious criticism. " These people spend entirely too much time *singing* ! " he complained. " This is no time to be singing ! "

It seemed to me to sum up a great deal about the youthful bravado of this singular " industrial centre " of Soviet Shensi. They had the spirit of Socialist industry, even if they lacked its materials !

PART EIGHT

WITH THE RED ARMY

1

The " Real " Red Army

At last, after two weeks of hacking and walking over the hills and plains of Kansu and Ninghsia, I came to Yu Wang Pao, a big walled town in southern Ninghsia, which was then the head-quarters of the 1st Front Red Army—and of its Commander-in-Chief, Peng Teh-huai.

Although in a strict military sense all Red warriors might be called " irregulars " (and some people would say " highly irregulars "), the Reds themselves made a sharp distinction between their front armies, independent armies, partisans, and peasant guards. During my first brief travels in Shensi I had not seen any of the " regular " Red Army, for its main forces were then moving in the west, nearly 200 miles from Pao An. I had planned a trip to the front, but news that Chiang Kai-shek was preparing to launch another major offensive from the south had inclined me toward the better part of valour, and an early de-parture while I could still get past the lines to write my story.

One day I had expressed these doubts to Wu Liang-p'ing, the young Soviet official who had acted as interpreter in my long official interviews with Mao Tse-tung. Although Wu was a rosy-cheeked lad of twenty-six, he was already the author of two books on dialectics. But, having found him a very likeable sort, with a sense of humour on everything but dialectics, I con-sidered him my friend, and I had frankly disclosed my appre-hensions to him.

He had been dumbfounded. " You have a chance to go to the front, and you wonder whether you should take it ? Don't make such a mistake ! Chiang Kai-shek has been trying to destroy us for ten years, and he is not going to succeed now. You can't go back without seeing the *real* Red Army ! " And he had produced evidence to show why I shouldn't. What had impressed me most was that the mere idea of going to the front had aroused such enthusiasm in him, a seasoned Bolshevik and veteran of the Long March. I had decided there must be something to see. And so I had made the long trip, and safely reached the scene of operations of Wu Liang-p'ing's *real* Red Army.

It was well that I took his advice. Had I not done so I would have left Pao An still wondering how the Reds had won their reputation for invincibility. I would have left still unconvinced of the youth, the spirit, the training, the discipline, the excellent equipment, and especially the high political morale, of the regular Red Army. I would have left without understanding that this is the only *politically* iron-clad army in China.

Perhaps the best way to approach an understanding of these so-called bandits is—statistical. For I found the Reds had complete data on all their regularly enlisted men. The facts I shall assemble below, which seem to me highly interesting and significant, were furnished from his files by Yang Shan-kun, the Russian-speaking, twenty-nine-year-old chairman of the political department of the 1st Front Red Army. With a few exceptions, I confine this statistical report to matters which I had some opportunity to verify from personal impression and observation.

First of all, many people suppose the Reds to be a hard-bitten lot of outlaws and malcontents. I vaguely had some such notion myself. But I soon discovered I was quite mistaken. The great mass of the Red soldiery was made up of young peasants and workers who believed themselves to be fighting for their homes, their land, and their country.

According to Yang, the average age of the rank and file was nineteen. This was easily believable. Although many men with the Reds had fought for seven or eight or even ten years, they were balanced by a vast number of youths still in their middle teens. And even most of the " old Bolsheviks," veterans of many battles, were only now in their early twenties, the majority having joined the Reds as Young Vanguards, or enlisted at the age of fifteen or sixteen.

In the 1st Front Army, a total of 38 per cent of the men came from either the agrarian working class (including craftsmen, muleteers, apprentices, farm labourers, etc.) or from the industrial working class, while 58 per cent came from the peasantry. Only 4 per cent were from the petty-bourgeoisie—sons of merchants, intellectuals, small landlords, and such. In this army over 50 per cent of the troops, including commanders, were members of the Communist Party or the Communist Youth League.

Between 60 and 70 per cent of the soldiers were literate—that is, they could write simple letters and texts, posters, handbills, etc. This was much higher than the average among ordinary troops in the White districts, and it was very much higher than the average in the peasantry of the North-west. Red soldiers began to study characters from Red texts, specially prepared for them, from the day of their enlistment. Prizes were offered (cheap notebooks, pencils, tassels, etc., but much valued by the soldiers) for rapid advancement, and a great effort was made to stimulate the spirit of ambition and competition.

Red soldiers, like their commanders, received no regular salaries. But every enlisted man was entitled to his portion of land, and some income from it. This is tilled in his absence, either by his family or his local Soviet. If he was not a native of the Soviet districts, however, his remuneration came from a share in the proceeds of crops from " public lands " (confiscated from the great landlords), which also helped provision the Red Army. Public lands were tilled by villagers in the local Soviets. Such free labour was obligatory, but the majority of the peasants, having benefited in the land redistribution, co-operated willingly enough to defend a system that had bettered their livelihood.

The average age of the officers in the Red Army was twenty-four. This included squad leaders and all officers up to army commanders, but despite their youth these men had behind them an average of eight years fighting experience each. All company commanders or higher were literate, though I met several who had not learned to read and write till after they had entered the Red Army. About a third of the Red commanders were former Kuomintang soldiers. Among Red commanders were many graduates of Whampoa Academy (Chiang Kai-shek's officers' training school), graduates of the Red Army Academy in Moscow, former officers of Chang Hsueh-liang's " North-eastern Army," cadets of the Paoting Military Academy, former Kuominchun (" Christian General " Feng Yü-hsiang's army) men, and a number of returned students from France, Soviet Russia, Germany and England. I met only one returned student from America. The Reds don't call themselves *ping*, or " soldiers "—a word to which there is attached much odium in China—but *chan-shih*, which means " fighters " or " warriors."

The majority of the soldiers as well as officers of the Red Army were unmarried. Many of them were " divorced "—that is, they had left their wives and families behind them. In several cases I had serious suspicions that the desire for this kind of divorce, in fact, may have had something to do with their joining the army, but this may be a cynical opinion.

My impression, from scores of conversations on the road and at the front, was that over half of these " Red fighters " were still 'virgins. There were few Communist women at the front with the army, and they are nearly all Soviet functionaries in their own right or married to Soviet officials.

So far as I could see or learn, the Reds treated the peasant women and girls with respect, and the peasantry seemed to have a good opinion of Red Army morality. I heard of no cases of rape or abuse of the peasant women, though I heard from some of the southern soldiers of " sweethearts " left behind them. Very few of the Reds smoked or drank: abstention was one of the " eight disciplines " of the Red Army, and, although no special punishment was provided for either vice, I read in the " black column " of wall newspapers several grave criticisms of habitual smokers. Drinking was not forbidden, but discouraged. Drunkenness, as nearly as I could see or learn, was utterly unheard of.

Commander Peng Teh-huai, who used to be a Kuomintang general, told me that the extreme youth of the Red Army explained much of its capacity for withstanding hardship, and that was quite believable. It also made the problem of feminine companionship less poignant. Peng himself had not seen his own wife since 1928, when he led an uprising of Kuomintang troops and joined the Reds.

Casualties among Red Army commanders were very high. They customarily went into battle side by side with their men, from regimental commanders down. A foreign military attaché has said that one thing alone might explain the fighting power of the Reds against an enemy with vastly superior resources. That is the Red officers' habit of saying " Come on, boys ! " instead of " Go on, boys ! " During Nanking's First and Second " final annihilation " Campaigns, casualties among Red officers were often as high as 50 per cent. But the Red Army could not stand these sacrifices, and later adopted tactics tending somewhat to reduce the risk of life by experienced commanders. Nevertheless, in the Fifth Kiangsi Campaign, Red commanders' casualties averaged about 23 per cent of the total. You can see plenty of evidence of this in the Red districts to-day. Common sights are youths still in their early twenties with an arm or a leg missing, or fingers shot away, or with ugly wounds on the head or anatomy—but still cheerful optimists about their revolution !

Nearly every province in China was represented in the various Red armies. In this sense it was probably the only really *national* army in China. It was also the " most widely travelled " ! Veteran cadres had crossed parts of eighteen provinces. They probably knew more about Chinese geography than any other army. On their Long March they found most of the old Chinese maps quite useless, and Red cartographers remapped many hundreds of miles of territory, especially in aboriginal country, and on the western frontiers.

In the 1st Front Army, consisting of about 30,000 men, there was a big percentage of southerners, about one-third coming from Kiangsi, Fukien, Hunan or Kweichow. Nearly 40 per cent were from the western provinces of Szechuan, Shensi, and Kansu. The 1st Front Army included some aborigines—Miaos and Lolos—and also attached to it was a newly organized Mohammedan Red Army. In the independent armies the percentage of natives was much higher, averaging three-fourths of the total.

From the highest commander down to the rank and file these men ate and dressed alike. Battalion commanders and higher, however, were entitled to the use of a horse or a mule. I noticed there was even an equal sharing of the delicacies available— expressed, while I was with the Red Army, chiefly in terms of water-melons and plums ! There was very little difference in living-quarters of commanders and men, and they passed freely back and forth without any formality.

One thing had puzzled me. How did the Reds manage to feed, clothe and equip their armies ? Like many others, I had assumed that they must live entirely on loot. This I discovered to be wrong, as I have already shown, for they start to construct a self-supplying economy of their own as soon as they occupy a district, and this single fact makes it possible for them to hold a base despite enemy blockade. I had also failed to realize on what almost unbelievably modest sums it is possible for a Chinese proletarian army to exist.

From enemy troops the Reds claimed to capture more than 80 per cent of their guns, and more than 70 per cent of their ammunition. If this is hard to believe, I can bear witness to the fact that the regular troops I saw were equipped with the latest-type British, Czecho-Slovakian, German and American machine guns, rifles, automatic rifles, mausers, and mountain cannon, such as have been sold in large quantities to the Nanking Government.

The only Russian-made rifles I saw with the Reds were the vintage of 1917. These had been captured from the troops of General Ma Hung-kuei, as I heard directly from some of Ma's ex-soldiers themselves. General Ma, governor of what remains of Kuomintang Ninghsia, had inherited these rifles from " Christian General " Feng Yü-hsiang, who ruled this region in 1924, and got some arms from Outer Mongolia. Red regulars disdained to use these ancient weapons, which I saw only in the hands of the partisans.

While I was in the Soviet districts any contact with a Russian source of arms was physically impossible, for the Reds were encompassed by various enemy troops totalling nearly 400,000 men, and the enemy controlled every road to Outer Mongolia, Sinkiang or the U.S.S.R. I gathered that they would be glad to get some of the manna they are frequently accused of receiving by some miracle from Russia. But it was quite obvious from a glance at the map that, until the Chinese Reds possessed much more territory to the north and to the west, Moscow would be unable to fill any orders, assuming Moscow to be so inclined, which is open to serious doubts.

Secondly, it is a fact that the Reds have no high-paid and squeezing officials and generals, who in other Chinese armies absorb most of the military funds. The greatest imaginable frugality is practised both in the army and the Soviets. In effect, about the only burden of the army upon the people is the necessity of feeding and clothing it.

Actually, as I have already said, the entire budget of the North-west Soviets, occupying an area about the size of England, was then only $320,000 a month ! Of the staggering sum mentioned, nearly 60 per cent went to the maintenance of the armed forces. Old Lin Pai-ch'u, the finance commissioner, was apologetic about this, but said it was " inevitable until the revolution has been consolidated " ! The armed forces then numbered (not including peasant auxiliaries) about 40,000 men. This was before the arrival in Kansu of the 2nd and 4th Front Armies, after which Red territory greatly expanded, and the main Red forces in the North-west soon approached a total of 90,000 men.

So much for statistics. But really to understand why the Chinese Reds have survived all these years it is necessary to get a glimpse of their inner spirit, their morale and fighting will and their methods of training. And, perhaps still more important, their political and military leadership.

For example, what sort of man is Peng Teh-huai, Red Commander-in-Chief, for whose head Nanking once offered a reward sufficient to maintain his whole army (if Finance Commissioner Liu Pai-ch'u's figures are correct) for more than a month ?

2

Impression of Peng Teh-huai

THE consolidation of command of the 1st, 2nd and 4th Front Red Armies had not yet occurred when I visited the front in August and September. Eight divisions of the 1st Front Red Army were then holding a line from the Great Wall in Ninghsia down to Kuyuan and Pingliang in Kansu. A vanguard of the 1st Army Corps was moving southward and westward, to clear a road for Chu Teh, who was leading the 2nd and 4th Front Armies up from Sikong and Szechuan, breaking through a deep cordon of Nanking troops in southern Kansu. Yu Wang Pao, an ancient Mohammedan walled city in south-east Ninghsia, was headquarters of the 1st Front Army, and here I found its staff and Commander Peng Teh-huai.

Peng's career as a Red-bandit began almost a decade ago, when he led an uprising in the Kuomintang army of the polygamous warlord-governor, General Ho Chien. Peng had risen from the ranks, won commissions to a military school, first in Hunan, later on at Nanchang. After graduation he had quickly distinguished himself and secured rapid promotions. By 1927, when he was twenty-eight years old, he was already a brigade commander, and noted throughout the Hunanese army as the " liberal " officer who actually consulted his soldiers' committee.

Peng's influence in the then Left wing Kuomintang, in the army, and in the Hunan military school, were serious problems for Ho Chien. In the winter of 1927 General Ho began a drastic purgation of Leftists in his troops, and launched the notorious Hunan " Peasant Massacre," in which thousands of radical farmers and workers were killed as " Communists." Against Peng he hesitated to act, however, because of his widespread popularity. It was a costly delay. In July 1928, with his own famous 1st Regiment as nucleus, and joined by parts of the 2nd and 3rd Regiments and the cadets of the military school, Peng Teh-huai directed the P'in-kiang Insurrection, which united with a peasant uprising, and established the first Hunan Soviet Government.

Two years later Peng had accumulated an "iron brotherhood" of about 8,000 followers, and this was the 5th Red Army Corps. With this force he attacked and captured the great walled city of Changsha, capital of Hunan, and put to rout Ho Chien's army of 60,000 men—then mostly opium-smokers. The Red Army held this city for ten days, against counter-attacks by combined Nanking–Hunan forces, but was finally forced to evacuate under a fierce bombardment of the city by Japanese, British and American gunboats.

It was shortly afterwards that Chiang Kai-shek began his First " grand annihilation " Campaign against the Red-bandits. The story of these campaigns has been outlined. On the Long March of the southern Reds, Peng Teh-huai was commander of the vanguard 1st Army Corps. He broke through lines of tens of thousands of enemy troops, captured vital points on the route of advance, and secured communications for the main forces, at last winning his way to Shensi and a refuge in the base of the North-west Soviets. Men in his army told me that he walked most of the 6,000 miles of the Long March, frequently giving his horse to a tired or wounded comrade.

With such a history of struggle behind him, I expected Peng to be a weary, grim, fanatical leader, perhaps physically a wreck. I found him, on the contrary, a gay, laughter-loving man, in excellent health except for a delicate stomach—the result of a week's forced diet of uncooked wheat grains and grass during the Long March, and of semi-poisonous food, and of a few days of no food at all. Veteran of scores of battles, he had been wounded but once, and then only superficially.

I stayed in the compound where Peng had his headquarters in Yu Wang Pao, and so I saw a great deal of him at the front. This headquarters, by the way—then in command of over 30,000 troops—was a simple room furnished with a table and wooden bench, two iron dispatch-boxes, maps made by the Red Army, a field telephone, a towel and wash-basin, and the *k'ang* on which was spread his blankets. He had only a couple of uniforms, like the rest of his men, and they bore no insignia of rank. One personal article of attire, of which he was childishly proud, was a vest made from a parachute, captured from an enemy aeroplane shot down during the Long March.

We shared many meals together. He ate sparingly and simply, of the same food his men were given—consisting usually of cabbage, noodles, beans, mutton, and sometimes bread. Ninghsia grew beautiful melons of all kinds, and Peng was very fond of these. Your pampered investigator, however, found Peng poor competition in the business of melon-eating, but had to bow before greater talents of one of the doctors on Peng's staff, whose capacity had won him the nickname of Han Ch'ih-kua-ti (Han the Melon-Eater).

I must admit that Peng impressed me. There was something open, forthright, and undeviating in his manner and speech— rare qualities among Chinese—which I liked. Quick in his movements and speech, full of laughter and a great wit, he was physically very active, an excellent rider, a man of endurance. Perhaps this was partly because he was a non-smoker and a teetotaller. I was with him one day during manœuvres of the Red 2nd Division, when we had to climb a very steep hill. " Run to the top ! " Peng suddenly called out to myself and his panting staff. He bounded off like a rabbit, and beat us all to the summit. Another time, when we were riding, he yelled out a similar challenge. In this way and others he gave the impression of great unspent energy.

Peng retired late and arose early, unlike Mao Tse-tung who retired late and also got up late. As far as I could learn, Peng slept an average of only four or five hours a night. He never seemed rushed, but he was always busy. I remember how astonished I was the morning of the day the 1st Army Corps received orders to advance 200 *li* to Haiyuan, in enemy territory: Peng issued all the commands necessary before breakfast and came down to eat with me; immediately afterwards he started off on the road, as if for an excursion to the countryside, walking along the main street of Yu Wang Pao with his staff, stopping to speak to the Moslem priests who had assembled to bid him good-bye. The big army seemed to run itself.

Incidentally, although Government aeroplanes frequently dropped leaflets, over Red lines, offering from $50,000 to $100,000 for Peng, dead or alive, he had only one sentry on duty before his headquarters, and he walked up and down the streets of the city without any bodyguard. While I was there, when thousands of handbills had been dropped offering rewards for himself, Hsu Hai-tung, and Mao Tse-tung, Peng Teh-huai ordered that these be preserved. They were printed on only one side, and there was a paper shortage in the Red Army. The blank side of these handbills was used later for printing Red Army propaganda.

Peng was very fond of children, I noticed, and he was often followed by a group of them. Many of these youngsters, who act as mess-boys, buglers, orderlies, and grooms, are organized as regular units of the Red Army, in groups called the *Shao-nin Hsien-feng-tui*, or Young Vanguards. I often saw Peng seated with two or three " little Red devils," seriously talking to them about politics or their personal troubles. He treated them with great dignity.

One day I went with Peng and part of his staff to visit a small arsenal near the front, and to inspect the workers' recreation room, their own *Lieh-ning T'ang*, or Lenin Club. There was a big cartoon, drawn by the workers, on one side of the room. It showed a kimonoed Japanese with his feet on Manchuria, Jehol and Hopei, and an upraised sword, dripping with blood, poised over the rest of China. The caricatured Japanese had an enormous nose.

" Who is *that* ? " Peng asked a Young Vanguard whose duty it was to look after the Lenin Club.

" That," replied the lad, " is a Japanese imperialist ! "

" How do you know ? " Peng demanded.

" Just look at his big nose ! " was the response.

Peng laughed and looked at me. " Well," he said, indicating me, " here is a *yang kuei-tzu* [foreign devil], is he an imperialist ? "

" He is a foreign devil all right," the Vanguard replied, " but not a Japanese imperialist. He has a big nose, but it isn't big enough for a Japanese imperialist ! "

Peng shouted in delight, and thereafter jokingly called me *ta pi-tzu*, the Big Nose. As a matter of fact my proboscis is regular and inoffensive enough in Occidental society, but to Chinese all foreigners are *ta pi-tzu*. I pointed out to Peng that such cartoons might result in serious disillusionment when the Reds actually came into contact with the Japanese and found

Japanese noses quite as reasonable as their own. They might not recognize the enemy and refuse to fight.

"Don't worry!" said the commander. "We will know a Japanese, whether he has a nose or not!"

Once I went to a performance of the 1st Army Corps' Anti-Japanese Theatre with Peng, and we sat down with the other soldiers on the turf below the improvised stage. He seemed to enjoy the plays immensely, and he led a demand for a favourite song. It grew quite chilly after dark, although it was still late August. I wrapped my padded coat closer to me. In the middle of the performance I suddenly noticed with surprise that Peng had removed his own coat. Then I saw that he had put it around a little bugler sitting next to him.

I understood Peng's affection for these "little devils" later on, when he yielded to persuasion one night and told me something of his childhood. The trials of his own youth may amaze an Occidental ear, but they are typical enough of background events which explain many of the young Chinese who "see Red" to-day.

3

Why Is a Red?

PENG TEH-HUAI was born in a village of Hsiang T'an hsien, about ninety *li* from Changsha, beside the blue-flowing Hsiang River, and in a wealthy farming community. Hsiang T'an is one of the prettiest parts of Hunan—a green countryside quilted with deep rice-lands and thickets of tall bamboo. It is densely populated. More than a million people live in this one county. But, though the soil of Hsiang T'an is rich, the majority of the peasants are miserably poor, illiterate and " little better than serfs," according to Peng. Landlords are all-powerful there, own the finest lands, and charge exorbitant rents and taxes, for they are in many cases also the officials.

" Several great landlords in Hsiang T'an have incomes of from forty to fifty thousand *tan* of rice annually, and some of the wealthiest grain merchants in the province live there."

Peng's own family were rich peasants. His mother died when he was six, his father remarried, and this second wife hated Peng because he was a constant reminder of her predecessor. She sent him to an old-style Chinese school, where the teacher frequently beat him. Peng was apparently quite capable of looking after his own interests: in the midst of one of these beatings he picked up a stool, scored a hit, and fled. The teacher brought a law-suit against him in the local courts, and his stepmother denounced him.

His father was rather indifferent in this quarrel, but to keep peace with his wife he sent the young stool-tosser off to live with an aunt, whom he liked. She put the boy into a so-called modern school. There he met a " radical " teacher, who did not believe in filial worship. One day, when Teh-huai was playing in the park, this teacher came along and sat down to talk with him. Peng asked whether he worshipped his parents, and whether he thought Peng should his. As for himself, said the teacher, he did not believe in such nonsense. Children were brought into the world while their parents were playing, just as Teh-huai had been playing in this park.

" I liked this notion," said Peng, " and I mentioned it to my aunt when I went home. She was horrified, and the very next day had me withdrawn from the evil ' foreign influence.' " Hearing something of the young man's objection to filial worship, his grandmother, who seems to have been a rather bloodthirsty old tyrant, began to pray regularly " on the first and fifteenth of each month, and at festivals, or when it stormed," for heaven to strike this unfilial child and destroy him.

And then occurred an amazing thing, which can best be told in Peng's own words:

" My grandmother regarded us all as her slaves. She was a heavy smoker of opium. I hated the smell of it, and one night, when I could stand it no longer, I got up and kicked a pan of her opium from the stove. She was furious. She called a meeting of the whole clan, and formally demanded my death by drowning, because I was an unfilial child. She made a long list of charges against me.

" The whole clan was about ready to carry out her demand. My stepmother agreed that I should die, and my father said that since it was the family will he would not object. Then an uncle, my own mother's brother, stepped forward and he bitterly attacked my parents for their failure to educate me properly. He said that it was their fault and that in this case no child could be held responsible.

" My life was spared, but I had to leave home. I was nine years old, it was cold October, and I owned nothing but my coat and trousers. My stepmother tried to take those from me, but I proved that they did not belong to her, but had been given to me by my own mother."

Such was the beginning of Peng Teh-huai's life in the great world. He got a job first as a cowherd, and next as a coal-miner, where he pulled a bellows for fourteen hours a day. Weary of these long hours he fled from the mine to become a shoemaker's apprentice, working only twelve hours a day, a big improvement. He received no salary, and after eight months he ran away again, this time to work in a sodium-mine. The mine closed; he was forced to seek work once more. Still owning nothing but the rags on his back, he became a dyke-builder. Here he had a " good job," actually received wages, and in two years had saved 1,500 *cash*—about $12 ! But he " lost everything " when a change of warlords rendered the currency worthless. Very depressed, he decided to return to his native district.

Now sixteen, Peng went to call on a rich uncle—the uncle who had saved his life. This man's own son had just died; he had always liked Teh-huai, and he welcomed him and offered him a home. Here Peng fell in love with his own cousin, and the uncle was favourably disposed to a betrothal. They studied under a Chinese tutor, played together, and planned their future.

These plans were interrupted by Peng's irrepressible impetuosity. Next year there was a big rice famine in Hunan, and thousands of peasants were destitute. Peng's uncle helped many, but the biggest stores of rice were held by a great landlord-merchant, who fabulously profiteered. One day a crowd of over 200 peasants gathered at his house, demanding that the merchant sell them rice without profit—traditionally expected of a virtuous man in time of famine. The rich man refused to discuss it, had the people driven away, and barred his gates.

Peng went on: " I was passing his place, and paused to watch the demonstration. I saw that many of the men were half starved, and I knew this man had over 10,000 *tan* of rice in his bins, and that he had refused to help the starving at all. I became infuriated, and led the peasants to attack and invade his house. They carted off most of his stores. Thinking of it afterwards, I did not know exactly why I had done that. I only knew that he should have sold rice to the poor, and that it was right for them to take it from him if he did not."

Peng had to flee once more for his life, and this time he was old enough to join the Army. His career as a soldier began. Not long afterward he was to become a revolutionary.

At eighteen he was made a platoon commander and was involved in a plot to overthrow the ruling governor—*Tuchün* Hu. Peng had been deeply influenced by a student leader in his army, whom the *tuchün* had killed. Entrusted with the task of assassinating Hu, he entered Changsha, waited for him to pass down the street one day, and threw a bomb at him. The bomb proved to be anti-climatic, like Chinese fiction: it failed to explode. Peng escaped.

Not long afterwards Dr. Sun Yat-sen became Generalissimo of the allied armies of the South-west, and succeeded in defeating Tuchün Hu, but was subsequently driven out of Hunan again by the northern militarists. Peng fled with Sun's army. Sent upon a mission of espionage by Ch'êng Ch'ien,[1] one of Sun's commanders, Peng returned to Changsha, was betrayed, and arrested. Chang Ching-yao was then in power in Hunan. Peng described his experiences:

" I was tortured every day for about an hour in many different ways. One night my feet were bound and my hands were tied behind my back. I was hung from the roof with a rope around my wrists. Then big stones were piled on my back, while the jailers stood around kicking me and demanding that I confess—for they still had no evidence against me. Many times I fainted.

" This torture went on for about a month. I used to think after every torture that next time I would confess, as I could not stand it. But each time I decided that I would not give up till the next day. In the end they got nothing from me, and to my surprise I was finally released. One of the deep satisfactions of my life came some years later when we captured Changsha and destroyed that old torture-chamber. We released several hundred political prisoners there—many of them half-dead from beatings, fiendish treatment and starvation."

When Peng regained his freedom he went back to his uncle's home, to visit his cousin. He intended to marry her, as he still considered himself betrothed. He found that she had died. Re-enlisting in the Army, he soon afterwards received his first commission and was sent to the Hunan military school. Following his graduation he became a battalion commander in the 2nd Division, under Lu Ti-p'ing, and was assigned to duty in his native district.

" My uncle died and, hearing of it, I arranged to return to attend the funeral. On the way there I had to pass my childhood home. My old grandmother was alive, now past eighty, and still very active. Learning that I was returning, she walked down the road ten *li* to meet me, and begged my forgiveness for the past. She was very humble and very respectful. I was quite surprised by this change. What could be the cause of it ?

---

[1] Lin Pai-chu was chief-of-staff of Ch'êng Ch'ien's army.

Then I reflected that it was not due to any change in her personal feeling, but to my rise in the world from a social outcast to an army officer with a salary of $200 a month. I gave the old lady a little money, and she sang my praises in the family as a model ' filial son ' ! "

I asked Peng what reading had influenced him. He said that when as a youth he read Ssu Ma-kuang's *Sze Chih Chien* (or *History of Governing*), he began for the first time to have some serious thoughts concerning the responsibility of a soldier to society. " The battles by Ssu Ma-kuang were completely pointless, and only caused suffering to the people—very much like those that were being fought between the militarists in China in my own time. What could we do to give purpose to our struggles, and bring about a permanent change ? "

Peng read Liang Ch'i-ch'ao and K'ang Yu-wei and many of the writers who had influenced Mao Tse-tung. For a time he had some faith in anarchism. Ch'en Tu-hsiu's *New Youth* interested him in Socialism, and from that point he began to study Marxism. The Nationalist Revolution was forming, he was a regimental commander, and he felt the necessity of a political doctrine to give morale to his troops. Sun Yat-sen's *San Min Chu I* " was an improvement over Liang Ch'i-ch'ao," but Peng felt that it was " too vague and confused," although he was by then a member of the Kuomintang. Bukharin's *A B C of Communism* seemed to him " for the first time a book that presented a practicable and reasonable form of society and government."

By 1926, Peng had read the *Communist Manifesto*, an outline of *Capital*, *A New Conception of Society* (by a leading Chinese Communist), Kautsky's *Class Struggle*, and many articles and pamphlets giving a materialist interpretation of the Chinese Revolution. " Formerly," said Peng, " I had been merely dissatisfied with society, but saw little chance of making any fundamental improvement. After reading the *Communist Manifesto* I dropped my pessimism and began working with a new conviction that society could be changed."

Although Peng did not join the Communist Party until 1927, he enlisted the aid of Communist youths in his troops, began Marxist courses of political training, and organized soldiers' committees. In 1926 he married a middle-school girl who was a member of the Socialist Youth, but during the revolution they became separated. Peng has not seen her since 1928. It was in July of that year that Peng revolted, seized P'in Kiang, and began his long career as a rebel, or bandit—as you prefer.

He had been pacing back and forth, grinning and joking as he told me these incidents of his youth and struggle, and carrying in his hand a Mongolian horse-hair fly-swatter, which he brandished absent-mindedly for emphasis. A messenger now brought in a sheaf of radiograms, and he suddenly looked the serious commander again as he turned to read them.

" Well, that's about all, anyway," he concluded. " That explains something about how a man becomes a ' Red-bandit' ! "

4

Tactics of Partisan Warfare

AND here I want to tell of an extremely interesting interview
I had with Peng Teh-huai on how and why the Red Army grew.
My recollection is that we sat in the house of a former magistrate,
in Yu Wang Pao, in a two-storied edifice with a balustraded
porch—a porch from which you could look out toward Mongolia,
across the plains of Ninghsia.

On the high stout walls of Yu Wang Pao a squad of Red
buglers was practising, and from a corner of the fort-like city
flew a big scarlet flag, its yellow hammer and sickle cracking
out in the breeze now and then as though a fist were behind it.
We could look down on one side to a clean courtyard, where
Mohammedan women were hulling rice and baking. Washing
hung from a line on another side. In a distant square some Red
soldiers were practising wall-scaling, broad-jumping, and
grenade-throwing.

Peng Teh-huai is a native of the same county of Hunan as
Mao Tse-tung, though they did not meet until the Red Army
was formed. He speaks with a pronounced southern dialect,
and machine-gun rapidity. I could only understand him clearly
when he spoke slowly and simply, which he was generally too
impatient to do. For this interview a young graduate of a
Peiping university, whose English was excellent, acted as my
interpreter. I hope he is still alive, and will some time read this
acknowledgment of my deepest thanks to him.

"The main reason for partisan warfare in China," Peng
began, "is economic bankruptcy, and especially rural bankruptcy. Imperialism, landlordism, and militaristic wars have
combined to destroy the basis of rural economy, and it cannot
be restored without eliminating its chief enemies. Enormous
taxes, together with Japanese invasion, both military and
economic, have accelerated the rate of this peasant bankruptcy,
aided by the landlords. The gentry's exploitation of power in
the villages makes life difficult for the majority of the peasants.
There is tremendous unemployment in the villages. There is a
readiness among the poor classes to fight for a change.

" Secondly, partisan warfare has developed because of the backwardness of the hinterland. Lack of communications, roads, railways and bridges makes it possible for the people to arm and organize.

" Thirdly, although the strategic centres of China are all more or less dominated by the imperialists, this control is uneven and not unified. Between the imperialist spheres of influence there are wide gaps, and in these partisan warfare can quickly develop.

" Fourthly, the Great Revolution (1926-7) fixed the revolutionary idea in the minds of many, and even after the counter-revolution in 1927 and the killings in the cities, many revolutionaries refused to submit, and sought a method of opposition. Owing to the special system of joint imperialist-comprador control in the big cities, and the lack of an armed force in the beginning, it was impossible to find a base in urban areas, so many revolutionary workers, intellectuals and peasants returned to the rural districts to lead the peasant insurrections. Intolerable social and economic conditions had created the conditions for revolution: it was only necessary to give leadership, form and objectives to this rural mass movement.

" All these factors contributed to the growth and success of revolutionary partisan warfare. They are, of course, quite simply stated, and do not go into the deeper problems behind them.

" Besides these reasons, partisan warfare has succeeded and partisan detachments have developed their invincibility because of the identity of the masses with the fighting forces. Red partisans are not only warriors; they are at the same time political propagandists and organizers. Wherever they go they carry the message of the revolution, patiently explaining to the mass of the peasantry the real missions of the Red Army, and making them understand that only through revolution can their needs be realized, and explaining why the Communist Party is the only party which can lead them.

" But, as regards the specific tasks of partisan warfare, you have asked why in some places it developed very rapidly, and became a strong political power, while in others it was easily and quickly suppressed. This is an interesting question.

" First of all, partisan warfare in China can only succeed under the revolutionary leadership of the Communist Party, because only the Communist Party wants to and can satisfy the demands of the peasantry, understands the necessity for deep, broad, constant political and organizational work among the peasantry, and can fulfil the promises of its propaganda.

" Secondly, the active field leadership of partisan units must be determined, fearless and courageous. Without these qualities in the leadership, partisan warfare not only cannot grow, but it must wither and die under the reactionary offensive.

" Because the masses are interested only in the practical solution of their problems of livelihood, it is possible to develop partisan warfare only by the *immediate* satisfaction of their most urgent demands. This means that the exploiting class must be promptly disarmed and immobilized.

" Partisans can never remain stationary; to do so is to invite destruction. They must constantly expand, building around themselves ever-new peripheral and protective groups. Political training must accompany every phase of the struggle, and local leaders must be developed from every new group added to the revolution. Leaders from the outside can be introduced to a limited extent, but no lasting success can be achieved if the movement fails to inspire, awaken and constantly create new leaders from the local mass."

These statements were interesting, they were undoubtedly important. But I wanted to know, if possible, the military principles which guide the Reds, and which have made them so difficult an enemy for the many times more formidably equipped Nanking troops. People who have read much about Colonel Lawrence and his campaigns invariably compare Red tactics to those of the great English genius of manœuvring warfare. Like the Arabs, the Reds have given but mediocre performances in their few big ventures at positional warfare; but, like the Arabs, they have proved invincible in the war of manœuvre.

One of the chief reasons why Marshal Chang Hsueh-liang began to respect the Reds (the enemy he had been sent to destroy) was because he had been impressed with their skill at this type of combat, and had come to believe they could be utilized in fighting Japan. After he had reached a kind of truce with them he invited Red instructors to teach in the new officer-training-school opened for his Manchurian army in Shensi, and here the Communist influence rapidly developed. Marshal Chang and most of his officers, bitterly anti-Japanese, had become convinced that it was superior mobility and manœuvring ability on which China would ultimately have to depend in a war with Japan. They were anxious to know all that Reds had learned about the tactics and strategy of manœuvring warfare during ten years of fighting experience.

Concerning these points I had questioned Peng. Was it possible, I had asked him, to summarize the " principles of Red partisan warfare " ? He had promised to do so and had written down a few notes from which he now read. For a fuller discussion of the subject he referred me to a small book written by Mao Tse-tung and published in the Soviet districts; but this I was unable to get.

" There are certain rules of tactics which must be followed," Peng explained, " if the newly developing partisan army is to be successful. These we have learned from our long experience, and though they are variable, according to conditions, I believe that departures from them generally lead to extinction. The main principles can be summarized under ten points, like this:

" First, partisans must not fight any losing battles. Unless there are strong indications of success, they should refuse any engagement.

" Second, surprise is the main offensive tactic of the well-led partisan group. Static warfare must be avoided. The partisan brigade has no auxiliary force, no rear, no line of supplies and communications except that of the enemy. In a lengthy positional war the enemy has every advantage, and in general the chances of partisan success diminish in proportion to the duration of the battle.

" Third, a careful and detailed plan of attack, and especially of retreat, must be worked out before any engagement is offered or accepted. Any attack undertaken without full preliminary precautions opens the partisans to outmanœuvre by the enemy. Superior manœuvring ability is a great advantage of the partisans, and errors in its manipulation mean extinction.

" Fourth, in the development of partisan warfare the greatest attention must be paid to the *min-t'uan*,[1] the first, last, and most determined line of resistance of the landlords and gentry. The *min-t'uan* must be destroyed militarily, but must, if at all possible, be won over politically on the side of the masses. Unless the *min-t'uan* in a district is disarmed and demobilized it is impossible to mobilize the masses.

" Fifth, in a regular engagement with enemy troops the partisans must exceed the enemy in numbers. But if the enemy's regular troops are moving, resting, or poorly guarded, a swift, determined, surprise flank-attack on an organically vital spot of the enemy's line can be made by a much smaller group. Many a Red ' short-attack ' has been carried out with only a few hundred men against an enemy of thousands. Surprise, speed, courage, unwavering decision, flawlessly planned manœuvre, and the selection of the most vulnerable and vital spot in the enemy's ' anatomy,' are absolutely essential to the complete victory of this kind of attack. Only a highly experienced partisan army can succeed at it.

" Sixth, in actual combat, the partisan line must have the greatest elasticity. Once it becomes obvious that their calculation of enemy strength or preparedness or fighting power is in error, the partisans should be able to disengage and withdraw with the same speed as they began the attack. Reliable cadres must be developed in every unit, fully capable of replacing any commander eliminated in battle. Resourcefulness of subalterns must be greatly relied upon in partisan warfare.

" Seventh, the tactics of distraction, decoy, diversion, ambush, feint, and irritation must be mastered. In Chinese these tactics are called ' the principle of pretending to attack the east while attacking the west.'

" Eighth, partisans must avoid engagements with the main force of the enemy, concentrating on the weakest link, or the most vital.

" Ninth, every precaution must be taken to prevent the enemy from locating the partisans' main forces. For this reason, partisans should avoid concentrating in one place when the enemy is

---

[1] Peng Teh-huai estimated that the *min-t'uan* number at least 3,000,000 men (in addition to China's huge regular army of 2,000,000 men).

advancing, and should change their position frequently—two or three times in one day or night, just before an attack. Secrecy in the movements of the partisans is absolutely essential to success. Well worked out plans for dispersal after an attack are as important as plans for the actual concentration to meet an enemy advance.

" Tenth, besides superior mobility, the partisans, being inseparable from the local mass, have the advantage of superior Intelligence, and the greatest use must be made of this. Ideally, every peasant should be on the partisans' Intelligence staff, so that it is impossible for the enemy to take a step without the partisans knowing of it. Great care should be taken to protect the channels of information about the enemy, and several auxiliary lines of Intelligence should always be established."

These were the main principles, according to Commander Peng, on which the Red Army had built up its strength, and it was necessary to employ them in every enlargement of Red territory. He finished up:

" So you see that successful partisan warfare demands these fundamentals: fearlessness, swiftness, intelligent planning, mobility, secrecy, and suddenness and determination in action. Lacking any of these, it is difficult for partisans to win victories. If in the beginning of a battle they lack quick decision, the battle will lengthen. They must be swift, otherwise the enemy will be reinforced. They must be mobile and elastic, otherwise they will lose their advantages of manœuvre.

" Finally, it is absolutely necessary for the partisans to win the support and participation of the peasant masses. If there is no movement of the armed peasantry, in fact, there is no partisan base, and the army cannot exist. Only by implanting itself deeply in the hearts of the people, only by fulfilling the demands of the masses, only by consolidating a base in the peasant Soviets, and only by sheltering in the shadow of the masses, can partisan warfare bring revolutionary victory."

Peng had been pacing up and down the balcony, delivering one of his points each time he returned to the table where I sat writing. Now he suddenly stopped, and stood thoughtfully reflecting.

" But nothing, absolutely nothing," he said, " is more

important than this—that the Red Army is a people's army, and has grown because the people helped us.

" I remember the winter of 1928, when my forces in Hunan had dwindled to a little over two thousand men, and we were surrounded. The Kuomintang troops burned down all the houses in a surrounding area of about 300 *li*, seized all the food there, and then blockaded us. We had no cloth, we used bark to make short tunics, and we cut up the legs of our trousers to make shoes. Our hair grew long, we had no quarters, no lights, no salt. We were sick and half starved. The peasants were no better off, and we would not touch what little they had.

" But the peasants encouraged us. They dug up from the ground the grain which they had hidden from the White troops, and gave it to us, and they ate potatoes and wild roots. They hated the Whites for burning their homes and stealing their food. Even before we arrived they had fought the landlords and tax-collectors, so they welcomed us. Many joined us, and nearly all helped us in some way. They wanted us to win ! And because of that we fought on and broke the blockade."

He turned to me and ended simply. " Tactics are important, but we could not exist if the majority of the people did not support us. We are nothing but the fist of the people beating their oppressors ! "

5

Life of the Red Warrior

THE Chinese soldier has a poor reputation abroad. Many people think his gun is chiefly ornamental, that he does his only fighting with an opium-pipe, that any rifle shots exchanged are by mutual agreement and in the air, that battles are fought with silver and the soldier is paid in opium. Some of this was true enough of most armies in the past, but the well-equipped first-class Chinese soldier of to-day (White as well as Red) is no longer a vaudeville joke, as the world may presently be shown. China's failure to repulse Japan is no criterion: with the exception of the sabotaged struggle at Shanghai, no serious resistance has thus far been attempted.

There are still plenty of comic-opera armies in China, but in recent years there has arisen a new type of Chinese warrior, who will soon supplant the old. Civil war, especially the class war between Reds and Whites, has been very costly, and at times heavily and bitterly fought, with no quarter or umbrella-truces given by either side. These ten years of strife in China have, if nothing else, created the nucleus of a fighting force and military brains experienced in the use of modern technique and tactics, which will before long build a powerful army that can no longer be dismissed as a tin-soldier affair.

The trouble has never been with the human material itself. The Chinese can fight as well as any people, as I learned during the Shanghai War in 1932. Technical limitations disregarded, the trouble has been entirely the inability of the command to train that human material at its disposal and give to it military discipline, political morale, and the *will to victory*. Therein lay the superiority of the Red Army. It was so often the only side in a battle that believed it was fighting for something. It was the Reds' greater success at the educative tasks in the building of an army that enabled them to withstand the tremendous technical and numerical superiority of their enemy.

For sheer dogged endurance, and ability to stand hardship without complaint, the Chinese peasants, who compose the greater part of the Red Army, are unbeatable. This was shown by the Long March. It is also demonstrated by the rigours and impositions of daily life in the Red Army. There may be foreign troops that can survive the same exposure and rough food, crude housing, and continuous suffering, but I have not seen them. I know American, British, French, Japanese, Italian and German troops fairly well, but only the very best, I am convinced, could stand up under the exhausting routine of the Red soldiers.

The Red troops I saw in Ninghsia and Kansu were quartered in caves, former stables of wealthy landlords, hastily erected barracks of clay and wood, and in compounds and houses abandoned by former officials or garrison troops. They slept on hard k'angs, without even straw mattresses, and with only a cotton blanket each—yet these rooms were fairly neat, clean and orderly, although their floors, walls and ceilings were of whitewashed clay. They seldom had tables or desks, and piles of bricks or rocks served as chairs, most of the furniture having been destroyed or carted off by the enemy before his retreat.

Every company had its own cook and commissariat. The Reds' diet was extremely simple. Coffee, tea, cake, sweets of any kind, or fresh vegetables, were almost unknown, but also unmissed. Coffee tins were more valued than their contents, for nobody liked coffee, it tasted like medicine, but a good tin could be made into a serviceable canteen ! Hot water was almost the only beverage consumed, and the drinking of cold water was specifically forbidden.

The Red soldier, when not fighting, had a full and busy day. Actually, in the North-west, as in the South, he had long periods of inactivity. When a new district was occupied, the Red Army settled down for a month or two to establish Soviets and otherwise " consolidate " it, and only put a small force on outpost duty. The enemy was nearly always on the defensive, except when one of the periodic big " annihilation drives " was launched, but, in the interim between offensives of their own or the enemy, there were big gaps of leisure.

When not in the trenches or on outpost duty, the Red soldier observed a six-day week. He arose at five, and retired to a " Taps " sounded at nine. The schedule of the day included: an hour's exercise immediately after rising; breakfast, two hours of military drill; two hours of political lectures and discussion; lunch; an hour of rest; two hours of character-study; two hours of games and sport; dinner; songs and group meetings; and " Taps."

Keen competition was encouraged in broad-jumping, high-jumping, running, wall-scaling, rope-climbing, rope-skipping, grenade-throwing, and marksmanship. Watching the leaps of the Reds over walls, bars, and ropes, you could easily understand why the Chinese Press had nicknamed them " human monkeys," for their agile feats at mountain-climbing and swift movement. Pennants were given in group competitions, from the squad up to the regiment, in sports, military drill, political knowledge, literacy, and public health. I saw these banners displayed in the Lenin Clubs of units that had won such distinctions.

There was a Lenin Club for every company and for every regiment, and here all social and " cultural " life had its centre. The regimental Lenin rooms were the best in the unit's quarters, but that says little; such as I saw were always crude, makeshift affairs, and what interest they aroused derived from the human activity in them, rather than from their furnishings. They all had pictures of Marx and Lenin, drawn by company or regimental talent. Like some of the Chinese pictures of Christ, they generally bore a distinctly Oriental appearance, with eyes like stitches, and either bulbous foreheads like an image of Confucius, or no foreheads at all. Marx, whose Chinese moniker is Ma K'e-ssu, was nicknamed by the Red soldiers " Ma Ta Hu-tzu," or " Ma the Big Beard." They seemed to have an affectionate awe for him. That was especially true of the Mohammedans, who appear to be the only people in China capable of growing luxuriant beards as well as appreciating them.

Another feature of the Lenin Club was a corner devoted to the study of military tactics, in models of clay. The Chinese are very good at this sort of thing. Miniature towns, mountains, forts, rivers, lakes, and bridges were constructed in these corners, and toy armies battled back and forth, while the class studied some tactical problem given to it. Thus in some places you saw the Sino-Japanese battles of Shanghai refought, in another the battles on the Great Wall, but most of the models were, of course, devoted to past battles between the Reds and the Kuomintang. They were also used to explain the geographical features of the district in which the army was stationed, to dramatize the tactics of a hypothetical campaign, or merely to animate the geography and political lessons which Red soldiers got as part of their military training. In a hospital company's Lenin room I saw displays of clay models of various parts of the anatomy, showing the effects of certain diseases, illustrating body hygiene, and so on.

Another corner of the club was devoted to character-study, and here you could see the notebook of each warrior hanging on its appointed peg on the wall. There were three character-study groups: those who knew less than 100 characters; those who knew from 100 to 300; and those who could read and write more than 300 characters. The Reds had printed their own textbooks (using political propaganda as materials of study) for each of these groups. The political department of each company, battalion, regiment and army was responsible for mass education, as well as political training. Only about 20 per cent of the 1st Army Corps, I was told, was still in the *hsia-tzu* class, or " blind men," as the Chinese call total illiterates.

" The principles of the Lenin Club," it was explained to me by Hsia Hua, the twenty-two-year-old political director of the 2nd Division, " are quite simple. All the life and activity in them must be connected with the daily work and development of the men. It must be done by the men themselves. It must be simple and easy to understand. It must combine recreational value with practical education about the immediate tasks of the army."

There was also a wall newspaper in every club, and a committee of soldiers was responsible for keeping it up to date. It was at least much more recent than the " library " of the average Lenin Club. That consisted chiefly of standard Chinese Red Army textbooks and lectures, a History of the Russian Revolution, miscellaneous magazines which may have been smuggled in or captured from the White areas, and files of Chinese Soviet publications like the *Red China Daily News, Party Work, Struggle,* and others.

The wall newspaper of a Lenin Club gave you a real insight into the soldier's problems and a measure of his development. I took down full notes, in translation, of many of these papers. A typical one was in the Lenin Club, 2nd Company, 3rd Regiment, 2nd Division, in Yu Wang Pao, for September 1. Its contents included daily and weekly notices of the Communist Party and the Communist Youth League; a couple of columns of crude contributions by the newly literate, mostly revolutionary exhortations and slogans; radio bulletins of Red Army victories in south Kansu; new songs to be learned; political news from the White areas; and, perhaps most interesting of all, two sections called the red and black columns, devoted respectively to praise and criticism.

" Praises " consisted of tributes to the courage, bravery, unselfishness, diligence or other virtues of individuals or groups. In the black column comrades lashed into each other and their officers (by name) for such things as failure to keep a rifle clean, slackness in study, losing a hand-grenade or bayonet, smoking on duty, " political backwardness," " individualism," " reactionary habits," etc. On one black column I saw a cook denounced for his " half-done " millet; in another a cook denounced a man for " always complaining " about his productions.

Many people have been amused to hear about the Reds' passion for the English game of table-tennis. It is bizarre, somehow, but every Lenin Club had in its centre a big ping-pong table, usually serving double-duty as dining-table. The Lenin Clubs were turned into mess halls at chow time, but there were always four or five " bandits," armed with bats, balls and the net, urging the comrades to hurry it up; they wanted to get on with their game. Each company boasted a ping-pong champion, and I was no match for them.

Some of the Lenin Clubs had gramophones, confiscated from the homes of former officials or White officers. One night I was entertained with a concert on a captured American Victrola, described as a " gift " from General Kao Kuei-Tzu, who was then in command of a Kuomintang army fighting the Reds on the Shensi–Suiyuan border. General Kao's records were all Chinese, with two exceptions, both French. One had on it the " Marseillaise " and " Tipperary." The other was a French comic song, and this brought on a storm of laughter from the astonished listeners, who understood not a word of it.

The Reds had many games of their own, and were constantly inventing new ones. One of these was called *Shih-tzu P'ai*, or " Know Characters," a card game which helped the illiterate learn his basic hieroglyphics. Another card game was somewhat like poker, but the high cards were marked " Down with Japanese Imperialism," " Down with Landlords," " Long live the Revolution," and " Long live the Soviets " ! Minor cards carried slogans that changed according to the political and military objectives. There were many group games. The Communist Youth League members were responsible for the programme of the Lenin Clubs, and likewise led mass singing every day. Many of their words, by the way, were sung to Christian hymns !

All these activities keep the mass of the soldiers fairly busy and fairly healthy. There were no camp followers or prostitutes with the Red troops I saw. Opium-smoking was prohibited. I saw no opium or opium-pipes with the Reds on the road, nor in any barracks I visited. Cigarette-smoking was not forbidden while on duty, but there was propaganda against it, and few Red soldiers seemed to smoke, most of them refusing when I offered them a fag.

Such was the organized life of the regular Red soldiers behind the front. It may strike you as not so very exciting, perhaps, but it is rather different from the propagandists' tales, from which one might gather that the Reds' life consists of wild orgies, entertainment by naked dancers, and rapine before and after meals. This may be dismissed as pure drivel—and not so pure at that. The fact is that a revolutionary army anywhere is always in danger of becoming too puritanical, rather than the contrary.

Some of the Reds' ideas have now been copied—with much better facilities for realizing them—by Chiang Kai-shek's crack " new army " and his New Life movement. But one thing the White armies cannot copy, the Reds claimed, was their " revolutionary consciousness," on which stood their main fortress of morale. What this was like could best be seen at a political session of Red troops—where you could hear the simple but firmly implanted credos that these youths fought and died for.

6

Session in Politics

FINDING myself with an idle afternoon, I went round to call on Liu Hsiao, a member of the Red Army political department, with offices in a guard house on the city wall of Yu Wang Pao.

I had been seeing too much of commanders and party leaders, and not enough of the mass of the soldiery. By now it was obvious that the Red commanders were loyal Marxists, and were effectively under the guidance of the Communist Party, through its representatives in the political department of every unit of the Army. Of course, Mr. Trotsky might dispute whether they were good Marxists or bad Marxists, but right here I shall not split that particular hair. The point is that they were conscious fighters for Socialism, in their fashion; they knew what they wanted, and believed themselves to be part of a world movement.

" Liu," I said, " I've been to too many meetings of commanders, and not enough of the rank and file. What about the ordinary soldier ? How much of this anti-imperialism and class-war business does he believe in ? I'm going to one of their political discussions, and I want you to come with me. There are too many dialects around here for me to follow alone."

Liu was one of the most serious-minded young men I had met among the Reds, and one of the hardest working, an intensely earnest youth of twenty-five, with an æsthetic intellectual face. He was extremely courteous, gentle and inoffensive. Yet I sensed an immense inner spiritual pride in him about his connection with the Red Army. He had a pure feeling of religious absolutism about Communism, and I believe he would not have hesitated, on command, to shoot any number of " counter-revolutionaries " or " traitors."

I had no right to break in on his day, but I knew he had orders to assist me in any way possible—he had several times acted as my interpreter—so I made the most of it. I think also that he disliked foreigners, and, when later on he gave me a brief biography of himself, I could not blame him. He had been twice arrested and imprisoned by foreign police in his own country !

Liu was an ex-student of Eastview Academy, an American missionary school in Shengchoufu, Hunan. He had been a devout Christian, a fundamentalist, and a good Y.M.C.A. man until 1926 and the Great Revolution. One day he led a student strike, was expelled, and disowned by his family. Awakened to the " imperialistic basis of missionary institutions " in China, he went to Shanghai, became active in the student movement there, joined the Communist Party, and was imprisoned by police in the French concession. Released in 1929, he rejoined his comrades, worked under the provincial committee of the Communist Party, was arrested by British police, put in the notorious Ward Road jail, tortured by electricity to extort a confession, handed over to the Chinese authorities, jailed again, and did not get his freedom till 1931. He was then just twenty years old. Shortly afterwards he was sent by the Reds' " underground railway " to the Fukien Soviet district, and had ever since been with the Red Army.

Liu agreed to accompany me, and together we found our way to a Lenin Club where there was a political class in session. It was a meeting of a company in the 2nd Regiment of the 2nd Division, 1st Army Corps, and sixty-two were present. This was the " advanced section " of the company; there was also a " second section." Political education in the Red Army is conducted through three main groups, each of which is divided into the two sections mentioned. Each elects its soldiers' committee, to consult with its superior officers and send delegates to the Soviets. The three groups are for: company commanders and higher; squad commanders and the rank and file; and the service corps—cooks, grooms, muleteers, carriers, sweepers, and Young Vanguards.

Green boughs decorated the room, and a big red paper star was fixed over the doorway. Inside were the usual pictures of Marx and Lenin, and on another wall were photographs of Tsai Ting-kai and Chiang Kuang-nai, heroes of the Shanghai War. There was a big picture of the Russian Red Army massed in the Red Square in an October anniversary demonstration—a photograph torn from a Shanghai magazine. Finally, there was a large lithographed photo of General Feng Yü-hsiang, with a slogan under it, " *Huan Wo Shan Ho* "—" Give back our mountains and rivers ! "—an old Classical phrase, now revived by the anti-Japanese movement.

The men sat on brick seats, which they had brought with them (you often saw these soldier students going to school with note-books in one hand and a brick in the other !) and the class was led by the company commander and the political commissioner, both members of the Communist Party. The subject, I gathered, was "Progress in the Anti-Japanese Movement." A lanky, gaunt-faced youth was speaking. He seemed to be summarizing five years of Sino-Japanese "undeclared war," and he was shouting at the top of his lungs. He told of the Japanese invasion of Manchuria, and his own experiences there, as a former soldier in the army of Marshal Chang Hsueh-liang. He condemned Nanking for ordering "non-resistance." Then he described the Japanese invasion of Shanghai, Jehol, Hopei, Chahar and Suiyuan. In each case, he maintained, the "Kuomintang dog-party" had retreated without fighting. They had "given the Japanese bandits a fourth of our country."

"Why ? " he demanded, intensely excited, his voice breaking a little. " Why don't our Chinese armies fight to save China ? Because they don't want to ? No ! We Tungpei men asked our officers nearly every day to lead us to the front, to fight back to our homeland. Every Chinese hates to become a Japanese slave ! But China's armies cannot fight because of our *mai-kuo chêng-fu* " (which means, literally, " sell-country government ").

" But the people will fight if our Red Army leads. . . ." He ended up with a summary of the growth of the anti-Japanese movement in the North-west, under the Communists.

Another arose, stood at rigid attention, his hands pressed closely to his sides. Liu Hsiao whispered to me that he was a squad leader—a corporal—who had made the Long March. " It is only the traitors who do not want to fight Japan. It is only the rich men, the militarists, the tax-collectors, the land-lords and the bankers, who start the ' co-operate-with-Japan ' movement, and the ' joint-war-against-Communism ' slogan. They are only a handful, they are not Chinese.

" Our peasants and workers, every one, want to fight to save the country. They only need to be shown a road. . . . Why do I know this ? In our Kiangsi Soviets we had a population of only

8,000,000, yet we recruited volunteer partisan armies of 500,000 men ! Our loyal Soviets enthusiastically supported us in the war against the traitorous White troops. When the Red Army is victorious over the whole country our partisans will number over ten millions. Let Japan dare to try to rob us then ! "

And much more of it. One after another they stood up to utter their hatred against Japan, sometimes emphasizing, sometimes disagreeing, with a previous speaker's remark, sometimes giving their answer to a question from the discussion leaders, making suggestions for " broadening the anti-Japanese movement," and so on.

One youth told of the response of the people to the Red Army's anti-Japanese Shansi expedition last year. " The *lao-pai-hsing* [the people] welcomed us," he shouted. " They came by the hundreds to join us. They brought us tea and cakes on the road, as we marched. Many left their fields to come to join us, or cheer us. . . . They understood quite clearly who were the traitors and who the patriots—who want to fight Japan, and who want to sell China to Japan. Our problem is to awaken the whole country as we awakened the people of Shansi. . . ."

One talked about the anti-Japanese student movement in the White districts, another about the anti-Japanese movement in the South-west, and a Tungpei man told of the reasons why Marshal Chang Hsueh-liang's Manchurian soldiers refused to fight the Reds any more. " Chinese must not fight Chinese, we must all unite to oppose Japanese imperialism, we must win back our lost homeland ! " he concluded with terse eloquence. A fourth spoke of the Manchurian anti-Japanese volunteers, and another of the strikes of Chinese workers in the Japanese mills of China.

The discussion continued for over an hour. Occasionally the commander or political commissar interrupted to summarize what had been said, to elaborate a point, or to add new information, occasionally to correct something that had been said. The men took brief laborious notes in their little notebooks, and the serious task of thought furrowed their honest peasant faces. The whole session was crudely propagandist, and exaggeration of fact did not bother them in the least. It was even evangelical in a way, with materials selected to prove a single thesis. But that it was potent in its effects was manifest. The logical shape of simple but powerful convictions were forming in these young, little-tutored minds—credos such as every great crusading army has found necessary in order to stiffen itself with that spiritual unity, that courage, and that readiness to die in a cause, which we call morale.

At last I interrupted to ask some questions. They were answered by a show of hands. I discovered that of the sixty-two present, nine were from urban working-class families, while the rest were peasants, straight from the land. Twenty-one were former White soldiers, and six were from the old Manchurian army. Only eight of this group were married, while twenty-one were from Red families—that is, from families of poor peasants who had shared in the land redistribution under some Soviet. Thirty-four of the group were under twenty years of age, twenty-four were between twenty and twenty-five, but only four were over thirty.

" In what way," I asked, " is the Red Army better than other armies of China ? " This brought half a dozen men to their feet at once. And here, briefly stated, are some of the replies of which I made notes at the time:

" The Red Army is a revolutionary army."

" The Red Army is anti-Japanese."

" The Red Army helps the peasants."

" Living conditions in the Red Army are entirely different from the White Army life. Here we are all equals; in the White Army the soldier masses are oppressed. Here we fight for ourselves and the masses. The White Army fights for the gentry and the landlords. Officers and men live the same in the Red Army. In the White Army the soldiers are treated like slaves."

"Officers of the Red Army come from our own ranks, and win their appointments by merit alone. White officers buy their jobs, or use political influence."

" Red soldiers are volunteers; White soldiers are conscripted."

" Capitalist armies are for preserving the capitalist class. The Red Army fights for the proletariat."

" The militarists' armies' work is to collect taxes and squeeze the blood of the people. The Red Army fights to free the people."

" The masses hate the White Army; they love the Red Army."

" But how," I interrupted once more, " do you know the peasants really like the Red Army ? " Again several jumped up to answer. The political commissar recognized one.

" When we go into a new district," he said, " the peasants always volunteer to help our hospital service. They carry our wounded back to our hospitals, from the front."

Another: " On our Long March through Szechuan the peasants brought us grass shoes, made by themselves, and they brought us tea and hot water, along the road."

A third: " When I fought in Liu Tze-tan's 26th Army, in Tingpien, we were a small detachment defending a lonely outpost against the Kuomintang general, Kao Kuei-tzu. The peasants brought us food and water. We did not have to use our men to bring supplies, the people helped us. Kao Kuei-tzu's men were defeated. We captured some and they told us they had had no water for almost two days. The peasants had poisoned the wells and run away."

A Kansu peasant-soldier: " The people help us in many ways. During battles they often disarm small parties of the enemy, cut their telephone and telegraph wires, and send us news about the movements of the White troops. But they never cut our telephone lines; they help us put them up ! "

Another: " When an enemy aeroplane crashed against a mountain in Shensi recently, nobody saw it but a few farmers. They were armed only with spears and spades, but they attacked the aeroplane, disarmed the two aviators, arrested them, and brought them to us in Wa Ya Pao ! "

Still another: " Last April, in Yen Ch'ang, five villages formed Soviets, where I was stationed. Afterwards we were attacked by T'ang En-p'o, and had to retreat. The *min-t'uan* returned, arrested eighteen villagers, and cut off their heads. Then we counter-attacked. The villagers led us by a secret mountain path to attack the *min-t'uan*. We took them by surprise, and we attacked and disarmed three platoons."

Then one youth with a long scar on his cheek got up and told of some experiences on the Long March. " When the Red Army was passing through Kweichow," he said, " I was wounded with some other comrades, near Tsunyi. The army had to move on; it could not take us along. The doctors bandaged us, and left us with some peasants, asking them to look after us. They fed us and treated us well, and when the White troops came to that village they hid us. In a few weeks we recovered. Later on, the Red Army returned to that district and captured Tsunyi a second time. We rejoined the army, and some of the young men of the villages went with us."

Another: " Once we were staying in a village of An Ting [north Shensi] and we were only a dozen men and rifles. The peasants there made bean curd for us, and gave us a sheep. We had a feast and we ate too much and went to sleep, leaving only one sentry on guard. He went to sleep too. But in the middle of the night a peasant boy arrived and woke us up. He had run ten *li* from —— [some mountain] to warn us that *min-t'uan* were there and intended to surround us. The *min-t'uan* did attack us about an hour later, but we were ready for them and drove them off."

A bright-eyed lad without a shadow of whisker on his face arose and declared: " I have only this to say. When the White Army comes to a village in Kansu, nobody helps it, nobody gives it any food, and nobody wants to join. When the Red Army comes, the peasants organize, and form committees to help us, and young men volunteer to join. Our Red Army *is* the people, and this is what I have to say ! "

Every youth there seemed to have a personal experience to relate to prove that " the peasants like us." I see from my notes that I wrote down seventeen different answers to that question. It proved so popular that another hour had passed before I realized that these warriors had been delayed long past their dinner call. I apologized, and prepared to leave, but one " small devil " attached to the company stood up and said: " Don't worry about ceremony. We Reds don't care about going with-out food when we are fighting, and we don't care about missing our food when we can tell a foreign friend about our Red Army ! "

It was a nice speech, and probably the *hsiao-kuei* meant every word of it. But it did not in the least interfere with him putting away at terrific speed an enormous bowl of steaming millet which, a few minutes later, I saw served to him in the company mess.

PART NINE

WITH THE RED ARMY

1

Hsü Hai-tung, the Red Potter

ONE morning I went to Peng Teh-huai's headquarters, and found several members of his staff there, just finishing up a conference. They invited me in, and opened a water-melon. As we sat around tables, wickedly spitting out seeds on the *k'ang*, I noticed a young commander I had not seen before.

Peng Teh-huai saw me looking at him, and he said banteringly: " That's a famous Red-bandit over there. Do you recognize him? " The new arrival promptly grinned, blushed crimson, and in a most disarming way exposed a big cavern where two front teeth should have been. It gave him a childish and impish appearance, and everybody smiled.

" He is the man you have been anxious to meet," supplied Peng. " He wants you to visit his army. His name is Hsü Hai-tung."

Now, of all the Red military leaders of China, probably none was more " notorious," and certainly none was more of a mystery, than Hsü Hai-tung. Scarcely anything was known of him to the outside world except that he once worked in a Hupeh pottery. Chiang Kai-shek had branded him a scourge of civilization. Recently Nanking aeroplanes had visited the Red lines, to drop leaflets containing, among other inducements to deserters (including $100 to every Red soldier who brought his rifle with him to the Kuomintang), the following promise:

> " Kill Mao Tse-tung or Hsü Hai-tung and we will give you $100,000 when you join our army. Kill any other bandit leader and we will reward you accordingly."

And here, poised shyly over a pair of square boyish shoulders, sat that head which Nanking apparently valued no less than Peng Teh-huai's.

I acknowledged the pleasure, wondering what it felt like to have a life worth that much to any one of your subordinates, and asked Hsü whether he was really serious about the invitation to visit his army. He was commander of the 15th Red Army

Corps, with headquarters then located about eighty *li* to the North-west, in a town called Yuwang Hsien.

" I already have a room arranged for you in the bell-tower," he responded. " Just let me know when you want to come, and I'll send an escort for you."

We made it a bargain on the spot.

Thus it happened that a few days later, carrying a borrowed automatic (a " confiscation " of my own from a Red officer), I set out for Yuwang Hsien, accompanied by ten Red troopers, armed with rifles and mausers—for in places our road skirted Red positions only a short distance behind the front lines. In contrast with the eternal hills and valleys of Shensi and Kansu, the road we followed—a road that led to the Great Wall, and the historic grasslands of Inner Mongolia—crossed high tablelands, striped with long green meadows, and dotted with tall bunch-grass and softly rounded hills, on which great herds of sheep and goats grazed. Eagles and buzzards sometimes flew overhead. Once a herd of wild gazelles came near us, sniffed the air, and then swooped off with incredible speed and grace, round a protecting mountain-side.

In five hours we reached Yuwang Hsien, an ancient Mohammedan city of four or five hundred families, with a magnificent wall of stone and brick. Outside the city was a Mohammedan temple, with its own walls of beautiful glazed brick, quite unscarred. But other buildings showed signs of the siege this city underwent before it was taken by the Reds. A two-storeyed building that had been the magistrate's headquarters was partly ruined, and its façade was pitted with bullet-holes. I was told that this and other buildings on the outskirts had been destroyed by the defending troops of General Ma Hung-kuei, when the Red siege had first begun. The enemy had withdrawn from all extramural buildings, after setting fire to them, to prevent the Reds occupying them as positions of attack against the city walls.

" Actually, when the city fell," Hsü Hai-tung told me later on, " there was only a very minor battle. We surrounded and blockaded Yuwang Hsien for ten days. Inside there was one brigade of Ma Hung-kuei's cavalry, and about 1,000 *min-t'uan*. We made no attack at all until the tenth night. It was very dark.

We put a ladder on the wall, a company scaled it before the enemy guards discovered it, and then they defended the ladder with a machine gun, while a regiment of our troops mounted the wall.

" There was little fighting. Before dawn we had disarmed all the *min-t'uan* and surrounded the brigade of cavalry. Only one of our men was killed, and only seven were wounded. We gave the *min-t'uan* a dollar apiece and sent them back to their farms, and we gave Ma's men two dollars each. Several hundred of them stayed and enlisted with us. The magistrate and the brigade commander escaped over the east wall while their troops were being disarmed."

I spent five days with the 15th Army Corps, and found every waking hour intensely interesting. And of it all nothing was better material for an " investigator of the Red regions," as I was labelled in Yuwang Hsien, than the story of Hsü Hai-tung himself. I talked with him every night when his duties were finished, I rode with him to the front lines of the 73rd Division, and I went to the Red theatre with him. He told me for the first time the history of the Honan-Anhui-Hupeh Soviet Republic, which has never been fully known. As organizer of the first partisan army of that great Red area, which was second in size only to the Central Soviets of Kiangsi, Hsü Hai-tung knew nearly every detail of its development.

Hsü struck me as the most strongly " class-conscious " man— in manner, appearance, conversation, and background—of all the Red leaders I met. With the exception of Ho Lung, in fact, he was probably the only " pure proletarian " among the army commanders. While the majority of the subordinate officers were of proletarian origin, many of the higher commanders were from middle-class, or middle-peasant, families, or from the intelligentzia.

Hsü was a very obvious exception. He was quite proud of his proletarian origin, and he often referred to himself, with a grin, as a " coolie." You could tell he sincerely believed that the poor of China, the peasants and the workers, were the good people— kind, brave, unselfish, honest—while the rich had a monopoly of all the vices. It was as simple as that for him, I think: he was fighting to get rid of the vices. This absolutism of faith kept his cocky comments about his own dare-deviltry, and his army's superiority, from sounding like vanity and conceit. When he said, " One Red is worth five Whites," you could see that to him it was a statement of irrefutable fact.

His prideful enthusiasms were a little naïve, but intensely sincere, and in them perhaps was the secret of the devotion his men seemed to have for him. He was immensely proud of his army—the men as individuals, their skill as soldiers, as horse-men, and as revolutionaries. He was proud of their Lenin Clubs, and their artistically made posters—which were really very good. And he was proud of his division commanders, two of whom were " coolies like himself," and one of whom—a Red for six years—was only twenty-one years old.

Hsü valued very highly any act of physical prowess, and it was his regret that eight wounds he had collected in ten years of fighting now slightly handicapped him. But he did not smoke or drink, and he still had a slender, straight-limbed body, every inch of which seemed to be hard muscle. He had been wounded in each leg, in each arm, in the chest, a shoulder, and a hip. One bullet had entered his head just below the eye and emerged behind his ear. And yet he still gave you the impression of a peasant youth who had but recently stepped out of the rice-fields, rolled down his trouser-legs, and joined a passing " free company " of warriors.

I found out also about the missing teeth. They had been lost during a riding accident. Galloping along the road one day, his horse's hoof struck a soldier, and Hsü turned in the saddle to see whether he had been hurt. The horse shied, and knocked Hsü into a tree. When he regained consciousness two weeks later, it was to discover that his upper incisors had been left with the tree.

" Aren't you afraid you'll be hurt some day ? " I asked him.

" Not much," he laughed. " I've been taking beatings ever since I was a child, and I'm used to it by now."

His childhood, in fact, explains much of why he is a revolu-tionary to-day. I asked him about his life—forcing answers from him with great difficulty, for, like all Reds, he only wanted to talk about battles. From the hundreds of words of notes I put down I select a few facts that seem significant.

Hsü Hai-tung was born in 1900 in Huangpi Hsien—Yellow Slope County—near Hankow. His family had for generations been potters, and in his grandfather's day had owned land, but since then, through drought, flood, and taxation, had been completely proletarianized. His father and five brothers worked in a pottery of Huangpi, and made enough to live. They were all illiterate, but ambitious for Hai-tung, a bright child and the youngest of the six sons, and they scraped together the money necessary to send him to school.

" My fellow students," Hsü told me, " were nearly all the sons of landlords or merchants, as few poor boys ever got to school. I studied at the same desks with them, but many hated me because I seldom had any shoes and my clothes were poor and ragged. I could not avoid fighting with them, when they cursed me. If I ran to the teacher for help, I was invariably beaten by him. But if the landlords' sons got the worst of it, and went to the teacher, I was also beaten !

" In my fourth year in school, when I was eleven, I got involved in a ' rich-against-poor ' quarrel, and was driven to a corner by a crowd of ' rich sons.' We were throwing sticks and stones, and one I threw cut the head of a child named Huang, son of a wealthy landlord. This boy went off crying, and in a short time returned with his family. The elder Huang said that I had ' forgotten my birth,' and he kicked and beat me. The teacher then gave me a second beating. After that I ran away from school, and refused to return. The incident made a deep impression on me. I believed from then on that it was impossible for a poor boy to get justice."

Hsü became an apprentice in a pottery, where he worked for nothing during his " thanking-the-master years." At sixteen he was a full journeyman, and the highest-paid potter among 300 workers. " I can turn out a good piece of pottery as fast as anyone in China," Hsü smilingly boasted, " so when the revolution is over I'll still be a useful citizen ! "

He recalled an incident that did not increase his love for the gentry: " A travelling theatrical troupe came to our neighbourhood, and the workers went to see it. Wives of the gentry and officials were also there. Naturally the workers were curious to see what these closely-guarded wives of the great ones looked

like, and they kept staring into the boxes. At this, the gentry
ordered the *min-t'uan* to drive them out of the theatre, and there
was a fight. Later on our factory master had to give a banquet for
the offended ' nobility,' and shoot off some fire-crackers, to
compensate for the ' spoiled purity ' of those women who had
been gazed upon by the people. The master tried to take the
money for this banquet from our wages, but we threatened to
strike, and he changed his mind. This was my first experience of
the power of organization as a weapon of defence for the poor."

When he was twenty-one, angered by a domestic quarrel, Hsü
left home. He walked to Hankow, then made his way to Kiangsi,
where he worked for a year as a potter, saved his money, and
planned to return to Huangpi. But he caught cholera, and
exhausted his savings while recovering. Ashamed to return
empty-handed, he joined the army, where he was promised $10
a month. He received " only beatings." Meanwhile the Nationalist Revolution was beginning in the South, and Communists were propagandizing in Hsü's army. Several of them
were beheaded, and he became interested. Disgusted with the
warlord army, he deserted with one of the officers, fled to Canton,
and joined the 4th Kuomintang Army under Chang Fa-kuei.
There he remained till 1927. He had become a platoon commander.

In the spring of 1927 the Nationalist forces were breaking into
Left-wing and Right-wing groups, and this conflict was especially sharp in Chang Fa-kuei's Army, which had reached the
Yangtze River. Siding with the radicals, Hsü was forced to flee,
and secretly he returned to Yellow Slope. By now he had become
a Communist, having been much influenced by some student
propagandists, and in Huangpi he at once began building up a
local branch of the Party.

The Right *coup d'état* occurred in April 1927, and Communism
was driven underground. But not Hsü Hai-tung. He decided all
by himself that the time had come for independent action. He
had organized most of the workers in the potteries, and some
local peasants. From these he now recruited the first " workers'
and peasants' army " of Hupeh. They numbered in the beginning only seventeen men, and they had one revolver and eight
bullets—Hsü's own.

This was the nucleus of what later became the Fourth Front Red Army of 60,000 men, which in 1933 had under its control a Sovietized territory the size of Ireland. It had its own post office, credit system, mints, co-operatives, textile factories, and in general a well-organized economy, under an elected Government. Hsu Hsiang-ch'ien, a Whampoa graduate and former Kuomintang officer, had become commander-in-chief, while Chang Kuo-t'ao, a returned student from Moscow, and one of the great leaders of the Chinese cultural renaissance of 1917, was chairman of the Government.

Like Kiangsi, this Hupeh-Anhui-Honan Red Republic withstood the first four " annihilation campaigns " launched by Nanking, and actually strengthened itself in the process. And like Kiangsi, much the same tactics and strategy, in the Fifth Campaign, forced the eventual " strategic retreat " of the main forces of the Fourth Front Red Army, first to Szechuan, and later to the North-west.

But besides the economic blockade, daily air-bombing, and the construction of a network of thousands of forts around this Soviet area, the Nanking generals evidently pursued a policy of almost complete annihilation of the civilian population of the Red districts. Realizing at last that the Reds' only real base was in the mass of the peasantry, they set out methodically to destroy the population. During the Fifth Campaign the anti-Red forces in Hupeh and Anhui, then numbering about 300,000, were stiffened with Fascist-trained officers, whom Chiang Kai-shek had spent a year indoctrinating with anti-Red propaganda in his Nanchang and Nanking military academies. The result was a civil war the barbarity and intensity of which rivalled the Fascist invasion of Spain.

The revenge of a ruling class, once its power is threatened, seems to follow much the same barbaric forms everywhere, regardless of race or colour. But some of the variations in technique are instructive, and here a few pages may be devoted to show how it was done in China.

2

Class War in China

FOR three days, several hours every afternoon and evening, I had been asking Hsü Hai-tung and his staff questions of their personal histories, about their troops, of the struggle of the former Hupeh-Honan-Anhui Soviet districts—the Oyüwan Soviet Republic,[1] as the Reds called it—and about their present situation in the North-west. I was the first foreign newspaperman to interview them. They had no Press " dope," no " story " to peddle (they would not have understood the expression), no pretty, formulated speeches, and I had to worm everything out of them by hard interrogation. But it was refreshing, I reflected, to get straight, unadorned statements in response from men untutored in the art of propagandizing the foreigner. You felt you could believe what they said.

And because of that, I suppose, I sat up with sudden interest when Hsü Hai-tung answered my question, " Where is your family now ? " His reply was so matter-of-fact, so obviously uncalculated, that I could not doubt its honesty.

" All of my clan have been killed except one brother, who is with the Fourth Front Army."

" You mean killed in fighting ? "

" Oh, no; only three of my brothers were Reds. The rest of the clan were executed by Generals T'ang En-p'o and Sha Tou-yin. Altogether the Kuomintang officers killed sixty-six members of the Hsü clan."

" Sixty-six ! " I repeated incredulously.

" Yes, twenty-seven of my near relatives were executed, and thirty-nine distant relatives—everyone in Huangpi Hsien named Hsü. Old and young men, women, children, and even babies were killed. The Hsü clan was wiped out, excepting my wife and three brothers in the Red Army, and myself. Two of my brothers were killed in battle later on."

" And your wife ? "

" I don't know what happened to her. She was captured when

[1] *O*, *Yu*, and *Wan* are the historic names of Hupeh, Anhui, and Honan. The Reds named their provincial Soviet on the borders of those three provinces by combining these ancient names.

the White troops occupied Huangpi Hsien in 1931. Afterwards I heard that she had been sold as a concubine to a merchant near Hankow. My brothers who escaped told me about that, and about the other killings. During the Fifth Campaign, thirteen of the Hsü clan escaped from Huangpi and fled to Lihsiang Hsien, but were all arrested there. The men were beheaded; the women and children were shot."

Hsü noticed the shocked look on my face and he grinned mirthlessly. " That was nothing unusual," he said. " That happened to the clans of many Red officers, though mine had the biggest losses. Chiang Kai-shek had given an order that when my district was captured no one named Hsü should be left alive."

So it was in this manner that we began to speak of class revenge. Here I must admit that I would more happily skip over the subject entirely, for collecting atrocity tales is a melancholy business anywhere. Yet, in common justice to the Reds, something should be said about the methods used by their enemy to destroy them. For a decade the Kuomintang maintained a complete news blockade around the Red districts, and flooded the country with propaganda " horror " stories, attributing much of the destruction of life and property by its own aeroplanes and heavy artillery—of which the Reds had none—to the " bandits." It cannot be an unhealthful thing to listen for once to what the Reds have to say about the Kuomintang.

I wrote down pages and pages of notes, collected from Hsü and his officers, containing dates, places, and detailed accounts of outrages committed on the population by the Kuomintang troops fighting in the Oyüwan district. But I cannot repeat the worst crimes I heard described. Not only are they unprintable, but (like the daily events in Spain) they are likely to prove incredible to the innocent sceptic who does not know the terrible depth of class hatred in class warfare.

We must remember that it is now well known that in the Fifth Anti-Red Campaign the Nanking officers gave orders in many areas to exterminate the civilian population. This was held to be militarily necessary because, as the Generalissimo remarked in one of his speeches, where the Soviets had been long-established

" it was impossible to tell a Red-bandit from a good citizen."
The method appears to have been applied with peculiar savagery
in the Oyüwan Republic, chiefly because some of the leading
Kuomintang generals in charge of anti-Red operations were
natives of that region, sons of landlords who lost their land to
the Reds, and hence had an insatiable desire for revenge. The
population in the Soviets had decreased by about 600,000 at the
end of the Fifth Campaign.

Red tactics in Oyüwan had depended upon mobility over a
wide territory, and at the beginning of every " annihilation
drive " their main forces had moved out of the Red districts,
to engage the enemy on its own ground. They had no important
strategic bases to defend, and readily moved from place to place,
to decoy, divert, distract, and otherwise gain manœuvring
advantages. This did, however, leave the periphery of their
" human base " very much exposed. But in the past the Kuomintang troops had not killed the farmers and townsmen whom they
found peacefully pursuing their tasks in Soviet areas they
occupied.

In the Fifth Campaign, as in Kiangsi, new tactics were
adopted. Instead of engaging the Red Army in the open field,
the Nanking troops advanced in heavily concentrated units,
behind extensive fortifications, bit by bit penetrating into Red
territory, systematically either annihilating or transporting the
entire population in wide areas inside and outside the Red
borders. They sought to make of such districts a desolate,
uninhabited wasteland, incapable of supporting the Red troops,
if they should later recapture it. Nanking had fully understood
at last that the only Red bases were in the peasant population—
and that such bases must be destroyed.

Thousands of children were taken prisoner, and driven to
Hankow and other cities, where they were sold into " apprentice-
ships." Thousands of young girls and women were transported
and sold into the factories as slave girls and as prostitutes. In the
cities they were pawned off as " famine refugees," or " orphans
of people killed by the Reds ": I remember hundreds of them
reaching the big industrial centres in 1934. A considerable trade
grew up, with middle-men buying the boys and women from
Kuomintang officers. It became a very profitable business for a

while, but threatened to corrupt the ranks of the army. Missionaries began talking about it. Christian General Chiang Kai-shek was finally obliged to issue a stern order forbidding this " bribe-taking," and ordering strict punishment for officers engaged in the traffic.

" By December 1933," said Hsü Hai-tung, " about half of Oyüwan had become a vast wasteland. Over a once rich country there were very few houses left standing, cattle had all been driven away, the fields were unkept, and there were piles of bodies in nearly every village that had been occupied by the White troops. Four counties in Hupeh, five in Anhui, and three in Honan, were almost completely ruined. In an area some 400 *li* from east to west and about 300 *li* from north to south the whole population was being killed or removed.

" During the year's fighting we recaptured some of these districts from the White troops, but when we returned we found the fertile lands had become semi-deserts. Only a few old men and women remained, and they would tell tales that horrified us. We could not believe such crimes had been committed by Chinese against Chinese.

" In November 1933 we retreated from Tien Tai Shan and Lao Chün Shan, Soviet districts where there were then about 60,000 people. When we returned, two months later, we found that these peasants had been driven from their land, their houses had been burned, or destroyed by bombing, and there were not more than 300 old men and a few sickly children in all that region. From them we learned what had happened.

" As soon as the White troops had arrived the officers had begun dividing the women and girls. Those with bobbed hair or natural feet had been shot as Communists. Higher officers had looked over the others, and picked out pretty ones for their own, and then the lower officers had been given their choice. The rest had been turned over to the soldiers to use as prostitutes. They had been told that these women were ' bandit-wives,' and therefore they could do what they liked with them.

" Many of the young men in those districts had joined the Red Army, but many of those left, and even some of the old men, tried to kill the White officers for these crimes. Those who protested were all shot as Communists. The survivors told us that many fights had occurred among the Whites, who had quarrelled among themselves about the distribution of women. After they had despoiled these women and girls they were sent to the towns and cities, where they were sold, only the officers keeping a few pretty ones for concubines."

" Do you mean to say these were the troops of the National Government ? " I interrupted.

" Yes, they were the 13th Army Corps of General T'ang En-p'o, and the 3rd Army Corps of General Wang Chün. Generals Sha Tou-yin, Liang Kuan-yin, and Sung T'ien-tsai were also responsible."

Hsü told of another district, Huan Kang Hsien, in Hupeh, which the Reds recovered from General Wang Chün in July 1933: " In the town of Tsu Yun Chai, where there was once a street of flourishing Soviet co-operatives and a happy people, everything was in ruins and only a few old men were alive. They led us out to a valley and showed us the scattered bodies of seventeen young women lying half-naked in the sun. They had all been raped and killed. The White troops had evidently been in a great hurry; they had taken the time to pull off only one leg of a girl's trousers. That day we called a meeting, the army held a memorial service there, and we all wept.

" Not long afterwards, in Ma Cheng, we came to one of our former athletic fields. There in a shallow grave we found the bodies of twelve comrades who had been killed. Their skin had been stripped from them, their eyes gouged out, and their ears and noses cut off. We all broke into tears of rage at this barbaric sight.

" In the same month, also in Huan Kang, our 25th Red Army reached Ao Kung Chai. This had once been a lively place, but it was now deserted. We walked outside the town and saw a peasant's hut with smoke coming from it, on a hillside, and some of us climbed up to it, but the only occupant was an old man who had apparently gone insane. We walked down into the valley again until we came upon a long pile of dead men and women. There were more than 400 bodies lying there, and they had evidently been killed only a short time before. In some places the blood was several inches deep. Some women were lying with their children still clutched to them. Many bodies were lying one on top of another.

" Suddenly I noticed one of the bodies move, and, going over to it, found that it was a man still alive. We found several more alive after that, altogether more than ten. We carried them back with us and treated their wounds, and they told us what had happened. These people had fled from the town to hide in this valley, and had encamped in the open. Afterwards the White officers had led their troops to the spot, ordered them to put up their machine guns on the mountain-sides, and had then opened fire on the people below. They had kept firing for several hours until they thought everybody was dead. Then, without even coming down to look at them, they had marched away again."

The next day Hsü led his whole army out to that valley, and showed them the dead, among whom some of the soldiers recognized peasants they had known, men and women who must have given them shelter at one time, or sold them melons, or traded at the co-operatives. They were deeply moved. Hsü said that this experience steeled his troops with a stubborn morale and a determination to die fighting, and that throughout the entire twelve months of the last great annihilation drive not a single man had deserted from the 25th Army.

" Toward the end of the Fifth Campaign," he continued, " nearly every house had dead in it. We used to enter a village that seemed empty until we looked into the ruined houses. Then we would find corpses in the doorways, on the floor, or on the k'ang, or hidden away somewhere. Even the dogs had fled from many villages. In those days we did not need spies to watch the enemy's movements. We could follow them quite easily by the skies filled with smoke from burning towns and hamlets."

This is only a little—only a very small part—of the stories I heard from Hsü Hai-tung and others who fought through that terrible year, and finally trekked westward, not their army but human " base " destroyed, its hills and valleys stained with the blood of its youth, the living heart of it torn out. Later on I talked to many warriors from Oyüwan, and they told tales more pitiful still. They did not like to talk of what they had seen; they did so only under questioning, and it was clear their experiences had permanently marked the matrix of their minds with a class hatred ineradicable for life.

Does this mean, however, that the Reds are innocent of

atrocity and class revenge themselves ? I think not. It is true that during my four months with them, as far as I could learn from unrestricted inquiry, they executed but two civilians. It is also true that I did not see a single village or town burned by them, or hear, from the many farmers I questioned, that the Reds were addicted to arson. But my personal experience with them starts and ends with the North-west: what " killing and burning " may have been done elsewhere I cannot affirm or deny. At the same time it would be naïve not to suspect about 90 per cent of the anti-Red propaganda published these many years in the Kuomintang and foreign Press as being pure poppy-cock, since at least that much of it has lacked any reliable confirmation.

And, to be accurate, one of the two ill-fated " counter-revolutionaries " mentioned above was not killed by the Reds, but by some Ninghsia Moslems with a strong distaste for tax-collectors. Farther on it will be told in what manner he met his demise, but first let us see how these Moslems have been ruled, and perhaps we shall understand the economics of the execution.

3

Four Great Horses

You might facetiously say that Chinghai, Ninghsia, and northern Kansu are the prototype of that fantasia of Swift's, the land of Houyhnhnm, for they are ruled as the satrapy of Four Great Horses whose fame is widespread in China. Over the areas mentioned power is divided (or was, before the Reds began edging the Houyhnhnms out of considerable portions of their domain) by a family of Mohammedan generals named Ma—the Messrs. Ma Hung-kuei, Ma Hung-ping, Ma Pu-fang, and Ma Pu-ching. And this particular *Ma* of course means *horse*.[1]

Ma Hung-kuei is governor of Ninghsia, and his cousin, Ma Hung-ping, former governor of the same province, is now ruler of a shifting fiefdom in northern Kansu. They are distantly related to Ma Pu-fang, many-wived son of the famous Mohammedan leader Ma Keh-chin. Ma Pu-fang inherited his father's toga and is now the Nanking-appointed Pacification Commissioner of that province, while his brother, Ma Pu-ching, helps out in Chinghai and in addition exploits the great Kansu panhandle which in the west separates Chinghai from Ninghsia. For a decade this distant country has been run like a medieval sultanate by the Ma family, with some assistance from an Allah of their own.

Two of the Great Horses claim to be nobles, descendants of a Mohammedan aristocracy which sometimes played a decisive rôle in the history of China's North-west, and, since something about that history is necessary background to an understanding of Chinese Mohammedans to-day, and especially of the Ma family itself—which is as numerous as the grasses of Ninghsia or the Smiths of the West—we may pause for a moment and briefly review it.

The brothers Ma, like most Moslems in China, have Turkish blood in them. As early as the sixth century a race which we now know as the Turks had become powerful enough on China's North-west frontier to make important demands on the monarchs

---

[1] It is an interesting character, written thus 馬, and deriving from an ancient form 馬 , in which one clearly sees its evolution from the original ideograph.

of the plains. In a couple of centuries they had built up an empire extending from eastern Siberia across part of Mongolia and into Central Asia. Gradually they filtered southward, and by the seventh century their Great Khan was received almost as an equal at the Court of Yang Ti, last Emperor of the Sui Dynasty. It was this same Turkish Khan who helped the half-Turkish General Li Yuan overthrow the Emperor Yang Ti and establish the celebrated T'ang Dynasty, which for three centuries reigned over Eastern Asia from Ch'ang An (now Sianfu)—then the most cultured capital on earth.

Mohammedan mosques had already been built in Canton by seafaring Arab traders before the middle of the seventh century. With the advent of the tolerant T'ang power the religion rapidly penetrated by land routes through the Turks of the North-west. Mullahs, traders, embassies, and warriors brought it from Persia, Arabia, and Turkestan, and the T'ang emperors formed close ties with the caliphates to the west. Especially in the ninth century, when vast hordes of Ouigour Turks (whose great leader Seljuk had not yet been born) were summoned to the aid of the T'ang Court to suppress rebellion, Islamism entrenched itself in China. Following their success, many of the Ouigours were rewarded with titles and great estates and settled in the North-west and in Szechuan and Yunnan.

Over a period of centuries the Mohammedans stoutly resisted Chinese absorption, but gradually lost their Turkish culture, adopted much that was Chinese, and became more or less submissive to Chinese law. Yet in the nineteenth century they were still powerful enough to make two great bids for power: one, in Yunnan, where Tu Wei-hsiu for a time set up a kingdom and proclaimed himself Sultan Suleiman; and the last, in 1864, when Mohammedans seized control of all the North-west and even invaded Hupeh. The latter rebellion was put down after a campaign lasting eleven years. At that time of waning Manchu power the able Chinese General Tso Chung-t'ang astounded the world by recapturing Hupeh, Shensi, Kansu, and eastern Tibet, finally leading his victorious army across the desert roads of Turkestan, where he re-established Chinese power on that far frontier in Central Asia.

Since then no single leader has been able to unite the Moslems of China in a successful struggle for independence, but there have been sporadic uprisings against Chinese rule, with savage and bloody massacres on both sides. The most serious recent rebellion occurred in 1928, when General Feng Yü-hsiang was warlord of the North-west. It was under Feng that the Wu-Ma, or " Five Ma,"[1] combination acquired much of its influence and secured the nucleus of its present wealth and power.

Although theoretically the Chinese consider the Hui or Moslem people one of the five great races[2] of China, most Chinese seem to deny Moslem racial separateness, claiming that they have been Sinicized. In practice, Nanking decidedly follows out a policy of absorption, even more direct (though perhaps less successful) than that pursued toward the Mongolians. The Chinese official attitude toward the Mohammedans seems to be that they are a " religious minority " but not a " national minority." However, it is quite evident to anyone who sees them in their own domain in the North-west that their claims to racial unity and the right to nationhood as a people are not without substantial basis in fact and history.

The Mohammedans of China are said to number about 20,000,000, and of these at least half are now concentrated in the provinces of Shensi, Kansu, Ninghsia, Szechuan, and Sinkiang. In many districts—particularly in Kansu and Chinghai— they are a majority, and in some very big areas they outnumber the Chinese as much as ten to one. Generally their religious orthodoxy seems to vary according to their strength of numbers in a given spot, but in the dominantly Mohammedan region of northern Kansu and southern Ninghsia the atmosphere is distinctly that of an Islamic country.

It may, in fact, be said that the Mohammedans are the largest people left in China among whom priest and bishop are the real arbiters of temporal as well as spiritual life, with religion a deciding factor in their culture, politics, and economy. Mohammedan society revolves around the *men-huang* and the *ahun* (ameer and mullah), and their knowledge of the Koran and of

---

[1] Ma Chung-ying was the fifth Ma, but has now been eliminated from an active rôle by tribal politics and international intrigue. Sven Hedin gives an interesting account of him in *Flight of the Big Horse*.

[2] These are the Han (Chinese), Man (Manchu), Mêng (Mongol), Hui (Mohammedan), and Tsang (Tibetan).

Lc

Turkish or Arabic (scant as it usually is) are the mechanisms of magic and authority. Mohammedans in the North-west pray daily in the hundreds of well-kept mosques, observe Mohammedan feast days, fast days, and marriage and funeral ceremonies, reject pork, and are offended by the presence of pigs or dogs. The pilgrimage to Mecca is an ambition of all, and is frequently realized by rich men and *ahuns*, who thereby strengthen their political and economic power. To most of them Turkey, not China, seems to be still the fatherland, and pan-Islamism rather than pan-Hanism the ideal.

Chinese influence is nevertheless very marked. Moslems dress like Chinese (except for round white caps or ceremonial fezes worn by the men and white turbans by the women), all speak Chinese as the language of daily life (although many know a few words from the Koran), and, while markedly Turkish features are not infrequent among them, the physiognomy of the majority is hardly distinguishable from the Chinese, with whom they have for centuries intermarried. Owing to their law that any Chinese who marries a Mohammedan must not only adopt the faith, but also be adopted into a Mohammedan family, cutting away from his or her own kinsmen, the children of these mixed marriages tend to grow up regarding themselves as a species quite different from their Chinese relatives.

To-day the struggle of three sects among the Chinese Moslems somewhat weakens their unity, and creates a convenient alignment for the Chinese Communists to work among them. The three sects are simply the Old, New, and Modern[1] schools. Old and New recently formed a kind of " united front " of their own to oppose the heretical Modern school. The latter nominally advocates giving up many of the ceremonies and customs of Mohammedanism and embracing " science," but its real objectives are evidently to destroy the temporal power of the clergy, which the Mas find inconvenient, and, since it is supported by the Kuomintang, many Mohammedans believe its aim to be the unwelcome doctrine of so-called " pan-Hanism "—absorption of the national minorities by the Chinese. In the North-west the Four Mas are leaders of this Modern school, and around them have grouped their own satellites, bureaucrats, and the

[1] *Hsin-hsin chiao*, literally, " New-new faith."

wealthy landowners and cattle barons upon whom their régime depends. And yet the Great Horses are not precisely the men you would expect to lead a reform movement in religion.

For example, consider Ma Hung-kuei, probably the richest and strongest of the quartet. He has numerous wives, is said to own about 60 per cent of the property of Ninghsia city, and has made a fortune of millions from opium, salt, furs, taxes, and his own paper currency. Still, he proved himself modern enough in one sense when recently he chose a new " picture bride." Importing a secretary from Shanghai, he had him gather photographs of eligible educated beauties, and made his choice. The price was fixed at $50,000. Old Ma hired an aeroplane, flew out of the northern dust-clouds to Soochow, where he swooped up the latest addition to his harem—a graduate of Soochow Christian University—and then swept back again to Ninghsia like an Aladdin on his carpet, amid a blaze of publicity.

But although this may seem charming enough to an Occidental, it is doubtful whether either Ma Hung-kuei's peasants or soldiers fully appreciated the romance of it all, for the peasants knew where the $50,000 came from, and the soldiers wondered why, if the Great Horse had money to pay for a Christian bride, he could not pay them wages. When, a few months later, the Reds began their westward drive into Ma's territory in southern Ninghsia and northern Kansu, it was perhaps not entirely surprising that his troops—which he had boasted would annihilate the " bandits "—put up little fight. There were reasons.

Here I shall not become involved in tables of statistics, but it is worth referring to a significant article in the Government bulletin of Ninghsia,[1] which lists the levies collected in that province by General Ma. They include the following taxes: sales, domestic animals, camels, salt-carrying, salt-consumption, opium-lamps, sheep, merchants, porters, pigeons, land, middlemen, food, special food, additional land, wood, coal, skins, slaughter, boats, irrigation, millstones, houses, wood, milling, scales, ceremonies, tobacco, wine, stamp, marriage, and vegetables. This does not exhaust the inventory of petty taxes collected, but it is enough to suggest that people might have comparatively little to fear from the Reds.

[1] *Ninghsia Kung Pao* (December 1934, Ninghsia City).

Ma Hung-kuei's method of salt-distribution was unique. Salt was not only a monopoly, but every person was required to buy half a pound per month, whether he could consume it or not. He was not allowed to resell; private trade in salt was punishable by whipping, or even death. Other measures against which the inhabitants protested were the collection of a 30 per cent tax on the sale of a sheep, cow, or mule, a 25-cent tax on the ownership of a sheep, a dollar tax for the slaughter of a pig, and 40 cents tax on the sale of a bushel of wheat.

But probably the most fiercely resented measure was General Ma's conscription. He had a total of about 40,000 troops (with Ma Hung-ping's), and an indefinite number of " gate guards," who policed the many walled towns and cities. Nearly all were conscripts. Every family with sons had to contribute, or hire a substitute, at a cost which had risen to about $150. The poor could borrow the sum—at rates from 40 per cent to 60 per cent annually—from a pawnshop usually owned by one of the Mas. Not only did the soldiers get no pay; they had to furnish their own food and clothing. Ma was evidently wasting no money, except on brides.

Excessive taxation and indebtedness had forced many farmers to sell all their cattle and abandon their lands. Great areas had been bought over by officials, tax-collectors, and lenders at very cheap rates, but much of it remained wasteland, because no tenants could be found to work under the tax-burden and rents imposed. An acceleration in the concentration of land, cattle, and capital was taking place, and a big increase in hired farm labourers. In one district[1] investigated it was found that over 70 per cent of the farmers were in debt, and about 60 per cent were living on food bought on credit. In the same district 5 per cent of the people owned from 100 to 200 *mou* of land, 20 to 50 camels, 20 to 40 cows, 5 to 10 horses, 5 to 10 carts, and had from $1,000 to $2,000 in trading capital, while at the same time about 60 per cent of the population had less than 15 *mou* of land, no livestock other than one or two donkeys, and an average indebtedness of $35 and 366 pounds of grain—much more than the average value of their land.

[1] " A Survey of Yuwang Hsien," by Liu Hsiao, *Tang-ti Kung-Tso* (August 3, 1936, Pao An).

Finally, it was suspected that Ma Hung-kuei was intriguing for support from the Japanese against the Reds. A Japanese military mission had been established in Ninghsia City, and General Ma had given them permission to build an aerodrome north of the city, in the Alashan Mongol territory. Some of the Moslems and Mongols feared an actual armed Japanese invasion.

Had the picture been otherwise when the Reds arrived, it is doubtful if they would have made much headway with the Mohammedans. Ma's troops, however, had little interest in fighting, and only that 5 per cent of the people had much at stake in resistance. But it still remained for the Communists to overcome the Moslems' natural aversion to co-operating with Chinese, and to offer them a suitable programme. This the Reds were trying hard to do, for the strategic significance of the Mo-. hammedan areas was manifest. They occupied a wide belt in the North-west which dominated the roads to Sinkiang and Outer Mongolia—and direct contact with Soviet Russia. As the Communists themselves saw it then:

" There are more than ten million Mohammedans in the North-west occupying an extremely important position. Our present mission and responsibility is to defend the North-west and to create an anti-Japanese base in these five provinces, so that we can more powerfully lead the anti-Japanese movement of the whole country and work for an immediate war against Japan. At the same time, in the development of our situation we can get into connection with the Soviet Union and Outer Mongolia. However, it would be impossible to carry out our mission if we failed to win over the Mohammedans to our sphere and to the anti-Japanese front."[1]

Communist work among the Mohammedans began several years ago in the North-west. Early in 1936, when the Red Army moved across Ninghsia and Kansu toward the Yellow River, vanguards of young Moslems were already propagandizing among the Ninghsia troops, urging the overthrow of the " Kuomintang running-dog " and " traitor to Mohammedanism," Ma Hung-kuei—and some of them losing their heads for it. These are the main promises which the Reds made to them:

[1] *Company Discussion Materials*: " The Mohammedan Problem," p. 2, 1st Army Corps, Pol. Dept., June 2, 1936.

To abolish all sur-taxes.

To help form an autonomous Mohammedan Government.

To prohibit conscription.

To cancel old debts and loans.

To protect Mohammedan culture.

To guarantee religious freedom of all sects.

To help create and arm an anti-Japanese Mohammedan army.

To help unite the Mohammedans of China, Outer Mongolia, Sinkiang, and Soviet Russia.

Here was something to appeal to nearly every Moslem. Even some of the *ahuns* saw in it an opportunity to get rid of Ma Hung-kuei (punishing him for burning the mosques of the Old and New schools), and also a chance to realize an old aspiration—to re-establish direct contact with Turkey through Central Asia. By May the Communists were claiming that they had achieved what sceptics had said was impossible. They boasted that they had created the nucleus of a Chinese Moslem Red Army.

4

Moslem and Marxist

ONE morning I went with an English-speaking member of Hsü Hai-tung's staff to visit the Moslem training regiment attached to the 15th Army Corps. It was quartered in the compound of a Moslem merchant and official—a thick-walled edifice with Moorish windows looking down on a cobbled street through which filed donkeys, horses, camels, and men.

Inside, the place was cool and neatly kept. Every room had in the centre of its brick floor a place for a cistern, connected to a subterranean drain, to be used for bathing. Properly orthodox Moslems shower themselves five times daily, but, although these soldiers were still loyal to their faith and obviously made use of the cistern occasionally, I gathered that they did not believe in carrying a good thing to extremes. Still, they easily had the cleanest habits of any soldiers I had seen in China, and carefully refrained from the national gesture of spitting on the floor.

The Reds had organized two training regiments of Mohammedans at the front, both recruited largely from former troops of Ma Hung-kuei and Ma Hung-ping. They were taller and more strongly built than the Chinese, heavier of beard, and darker-skinned, some of them very handsome in a distinctly Turkish way, with large black almond-shaped eyes and strong sharp Caucasian features. They all carried the big sword of the North-west, and gave a skilful demonstration of various strokes by which you can remove at one swift blow your enemy's head.

Cartoons, posters, maps, and slogans covered the walls of their barracks. " Down with Ma Hung-kuei ! " " Abolish Ma Hung-kuei's Kuomintang Government ! " " Oppose Japan's building of aerodromes, map-making, and invasion of Ninghsia ! " " Realize the independent Government of the Mohammedan people ! " " Build our own anti-Japanese Mohammedan Red Army ! " Such were the exhortations which had attracted what Moslem following the Communists had, and answers given to me by Moslem soldiers concerning their reasons for joining the Reds centred on them as main issues.

From this it may be gathered that there was some dissatisfaction with General Ma Hung-kuei among his soldiers (no doubt somewhat exaggerated by the Reds), and this seemed to be shared by the Ninghsia peasants. I remember stopping on the road one morning to buy a melon from a Moslem farmer who had a whole hillside covered with them. He was an engaging old rustic with a jolly face, a humorous manner, and a really beautiful daughter—so rare an apparition in those parts that I stayed and bought three melons. I asked him if Ma Hung-kuei's officials were really as bad as the Reds claimed. He threw up his hands comically in indignation, spluttering water-melon seeds between his gums. " Ai-ya ! Ai-ya ! Ai-ya ! " he cried. " Ma Hung-kuei, Ma Hung-kuei ! Taxing us to death, stealing our sons, burning and killing ! *Ma-ti Ma Hung-kuei !* " By which last expression he meant you could defile his mother and it would be too good for him. Everyone in the courtyard laughed at the old man's agitation.

The Moslem soldiers with the Reds had originally been won over by subversive propaganda conducted among Ma's troops, and by political lectures when they reached the Red camp. I asked one commander why he had joined.

" In order to fight Ma Hung-kuei," he said. " Life is too bitter for us *Hui-min* under Ma Hung-kuei. No family is secure. If a family has two sons, one of them must join his army. If it has three sons, two must join. There is no escape—unless you are rich and can pay the tax for a substitute. What poor man can afford it ? Not only that, but every man must bring his own clothes, and his family must pay for his food, fires, and lighting. This costs several tens of dollars a year."

Although these Red Moslem regiments had been organized less than half a year, they had already achieved considerable " class consciousness," it seemed. They had read, or heard read, the *Communist Manifesto*, brief lessons from *Class Struggle*, and daily political lectures, *à la* Marxism, on the immediate problems of the Mohammedan people. This instruction was given to them, not by Chinese, but by Mohammedan members of the Communist Party—men who had been through the Reds' Party school. Over 90 per cent of Ma Hung-kuei's troops were quite illiterate, and most of the Moslem recruits to the Red Army had been unable to read at all when they joined, but they now knew a few hundred characters each, and could study the simple lessons given to them. Out of their two training regiments the Communists hoped to develop cadres for a big Moslem Red Army, to defend the autonomous Moslem republic they dreamed of seeing established in the North-west. Already nearly 25 per cent of these Moslems had joined the Communist Party.

With the autonomy slogan the Moslem population was naturally in sympathy, for this has been their demand for many years. Whether the majority of them believed the Reds were sincere in their promises is quite another matter. I doubted it. Years of maltreatment by the Chinese militarists, and racial hatreds between Han and Hui (Chinese and Moslem), had left among them a deep and justified distrust of the motives of all Chinese, and it was unbelievable that the Communists had been able to break down this Moslem scepticism in so short a time.

Such Moslems as co-operated with the Reds probably had reasons of their own. If Chinese offered to help them drive out the Kuomintang, help them create and equip an army of their own, help them get self-government, and help them despoil the rich (they no doubt said to themselves), they were prepared to take the opportunity—and later on turn that army to uses of their own, if the Reds failed to keep their bargain. But it was apparent from the friendliness of the farmers, and their readiness to organize under the Reds, that their programme had a distinct attraction, and that their careful policy of respecting Moslem institutions had made an impression on even the most suspicious peasants and *ahuns*.

Among the soldiers themselves it appeared that some of the historic racial animosity was being overcome, or gradually metamorphosed into class antagonism. Thus, when I asked some Moslem soldiers whether they thought the Hui and Han peoples could co-operate under a Soviet form of government, one replied:

" The Chinese and the Moslems are brothers; we Moslems also have Chinese blood in us; we all belong to Ta Chung Kuo [China], and therefore why should we fight each other ? Our common enemies are the landlords, the capitalists, the money-lenders, our oppressive rulers, and the Japanese. Our common aim is revolution."

" But what if the revolution interferes with your religion ? "

" There is no interference. The Red Army does not interfere with Mohammedan worship."

" Well, I mean something like this. Some of the *ahuns* [priests] are wealthy landlords and moneylenders, are they not ? What if they oppose the Red Army ? How would you treat them ? "

" We would persuade them to join the revolution. But most *ahuns* are not rich men. They sympathize with us. One of our company commanders was an *ahun*."

" Still, suppose some *ahuns* can't be persuaded, but join with the Kuomintang to oppose you ? "

" We would punish them. They would be bad *ahuns*, and the people would demand their punishment."

Meanwhile intensive instruction was going on throughout the 1st and 15th Army Corps to educate the soldiers to an understanding of the Communist policy toward Moslems, and their effort to create a " Hui-Han United Front." I attended several political sessions in which soldiers were discussing the " Mohammedan revolution," and they were quite interesting. At one session there were long debates, especially about the land question. Some argued that the Red Army should confiscate the land of great Mohammedan landlords; others opposed it. The political commissar then gave a concise statement of the Party's position, explaining why it was necessary for the Mohammedans themselves to carry on their own land revolution, led by a strong revolutionary organization of their own, with a base in the Moslem masses.

Another company reviewed a brief history of relationships between the Moslems and Chinese, and another discussed the necessity for strict observance of the rules of conduct which had been issued to all soldiers stationed in Mohammedan districts. These latter decreed that Red soldiers must not: enter the home of a Moslem without his consent; molest a mosque or a priest in any way; say " pig " or " dog " before Moslems, or ask them why they don't eat pork; or call the Moslems " small faith " and the Chinese " big faith."

Besides these efforts to unite the whole army intelligently behind the Moslem policy of the Reds, there was incessant work with the peasantry. The two Moslem training regiments led in this propaganda, but companies in the Red Army also sent their propaganda corps from house to house, explaining Communist policies and urging the farmers to organize; the army dramatic clubs toured the villages, giving Mohammedan plays, based on local situations and incidents of history, and designed to " agitate " the population; leaflets, newspapers, and posters were distributed, written in Chinese and Arabic; and mass meetings were frequently called to form revolutionary committees and village Soviets. The peasant, Chinese or Moslem, had a hard squeeze of it to avoid indoctrination to at least some degree. It was certainly " a system "—but it seemed to be working. By July several dozen Mohammedan communities in Ninghsia had elected village Soviets, and were sending delegates to Yu Wang Pao to confer with the Moslem Communists there.

Four months later the Fourth Front Red Army was to cross the Yellow River, move over 200 miles farther west, and reach Hsuchow, in Ma Pu-fang's territory, astride the main road to Sinkiang, and their rapid advance was to be due to a large extent to good relations established at this early stage with the Moslem people. One of the most significant events in the development of that relationship occurred while I was in Ninghsia. Early in September enough progress had been made in Ninghsia to convene a meeting of over 300 Moslem delegates from Soviet committees elected by the villages then under the Red Army. A number of *ahuns*, teachers, merchants, and two or three small landlords were among them, but mostly they were poor farmers, members of the wealthier class having fled with the arrival of the " Han bandits." The meeting of delegates elected a chairman and a provisional Moslem Soviet Government Committee. They passed resolutions to co-operate with the Red Army and accept its offer to help create an anti-Japanese Mohammedan army, and to begin at once the organization of a Chinese-Moslem unity league, a poor people's league, and a mass anti-Japanese society.

Now, the last item of business attended to by this historic little convention—and I suspect the most important to the peasants there—was the disposal of a Kuomintang tax-collector. This man had evidently earned himself considerable enmity before the Reds arrived, and after that he had fled to a place called Changchia Cha, into some of the neighbouring hill villages, and there continued to collect his taxes. It was alleged that he had doubled his levies—and announced that this was due to the regulations of the new Red Government which he claimed to represent! But the Mohammedan farmers learned that the Reds appointed no tax-collectors, and half a dozen of them captured this miscreant and brought him into Yu Wang Pao for a mass trial. My personal reaction to the story was that any man who had sufficient nerve to act as an impostor in such a rôle at such a time had talents that should be preserved. The Moslems thought otherwise. There was no dissenting vote when the delegates took the decision to execute him.

But he was the only civilian shot during the two weeks I spent in Yu Wang Pao.

PART TEN

WAR AND PEACE

1

More about Horses

On August 29 I rode out to Hung Ch'eng Shui (Red City Waters), a pretty little town in Weichow county, famous for its beautiful fruit gardens of pears, apples, and grapes, irrigated by crystal springs that bubbled through the canals. Here part of the 73rd Division was encamped. Not far away was a fortified pass, and a temporary line with no trenches but with a series of small mole-like machine-gun nests, and round hilltop forts—low-walled earthwork defences—from which the Reds faced an enemy that had generally withdrawn from five to ten miles to the walled towns. There had been no movement on this front for several weeks, while the Reds rested and " consolidated " the new territory.

Back in Yuwang Hsien again, I found the troops celebrating with a melon feast the radio news from south Kansu that a whole division of Ma Hung-kuei's Chinese troops had turned over to Chu Teh's Fourth Front Red Army. Li Tsung-yi, the commander of this Kuomintang division, had been sent to impede Chu Teh's march to the north. His younger officers, among whom were secret Communists, led an uprising and took some 3,000 troops, including a battalion of cavalry, to join the Reds near Lung Hsi. It was a big blow to Nanking's defences in the south, and hastened the northward advance of the two southern armies.

Two days later two of the three divisions of Hsü Hai-tung's 15th Army Corps were prepared to move again, one column toward the south, to break open a path for Chu Teh, and the other to the west, and the valley of the Yellow River. Bugles began sounding at about three in the morning, and by six o'clock the troops were already marching. I was myself returning to Yu Wang Pao that morning with two Red officers who were reporting to Peng Teh-huai, and I left the city by the south gate with Hsü Hai-tung and his staff, marching toward the end of the long column of troops and animals that wound like a grey dragon across the interminable grasslands, as far as you could see.

The big army left the city quietly, except for the bark of bugles that never ceased, and gave an impression of efficient command. Plans for the march had been completed days ago, I was told; every detail of the road had been examined, the enemy's concentrations were all carefully charted on maps prepared by the Reds themselves, and guards had stopped all travellers from moving across the lines (which the Reds permit, to encourage trade, except during battles or troop movements), and now they went ahead unknown to the Kuomintang troops, as later surprise captures of enemy outposts were to prove.

With this army I saw no camp followers except thirty or more Kansu greyhounds, who ran in a closed pack, ranging back and forth across the plain in chase of an occasional distant gazelle or a prairie hog. They barked joyously and scrapped in excellent humour, evidently liking the idea of going to war. Many of the soldiers carried their pets along with them. Several had little wonks on leashes of string, one had a pet slate-coloured pigeon perched on his shoulder; some had little white mice, and some had rabbits. Was this an army? From the youth of the warriors, and the bursts of song that rang down the long line, it seemed more like a prep. school on a holiday excursion.

A few *li* beyond the city an order was suddenly given for a practice air-raid defence. Squads of soldiers left the road and melted into the tall grass, donning their big wide camouflage hats made of grass, and their grass shoulder-capes. Machine guns (they had no anti-aircraft) were pitched at angles on grassy knolls beside the road in hopeful anticipation of a low-flying target. In a few moments that whole dragon had simply been swallowed up on the landscape, and you could not distinguish men from the numerous clumps of bunch-grass. Only the mules, camels, and horses remained visible on the road, and aviators might have taken these for ordinary commercial caravans. The cavalry (which was then in the vanguard, out of sight) had to take it in the neck, however, their only possible precautionary measure being to seek cover if it was available, otherwise merely to scatter as widely as possible, but always remaining mounted. Unmounted during an air raid, these Mongolian ponies are impossible to manage, and a whole regiment can be thrown into complete disorder. The first command to a cavalry unit at the drone of aeroplanes is " *Shang ma !* " (" Mount horse ! ")

The manœuvre having been pronounced satisfactory, we marched on.

Li Chiang-lin had been right. The Reds' good horses were all at the front. Their cavalry division was the pride of the army, and every man aspired to promotion to it. They were physically the pick of the army, mounted on about 3,000 beautiful Ninghsia ponies, fine fleet animals taller and stronger than the Mongolian ponies you see in North China, with sleek flanks and well-filled buttocks. Most of them had been captured from Ma Hung-kuei and Ma Hung-ping, but three whole battalions of horses had been taken in a battle nearly a year before with General Ho Chu-kuo, commander of Nanking's 1st Cavalry Army, including one battalion of all-white animals and one of all-blacks. They were the nucleus of the 1st Red Cavalry.

People outside the Red districts had predicted, when the Reds went into Kansu and Ninghsia, that the Moslem cavalry would break them to pieces. Events had proved otherwise. In 1935 a school had been opened in Shensi, and the nucleus of a Red cavalry had been trained by the German adviser, Li Teh, an expert horseman who was once in the Red Russian cavalry. Shensi and Kansu natives are many of them born to the saddle —unlike most southerners, who cannot ride—and a crack corps was soon developed out of this local material. In 1936 they took the field and introduced a new mode of mounted warfare in the North-west.

The Moslems are superb horsemen, but they are not trained to fire from the saddle or to use sabres, nor is the Chinese cavalry. Their tactic is to ride swiftly in flank attacks co-ordinated with the infantry, and, if this fails to rout the enemy, they dismount and fire from the ground, thus losing their mobility. Li Teh trained the Red cavalry to use sabres, crude affairs made in the Red arsenal, but serving the purpose well enough. Red cavalrymen quickly became respected for their phalanx sabre charge, and in a brief period of a year had a short string of victories to their credit, and many new horses.

I rode with the Red cavalry several days in Kansu—or more correctly, I walked with it. They lent me a fine horse with a captured Western saddle, but at the end of each day I felt that I had been giving the horse a good time instead of the contrary. This was because our battalion commander was so anxious not to tire his four-legged charges that we two-legged ones had to lead horse three or four *li* for every one we rode. He treated his horses as if they had been Dionne quintuplets, and I concluded that any one who qualified for this man's cavalry had to be a nurse, not a *mafoo*, and an even better walker than rider. I paid them due respect for kindness to animals—no common phenomenon in China—but I was glad to disengage myself and get back to free-lance movement of my own, in which occasionally I could actually ride a horse.

I had been grumbling about this mildly to Hsü Hai-tung, and I suspect he decided to play a joke on me. To return to Yu Wang Pao he lent me a splendid Ninghsia pony, strong as a bull, that gave me one of the wildest rides of my life. My road parted with the 15th Army Corps near a big fort in the grassland. There I bade Hsü and his staff good-bye. Shortly afterwards I got on my borrowed steed, and from then on it was touch and go to see which of us reached Yu Wang Pao alive.

The road lay level across the plain for over fifty *li*. In that whole distance we got down to a walk just once. He raced at a steady gallop for the last five miles, and at the finish I swept up the main street of Yu Wang Pao with my companions trailing far behind. Before Peng's headquarters I slithered off and examined my mount, expecting him to topple over in a faint. He was puffing very slightly and had a few beads of sweat on him, but was otherwise quite unruffled, the beast.

The real trouble with the ride had been the wooden Chinese saddle. It was so narrow that I could not sit in the seat, but literally had to ride on my inner thighs the whole distance. The short, heavy iron stirrups had cramped my legs, which now felt like logs. All I wanted was rest and sleep—but I did not get it.

2

" *Little Red Devils* "

ONE morning I climbed the wide, thick, yellow wall of Yu Wang Pao, from the top of which you could look down thirty feet and see at a glance a score of different and somehow incongruously prosaic and intimate tasks being pursued below. It was as if you had prized off the lid of the city. A big section of the wall was being demolished, in fact, for this is one act of destruction the Reds do carry out. Walls are impediments to guerilla warriors like the Reds, who endeavour to come to battle with an enemy in open country, and if they fail there, they do not waste men in an exhausting defence of the walled city, where they can be endangered by blockade or annihilation, but withdraw and let the enemy put himself in that position if he likes. In any case, the broken wall simplifies their work if and when they are strong enough to attempt a reoccupation of the city.

Half-way round the crenellated battlement I came upon a squad of buglers—at rest for once, I was glad to observe, for their plangent calls had been ringing incessantly for days. They were all Young Vanguards, mere children, and I assumed a somewhat fatherly air toward one to whom I stopped and talked. He wore tennis shoes, grey shorts, and a faded grey cap with a dim red star on it. But there was nothing faded about the bugler under the cap: he was rosy-faced and had bright shining eyes, a lad toward whom your heart naturally warmed as toward a plucky waif in need of affection and a friend. How homesick he must be ! I thought. But I was soon disillusioned. He was no mama's boy, but already a veteran Red. He told me he was fifteen, and that he had joined the Reds in the South four years ago.

" Four years ! " I exclaimed incredulously. " Then you must have been only eleven when you became a Red ? And you made the Long March ? "

" Right," he responded with comical swagger. " I have been a *hung-chun* for four years."

" Why did you join ? " I asked.

" My family lived near Changchow, in Fukien. I used to cut wood in the mountains, and in the winter I went there to collect bark. I often heard the villagers talk about the Red Army. They said it helped the poor people, and I liked that. Our house was very poor. We were six people, my parents and three brothers, older than I. We owned no land. Rent ate more than half our crop, so we never had enough. In the winter we cooked bark for soup and saved our grain for planting in the spring. I was always hungry.

" One year the Reds came very close to Changchow. I climbed over the mountains and went to ask them to help our house because we were very poor. They were good to me. They sent me to school for a while, and I had plenty to eat. After a few months the Red Army captured Changchow, and went to my village. All the landlords and moneylenders and officials were driven out. My family was given land and did not have to pay the tax-collectors and landlords any more. They were happy and they were proud of me. Two of my brothers joined the Red Army."

" Where are they now ? "

" Now ? I don't know. When we left Kiangsi they were with the Red Army in Fukien; they were with Fang Chih-min. Now, I don't know."

" Did the peasants like the Red Army ? "

" Like the Red Army, eh ? Of course they liked it. The Red Army gave them land and drove away the landlords, the tax-collectors, and the exploiters." (These " little devils " all had their Marxist vocabulary !)

" But, really, how do you *know* they liked the Reds ? "

" They made us a thousand, ten thousands, of shoes, with their own hands. The women made uniforms for us, and the men spied on the enemy. Every home sent sons to our Red Army. That is how the *lao-pai-hsing* treated us ! "

No need to ask him whether *he* liked his comrades: no lad of thirteen would tramp 6,000 miles with an army he hated.

Scores of youngsters like him were with the Reds. The Young Vanguards were organized by the Communist Youth League, and altogether, according to the claims of Fang Wen-ping, secretary of the C.Y., there were some 40,000 in the North-west

Soviet districts. There must have been several hundred with the Red Army alone: a " model company " of them was in every Red encampment. They were youths between twelve and seventeen (really eleven to sixteen by foreign count), and they came from all over China. Many of them, like this little bugler, survived the hardships of the march from the South. Many joined the Red Army during its expedition to Shansi.

The Young Vanguards worked as orderlies, mess-boys, buglers, spies, radio-operators, water-carriers, propagandists, actors, *mafoos*, nurses, secretaries, and even teachers ! I once saw such a youngster, before a big map, lecturing a class of new recruits on world geography. Two of the most graceful child dancers I have ever seen were Young Vanguards in the dramatic society of the 1st Army Corps, and had marched from Kiangsi.

You might wonder how they stood such a life. Hundreds must have died or been killed. There were over 200 of them in the filthy jail in Sianfu, who had been captured doing espionage or propaganda, or as stragglers unable to keep up with the army on its march. But their fortitude was amazing, and their loyalty to the Red Army was the intense and unquestioning loyalty of the very young.

Most of them wore uniforms too big for them, with sleeves dangling to their knees and coats dragging nearly to the ground. They washed their hands and faces three times a day, they claimed, but they were always dirty, their noses were usually running, and they were often wiping them with a sleeve, and grinning. The world nevertheless was theirs: they had enough to eat, they had a blanket each, the leaders even had a pistol, and they wore red bars, and a broken-peaked cap a size or more too large, but with a red star on it. They were often of uncertain origin: many could not remember their parents, many were escaped apprentices, some had been slaves, most of them were runaways from huts with too many mouths to feed, and all of them had made their own decisions to join, sometimes a whole group of youngsters running off to the Reds together.

Many stories of courage were told of them. They gave and asked no quarter as children, and many had actually participated in battles. They say that in Kiangsi, after the main Red Army left, hundreds of Young Vanguards and Young

Communists fought with the partisans, and even made bayonet charges—so that the White soldiers laughingly said they could grab their bayonets and pull them into their trenches, they were so small and light. Many of the captured " Reds " in Chiang's reform schools for bandits in Kiangsi were youths from ten to fifteen years old.

Perhaps the Vanguards liked the Reds because among them they were treated like human beings probably for the first time. They ate and lived like men; they seemed to take part in everything; they considered themselves any man's equal. I never saw one of them struck or bullied. They were certainly " exploited " as orderlies and mess-boys (and it was surprising how many orders starting at the top were eventually passed on to some Young Vanguard), but they had their own freedom of activity, too, and their own organization to protect them. They learned games and sports, they were given a crude schooling, and they acquired a faith in simple Marxist slogans—which in most cases meant to them simply helping to shoot a gun against the landlords and masters of apprentices. Obviously it was better than working fourteen hours a day at the master's bench, and feeding him, and emptying his " defile-mother " night-bowl !

I remember one such escaped apprentice I met in Kansu who was nicknamed the Shansi Wa-wa—the Shansi Baby. He had been sold to a shop in a town near Hung T'ung, in Shansi, and when the Red Army came he had stolen over the city wall, with three other apprentices, to join it. How he had decided that he belonged with the Reds I do not know, but evidently all of Yen Hsi-shan's anti-Communist propaganda, all the warnings of his elders, had produced exactly the opposite effect from that intended. He was a fat roly-poly lad with the face of a baby, and only twelve, but he was quite able to take care of himself, as he had proved during the march across Shansi and Shensi and into Kansu. When I asked him why he had become a Red he said: " The Red Army fights for the poor. The Red Army is anti-Japanese. Why should any man not want to become a Red soldier ? "

Another time I met a bony youngster of fifteen, who was head of the Young Vanguards and Young Communists working in the hospital near Holienwan, Kansu. His home had been in Hsin

Kuo, the Reds' model *hsien* in Kiangsi, and he said that one of
his brothers was still in a partisan army there, and that his sister
had been a nurse. He did not know what had become of his
family. Yes, they all liked the Reds. Why? Because they " all
understood that the Red Army was our army—fighting for the
wu-ch'an chieh-chi "—the proletariat. I wondered what impressions the great trek to the North-west had left upon his young
mind, but I was not to find out. The whole thing was a minor
event to this serious-minded boy, a little matter of a hike over
a distance about twice the width of America.

" It was pretty bitter going, eh? " I ventured.

" Not bitter, not bitter. No march is bitter if your comrades
are with you. We revolutionary youths can't think about
whether a thing is hard or bitter; we can only think of the task
before us. If it is to walk 10,000 *li*, we walk it, or if it is to walk
20,000 *li*, we walk it! '"

" How do you like Kansu, then? Is it better or worse than
Kiangsi? Was life better in the South? "

" Kiangsi was good. Kansu is also good. Wherever the revolution is that place is good. What we eat and where we sleep is not
important. What is important is the revolution."

Copy-book replies, I thought. Here was one lad who had
learned his answers well from some Red propagandist. Next day
I was quite surprised when at a mass meeting of Red soldiers I
saw that he was one of the principal speakers, and a " propagandist " in his own right. He was one of the best speakers in the
army, I was told, and in that meeting he gave a simple but
competent explanation of the present political situation, and the
reasons why the Red Army wanted to stop civil war and form a
" united front " with all anti-Japanese armies.

I met a youth of fourteen who had been an apprentice in a
Shanghai machine-shop, and with three companions had found
his way, through various adventures, to the North-west. He was
a student in the radio school in Pao An when I saw him. I asked
whether he missed Shanghai, but he said no, he had left nothing
in Shanghai, and that the only fun he had ever had there was
looking into the shop-windows at good things to eat—which of
course he could not buy.

But best of all I liked the " little devil " in Pao An, who served as orderly to Li Ko-nung, chief of the communications department of the Foreign Office. This *hsiao-kuei* was a Shansi lad of about thirteen or fourteen, and he had joined the Reds I know not how. He was the Beau Brummell of the Vanguards, and he took his rôle with utmost gravity. He had inherited a Sam Browne belt from somebody, he had a neat little uniform tailored to a good fit, and a cap whose peak he regularly refilled with new cardboard whenever it broke. Underneath the collar of his well-brushed coat he always managed to have a strip of white linen showing. He was easily the snappiest-looking soldier in town. Beside him Mao Tse-tung looked a tramp.

But this *wa-wa's* name happened by some thoughtlessness of his parents to be Shang Chi-pang. There is nothing wrong with that, except that Chi-pang sounds very much like *chi-pa*, and so, to his unending mortification, he was often called *chi-pa*, which simply means " penis." One day Chi-pang came into my little room in the Foreign Office with his usual quota of dignity, clicked his heels together, gave me the most Prussian-like salute I had seen in the Red districts, and addressed me as " Comrade Snow." He then proceeded to unburden his small heart of certain apprehensions. What he wanted to do was to make it perfectly clear to me that his name was not Chi-pa, but Chi-pang, and that between these two there was all the difference in the world. He had his name carefully scrawled down on a scrap of paper, and this he deposited before me.

Astonished, I responded in all seriousness that I had never called him anything but Chi-pang, and had no thought of doing otherwise. I half expected him to offer me the choice of swords or pistols.

But he thanked me, made a grave bow, and once more gave that preposterous salute. " I wanted to be sure," he said, " that when you write about me for the foreign papers you won't make a mistake in my name. It would give a bad impression to the foreign comrades if they thought a Red soldier was named Chi-pa ! " Until then I had had no notion of introducing Chi-pang into this strange book, but with that remark I had no choice in the matter, and he walked into it right beside the Generalissimo, the dignity of history notwithstanding.

One of the duties of the Young Vanguards in the Soviets was

to examine travellers on roads behind the front, and see that they
had their road passes. They executed this duty quite determin-
edly, and marched anyone without his papers to the local Soviet
for examination. Peng Teh-huai told me of being stopped once
and being asked for his *lu-t'iao* by some Young Vanguards, who
threatened to arrest him.

" But I am Peng Teh-huai," he said. " I write those passes
myself."

" We don't care if you are Commander Chu Teh," said the
young sceptics; " you must have a road pass." They signalled
for assistance, and several boys came running from the fields to
reinforce them.

Peng had to write out his *lu-t'iao* and sign it himself before
they allowed him to proceed.

Altogether, as you may have gathered, the " little devils "
were one thing in Red China with which it was hard to find anything seriously wrong. Their spirit was superb. I suspect that
more than once an older man, looking at them, forgot his
pessimism and was heartened to think that he was fighting for
the future of lads like those. They were invariably cheerful and
optimistic, and they had a ready " *hao !* " for every how-are-
you, regardless of the weariness of the day's march. They were
patient, hard-working, bright, and eager to learn, and seeing
them made you feel that China was not hopeless, that no nation
was more hopeless than its youth. Here in the Vanguards was the
future of China, if only this youth could be freed, shaped, made
aware, and given a rôle to perform in the building of a new
world. It sounds somewhat evangelical, I suppose, but nobody
could see these heroic young lives without feeling that man in
China is not born rotten, but with infinite possibilities of
personality.

3

United Front in Action

IN the beginning of September 1936, while I was at the front in Ninghsia and Kansu, the army under Peng Teh-huai commenced moving westward toward the Yellow River, and southward toward the Sian-Lanchow highway, to establish connections with Chu Teh's troops, coming up from the South—a manœuvre which was to be brilliantly concluded at the end of October, when the combined Red Armies occupied nearly all north Kansu above the Sian-Lanchow highway.

But having now decided to seek a compromise with the Kuomintang in an attempt to " coerce " the latter into resistance against Japan, the Reds were becoming every day more of a force of political propagandists and less of an army intent on seizing power by conquest. New instructions from the Party ordered the troops to observe " United Front tactics " in their future movements. And what were " United Front tactics " ? Perhaps a day-by-day diary account of the manœuvres of the army at this time best answers that question:

Pao Tou Shui, September 1. Leaving Yu Wang Pao, the headquarters of the First Front Army, walked for about forty *li*, Commander Peng Teh-huai joking with the muleteers and generally having a lark. Most of the region travelled was hilly and mountainous. Peng made his headquarters for the night in a Mohammedan peasant's home in this little village.

Maps immediately were put up on the wall and the radio began functioning. Messages came in. While Peng was resting, he called in the Mohammedan peasants, and explained the Red Army's policies to them. An old lady sat and talked with him for nearly two hours, pouring out her troubles. Meanwhile a Red Army harvesting brigade passed by, on its way to reap the crop of a landlord who had run away, thus making his land subject to confiscation as a " traitor." Another squad of men has been appointed to guard and keep clean the premises of the local mosque. Relations with the peasants seem good. A week ago the peasants in this *hsien*, who have now lived under the Reds for several months without paying taxes, came in a delegation to present Peng with six cartloads of grain and provisions as an expression of gratitude for the relief. Yesterday some peasants presented Peng with a handsome wooden bed—which amused him very much. He turned it over to the local *ahun*.

Li Chou K'ou, September 2. On the road at four a.m. Peng up long before. Met ten peasants, who had come with the army from Yu Wang Pao to help carry the wounded back to the hospital. They voluntarily asked to do this in order to fight Ma Hungkuei, hated because he'd forced their sons to join the army. A Nanking bomber flew overhead, spotted us, and we scattered for cover. The whole army melted into the landscape. The plane circled twice and dropped one bomb—" laid an iron egg," or " dropped some bird-dung," as the Reds say—then strafed the horses and flew on to bomb our vanguard. One soldier, slow in taking cover, was wounded in the leg—a slight injury— and after it was dressed he walked without assistance.

From this village, where we are spending the night, very little can be seen. One regiment of the enemy is holding a fort near here, a 15th Army Corps detachment attacking.

From Yu Wang Pao comes a radio message reporting the visit of enemy bombers, which attacked the city and dropped ten bombs this morning. Some peasants were killed and wounded; no soldiers hit.

Tiao Pao Tzu, September 8. Left Li Chi K'ou, and on the way many peasants came out and brought the soldiers *pai ch'a* (white tea)—i.e. hot water, the favourite beverage in these parts. Mohammedan schoolteachers came over to bid Peng good-bye and thank him for protecting the school. As we neared Tiao Pao Tzu (now over 100 *li* west of Yu Wang Pao) some of Ma Hung-kuei's cavalry, withdrawing from an isolated position, ran into our rear. They were only a few hundred yards from us. Nieh (chief-of-staff) sent a detachment of headquarters cavalry to chase them, and they galloped off in a whirl of dust. A Red pack-train was attacked, and another detachment of soldiers was sent to recover the mules and loads. The caravan returned intact.

To-night some interesting items of news were posted on the bulletin board. Li Wang Pao is now surrounded, and in a fort near there a trench-mortar shell fell almost directly on Hsü

Hai-tung's headquarters. One young Vanguard was killed and three soldiers were wounded. In another place near by a White platoon commander, reconnoitring the Reds' position, was captured by a surprise attack party. The Reds slightly wounded him and sent him back to headquarters. Peng raised hell over the radio because he was wounded. " Not good United Front tactics," he commented. " One slogan is worth ten bullets." He lectured the staff on the United Front and how to work it out in practice.

Peasants sold fruit and melons on the road, the Reds paying for everything they bought. One young soldier traded his pet rabbit for three melons in a long transaction with a peasant. After he'd eaten the melons he was very dour, wanting his rabbit back !

A report by phone said that a regiment of enemy had been surrounded by part of the 2nd Division (1st Army Corps). Shouts of welcome, friendly slogans, and bugle calls were used as " greetings " to the enemy. The Reds sent them 200 sheep because they had no food, and with the sheep went a letter explaining Red Army policies. The Whites promised to reply that afternoon. In their letter the Reds proposed the programme of a United Front, peace between them, and agreed not to fire if they withdrew. At two o'clock these troops (some of Ma Hung-kuei's men) retreated. " This is a successful step in the United Front struggle," Peng remarked jubilantly. Some Reds did after all fire on them, but these seem to have been a few " individualists." They could not see why they should let all those arms out of their hands. For this they were severely reprimanded and given more lectures on the United Front. Some soldiers could not understand, and wanted to capture the Whites, but they were prevented from doing this. Here the Reds could have captured a cavalry detachment also, but were ordered not to do so.

This tendency of the rank and file to oppose the United Front programme was discussed by Peng and the political department to-night. It is realized that " more educational work must be done."

Another item: at Ma Liang Wu one group of the enemy came over to the Red lines to attend an anti-Japanese mass meeting.

They left their rifles behind, and at the invitation of the Reds came to listen to lectures, accompanied by their regimental commander. He said, " So far as these Japanese are concerned, we are ready to fight them. Just tell us how." He told the Reds that his regiment and all Ma Hung-kuei's regiments, both Chinese and Moslem, had at least three Fascist (Blueshirt) spies each, and hence must co-operate secretly.

Hsü Hai-tung rode over on his big mule for a conference with Peng and Tso Chuan (commander of the 1st Army Corps). Afterwards he told a story of one of the 15th Army Corps' " little devils," a dispatch-bearer on the front. He was given some messages to carry, and on the way he had to circle round a *pao* (fort) held by the enemy. Instead of taking the mountain path, he deliberately took the main road that led right in front of the enemy guns on the fort. As soon as they saw him the Whites sent out a squad of cavalry to pursue him, but he had a fast horse and rode bareback, and he left them far behind. " He always does this," Hsü complained, " but he is the best dispatch-rider on the front."

To-day's news was celebrated by Peng Teh-huai with a large water-melon feast: the melons here are cheap and excellent.

Tiao Pao Tzu, September 4-5. Liu Hsiao (of the political department) is now working among the Mohammedans near Li Wang Pao. To-day he sent a report of some recent developments there. One of Ma's regiments asked to have a Mohammedan sent from the Red Moslem regiment to talk to them. Ma's regimental commander refused to meet the Red delegate, but permitted him to talk to his men.

Wang (this Red Moslem delegate) returned and reported that he had seen Red handbills all over the troops' quarters. He said that after talking to the troops for a few hours they became more and more interested, and finally the commander listened in, too, but, getting worried, decided to have him arrested. The men protested, and he was safely escorted back to the Red lines. The regiment sent a letter in reply to the one which Wang had carried to them from Liu Hsiao. They said they would not retreat because they had been ordered to hold this district, and must do so; that they were ready to make an agreement to fight Japan, but the Reds should negotiate with their division commander; that if the Reds would not fight them, they would not fight the Reds; and that letters and pamphlets sent by the Reds had been distributed among the men.

Two planes bombed a Red cavalry detachment near here to-day. No men nor horses were hit, but one bomb struck a corner of a village mosque, and three old Moslem attendants were killed. This doesn't increase local affection for Nanking.

Tiao Pao Tzu, September 6. A day of rest and recreation. All commanders of the 1st Army Corps met at Peng's head-quarters for a melon feast, while the soldiers rested and had sports and a melon feast of their own. Peng called a meeting of all company commanders and higher, and there was a political session. They permitted me to attend. A summary of Peng's speech follows:

" Reasons for our movement to these districts are first to enlarge and develop our Soviet districts, secondly to co-operate with movement and advance of the Second and Fourth Front Armies (in south Kansu), thirdly to liquidate the influence of Ma Hung-kuei and Ma Hung-ping in these regions and form a United Front directly with their troops.

" We must enlarge the basis of the United Front here. We must decisively influence those White commanders who are now sympathetic and win them over definitely to our side. We have good contacts with many of them now; we must continue our work, by letter, in our Press, through delegates, through the secret societies, etc.

" We must liberate the Mohammedan masses here as quickly as possible, arming them as soon as they have been organized, and have formed their own representative Government, and thus develop at an early stage an anti-Japanese Moslem army.

" We must intensify our educational work among our own troops. In several recent instances our men have violated the United Front policy by firing on troops that we had agreed to permit to withdraw. In other instances men were reluctant to return captured rifles and had to be ordered several times to do so. This is not a breach of discipline, but a lack of confidence in their commanders' orders, showing that the men do not fully understand the reasons for such actions, some men actually accusing their leaders of ' counter-revolutionary orders.' One company commander received a letter from a White commander and did not even read it, but tore it up, saying, ' They are all the same, these Whites.' This shows that we must more deeply instruct the rank and file; our first lectures have not made their position clear to them. We must ask for their criticism and make such modifications in our policy as they think necessary after thorough discussion and explanation. We must impress upon them that the United Front policy is no trick to fool the Whites, but that it is a basic policy and in line with the decisions of our Party.

" In Kiangsi, Chiang Kai-shek spread vile lies about us and our policies, and his blockade prevented us from giving any refutation to the Chinese people outside our areas. Now his Fascists are spreading lies about us here and attacking our anti-Japanese policy by comparing the resources of China and Japan. Chiang suppresses the truth, and he does not mention either that the Chinese anti-imperialist movement is not isolated, but has friends such as the Soviet Union and the Japanese proletariat itself. We must make the enemy troops understand clearly the basis of the anti-Japanese movement, and defeat these Fascist lies.

" After the East Attack (into Shansi) many of our comrades, coming here to Kansu and Ninghsia, felt discouraged because the contrast was so great compared with the response we received there. They felt depressed because of the poverty of the country here and the low level of political enthusiasm among the people. Don't be discouraged ! Work harder ! These people are also brothers, and will respond to the same treatment as other human beings. We must not miss a single opportunity to convince a White soldier or a Mohammedan peasant. We are not working hard enough.

" As for the masses, we must urge them to take the lead in every revolutionary action. We must not touch any Mohammedan landlord ourselves, but we must show the people clearly that they have the freedom to do so, that we will protect their mass organizations that do so, that this is their revolutionary right, that it is the product of their labour and belongs to them. We must intensify our efforts to raise the political consciousness of the masses. Remember that they have heretofore had no political consciousness except racial hatred. We must awaken a patriotic conciousness in them. We must deepen our work in the Kê Lao Hui and other secret societies and make them active, not merely passive, allies on the anti-Japanese front. We must consolidate our good relations with the *ahuns* and urge them to take places of leadership in the anti-Japanese movement. We must strengthen the basis of revolutionary power by organizing every Mohammedan youth."

Peng's statement was followed by long critical comments from the political commissars of the 1st and the 15th Army Corps. Both of them reviewed their efforts in " United Front educational work " and suggested improvements. All commanders took copious notes, and afterwards there was a session of long debate and argument which lasted till dinner. Peng moved that the two army corps be enlarged by 500 new enlistments each, and this was seconded and passed unanimously.

After dinner there was a new play by the dramatic club of the 1st Army Corps, based on experiences of the past week. It portrayed in an amusing way the mistakes of the commanders and men in carrying out the new policy. One scene showed an argument between a commander and a warrior; another between two commanders; a third showed a company commander tearing up a letter he had received from the Whites.

In the second act most of these mistakes were shown corrected and the Red Army and anti-Japanese Moslem Army were marching together, and singing and fighting side by side against the Japanese and the Kuomintang. Seemed magically quick work by the education-through-entertainment department.

A report came in that there was a heavy bombardment of Li Wang Pao (held by Kuomintang troops) by Nanking planes. Evidently the pilots thought their troops had already withdrawn, because the Reds are all around the place. During the bombardment some Mohammedan soldiers ran outside the walls and hid in the caves in the mountain, but the Reds did not fire on them. Peng said this often happened in Kiangsi, and sometimes whole towns and groups of *min-t'uan* or Nanking troops were destroyed by Chiang Kai-shek's own aeroplanes, whose pilots thought they were bombing Reds.

The vanguard has not yet reached Hai Yuan, but a few points of enemy defence are being cleared before proceeding farther. These positions are at Li Wang Pao and Mao Liang Wu. The whole Kuyuan valley and west to Kaiyuan are to be Sovietized first. The Reds are now moving into a wholly Mohammedan region, and will not be in thickly populated Chinese areas again until they reach the Yellow River valley, at Ching-yuan.

I am returning to Pao An to-morrow.

During the next month the attention of every Red in China was to be focused anxiously upon the series of manœuvres by which, for the first time in the history of the Soviets, all the main forces of the Red Army were eventually united and concentrated in a single great area. And here some illumination should be shed upon the leadership of this second great trek from the south—upon Chu Teh, commander-in-chief of the " All China " Red Army, who, after a heart-breaking winter spent on the frozen marches of Tibet, was now pouring the Second and Fourth Front Armies into the North-west in a drive of unexpected vigour and success.

Mc

4

Concerning Chu Teh

UNLIKE Shakespeare, Confucius held that names were of first importance. In Chu Teh, at least, there is much. It is a strong-sounding name which should really be spelled Ju Deh in English, for so it is pronounced. But it is an appropriate name, because by a strange accident of language these two characters in Chinese mean " Red Virtue," although for the fond parents who yclept him thus when he was born in far-away Ni Lung, Szechuan, it was impossible to foresee the political meaning which that name later on was to acquire. Impossible, or they would surely have changed it in terror.

Now the remarkable thing about Chu Teh as a study in character development is not that he " gave many years of his life to heavy exhausting labour as a coolie," and rose from this lowly status to champion the oppressed, as an inaccurate account of him in a Comintern publication[1] declares, but, on the contrary, the uniqueness of his career is this: that this scion of a family of landlords, rising to power and luxury and dissipation while still young, was nevertheless able, when past middle age, to discard the degenerate environment of his youth, to break, by a superb act of human will, a life-long addiction to narcotics, and finally even to forsake his family, and devote his entire fortune to a revolutionary ideal which he believed to animate the highest cause and purpose of his time. For the success of this mission which had seized, shaken, and remade his character he staked a head which came to be valued at $250,000 by his infuriated enemies.

As a youth Chu Teh was reckless, adventurous, and courageous, moved by the legends of his people, by the tales of " free companions " of the *Shui Hu Chuan,* and by the exploits of the heroes of the *Romance of Three Kingdoms,* who had fought over the fields and mountains of his native Szechuan. He gravitated naturally toward military life. Helped by his family's political influence, he was accepted in the new Yunnan Military Academy,

---

[1] *China at Bay,* January 1936, published in London as a special supplement to *The Communist International.* It contains an equally erroneous account of the life of Mao Tse-tung.

and he was among the first cadets in China to be given modern military training. Upon graduation from the Yunnan Academy he was commissioned a lieutenant, and entered what the natives referred to as the " foreign army "—" foreign " because it used Western methods of drill and tactics, because it did not go into battle accompanied by Chinese musicians, and because for arms it used " foreign spears "—rifles with fixed bayonets on them.

In the overthrow of the Manchu dynasty in 1912 this Modern Army of Yunnan played a prominent rôle, and Chu Teh, leading a battalion of braves, soon distinguished himself as a warrior of the republic. By 1916, when Yuan Shih-k'ai attempted to restore the monarchy, he was a brigadier-general, and his Yunnanese troops under the celebrated Ts'ai Ao were the first to raise the banner of revolt, which doomed Yuan's imperial ambitions to defeat. At this time Chu Teh first became known throughout the southern provinces as one of the " four fierce generals " of Ts'ai Ao.

With his prestige thus established, Chu Teh's political fortunes pyramided rapidly. He became director of the Bureau of Public Safety in Yunnanfu, and then Provincial Commissioner of Finance. People of Yunnan and Szechuan agree that there are two things certain about officials: one is that they are corrupt, the other that they are opium-smokers. Chu Teh was both. Reared in a region where opium was as commonly smoked as tea was drunk, and where parents customarily spread the drug on sugar-cane to soothe their bellowing infants, he had inevitably become a smoker. And, given office by a bureaucracy which looked upon plunder of public funds not so much as a right as a duty to one's family, he followed the example of superiors, and manipulated the privileges of office to enrich himself and his heirs.

He went in for a harem, too. He is said to have acquired nine wives and concubines, and he built for them and his numerous progeny a palatial home in the capital of Yunnan. One might have thought he had everything he desired: wealth, power, love, descendants, poppy dreams, eminent respectability, and a comfortable future in which to preach the proprieties of Confucianism. He had, in fact, only one really bad habit, but it was to prove his downfall. He liked to read books.

Pure realist though he had been till now, there seems to have been a strain of idealism and genuine revolutionary ardour latent in his character. Influenced by reading, influenced also by a few returned students who occasionally drifted into the backwash of Yunnan, Chu Teh gradually understood that the revolution of 1911 had been for the mass of the people a complete cipher; that it had merely replaced one despotic bureaucracy of exploitation with another. What is more, he seems to have worried about it—as anyone of feeling, living in Yunnanfu, a city of 40,000 slave girls and boys, might well have done. He seems to have been possessed by a sense of shame and simultaneously with an ambition to emulate the popular heroes of the West, and a desire to " modernize " China. The more books he read the more he realized his own ignorance and China's backwardness. He wanted to study and he wanted to travel.

By 1922 Chu Teh had unburdened himself of his wives and concubines, pensioning them off in Yunnanfu. To one who knows the conservatism of China, and especially the feudal taboos of Yunnan, this act of repudiation of tradition is hardly believable, and indicates in itself a personality of unusual independence and resolution. Leaving Yunnan, he went to Shanghai, where he met many young revolutionaries of the Kuomintang, which he had joined. Here also he came into contact with Left-wing radicals, who tended to look upon him condescendingly as an old-fashioned militarist. A corrupt official from feudal Yunnan, a many-wived general, an inveterate opium addict—could this also be a revolutionary ?

Taking his friends' advice, Chu Teh determined to break himself of the drug habit. It was not easy: he had been using opium almost since childhood. But this man had more steel in his will than his acquaintances supposed. For a week he lay almost unconscious as he fought his noxious craving; then, fearful that he would weaken, he moved to a British steamer on the Yangtze, and took passage for Hankow. No opium could be bought or sold on board, and for weeks he sailed back and forth, up and down the river, pacing the deck, never going ashore, fighting this hardest battle of his life. But after a month on board he left the ship with clear eyes, a ruddy glow on his cheeks, and a new confidence in his step. He was completely cured. He began a new life in earnest.

Chu Teh was now about forty, but he was in excellent health, and his mind was eagerly reaching out for new knowledge. Accompanying some Chinese students, he went to Germany, where he lived for a while near Hanover. There he met many Communists, and at this time seems to have seriously taken up the study of Marxism and become enamoured of new perspectives opened up by the theory of social revolution. In this study he was chiefly tutored by Chinese students young enough to be his own sons—for he never learned French, he knew only a smattering of German, and he was a poor linguist. One of his student-teachers in Germany told me how deadly in earnest he had been; how patiently, ploddingly, stubbornly, he struggled amid the confusion of an impact of a whole new world of ideas to integrate the basic truths and meanings, how great had been the intellectual effort with which he divested himself of all the prejudices and limitations of his traditional Chinese training.

In this way he read some histories of the Great War, and familiarized himself with the politics of Europe. One day a student friend of his came to see him, talking excitedly about a book called *State and Revolution*. Chu Teh asked him to help him read it, and thus he became interested in Marxism and the Russian Revolution. He read Bukharin's *A B C of Communism*, and his works on dialectical materialism, and then he read more of Lenin. The powerful revolutionary movement then active in Germany swept him, with hundreds of Chinese students, into the struggle for world revolution. He joined the Chinese branch of the Communist Party founded in Germany.

" Chu Teh had an experienced, disciplined, practical mind," a comrade who knew him in Germany told me.[1] " He was an extremely simple man, modest and unassuming. He always invited criticism; he had an insatiable appetite for criticism. In Germany he lived the simple life of a soldier. Chu Teh's original interest in Communism sprang from his sympathy for the poor, which had also brought him into the Kuomintang. He believed strongly in Sun Yat-sen for awhile, because of Sun's principles advocating land for the tillers, and the limitation of private

---

[1] This account is based chiefly on biographical notes given to me by Commander Li Chiang-lin (who was on Chu Teh's staff from the earliest days in Kiangsi), supplemented by brief data from Mao Tse-tung, Peng Teh-huai, and others.

capital. But not until he began to understand Marxism did he realize the inadequacy of Sun Yat-sen's programme."

Chu Teh also lived for some time in Paris, where he entered a school for Chinese students which had been established by Wu Tze-hui, a veteran national revolutionary of the Kuomintang. In France and in Germany he sat at the feet of his young German, French, and Chinese instructors, and he humbly listened, quietly interrogated, debated, sought clarity and understanding. " To be modern, to understand the meaning of the revolution," his youthful tutors kept repeating, " you must go to Russia. There you can see the future." And again Chu Teh followed their advice. In Moscow he entered the Eastern Toilers' University, where he studied Marxism under Chinese teachers. Late in 1925 he returned to Shanghai, and from that time on he worked under the direction of the Communist Party, to which he soon gave his fortune.

Chu Teh rejoined his former superior and fellow Yunnanese, General Chu Pei-teh, whose power in the Kuomintang Army was second only to that of Chiang Kai-shek. In 1927, when General Chu Pei-teh's forces occupied several provinces south of the Yangtze, he made Chu Teh chief of the Bureau of Public Safety in Nanchang, capital of Kiangsi. There also he took command of a training regiment of cadets, and there he made contact with the 9th Kuomintang Army, stationed farther south in Kiangsi. In the 9th Army were detachments that had formerly been under his personal command in Yunnan. Thus the stage was prepared for the August Uprising in Nanchang, in which Communist troops first began the long open struggle for power against the Kuomintang.

August 1, 1927, was a day of great decision for Chu Teh. He had either to execute the order of his commander-in-chief, Chu Pei-teh, and suppress the insurrectionists, or to join with them, renouncing the remaining connections with an unsavoury past, to come out openly as a Red. When he chose the latter, and after the defeat of Ho Lung headed his police and his training regiment southward with the rebels, the city gates which closed behind him were symbolic of the final break with the security and success of his youth. Ahead of him lay years of unceasing struggle.

Part of the 9th Army went with Chu Teh also, as the straggling band of revolutionaries swept down to Swatow, captured it, were driven out, and then withdrew again to Kiangsi and Hunan. Among Chu Teh's chief lieutenants at that time were Wang Erh-tso and Chien Yi, Whampoa cadets who were later killed in battle, and Lin Piao, who later became president of the Red Academy. They did not yet call themselves a Red Army, but renamed only as the National Revolutionary Army. After the retreat from Fukien, Chu Teh's forces were reduced, by desertions and casualties, to 900 men, with a fire power of only 500 rifles, one machine gun, and a few rounds of ammunition each.

In this situation Chu Teh accepted an offer to connect with General Fan Shih-sheng, another Yunnan commander whose big army was then stationed in southern Hunan, and who, though not a Communist, tolerated Communists in his army, hoping to use them politically against Chiang Kai-shek. As a Yunnanese he was also inclined to give haven to his fellow provincials. Here Chu Teh's troops were incorporated as the 140th Regiment, and he became chief political adviser to the 16th Army. And here he had the narrowest escape of his life.

Communist influence in Fan Shih-sheng's army rapidly increased, and soon an anti-Bolshevik faction, secretly connected with Chiang Kai-shek, planned a coup against Chu Teh. One night he was staying in an inn with only forty of his followers, when he was attacked by a force under Hu Chi-lung, leader of the coup. Shooting began at once, but it was dark and the assassins could not see clearly. When several of them aimed revolvers at Chu Teh's head he cried out excitedly, " Don't shoot me, I'm only the cook. Don't shoot a man who can cook for you ! " The soldiers, touched to the stomach, hesitated, and Chu Teh was led outside for closer inspection. There he was recognized by a cousin of Hu Chi-lung, who shouted, " Here is Chu Teh ! Kill him ! " But Chu Teh pulled out a concealed weapon of his own, shot the man, overcame his guard, and fled. Only five of his men escaped with him.

This incident explains the nickname by which Chu Teh has ever since been known in the Red Army—" Chief of the Cooks."

Rejoining his regiment, Chu Teh notified Fan Shih-sheng that he was withdrawing, whereupon Fan is said to have presented him with a gift of $50,000 to keep his goodwill, for the issue against Chiang Kai-shek was still not clearly decided, and free-lance allies like these young Communists, who had considerable influence on many of his officers and men, were not to be lightly spurned. But in the months ahead the money was to prove inadequate. The little army was now held together almost solely by loyalty to Chu Teh and a few of his commanders. Party affairs were in great confusion, no definite " line " had been established, and military strategy was undecided. Chu's troops still wore Kuomintang uniforms, but they were in rags; many of them had no shoes, and poor food, or often no food at all, caused steady desertions. But some encouragement had been provided by the news of the Canton Commune, however, which had suggested a clear line of action. Chu Teh re-formed his army into three sections, calling it the " Peasant Column Army," and moved to the Hunan–Kiangsi–Kwangtung border, where he united with some bandits led by a radical student, and began a programme of tax-abolition, redistribution of land, and confiscation of the property of the rich. Yih Chang Hsien was occupied as a base, after a bloody struggle, and the young army eked out the winter on squash and political debates.

Meanwhile Mao Tse-tung's peasant army had marched in-gloriously through Hunan, to come at last to sanctuary at Chingkanshan, on the southern Kiangsi–Hunan border, where with the help of the bandit leaders Wang Tso and Yuan Wen-tsai they had occupied two surrounding counties, and built up in the mountains a nearly impregnable base. To Chu Teh, not far away, the " Peasants' and Workers' Red Army " of Mao Tse-tung sent as delegate his brother, Mao Tse-ming. He brought instructions from the Party to unite forces, and news of a definite programme of partisan warfare, agrarian revolution, and the building of Soviets. When, in May 1928, the two armies combined at Chingkanshan, they were in control of five counties, and had some 50,000 followers. Of these about 4,000 were armed with rifles, some 10,000 being equipped only with spears, swords, and hoes, while the rest were unarmed Party workers, propa-gandists, or families of the warriors, including a large number of children.

Thus began the famous Chu-Mao combination which was to make history in South China for the next six years. The story thenceforth is fairly well known. Mao Tse-tung has related how the programme of the Soviets evolved and how the Red Army developed. Chu Teh's ascension as a formidable military leader followed the same curve of growth as the Soviets.

At the First Soviet Congress, in 1931, Chu Teh was unanimously elected commander-in-chief of the Red Army. Within two years four army corps had been built up, with a firing power of some 50,000 rifles and hundreds of machine guns, mostly captured from enemy troops, and the Soviets controlled vast areas of southern Kiangsi and parts of Hunan and Fukien. Intensified political training had begun, an arsenal had been erected, elementary social revolutionary economic and political reforms were being realized throughout the Soviets, Red Army uniforms were being turned out day and night to equip new partisans, and revolutionary morale was strengthening. In two years more the Red forces had been doubled.

During these years in the South, Chu Teh led the combined Red Armies in hundreds of skirmishes, through scores of major battles, and through the brunt of five great annihilation campaigns, in the last of which he faced an enemy with technical offensive power (including heavy artillery, aviation, and mechanized units) estimated at from eight to nine times greater than his own, and resources many, many times exceeding anything at his disposal. However his degree of success or failure is to be measured, it must be admitted that for tactical ingenuity, spectacular mobility, and richness of versatility in manœuvre, he repeatedly proved his superiority to every general sent against him, and established beyond any doubt the formidable fighting power of revolutionized Chinese troops in partisan warfare. The great mistakes of the Red Army in the South were strategic, and for those the political leadership must be held chiefly responsible. Even with such blunders, however, there is little doubt that had the Red Army been able to face their enemy on anything even approximating equal terms in the Fifth Campaign, the result would have been a catastrophic defeat for Nanking—Nazi advisers notwithstanding.

For pure military strategy and tactical handling of a great army in retreat nothing has been seen in China to compare with Chu Teh's splendid generalship of the Long March, already described.

And to sheer personal magnetism of leadership, and the rare human quality which inspires in followers that unquestioning faith and devotion that gives men the courage to die in a cause—to this must be attributed the unbroken unity with which the forces under him withstood the terrible winter of siege and hardship, eating nothing but yak meat, on the icy wind-driven plateaus of Tibet. For me at least it is utterly impossible to imagine Chiang Kai-shek, Pai Chung-hsi, Sung Cheh-yuan, or any other Kuomintang general in China surviving with an army under such circumstances, to say nothing of actually staging a come-back at the end of that ordeal, and launching a big attack to drive a wedge right through the defence lines of enemy troops that had been comfortably preparing for months to prevent it. Which was what Chu Teh was doing as I rode across the North-west.

No wonder Chinese legends credit him with all sorts of miraculous powers: the ability to see 100 *li* on all sides, the power to fly, and the mastery of Taoist magic, such as creating dust clouds before an enemy, or stirring a wind against them. Super-stitious folk believe he is invulnerable, for have not thousands of bullets and shells failed to destroy him? Others say he has the power of resurrection, for has not the Kuomintang repeatedly declared him dead, often giving minute details of the manner in which he expired? Millions know the name " Red Virtue " in China, and to each it is a menace or a bright star of hope, according to his status in life, but to all it is a name imprinted on the pages of a decade of history.

Yet everybody told me Chu was unimpressive in appearance— a quiet, modest, soft-spoken, old-shoe sort of man, large-eyed (" very kind eyes," was the frequent expression), short, rather stockily built, but with arms and legs of iron. He is now over fifty, perhaps as much as fifty-three or fifty-four, nobody knew exactly—but Li Chiang-lin laughingly told me that he has been saying he is forty-six ever since he could remember. It seemed to be a little jest of his own: and Li thought he had stopped counting his age when he married his present wife—a big-boned peasant girl, who is an excellent shot and an expert rider, an Amazon who has led a partisan brigade of her own, and carried wounded comrades on her shoulder, a woman with big hands and feet like a man, robust, in hearty health, and courageous. Chu Teh's devotion to his men is proverbial. Since assuming command of the Army he has lived and dressed like the rank and file, has shared all their hardships, often going without shoes in the early days, living one whole winter on squash, another on yak meat, never complaining, rarely sick. He likes to wander through the camp, they say, sitting with the men and telling stories, or playing games with them. He plays a good game of table tennis, and a wistful game of basket-ball. Any soldier in the Army can bring his complaints directly to the commander-in-chief—and frequently does. Chu Teh takes his hat off when he addresses his men. On the Long March he lent his horse to tired comrades, walking much of the way, seemingly tireless.

Yet people who have fallen victim to the Reds no doubt saw in him a fiend in human form. Class war knows little mercy. Many of the horror stories spread about the Reds have now been discredited, but it would be naïve to suppose that Chu Teh has not found it a " revolutionary necessity " to send men to the firing squad. To succeed in his mission he had to transfer his loyalty completely to the disinherited, and in that rôle he could have been no more merciful than the masses he sought to empower and obey. So unless you believe that the masses cannot also take life, Chu Teh is no man without blood on his hands, but it depends entirely on your own philosophy or religion or prejudice or human sympathy, whether you find it the blood of the surgeon or of the executioner. Chu Teh has been no saint in any case, but still among his own people, among the poor who are after all the vast majority in China, he has been a deeply loved man who for a while held high a torch of liberation, and his name is already immortalized among those who have fought for human freedom in China.

PART ELEVEN

BACK TO PAO AN

1

Casuals of the Road

FROM Ninghsia I turned southward again into Kansu. In four or five days I was back in Holienwan, where again I saw Tsai Chang and her husband, Li Fu-chen, and had another meal of French cooking with them, and met the young and pretty wife of Nieh Jung-chen, political commissar of the 1st Army Corps. She had but recently slipped into the Soviet districts from the White World, and had now just returned from a visit to her husband, whom she had not seen for five years.

I stayed three days in Holienwan with the supply commissariat, which was quartered in a big compound formerly owned by a Mohammedan grain merchant. Architecturally it was an interesting group of buildings of a generally Central Asian appearance, with flat heavy roofs, and deep Arabic windows set into walls at least four feet thick. As I led my horse into its spacious stables a tall white-bearded man, wearing a faded grey uniform, with a long leather apron that reached to the ground, stepped up and saluted his red-starred cap, while his sunburned face wreathed a toothless smile. He took charge of Ma Hung-kuei—my horse.

How on earth, I wondered, had this grandfather wandered into our boy-scout encampment? I stopped to ask, and forced a story from him. He was from Shansi, and had joined the Red Army during its expedition there. His name was Li, he was sixty-four, and he claimed the distinction of being the oldest Red " warrior." Rather apologetically he explained that he was not at the front just then " because Commander Yang thinks I am more useful here at this horse work, and so I stay."

Li had been a small pork-seller in the town of Hung T'ung, Shansi, before he became a Red, and he roundly cursed " Model Governor " Yen Hsi-shan and the local officials, and their ruinous taxes. " You can't do business in Hung T'ung," he said; " they tax a man's excrement." When old Li had heard the Reds were coming he had decided to join them. His wife was dead, and his two daughters were both married; he had no sons; he had no ties at all in Hung T'ung except his overtaxed

pork business; and Hung T'ung was a " dead-man " sort of
place anyway. He wanted something livelier, and so the
adventurer had crept out of the city to offer himself to the
Reds.

" When I wanted to enlist they said to me, ' You are old. In
the Red Army life is hard.' And what did I say ? I said, ' Yes,
this body is sixty-four years old, it's true, but I can walk like a
boy of twenty, I can shoot a gun, I can do the work of any man.
If it's men you need, I can also serve.' So they told me to come
along, and I marched through Shansi with the Red Army,
and I crossed the Yellow River with the Red Army, and here I
am in Kansu."

I smiled and asked him whether it was any better than pork-
selling. Did he like it ?

" Oh-ho ! Pork-selling is a turtle-man's sort of business ! Here is
work worth doing. A poor man's army fighting for the oppressed,
isn't it ? Certainly I like it." The old man fumbled in his breast.
pocket and brought forth a soiled cloth, which he carefully
unwrapped to reveal a worn little notebook. " See here," he said.
" I already recognize over 200 characters. Every day the Red
Army teaches me four more. In Shansi I lived for sixty-four
years and yet nobody ever taught me to write my name. Is the
Red Army good or isn't it ? " He pointed with intense pride to
the crude scrawl of his characters that resembled the blots of
muddy hens' feet on clean matting, and falteringly he read off
some newly inscribed phrases. And then, as a sort of climax, he
produced a stub of pencil and with an elaborate flourish he
wrote his name for me.

" I suppose you're thinking of marrying again," I joked with
him. He shook his head gravely and said no, what with one
defile-mother horse after another he had no time to think about
the woman problem, and with that he ambled away to look after
his beasts.

Next evening, as I was walking through an orchard behind the
courtyard, I met another Shansi man, twenty years Li's junior,
but just as interesting. I heard a *hsiao-kuei* calling out, " Li
Pai T'ang ! Li Pai T'ang ! " and looked in curiosity to see whom
he was addressing as the " House-of-Christian-Worship ! "
There upon a little hill I found a barber shaving a youth's head

clean as an egg. Upon inquiry I discovered that his real name was Chia Ho-chung, and that he had formerly worked in the pharmacy of an American missionary hospital in P'ing Yang, Shansi. The " little devils " had given him this nickname because he was a Christian, and still said his prayers daily.

Chia pulled up his trousers and showed me a bad wound on his leg, from which he still limped, and he yanked up his coat to display a wound on his belly, where he had also been hit. These, he explained, were souvenirs of battles, and that was why he was not at the front. This hair-cutting wasn't his real job at all: he. was either a pharmacist or a Red warrior.

Chia said that two other attendants in that Christian hospital had joined the Reds with him. Before leaving, they had discussed their intention with the American doctor in the hospital, whose Chinese name was Li Jen. Dr. Li Jen was " a good man, who healed the poor without charge and never oppressed people," and when Chia and his companions had asked his advice he had said, " Go ahead. I have heard that the Reds are good and honest men and not like the other armies, and you should be glad to fight with them." So off they had gone to become red, red Robin Hoods.

" Maybe Dr. Li Jen just wanted to get rid of you," I suggested.

The barber indignantly denied it. He said he had always got along very well with Li Jen who was an excellent man. He asked me to tell this Li Jen, if I ever saw him, that he was still alive, well, and happy, and that as soon as the revolution was over he was coming back to take his old job in the pharmacy. I left House-of-Worship with much reluctance. He was a fine Red, a good barber, and a real Christian.

Incidentally, I met several Christians and ex-Christians among the Reds. Many Communist leaders—Chou En-lai is an outstanding example—were educated in foreign missionary schools, and some of them were once active Christians. Dr. Nelson Fu, head of the Red Army Medical Corps, was formerly a doctor in a Methodist hospital in Kiangsi. Although he volunteered to work with the Reds, and enthusiastically supported them, he still adhered to his faith, and hence had not joined the Communist Party.

In Kiangsi the Soviets carried on an extensive " anti-God "

propaganda. All temples, churches, and Church estates were
converted into State property, and monks, nuns, priests,
preachers, and foreign missionaries were deprived of the rights of
citizenship, but in the North-west a much milder policy of religious toleration was practised. Freedom of worship was a primary
guarantee, in fact. All foreign mission property was protected,
and refugee missionaries were invited to return to their flocks.
The Communists reserved the right to preach anti-religious
propaganda of their own, holding the " freedom to oppose
.worship " to be a democratic privilege of the freedom to worship.

The only foreigners who took advantage of the new Communist
policy toward religious institutions were some Belgian missionaries who are among the great landlords of Suiyuan. They own
one vast estate of 20,000 *mou*, and another of some 5,000 *mou*
of land near Tingpien, on the Great Wall. After the Red Army
occupied Tingpien, one side of the Belgians' property lay
adjacent to Soviet territory and the other side was held by White
troops. The Reds did not attempt to expropriate the Belgians'
land, but made a " treaty " in which they guaranteed to protect
the Church property, provided the priests permitted them to
organize anti-Japanese societies among the tenants (in reality
virtually serfs) who tilled the land of this big Catholic missionary
fiefdom. Another stipulation of the curious agreement provided
that the Belgians would dispatch a message of congratulations
from the Chinese Soviet Government to Premier Blum, congratu-
lating him on the triumph of the People's Front.

There had been a series of raids by *min-t'uan* near Holienwan,
and one village only a short distance away had been sacked two
nights before I arrived. A band had crept up to the place just
before dawn, overpowered and killed the lone sentry, and had
then brought up bunches of dry brushwood, and set fire to the
huts in which about a dozen Red soldiers were sleeping. As the
Reds had run out, blinded by the smoke, the *min-t'uan* had shot
them down and seized their guns. Then they had joined with a
gang of some 400, most of them armed by the Kuomintang
general, Kao Kuei-tzu, who were raiding down from the north
and burning towns and villages. The 28th Army had sent a
battalion out to attempt to round them up, and the day I left

Holienwan these young warriors came back after a successful chase.

The battle had occurred only a few *li* from Holienwan, which the White-bandits were in fact preparing to attack. Some peasants had discovered the *min-t'uan* lair in the inner mountains and, acting on this information, the Reds had divided into three columns, the centre one meeting the bandits in a frontal clash. The issue was decided when the two flanking columns of Reds closed in and surrounded the enemy. Some forty *min-t'uan* were killed, and sixteen Reds, while many on both sides were wounded. The *min-t'uan* were entirely disarmed, and their two chieftains taken captive.

We passed the battalion returning with their captives as we rode back toward Shensi. A big welcome had been organized in the villages, and the peasants lined the road to cheer the victorious troops. Peasant Guards stood holding their long red-tasselled spears in salute, and the Young Vanguards sang Red songs to them, while girls and women brought refreshments, tea and fruit and hot water—all they had, but it creased the faces of the weary soldiers with smiles. They were very young, much younger than the front-line regulars, and it seemed to me that many who wore blood-stained bandages were no more than fourteen or fifteen. I saw one youth on a horse, half-conscious and held up by a comrade on each side, who had a white bandage round his forehead, in the exact centre of which was a round red stain.

There in the midst of this column of youngsters, who carried rifles almost as big as themselves, marched the two bandit chieftains. One of them was a grizzled middle-aged peasant, and you wondered whether he felt ashamed, being led by these warriors all young enough to be his sons. Yet there was something rather splendid about his fearless bearing, and I thought that he was, after all, possibly a poor peasant like the rest, perhaps one who had also believed in something when he fought them, and it was regrettable that he was, I supposed, to be killed. But Fu Chin-kuei shook his head when I asked him.

" We don't kill captured *min-t'uan*. We educate them and give them a chance to repent, and many of them later become good Red partisans."

It was fortunate that the Reds had erased this group of

bandits, for it cleared our road back to Pao An of any menace. We made the trip from the Kansu border in five days, doing more than a hundred *li* on the fifth, but though there was plenty of incident there was no event, and I returned to Pao An with nothing hanging from my trophy-belt but some cantaloups and melons I had bought along the road.

2

Life in Pao An

BACK in Pao An again, I settled down once more in the Waichiaopu—the Foreign Office—where I stayed through late September and half of October. I collected enough biographies to fill
a *Who's Who in Red China*, and every morning turned up a new
commander or Soviet official to be interviewed. But I was
becoming increasingly uneasy about departure: Nanking troops
were pouring into Kansu and Shensi, and were gradually
replacing the Tungpei troops everywhere they held a front with
the Reds, as Chiang Kai-shek made all preparations for a new
" annihilation drive " from the south and the west. Unless I got
out soon it might be impossible: the last fissure in the blockade
might be closed. I waited anxiously for arrangements to be
completed for me to leave.

Meanwhile life in Pao An went on tranquilly enough, and you
would not have supposed that these people were aware of their
imminent " annihilation." Not far from me a training regiment
of new recruits was quartered. They spent their time marching
and counter-marching all day, playing games and singing songs.
Some nights there were dramatics, and every night the whole
town rang with song, as different groups gathered in barracks or
in cave grottoes, yodelling down the valley. In the Academy the
cadets were hard at work on a ten-hour day of study. A new
mass education drive was beginning in the town, even the
"little devils " in the Waichiaopu being subjected to daily lessons
in reading, politics, and geography.

As for myself, I lived a holiday life, riding, bathing, and
playing tennis. There were two courts, one set up on the grassy
meadow, clipped close by the goats and sheep, near the Red
Academy, the other a clay court next door to the cottage of Po
Ku, the gangling chairman of the North-west Branch Soviet
Government. Here, every morning, as soon as the sun rose above
the hills, I played tennis with three faculty members of the Red
Army Academy: the German Li Teh, Commissar Tsai, and
Commissar Wu. The court was full of stones, it was fatal to run
after a fast ball, but the games were nevertheless hotly contested.

Tsai and Wu both spoke Russian to Li Teh, whose Chinese was fragmentary, while I talked to Li Teh in English and to Tsai and Wu in Chinese, so that we thus had a tri-lingual game.

A more corrupting influence I had on the community was my gambling club. I had a pack of cards, unused since my arrival, and one day I got these out and taught Commissar Tsai to play rummy. Tsai had lost an arm in battle, but it handicapped him very little either at tennis or cards. After he had learned rummy he easily beat me with one hand. For a while rummy was the rage. Even the women began sneaking up to the Waichiaopu gambling club. My mud *k'ang* became the rendezvous of Pao An's *élite*, and you could look around at the candle-lit faces there at night and recognize Mrs. Chou En-lai, Mrs. Po Ku, Mrs. Kai Feng, Mrs. Teng Fa, and even Mrs. Mao. It set tongues wagging.

But the real menace to Soviet morals didn't appear till Pao An took up poker. Our tennis quartet started this, alternating nights at Li Teh's hut and my own den of iniquity in the Foreign Office. Into this sinful mire we dragged such respectable citizens as Po Ku, Li Ko-nung, Kai Feng, Lo Fu, and others. Stakes rose higher and higher. One-armed Tsai finally cleaned up $120,000 from Chairman Po Ku in a single evening, and it looked as if Po Ku's only way out was embezzlement of the State funds. We settled the matter by ruling that Po Ku would be allowed to draw $120,000 on the treasury to pay Tsai, provided Tsai would use the money to buy aeroplanes for the non-existent Soviet air force. It was all in matches, anyway—and, unfortunately, so were the aeroplanes Tsai bought.

One-armed Tsai was an interesting, lovable, good-looking lad, quick-witted, excitable, full of repartee and badinage. He had been a Red for a decade, having joined while he was a railway worker in Hunan. Later on he had gone to Moscow, and studied there for two or three years, and found time to fall in love with, and marry, a Russian comrade. Sometimes he looked ruefully at his empty sleeve and wondered whether his wife wouldn't divorce him when she saw his arm missing. " Don't worry about a little thing like that," Professor Wu, who was also a returned Russian student, would comfort him. " If you haven't had your posterity shot when off you see her again you'll be lucky." Nevertheless,

Tsai kept urging me to send him an artificial arm when I got back to the White World.

This was only one of the impossible requests I had for things to be sent in. Lo Ting-yi wanted me to buy, equip, and man an air fleet for them from the proceeds of the sale of my pictures of the Reds. Hsü Hai-tung wanted a couple of false teeth to fill in the gap in his gums: he had fallen in love. Everybody had something wrong with his teeth; they hadn't seen a dentist for years. But actually their fortitude was amazing; you never heard anybody complaining, though most of them were suffering from some kind of ailment, a big number especially from ulcers and other stomach trouble, as a result of years of a dubious diet.

Personally I thrived on the food and put on weight, and my disgust at facing the unvaried menu every day did not prevent me from consuming embarrassing quantities of it. They made me the concession of graham flour unbaked bread, which when toasted was not bad, and occasionally I had pork or mutton shaslick. Besides that I lived on millet—boiled millet, fried millet, baked millet, and vice versa. Cabbage was plentiful, and peppers, onions, and beans. I missed coffee, butter, sugar, milk, eggs, and a lot of things, but I went right on eating millet.

A batch of copies of the *North China Daily News* arrived for the library one day, and I read a recipe for what seemed to be a very simple chocolate sponge cake. I knew Po Ku was hoarding a tin of cocoa in his hut, and I schemed that with some of this, and by substituting pig's fat for butter, I could make that cake. Accordingly I got Li Ko-nung to write out a formal application to the Chairman of the North-west Branch Soviet Government of the Chinese Soviet Republic to supply me with two ounces of chocolate. After several days of delay, and hemming and hawing, and doubts and aspersions cast upon my ability to bake a cake anyway, and a lot of unravelling of red tape, and conflicts with the bureaucracy in general, we finally forced those two ounces of cocoa out of Po Ku, and got other materials from the food co-operative. But before I could mix up the batter my bodyguard came in to investigate, and the wretch dumped the cocoa on the ground. Followed more red tape, but finally I got the order refilled and began the great experiment. Why labour the result. Any intelligent *Hausfrau* can foresee what happened. My improvised oven failed to function properly, the cake did not rise, and when I took it off the fire it was a two-inch layer of charcoal on the bottom, and a top still in a state of slimy fluidity. However, it was consumed by the interested onlookers in the Waichiaopu with great relish: there were too many good materials in it to be wasted. I lost immense face, and thereafter docilely consumed my millet.

Li Teh compensated by asking me to a " foreign meal " with him. He had a way of getting rice and eggs sometimes, and, being German, he must have his own sausages. You could see them swinging in strings, drying outside his door near the main street of Pao An. He was getting ready his winter's supply. He also built himself a fireplace and taught his Chinese wife, a girl who had come with him from Kiangsi, how to bake. He showed me that the materials were there for tolerable cooking. It was only that the food co-operative (where our meals were cooked in common) didn't know how it should be done. Mrs. Lo P'ing-hui, wife of a Red Army commander (and the only lily-footed woman who made the Long March), was chief chef of the co-operative, and I think Li Teh's wife had a pull with her, and that is how he garnered his eggs and sugar.

But Li Teh was of course more than a good cook and a good poker-player. Who was this mystery man of the Chinese Soviet districts ? Has his importance been exaggerated by the Kuomintang General Lo Cho-ying, who, after reading some of Li Teh's writings found in Kiangsi, described him as the " brain-trust " of the Reds ? What was his connection with Soviet Russia ? How much influence, in fact, did Russia exercise over the affairs of Red China ?

The Russian Influence

THIS volume does not have as one of its primary purposes an examination of relations between the Communist Party of China and the Communist Party of Russia, or the Comintern, or the Soviet Union as a whole. No adequate background has been provided here for such a task. But the book would be incomplete without some discussion of these organic connections, and their more significant effects on the revolutionary history of China.

Certainly and obviously Russia has for the past dozen years been a dominating influence—and particularly among educated . youth it has been *the* dominating external influence—on Chinese thought about the social, political, economic, and cultural problems of the country. This has been almost as true, though unacknowledged, in the Kuomintang areas as it has been an openly glorified fact in the Soviet districts. Everywhere that youth has any solid political beliefs in China the impact of Marxist ideology is apparent, both as a philosophy and as a kind of substitute for religion. Among young Chinese, Lenin is almost worshipped, Stalin is by far the most popular foreign leader, Socialism is taken for granted as the future form of Chinese society, and Russian literature has the largest following —Maxim Gorky's works, for example, outselling all native writers except Lu Hsün, who was himself a great social revolutionary.

And all this is quite remarkable for one reason especially. This is that, while America, England, France, Germany, Japan, Italy, and other capitalist or imperialist powers have sent thousands of political, cultural, economic, or missionary workers into China, actively to propagandize the Chinese masses with credos of their own States, yet for many years the Russians have not had a single school, church, or even a debating society in China where Marx-Leninist doctrines could legally be preached. Their influence, except in the Soviet districts, has been largely indirect. Moreover, it has been aggressively opposed everywhere by the Kuomintang. Yet few who have been in

China during this decade, and conscious of the society in which
they have lived, will dispute the contention that Marxism, the
Russian Revolution, and the triumphs of the Soviet Union
are influences which have made deeper and more profound
spiritual impressions on the Chinese people than all bourgeois
Christian influences combined.

Contrary to the ideas of many people obsessed with the Comintern bogey, even in the Red districts the influence of Russia
has probably been more spiritual and ideological than through
direct participation in the development of the Chinese Soviet
movement. Remember that the Chinese Communists' adherence
to the Comintern, and unity with the U.S.S.R., have always
been entirely voluntary, and could have been liquidated at any
time by the Chinese from within. The rôle of the Soviet Union
for them has been most potent as a living example, an ideal that
bred hope and faith. It has been the fire and forge that helped
anneal in them the steel-like qualities of heroic character that
many people had not supposed Chinese possessed. These Reds
stoutly believe that the Chinese revolution is not isolated, and
that hundreds of millions of workers, not only in Russia, but
throughout the world, are anxiously watching them, and when
the time comes will emulate them, even as they themselves
have emulated the comrades in Great Russia. In the day of
Marx and Engels it may have been correct to say that " the
workers have no country," but these Chinese Communists
to-day believe that, besides their own little bases of proletarian
rule, they have a mighty fatherland of their own in the Soviet
Union. These earnests have been a tremendous source of encouragement and revolutionary nourishment to them.

" The Soviet Government in China," reads the Constitution
adopted at the first All-China Soviet Congress, " declares its
readiness to form a revolutionary united front with the world
proletariat and all oppressed nations, and *proclaims the Soviet
Union, the land of proletarian dictatorship, to be its loyal ally.*"
How much the words italicized meant to the Chinese Soviets,
which in truth most of the time were completely isolated
geographically, economically, and politically, is hard to understand for any Westerner who has never known a Chinese Communist.

But I saw it, and heard it, and felt it. This idea of having behind them such a great ally—even though it has been less and less validated by any demonstrations of positive support from the Soviet Union—is of primary importance to the morale of the Chinese Reds. It has imparted to their struggle the universality of a religious cause, and they deeply cherish it. When they shout, " Long live the World Revolution ! " and " Proletarians of All Lands, Unite ! " it is an idea that permeates all their teaching and faith, and in it they reaffirm their allegiance to the dream of a Socialist world brotherhood.

It seemed to me that these concepts had already shown that they could change Chinese behaviour. I never suffered from any " anti-foreignism " in the Reds' attitude toward me. They were certainly anti-imperialist, and an American or European capitalist might have been uncomfortable among them, but no more so than a Chinese landlord or a Shanghai comprador. Racial prejudice seemed to have been thoroughly sublimated in class antagonism that knew no national boundaries. Even their anti-Japanese agitation was not directed against the Japanese on a racial basis. In their propaganda the Reds constantly emphasized that they opposed only the Japanese militarists, capitalists, and other " Fascist oppressors," and that the Japanese masses were their potential allies. Indeed, they derived great encouragement from that conviction. This raising of the level of national prejudice to a higher plane of antagonism was no doubt to a considerable degree traceable to the education in Russia of scores of the Chinese Red leaders, who had attended Sun Yat-sen University, or the Eastern Toilers' University, or the Red Academy, or some other school for training international cadres of Communism, and had returned as teachers to their own people.

One example of this spirit of internationalism was shown in the intense interest with which the Reds followed the events of the Spanish civil war. Bulletins were issued in the Press, were pasted up in the meeting-rooms of village Soviets, were announced to the armies at the front. Special lectures were given by the political department on the cause and significance of the Spanish war, and the " People's Front " in Spain was contrasted with the " United Front " in China. Mass meetings of the populace were summoned, demonstrations were held, and public discussions were encouraged. It was quite surprising sometimes to find, even far back in the mountains, Red farmers who knew a few rudimentary facts about such things ·as the Italian conquest of Abyssinia and the German-Italian invasion of Spain, and spoke of these powers as the " Fascist allies " of their enemy, Japan ! Despite their geographical isolation, these rustics now knew much more about world politics, thanks to radio news and wall newspapers and Communist lecturers and propagandists, than the rural population anywhere else in China.

The strict discipline of Communist method and organization —a discipline inherent in Communist ideology itself—had produced among Chinese Marxists a type of co-operation and a suppression of individualism which the average " Old China Hand," or treaty-port diehard, or missionary, who fancies he " knows Chinese psychology," would find it impossible to believe in without witnessing for himself. In their political life the existence of the individual was an atomic pulse in the social whole, the mass, and must bend to its will, either consciously in the rôle of leadership, or unconsciously as part of the material demiurge. There have been disputes and internecine struggles among the Communists, of course, but none of them has been severe enough to deal a permanent injury either to the Army or the Party. This phenomenon, this " un-Chinese " solidarity, was the result of a new conception of society as the arena of struggle between class forces for dominance, a struggle in which the most coherent, most compact, most purposeful and dynamic, the most consciously determined, in the end won victory. And this solidarity explained a good deal about the Communists' survival, if not their victory.

Had Nanking been able at any time to split their military and political strength into contradictory and warring factions, as it did with all other Opposition groups—as Chiang Kai-shek did with his own rivals to power within the Kuomintang—the task of Communist-suppression might have been rewarded with final success. But its attempts were failures. For example, a few years ago Nanking hoped to utilize the world-wide Stalin-Trotsky controversy to divide the Chinese Communists, but, although so-called Chinese " Trotskyites " did appear, they earned a very bad stigma as spies and traitors—many of them were led by the logic of their position to join the Blueshirts and betray former comrades to the police—and they never developed any important mass influence or following, and remained a curious agglomerate of tragic, cynical, and isolated intellectuals. To the leadership of the Communist Party they were unable to offer any serious threat of disruption at all.

The Reds had generally discarded all the feudal rubbish of so-called Chinese etiquette, and their psychology and character were quite different from traditional conceptions of Chinese. Alice Tisdale Hobart could never write a book about them, nor could the Chinese author of *Lady Precious Stream*. They were direct, frank, simple, undevious, and scientific-minded. They rejected nearly all the old Chinese philosophy that was the basis of what was once Chinese civilization, and most important of all, perhaps, they were implacable enemies of the old Chinese familism.[1] Most of the time I felt as completely at ease in their company as if I were with some of my own countrymen. Incidentally, my presence meant very much to them in one sense. They could point to me, and the interest that had brought me to the Soviet districts, as concrete evidence of the " internationalism " of their movement. They exploited me as a kind of Exhibit A for Doubting Thomases.

With this zealous adoration of the Soviet Union there has naturally been a lot of copying and imitating of foreign ideas, institutions, methods, and organizations. The Chinese Red Army is constructed on Russian military lines, and much of its tactical knowledge derives from Russian experience. Social organizations in general follow the pattern laid down by Russian Bolshevism. Many Red songs have been put to Russian music, and are widely sung in the Soviet districts. *So-wei-ai*—Chinese for Soviet—is only one example of many words transliterated directly from Russian into Chinese.

But in all this borrowing there was much adaptation; few Russian ideas or institutions have survived without drastic changes to suit the *milieu* in which they operate. The empirical process of a decade eliminated indiscriminate wholesale importations, and also resulted in the introduction of features in

---

[1] Of course, here I do not speak of the peasant masses as a whole, but only of a thoroughly Communist vanguard.

the Soviet system that are peculiarly Chinese. A process of imitation and adaptation of the West has, of course, been going on in the bourgeois world of China, too—for there is very little left even of poetry in the ancient feudal heritage, that " scrap material of a great history " as Spengler calls it, which is of much value in building either a modern bourgeois or a Socialist society capable of grappling with the vast new demands of the country to-day. Two ova have simultaneously shaped within the womb of Old China, and both have been fertilized from abroad. Thus it is significant, for example, that while the Reds leaned heavily on Russia for organizational methods with youth, Generalissimo Chiang Kai-shek used not only Italian bombing-planes to destroy them, but also borrowed from the Y.M.C.A. in building his anti-Communist New Life Movement.

And finally, of course, the political ideology, tactical line, and theoretical leadership of the Chinese Communists have been under the close guidance, if not positive detailed direction, of the Communist International, which during the past decade has become virtually a bureau of the Russian Communist Party. In final analysis this means that, for better or worse, the policies of the Chinese Communists, like Communists in every other country, have had to fall in line with, and usually subordinate themselves to, the broad strategic requirements of Soviet Russia, under the dictatorship of Stalin.

So much is obvious. Great benefits have undoubtedly accrued to the Chinese Reds from sharing the collective experience of the Russian Revolution, and from the leadership of the Comintern. But it is also true that the Comintern may be held responsible for serious reverses suffered by the Chinese Communists in the anguish of their growth.

4

Chinese Communism and the Comintern

IT is possible to divide the history of Sino-Russian relations from 1923 to 1937 roughly into three periods. The first, from 1923 to 1927, was a period of *de facto* alliance between the Soviet Union and the National Revolutionaries, consisting of a *bloc* composed of strange bedfellows aligned under the banners of the Kuomintang and the Communist parties, and aiming at the overthrow by revolution of the then extant Government of China, and the achievement of China's independence from foreign imperialism. This exciting enterprise ended with the triumph of the Right-wing Kuomintang, the founding of the Nanking Government, a compromise with imperialism, and the severance of Sino-Russian relations.

From 1927 to 1933 there was a period of isolation of Russia from China, and of complete insulation by Nanking against Russian influence. This era closed when Moscow resumed diplomatic relations with Nanking late in 1933. The third period began with a lukewarm Nanking–Moscow *rapprochement*, embarrassed considerably by the continued heavy civil war between Nanking and the Chinese Communists. It was to end dramatically early in 1937, when a partial reconciliation would be effected between the Communists and the Kuomintang, with new possibilities opened up for Sino-Russian co-operation. But the Communist serenade was still falling on deaf Kuomintang ears when I was with the Reds, and this new period can be reserved for discussion in its proper setting farther on.

The three periods of Sino-Russian relationship mentioned above accurately reflect also the changes that have taken place in the character of the Comintern during recent years, and its stages of transition from an organization of international incendiaries into an instrument of the national policy of the Soviet Union. It is impossible here to enter into the dialectics of the extremely complex series of causes, domestic and international, which have brought about these changes, both in the Soviet Union and in the Comintern, but it is pertinent to see how in the main they affected, and were affected by, the Chinese Revolution.

As everyone who has studied this subject knows, the crisis of the Chinese Revolution coincided with a crisis in Russia, and in the Comintern, expressed in the struggle between Trotskyism and Stalinism for theoretical and practical control of the forces of world revolution. Had Stalin not waited till 1924 to advance his slogan, "Socialism in one country," had the issue been fought out and had he been able to dominate the Comintern before then, quite possibly the " intervention " in China might never have begun. Such a speculation in any case is idle. When Stalin did develop his fight, the line in China had already been cast.

The active military, political, financial, and intellectual collaboration given to the Chinese Nationalist Revolution was until 1926 under the direction chiefly of Zinoviev, who was chairman of the Communist International, and was strongly influenced by Trotsky. Until then Stalin's adherents had not yet decisively overpowered the Trotsky theory of " permanent revolution." But from early 1926 onward Stalin became chiefly responsible for the affairs and policies of the Comintern as well as the Communist Party of the Soviet Union, and it will nowhere be disputed that he has tightened his grasp on both organizations ever since.

Stalin led the Comintern which gave the Chinese Communists their tactical line and " directives " throughout 1926, and on through the catastrophe of the spring of 1927. During these swift months, in which disaster gathered like a mighty typhoon above the heads of the Chinese Communists, Stalin's line was subjected to continuous bombardment from the Opposition, dominated by Trotsky, Zinoviev, and Kamenev. Although, while he had been Comintern chairman, Zinoviev had fully supported the line of Communist co-operation with the Kuomintang, he now violently attacked this same line as carried out by Stalin. Particularly after Chiang Kai-shek's first " treachery "—the abortive attempt at a *coup d'état* in Canton in 1926—Zinoviev predicted an inevitable counter-revolution, in which the national bourgeoisie would compromise with imperialism and turn traitor to the masses.

At least a year before Chiang Kai-shek's second and successful *coup d'état*, Zinoviev began demanding the separation of the Communists from the Kuomintang, the party of the national bourgeoisie, which he realized was incapable of carrying out the two main tasks of the revolution—anti-imperialism, i.e. the overthrow of foreign domination of China, and " anti-feudalism," or the destruction of the landlord-gentry rule in rural China. Just as early Trotsky began urging the formation of Soviets, and an independent Chinese Red Army. The Opposition in general foretold the failure of the " bourgeois-democratic " revolution—all they hoped for in this period—if Stalin's line was continued. And this prophecy was, of course, fulfilled.

There is, however, abundant reason to believe that had the Opposition's objections been made the basis of an early Jacobin policy in China the tragedy would have been even more severe. Trotsky's theoretical criticisms were, as usual, brilliant, and his advice had some connection with the actual peculiarities of the situation. But not, as often, very much. Certainly his *Problems of the Chinese Revolution*, which contains most of his remarks on the period, is a loosely argued work, full of an insouciant disregard for the objective limitations of the living situation at that time. It clearly suggests that the only alternative he had to offer to the Comintern policy, which ended in catastrophe, was a policy which would have ended in a much earlier and more complete catastrophe.

Stalin defended himself, after the *débâcle*, by ridiculing as non-Marxist the Trotskyist contentions that the tactical line of the Comintern had been the main cause of the failure. " Comrade Kamenev," declared Stalin, " said that the policy of the Communist International was responsible for the defeat of the Chinese Revolution, and that we ' bred Cavaigners in China.' . . . How can it be asserted that the tactics of a party can abolish or reverse the relation of class forces ? What are we to say of people who forget the relation of class forces in time of revolution, and who try to explain everything by the tactics of a party ? Only one thing can be said of such people—that they have abandoned Marxism."

It is, in fact, hard for any candid student of the whole epoch to escape the conclusion that the Trotskyists greatly exaggerated the importance of Comintern mistakes, while · they
Nc

minimized the overwhelmingly adverse factors in the objective
situation. They were obviously more interested in forging from
the Comintern's errors new shells for their artillery barrage
against Stalin than they were in the immediate fate of China.
Their assault was, anyway, unsuccessful. The Party as a whole
remained unconvinced of Stalin's incompetence. With the
failure of the Chinese Revolution, coupled with the earlier
destruction of Communist régimes in Bavaria and Hungary,
as well as the general defeat of the Comintern hopes throughout
the countries of the East, the Party grew weary of adventures
afar, and was ready to turn to construction at home. Stalin
triumphed. Trotsky was exiled—and, if we are to believe the
evidence of the Moscow trials, went into the railway-wrecking
business.

The important change that occurred in the Comintern after
Stalin's victory, and the adoption of five-year plans and a
passion for tractors, was that active schemes to promote immediate world revolution were temporarily set aside, while
the revolutionary energies of the Soviet Union were concentrated
in a mighty offensive of Socialist construction. The Comintern
ceased being the dominant thing, and instead became a kind
of bureau of the Soviet Union, gradually turning into a glorified
advertising agency for the prosaic labours of the builders of
Socialism in one country. Its main tasks altered from attempts
to create revolution by force, or active intervention, to bringing
about revolution by example. Because the Soviet Union, the
" base of the world revolution," needed peace, the Comintern
became a powerful organ of peace propaganda throughout the
world.

It is tedious here to enter further into Stalin-Trotsky polemics.
The important thing is that Stalin won, and his policy dominated the future activities of the Comintern in China. After
1927 these were for a while almost nil. Russian organs in China
were closed, Russian Communists were killed or driven from the
country, the flow of financial, military, and political help from
Russia ceased, and the Chinese Communist Party was thrown
into great confusion, and for a time lost contact with the Comintern. *The Soviet movement and the Chinese Red Army began
spontaneously, under purely Chinese leadership*, and they did

not in fact get much applause from Russia till after the Sixth Congress, when the Communist International gave its post-natal sanction.

The rôle of the Comintern in the Chinese Revolution since then has been colossally magnified. Some organs were, it is true, covertly restored; delegates were sent to a few big cities to contact Chinese Communists; Chinese students continued to be educated in Russia and secretly return to carry on revolutionary work; and a little money dribbled in. But it became utterly impossible for Russia to have any direct physical connection whatever with the Red areas, which had no seaport and were entirely surrounded by a ring of hostile troops. Whereas in the past there had been hundreds of Comintern workers in China, there were now two or three, often almost isolated from society as a whole, seldom able to risk a stay of more than a few months. Whereas millions of dollars had formerly gone to Chiang Kai-shek's Nationalists, now a thousand or so at a time trickled into the Reds. And whereas the whole Soviet Union had backed the great revolution of 1925–7, the Chinese Communist movement was now aided only by a Comintern which could no longer command the vast resources of the " base of the world revolution," but had to limp along as a kind of poor step-child which might be officially disinherited whenever it did anything malaprop.

Actually, the financial help given to the Chinese Reds by Moscow or the Comintern during this decade seems to have been amazingly small. When the Noulens were arrested in Shanghai in 1932 and convicted in Nanking as chief Far Eastern agents of the Comintern, the complete evidence which the police produced showed that total out-payments for the whole Orient (not just China) had not at most exceeded the equivalent of about U.S. $15,000 per month. This is a trifle compared with the vast sums poured into China to support Christian propaganda, which is mostly capitalist propaganda, or to support Japanese and Nazi-Fascist propaganda. It is rather pitiful also in contrast, for example, with America's $50,000,000 Wheat Loan to Nanking in 1933—the proceeds of which were of decisive value to Chiang Kai-shek's civil war against the Reds, according to reports of foreign military attachés.

.

America, England, Germany, and Italy sold Nanking great quantities of aeroplanes, tanks, guns and munitions, to destroy the Chinese Soviets, but they of course sold none to the Reds. The American Army released many officers to train the Chinese air force, which demolished hundreds of towns in Red China, and Italian and German instructors actually led some of the most destructive bombing expeditions themselves—just as they do in Spain to-day. To Chiang Kai-shek's aid Nazi Germany sent its ablest general, Von Seeckt, with a big staff of Prussian officers, who improved Nanking's technique of annihilation. In view of these well-known facts it seems to me rubbish to assert that Russia has been propping up the Chinese Reds. On the contrary, quite clearly Chiang Kai-shek was propped up for nearly ten years by the important aid which the foreign powers gave to him but denied the Reds.

It may be said categorically—and I believe no foreign military expert of intelligence can disagree with the statement—that the Chinese Reds have fought with less foreign help than any army in modern Chinese history.

5

That Foreign Brain-Trust

THE fact is that there was not a single foreign adviser actually with the Red Army during the first five years of its existence—years in which it built up the Soviets, created a disciplined revolutionary movement, and increased its forces by the process of demobilizing and disarming its enemy. Not until 1933 did Li Teh, the German adviser, and the only foreigner who ever fought with the Chinese Red Army, appear in the Soviet districts, to take a high position both politically and militarily.

Li Teh got into Juichin, the capital of Soviet Kiangsi, after an adventurous journey of six days and nights, while he lay hidden under some matting in a native river-junk which smuggled him from Canton to the Red front. Prior to his arrival in Juichin the Reds' only contact with the Comintern, except for irregular couriers, was by radio communication. In Shanghai there was an advisory committee under the direction of the Comintern, and this was of great value in keeping the Reds informed on important political and military movements of the enemy. It evidently functioned much more efficiently than any espionage organization Chiang Kai-shek ever managed to set up within the Soviets.

But this advisory committee, together with Li Teh, are held responsible for two great errors committed in the last days of the Kiangsi Red Republic. The first of these, as Mao Tse-tung has pointed out, was the failure of the Red Army to unite with the 19th Route Army, when it arose in revolt against Nanking in the autumn of 1933. The 19th Route Army, commanded by Ts'ai T'ing-K'ai and Chiang Kuang-nai, had made the heroic defence of Shanghai against Japan's invasion in 1932, and had demonstrated beyond all doubt its strongly anti-Japanese revolutionary character. Transferred to Fukien province, it had, after the humiliating Tangku Truce negotiated with Japan by Chiang Kai-shek and Ho Ying-chin, begun an anti-Nanking, anti-Japanese rebellion, and a movement for a democratic republic and the destruction of Chiang Kai-shek's military dictatorship. To the Red Army it had proposed not only a truce (the 19th

Route Army, after Nanking had sabotaged its struggle against Japan, and been sent to fight the Chinese Reds in Fukien), but also an alliance on the basis of the anti-Japanese front.

Most of the leaders of the Soviet Government, as well as the Red Army, were very sympathetic to these offers. They were prepared to move their main forces into Fukien, develop a strong flank attack on Nanking's troops, form a Coalition Government with the Fukien rebels, and in general give the 19th Route Army full military and political support. But the Comintern, for reasons not entirely clear, opposed this, through its advisory committee in Shanghai. Russia was just then renewing its flirtation with Nanking, Moscow had but recently recognized the Kuomintang régime, and it is the Trotskyist contention that this was the main reason for the Comintern line: i.e. that Moscow opposed the extension of large-scale civil war, still hoped to unite the Reds and Nanking in a common stand against Japan, did not want to be accused of fomenting insurrection at this time, and especially did not wish to face a situation in which the Reds, if they had got control of a seaport in Fukien, would clearly have looked to Russia for supplies. Evidence for this opinion, however, is lacking.

In any case, what happened was that instead of co-operating with the 19th Route Army, the Reds withdrew their main forces to western Kiangsi, and left Chiang Kai-shek's flank almost entirely free. Thus enabled to descend swiftly into neighbouring Fukien, with little impediment, the Generalissimo quickly squashed the insurgents, and the Reds lost their strongest potential allies. There is no doubt that this elimination of the revolutionary 19th Route Army very much facilitated the task of destroying the southern Soviets, to which Chiang Kai-shek at once turned with a new confidence.

The second severe mistake was the plan of tactical defence followed out during Nanking's Fifth Annihilation Campaign. In previous campaigns the Reds had triumphed by reliance on their superiority in manœuvring warfare, and their ability to take the initiative from Chiang Kai-shek in strong, swift concentrations and surprise offensives. Positional warfare and regular fighting had always played minor rôles in their operations.

But in the Fifth Campaign Li Teh insisted upon a reversal of tactics. He planned a large-scale defensive on the pivot of positional warfare, relegating partisan and guerilla tactics to subordinate tasks, and somehow he hammered his scheme through to acceptance against the unanimous opposition of the Red military council.

To-day it is quite obvious that Li Teh greatly over-estimated the resources of the Soviet base, the fighting power of the Red Army in immobile warfare, and the demoralization of the enemy, while he unforgivably under-estimated the improved offensive power of Nanking's new air force and mechanized units, and seriously miscalculated important factors in the political situation, which he expected to develop much more favourably for the Reds than was actually the case.

But how was it possible that Li Teh, a single foreigner, had sufficient influence to impose his will over the judgment of the entire military council, the Government, and the Party—a very dictatorial proceeding ? Li Teh was undoubtedly an exceptionally able military tactician and strategist. During the World War he had distinguished himself with the German Army; later on he had been a division commander in the Red Army of Russia, and he was a graduate of Moscow's Red Army Academy. As a German the Reds also respected his analysis of the tactics which General Von Seeckt had given to Generalissimo Chiang (how dramatic a thing it was, as these two German generals, one a Fascist to the soul, the other a Bolshevik, fought against each other through these two Chinese armies !), and events proved this faith to be correct. Nanking generals, when they found some of Li Teh's writings interpreting their tactics, admitted with admiring amazement that Li Teh had accurately anticipated every stage of the gigantic offensive.

Li Teh was a saddened and chastened ex-Prussian officer, and a wiser Bolshevik, when he mounted horse to ride with the Red Army on its Long March. In Pao An he admitted to me that Western methods of warfare do not always work in China. " Chinese psychology and tradition and the peculiarities of the Chinese military experience," he said, " have to decide the main tactics in a given situation. Chinese comrades know better than we do the correct tactics of revolutionary warfare in their own

country." He had by this time been degraded to a very subordinate position—but they had all buried ill-feelings of the past.

However, in justice to Li Teh, it may be suggested that the
actual degree of his responsibility in Kiangsi probably tends to
be over-emphasized. He is in fact an important part of the
defence-mechanism by means of which the Reds rationalize a
very adverse experience. He is the arrogant foreigner, the black
sheep, the scapegoat: and it is somehow comforting to be able to
cast most of the blame on him. Actually it is almost impossible
to believe that under any genius of command the Reds could
have emerged victorious from the Himalayan obstacles which
faced them throughout the year of the Fifth Campaign. In any
event, the experience has been a lesson, and one from which the
world Communist movement as a whole may benefit. The mistake of giving over to a foreigner the plenary tactical command
of a revolutionary army is hardly likely to be repeated.

So much for Kiangsi. During the next two years the Reds were
almost entirely cut off from contact even with their own Party
members in the coastal cities of China, and the Comintern confined its activities chiefly to publishing in *Inprecorr* the astounding reports of Wang Ming, the Chinese delegate to the International. Incidentally, I happened to be in Pao An one day
when some *Inprecorrs* arrived, and I saw Lo Fu, the American-
educated secretary of the Central Committee of the Party,
eagerly devouring them. He mentioned casually that he had not
seen a copy of *Inprecorr* for nearly three years !

And not until September 1936, while I was still with the Reds,
did the detailed account of the proceedings of the Seventh
Congress of the Communist International, held just a year
previously, finally reach the Red capital of China. It was these
reports which brought to the Chinese Communists for the first
time the fully developed thesis of the international anti-Fascist
united front tactics—tactics which were to guide them in their
policy during the exciting months ahead, when revolt was to
spread throughout the North-west, and to shake the entire
Orient. And once more the Comintern was to assert its will in
the affairs of China, in a manner that sharply affected the
development of the revolution.

But I was to view this episode from the sidelines again in Peiping.

6

Farewell to Red China

Two interesting things happened before I left Pao An. On October 9, radio messages from Kansu reached us, telling of the successful junction at Huining of the vanguard of the 4th Red Army with Ch'en Keng's 1st Division of the 1st Army Corps. A few days later Ch'en Keng and all the important officers of the First Front Army were holding a joyous reunion in Kansu with the leaders of the Second and Fourth Front Armies, including Chu Teh, Hsu Hsiang-ch'ien, Ho Lung, Chang Kuo-t'ao, Hsiao K'eh, and many others. The whole of north-eastern Kansu had fallen to the Reds, and a column of the Fourth Front Army was moving across the Yellow River into the panhandle of north-western Kansu. Government opposition had momentarily been overwhelmed.

All the regular Red Army forces were now concentrated in North-west China, with good lines of communications established. Orders for winter uniforms poured into the factories of Pao An and Wu Ch'i Chen. The combined forces of the Three Great Armies now numbered between 80,000 and 90,000 seasoned, well-equipped warriors. Celebrations and rejoicing were held in Pao An and throughout the Soviet districts. The long period of suspense during the fighting in south Kansu was ended. Everyone now felt a new confidence in the future. With the whole of the best Red troops in China concentrated in a big new territory, and near by another 100,000 sympathetic troops of the Tungpei Army, of whom they had come to think as allies, the Reds now believed that their proposals for a United Front would be heard with keener interest at Nanking.

The second important event was an interview I had with Mao Tse-tung, just before I left, in which, for the first time, he indicated concrete terms on the basis of which the Communists would welcome peace with the Kuomintang, and co-operation to resist Japan. Some of these terms had already been announced in a manifesto issued by the Communist Party in August. In my conversation with Mao, I asked him to explain the reasons for this new policy.

" First of all," he began, " the seriousness of Japanese aggression: it is becoming more intensified every day, and is so formidable a menace that before it all the forces of China must unite. Besides the Communist Party there are other parties and forces in China, and the strongest of these is the Kuomintang. Without its co-operation our strength at present is insufficient to resist Japan in war. Nanking must participate. The Kuomintang and the Communist Party are the two main political forces in China, and if they continue to fight now in civil war the effect will be unfavourable for the anti-Japanese movement.

" Secondly, since August 1935 the Communist Party has been urging, by manifesto, a union of all parties in China for the purpose of resisting Japan, and to this programme the entire populace has responded with sympathy, notwithstanding the fact that the Kuomintang has continued its attacks upon us.

" The third point is that many patriotic elements even in the Kuomintang now favour a reunion with the Communist Party. Anti-Japanese elements even in the Nanking Government, and Nanking's own armies, are to-day ready to unite because of the peril to our national existence.

" These are the main characteristics of the present situation in China, and because of them we are obliged to reconsider in detail the concrete formula under which such co-operation in the national liberation movement can become possible. The fundamental point of unity which we insist upon is the national liberation anti-Japanese principle. In order to realize it we believe there must be established a national defence democratic Government. Its main tasks must be to resist the foreign invader, to grant popular rights to the masses of the people, and to intensify the development of the country's economy.

" We will therefore support a parliamentary form of representative Government, an anti-Japanese salvation Government, a Government which protects and supports all popular patriotic groups. If such a republic is established, the Chinese Soviets will become a part of it. We will realize in our areas measures for a democratic parliamentary form of Government."

" Does that mean," I asked, " that the laws of such a [democratic] Government would also apply in Soviet districts ? "

Mao replied in the affirmative. He said that such a Government should restore and once more realize Sun Yat-sen's final will, and his three " basic principles " during the Great Revolu-. tions, which were: alliance with the U.S.S.R. and those countries which treat China as an equal; union with the Chinese Communist Party; and fundamental protection of the interests of the Chinese working class.

" If such a movement develops in the Kuomintang," he continued, " we are prepared to co-operate with and support it, and to form a United Front against imperialism such as existed in 1925-7. We are convinced that this is the only way left to save our nation."

" Is there any *immediate* cause for the new proposals ? " I inquired. " They must certainly be regarded as the most important decision in your Party's history in a decade."

" The immediate causes," Mao explained, " are the severe new demands of Japan, capitulation to which must enormously handicap any attempts at resistance in the future, and the popular response to this deepening Japanese invasion in the form of a great people's patriotic movement. These conditions have in turn produced a change in attitude among certain elements in Nanking. Under the circumstances it is now possible to hope for the realization of such a policy as we propose. Had it been offered in this form a year ago, or earlier, neither the country nor the Kuomintang would have been prepared for it.

" At present negotiations are being conducted. While the Communist Party has no great positive hopes of persuading Nanking to resist Japan, it is nevertheless possible. As long as it is, the Communist Party will be ready to co-operate in all necessary measures. If Chiang Kai-shek prefers to continue the civil war, the Red Army will also receive him."

In effect, Mao made a formal declaration of the readiness of the Communist Party, the Soviet Government, and the Red Army, to cease civil war, and further attempts to overthrow Nanking by force, and to submit to the high command of a representative central Government, provided there was created the political framework in which the co-operation of other parties besides the Kuomintang would be possible. At this time also, though not as part of the formal interview, Mao indicated that the Communists would be prepared to make such changes in nomenclature as would facilitate " co-operation," without fundamentally affecting the independent rôle of the Red Army and the Communist Party. Thus, if it were necessary, the Red Army would change its name to the National Revolutionary Army, the name " Soviets " would be abandoned, and the agrarian policy would be modified during the period of preparation for war against Japan. During the exciting weeks that lay ahead, this statement[1] was to have an important influence on events. Prior to its appearance, the Communists' own manifestos were suppressed from the public, and, among the few Nanking leaders who saw them, were received with deep scepticism. With the widespread publication of a foreigner's interview with the Communist leader himself, however, influential groups were to become more convinced of the Communists' sincerity. The demand for a " re-marriage " of the two parties was to gain many new adherents—for the proposal of a cessation of the costly civil war, and the peaceful achievement of unity to resist the menace of Japanese conquest, now appealed to all classes.

.   .   .   .

In the middle of October 1936, after I had been with the Reds nearly four months, arrangements were finally completed for my return to the White World. It had not been easy. Chang Hsueh-liang's friendly Tungpei troops had been withdrawn from nearly every front, and replaced by Nanking or other hostile forces. There was only one outlet then, through a Tungpei division which still had a front with the Reds near Lochuan, a walled city a day's motor-trip north of Sian.

I walked down the main street of Defended Peace for the last time, and the farther I got toward the gate, the more reluctantly I moved. People popped their heads out of offices to shout last remarks. My poker club turned out *en masse* to bid the *maestro* good-bye, and some " little devils " trudged with me to the walls of Pao An. I stopped to take a picture of Old Hsü and Old Hsieh, their arms thrown around each other's shoulders like schoolboys. Only Mao Tse-tung failed to appear; he was still asleep.

" Don't forget my artificial arm ! " called out Tsai.

" Don't forget my films ! " urged Lo Ting-yi.

[1] For the full text of the interview see *The China Weekly Review*, Shanghai, November 14 and 22, 1936.

" We'll be waiting for the air-fleet ! " laughed Yang Shang-k'un.

" Send me in a wife ! " demanded Li Ke-nung.

" And send back those four ounces of cocoa," chided Po Ku.

The whole Red Academy was seated out in the open, under a great tree, listening to a lecture by Lo Fu, when I went past. They all came over, and we shook hands, and I mumbled a few words. Then I turned and forded the stream, waved them a farewell, and rode up quickly with my little caravan. I might be the last foreigner to see any of them alive, I thought. It was very depressing. I felt that I was not going home, but leaving it.

In five days we reached the southern frontier, and I waited there for three days, staying in a tiny village and eating black beans and wild pig. It was a beautiful wooded country, alive with game, and I spent the days in the hills with some farmers and Red soldiers, hunting pig and deer. The bush was crowded with huge pheasants, and one day we even saw, far out of range, two tigers streaking across a clearing in a valley drenched with the purple-gold of autumn. The front was absolutely peaceful, and the Reds had only one battalion stationed here.

On the 20th I got through no man's land safely and behind the Tungpei lines, and on a borrowed horse next day I rode into Lochuan, where a lorry was waiting for me. A day later I was in Sianfu. At the Drum Tower I jumped down from the driver's seat and asked one of the Reds (who were wearing Tungpei uniforms) to toss me my bag. A long search, and then a longer search, while my fears increased. Finally there was no doubt about it. My bag was not there. In that bag were a dozen diaries and notebooks, thirty rolls of film—the first pictures ever taken of the Chinese Red Army—and several pounds of Red magazines, newspapers, and documents. It had to be found !

Excitement under the Drum Tower, while traffic policemen curiously gazed on a short distance away. Whispered consultations. Finally it was realized what had happened. The lorry had been loaded with gunny sacks full of broken Tungpei rifles and guns being sent for repairs, and my bag, in case of any search, had been stuffed into such a sack also. But back at Hsienyang, on the opposite shore of the Wei River, twenty miles behind us, the missing object had been thrown off with the other loads !

The driver stared ruefully at the lorry. "*T'a ma-ti*," he offered in consolation. " Rape its mother."

It was already dusk, and the driver suggested that he wait till morning to go back and hunt for it. Morning! Something warned me that morning would be too late. I insisted, and I finally won the argument. The lorry reversed and returned, and I stayed awake all night in a friend's house in Sianfu wondering whether I would ever see that priceless bag again. If it were opened at Hsienyang, not only would all my things be lost for ever, but that " Tungpei " lorry and all its occupants would be *huai-la*—finished. There were Nanking gendarmes at Hsienyang.

Luckily, as you will see from the pictures in this book, the bag was found. But my hunch about the urgency of the search had been absolutely correct, for early next morning all traffic was completely swept from the streets, and all roads leading into the city were lined with gendarmes and troops. Peasants were cleared out of their homes along the road. Some of the more unsightly huts were simply demolished, so that there would be nothing offensive to the eye. Generalissimo Chiang Kai-shek was paying a sudden call on Sianfu. It would have been impossible then for our lorry to return over that road to the Wei River, for it skirted the heavily guarded aerodrome.

This arrival of the Generalissimo made an unforgettable contrast with the scenes still fresh in my mind—of Mao Tse-tung, or Hsü Hai-tung, or Lin Piao, or Peng Teh-huai non-chalantly strolling down a street in Red China. And the Generalissimo did not even have a price on his head. It vividly suggested who really feared the people and who trusted them. But even all the precautions taken to protect the Generalissimo's life in Sian were to prove inadequate. He had too many enemies among the very troops who were guarding him.

PART TWELVE

WHITE WORLD AGAIN

1

A Preface to Mutiny

I EMERGED from Red China to find a sharpening tension between the Tungpei (ex-Manchurian) troops of Young Marshal Chang Hsueh-liang, and Generalissimo Chiang Kai-shek. The latter was now not only Commander-in-Chief of China's armed forces, but also chairman of the Executive Yuan—a position comparable to that of Premier.

The steps have been described[1] by which the Tungpei troops were gradually being transformed, militarily and politically, from mercenaries who had been shipped to half a dozen different provinces to fight the Reds, into an army infected by the national revolutionary anti-Japanese slogans of its enemy, convinced of the futility of continued civil war, stirred by only one exhortation, loyal to but one central idea—the hope of " fighting back to the old homeland," of recovering Manchuria from the Japanese who had driven them from their homes, and abused and murdered their families. These notions being directly opposed to the maxims then held by Nanking, it has been told how the Tungpei troops, naturally enough, had found themselves with a growing fellow feeling for the anti-Japanese Red Army.

The estrangement had been widened by important occurrences during the four months of my travels. In the South-west a revolt against Nanking had been led by Generals Pai Chung-hsi and Li Tsung-jen, whose chief political demands were based on opposition to Nanking's " pro-Japanese " non-resistance policies. After weeks of near-war, a compromise settlement had finally been reached, but the interim had provided a tremendous stimulus to the anti-Japanese movement throughout China. Three or four Japanese had been killed by angry mobs in various parts of the interior, and Japan had presented to Nanking strong demands for apologies, compensations, and new political concessions. A new Sino-Japanese " incident," followed by a Japanese invasion, seemed a possibility.

Meanwhile the anti-Japanese movement, led by the Left wing National Salvation Association, was, despite stern measures of

[1] Cf. especially, Part I, " Some Han Bronzes."

suppression, rising in strength everywhere, and considerable mass pressure was being indirectly exerted on Nanking to stiffen its attitude. This pressure multiplied when, in October, Japanese-led Mongol and Chinese puppet troops, equipped and trained in Japan's conquered Jehol and Chahar, began an invasion of northern Suiyuan. But the widespread popular demand that this be considered " the last extremity," and the signal for a " war of resistance " on a national scale, was ignored. No mobilization orders were forthcoming. Nanking's standing reply remained. " Internal unification "—i.e. extermination of the Reds—must come first. Many patriotic quarters began to urge that the Communists' proposals for an end to civil war, and the creation of a national front on the basis of " voluntary unification," be accepted by Nanking, in order to concentrate the entire energies of the people to oppose the common peril of Japan. Proponents of such opinions were arrested as " traitors."

But the highest degree of emotional excitement centred in the North-west. Few people realized then how closely the anti-Japanese sentiment of the Tungpei Army was connected with the determination to stop the war against the Reds. Sian seems a long way off to most Chinese as well as to foreigners in the big treaty ports of China, and it is little visited by journalists. No foreign correspondent had been to Sian in recent months, and none had any reliable background to the events that were to take place there—with one exception. That was Miss Nym Wales, an American writer, who in October journeyed to Sian and interviewed the Young Marshal. Miss Wales accurately reported the rising beat of pulse in the North-west:

" In Sianfu, the ' Western Capital' of China, a critical situation is developing in the ranks of Young Marshal Chang Hsueh-liang's bitterly anti-Japanese North-eastern Army, stationed here for suppression of the Reds. These troops, dwindled from 250,000 men in 1931 to 130,000 at present, are all ' men without a country,' homesick, sick of civil war, and in a high temper against the continued non-resistance policy of the Nanking Government toward Japan. The attitude of the lower rank and file might very easily be described as mutinous, and this feeling has permeated even to the high officers.

This condition has given rise to rumours that even Chang Hsueh-liang's previously good personal relations with Chiang Kai-shek have become strained, and that he is planning an alliance with the Red Army in an anti-Japanese United Front, under the direction of a National Defence Government.

" The serious anti-Japanese movement in China is formulating itself not in the various ' incidents ' ranging from North to South, but here in Sianfu among the North-eastern exiles from Manchuria—as one might expect that it logically should. While the movement is being suppressed in other parts of China, in Sianfu it is under the open and enthusiastic leadership of Young Marshal Chang Hsueh-liang—ardently supported by his troops, if not compelled by them to act in this direction."[1]

Reflecting on the significance of her interview with the Young Marshal, Miss Wales wrote:

" In effect, and read in relation to its background, this interview may be interpreted as an attempt to influence Chiang Kai-shek to lead active resistance . . . implying a threat (in his statement) that ' only by resistance to foreign aggression [i.e. not by civil war] can the *real* unification of China be manifested,' and that ' if the Government does not obey the will of the people it cannot stand.' Most significant, this Deputy Commander-in-Chief (second only to Chiang Kai-shek) said that ' if the Communists can sincerely co-operate to resist the common foreign invader, perhaps it is possible that this problem can be settled peacefully.' . . ."

Truly mutinous assertion ! But Chiang Kai-shek plainly underestimated the seriousness of the warning. In October he sent his crack 1st Army as vanguard to attack the Reds in Kansu, and when he arrived in Sianfu it was for the purpose of completing preliminary plans for his sixth general offensive against the Reds. In Sian and Lanchow arrangements were made to accommodate a fleet of over 100 bombers. Tons of torpedoes arrived. It was reported that poison gas was to be used. This was seemingly the only explanation of Chiang's queer boast that he would " destroy

[1] *New York Sun, circa* October 25, 1936.

the remnant Red-bandits in a couple of weeks, or at most a month."[1]

One thing Chiang must have understood after his October visit to Sian. That was that the Tungpei troops were becoming useless in the war against the Communists. In interviews with Tungpei commanders the Generalissimo could now discern a profound lack of interest in his new offensive. One of Chang Hsueh-liang's staff told me later that at this time the Young Marshal formally presented to the Generalissimo the programme for a national front, cessation of civil war, alliance with Russia, and resistance to Japan. Chiang Kai-shek replied, " I will never talk about this until every Red soldier in China is exterminated, and every Communist is in prison." Only then would it be possible to co-operate with Russia.

The Generalissimo went back to his headquarters in Loyang and supervised preparations for the new campaign. Twenty divisions of troops were to be brought into the North-west if necessary. By late November over ten full war-strength divisions had already been concentrated near Tungkuan, outside the historic pass at the gateway to Shensi. Trainloads of shells and supplies poured into Sian. Tanks, armoured cars, motor transport, were prepared to move after them.

But of all these plans for intensified civil war on an immense scale the public—except in the North-west—remained in ignorance. Little crept into the Press about the North-west. The Reds had already been officially " exterminated," and only a few " remnants " were being dispersed—so the official story went. Meanwhile, the Suiyuan (Inner Mongolian) defences were left to provincial troops—who put up a good fight. Not a single Nanking aeroplane rose to combat the Japanese planes daily bombing the Chinese lines. But a lively propaganda kept up the fiction that Nanking troops were leading the defence; at the same time Tokyo and Nanking exchanged assurances that the " local conflict " in Suiyuan must not spread. A few central Government troops—at most two divisions—entered Suiyuan, to be tactically disposed in such a manner as to prevent the provincial troops from really taking this " resistance " business too seriously. It was feared they might actually open an attack on Japanese-held

[1] Cf. Chiang's diary.

territory in Chahar and Jehol. Some Nanking troops were also arranged between the Suiyuan army and the Reds, whom Chiang thought might make a drive into Suiyuan from Shensi, and attempt to lead a real attack on the Japanese.

A flame of strong nationalist feeling swept through the country, and the Japanese demanded the suppression of the National Salvation Movement, which they held responsible for the anti-Japanese agitation. Nanking obliged. Seven of the most prominent leaders of the organization, all respectable bourgeois citizens, including a prominent banker, a lawyer, educators, and writers, were arrested. At the same time the Government suppressed fourteen nationally popular magazines at one stroke. Strikes in the Japanese mills of Shanghai, partly in patriotic protest against the Japanese invasion of Suiyuan, were also broken up with considerable violence by the Japanese, in cooperation with the Kuomintang. When other patriotic strikes occurred in Tsingtao, the Japanese landed their own marines, arrested the strikers, occupied the city. The marines were withdrawn only after Nanking had agreed virtually to prohibit all strikes in Japanese mills of Tsingtao in the future !

All these happenings had further repercussions in the Northwest. In November, under pressure from his own officers, Chang Hsueh-liang dispatched his famous appeal to be sent to the Suiyuan front. " In order to control our troops," this missive concluded, " we should keep our promise to them that whenever the chance comes they will be allowed to carry out their desire of fighting the enemy. Otherwise, they will regard not only myself, but also Your Excellency, as a cheat, and thus will no longer obey us. Please give us the order to mobilize at least a part, if not the whole, of the Tungpei Army, to march immediately to Suiyuan as enforcements to those who are fulfilling their sacred mission of fighting Japanese imperialism there. If so, I, as well as my troops, of more than 100,000, shall follow Your Excellency's leadership to the end." The earnest tone of this whole letter,[1] the burning ambition for *revanche*, the hope of restoring an army's lost prestige, were overwhelmingly evident. But Chiang rejected the suggestion. He still wanted the Tungpei Army to fight the Reds.

[1] Published in Sianfu, January 2, 1937, by the North-west Military Council.

Not long afterwards, importunate, the Marshal flew his plane to Loyang to repeat the request in person. At this time also he interceded for the arrested leaders of the National Salvation Association. Later on, after the arrest of the Generalissimo, Chang Hsueh-liang recounted that conversation:

" ' Recently Generalissimo Chiang arrested and imprisoned seven of our National Salvation leaders in Shanghai. I asked him to release those leaders. Now, none of the National Salvation leaders are my friends or relatives, and I do not even know most of them. But I protested at their arrest because their principles are the same as mine. My request that they be released was rejected. To Chiang I then said: " Your cruelty in dealing with the patriotic movement of the people is exactly the same as that of Yuan Shih-kai or Chang Tsung-chang."

" ' Generalissimo Chiang replied: " That is merely your viewpoint. I am the Government. My action was that of a revolutionary."

" ' Fellow countrymen, do you believe this ? '

" The question was answered by an angry roar from the assembled thousands."[1]

But Chang Hsueh-liang's flight to Loyang at that time had one positive result. The Generalissimo agreed that when he next came to Sian he would explain his plans and strategy to the Tungpei division generals in detail. The Young Marshal returned to impatiently await his superior's second visit. Before Chiang arrived, however, two occurrences intervened which further antagonized the North-west.

The first of these was the signing of the German-Japan anti-Communist agreement, and Italy's unofficial adherence thereto. Italy had already tacitly recognized Japan's conquest of Manchuria, in return for which Japan had acknowledged Italy's control of Abyssinia. The opening of Italian relations with Manchukuo had infuriated the Young Marshal, who had once been pals with Count Ciano. With receipt of this news he denounced both Ciano and Mussolini, and swore to destroy Italian influence in his country. " This is absolutely the end of the

---

[1] A speech reported by the *Hsiking Min Pao*, Sianfu, December 17, 1936.

Fascist movement in China ! " he had exclaimed in a speech before his cadets. The Tungpei people now added one more complaint to their list. German and Italian military advisers were training Chiang's army and his air force to bomb Chinese Reds. Were they not also furnishing Japan with all the military information they had about China ? Had Chiang Kai-shek not been informed in advance, in fact, of the German-Japan Pact, and approved of it ? It was rumoured that he had.

Then, in November also, came news of the disaster to Hu Tsung-nan's famed 1st Army, which on the 21st suffered a severe defeat from the Reds. General Hu, ablest of Nanking's tacticians, had for weeks been moving almost unimpeded into northern Kansu. The Reds had slowly withdrawn, refusing battle except in minor skirmishes. But in various ways they propagandized the Nanking troops about the " United Front," trying to persuade them to halt, issuing declarations that the Red Army would attack no anti-Japanese troops, urging the enemy to join them in resisting Japan. " Chinese must not fight Chinese ! " The propaganda was to prove highly effective.

But General Hu concluded that the Reds were finished—weak, afraid, with no fight left in them. He recklessly pushed on. The Reds continued to withdraw until they had almost reached Holienwan. There they decided to retreat no further; the enemy needed a lesson. It needed to be shown that the United Front also had teeth in it. Suddenly turning, they skilfully manœuvred General Hu's troops into a valley of loessland, surrounded them at dusk, when the air bombardment had ceased, and at night staged a surprise frontal attack, supported by bayonet charges from both flanks. It was zero weather, and the Reds' bare hands were so cold they could not pull the caps from their hand grenades. Hundreds of them went into the enemy lines using their potato-masher grenades for clubs. The fierce onslaught, led by the 1st Army Corps, resulted in the complete destruction and disarming of two infantry brigades and a regiment of cavalry, while thousands of rifles and machine guns were captured, and one Government regiment turned over intact to join the Reds. General Hu beat a hasty retreat, giving up in a few days all the territory which he had " recovered " over a period of weeks. He sat down to wait for the Generalissimo's reinforcements.

The Tungpei troops chuckled among themselves. It was just as they had said: the Reds had more punch in them than ever, and this inauspicious beginning of the new campaign showed how difficult the process of annihilation was going to be. A year, two years, three, and where would they be? Still fighting the Reds. And Japan? In occupation of new and greater areas of Chinese territory. Thus they reasoned. But the obstinate Generalissimo, angered by the humiliation of his best army, censured General Hu and only became more determined to destroy his ten-year enemy.

Into this main theatre of events Chiang Kai-shek stepped from his giant aeroplane on to the flying-field of Sian on December 7, 1936.

Meanwhile, important things had happened on both the right and left wings of the stage. Among the Tungpei commanders an agreement had been reached to present a common request for cancellation of civil war, and resistance to Japan. Into this agreement had come the officers of the army of General Yang Hu-cheng, the Pacification Commissioner of Shensi, who has already been described. General Yang's army, of about 40,000 men, had even less interest in continuing the war against the Reds than the Tungpei troops. To them it was Nanking's war, and they saw no good reason for wrecking themselves against the Reds—many of whom were Shensi people like themselves. It was to them also a disgraceful war, when Japan was invading the neighbouring province of Suiyuan. General Yang's troops, known as the Hsipei Chun, or North-west Army, had some months previously formed a close solidarity with the Tungpei troops, and secretly joined in the truce with the Reds.

All this must have been known in a general way to the Premier-Generalissimo. Although he had no regular troops in Sian, a few months earlier some 1,500 of the notorious Third Gendarmes, a so-called " special service " regiment of the Blueshirts, commanded by his nephew, General Chiang Hsiao-hsien, who was credited with the abduction, imprisonment, and killing of hundreds of radicals, had arrived in the city, established espionage headquarters throughout the province, and begun arrests and kidnappings of alleged " Communist " students, political workers, and soldiers. Shao Li-tzu, the Nanking-appointed governor of Shensi, was in complete control of the police force of the capital. As neither the Young Marshal nor Yang Hu-cheng had any troops but bodyguards in the city, the Generalissimo had practical command there. This situation helped to provoke a further incident. On the 9th, two days after Chiang's arrival, several thousand students held an anti-Japanese demonstration, and started to march to Lintung, to present a petition to the Generalissimo. Governor Shao ordered it to be dispersed. The police, assisted by some of Chiang Kai-shek's gendarmes, roughly handled the students, and at one stage opened fire on them. Two students were wounded, and, as they happened to be children of a Tungpei officer, the shooting was especially inflammatory. Chang Hsueh-liang intervened, stopped the fight, persuaded the students to return to the city, and agreed to present their petition to the Generalissimo. Infuriated, Chiang Kai-shek reprimanded Chang for his " disloyalty " in trying " to represent *both sides*." Chiang Kai-shek himself thinks that this incident between them was the immediate cause of the revolt.

The Generalissimo's whole staff, together with his personal bodyguards, were with him in Sianfu. Chiang refused to see the Tungpei and Hsipei commanders in a group, as they wished, but talked to them separately, and attempted, by various inducements, to break their solidarity. In this effort he failed. One and all acknowledged him as Commander-in-Chief, but each expressed his displeasure with the new campaign, and all asked to be sent to the anti-Japanese front in Suiyuan. For them all Chiang had but one command: " *Destroy the Reds*." " I told them," said Chiang in his own diary, " that the bandit-suppression campaign had been prosecuted to such a stage that it would require only the last five minutes to achieve the final success."

So, despite all the objections and warnings, the Generalissimo summoned a General Staff Congress on the 10th, when final plans were formally adopted to push ahead with the Sixth Campaign. A general mobilization order was prepared for the Hsipei, Tungpei, and Nanking troops already in Kansu and Shensi, together with the Nanking troops waiting at T'ungkuan. It was announced that the order would be published on the 12th. It was openly stated that if Marshal Chang refused these orders his troops would be disarmed by Nanking forces, and he himself would be dismissed from his command.[1] At the same time reports reached both Chang and Yang that the Blueshirts, together with the police, had prepared a " black list " of Communist sympathizers in their armies, who were to be arrested immediately after publication of the mobilization order.

Thus it was as the culmination of this complicated and historic chain of events that Chang Hsueh-liang called a joint meeting of the division commanders of the Tungpei and Hsipei armies at ten o'clock on the night of December 11. Orders had been secretly given on the previous day for a division of Tungpei troops, and a regiment of Yang Hu-cheng's army to move into the environs of Sianfu. The decision was now taken to use these forces to " arrest " the Generalissimo and his staff. The mutiny of 170,000 troops had become a fact.

[1] General Chiang Ting-wen had already been appointed to replace Chang Hsueh-liang as head of the Bandit Suppression Commission.

2

The Generalissimo is Arrested

WHATEVER we may say against its motives, or the political energies behind them, it must be admitted that the *coup de théâtre* enacted at Sian was brilliantly timed and brilliantly executed. It was infinitely less bloody and clumsy than Chiang Kai-shek's *coup d'état* at Nanking or Shanghai, or the Communists' seizure of Canton. No word of the rebels' plans reached their enemies until too late. By six o'clock on the morning of December 12 the whole affair was over. Tungpei and Hsipei troops were in control at Sian. The Blueshirts, surprised in their sleep, had been disarmed and arrested, practically the whole General staff had been surrounded in its quarters at the Sian Guest House, and was imprisoned, Governor Hsiao Li-tzu and the chief of police were also prisoners, the city police force had surrendered to the mutineers, and fifty Nanking bombers and their pilots had been seized at the aerodrome.

But the arrest of the Generalissimo was a bloodier affair. Chiang Kai-shek was staying ten miles from the city, at Lintung, a famous hot springs resort, which had been cleared of all other guests. To Lintung, at midnight, went twenty-six-year-old Captain Sun Ming-chiu, commander of the Young Marshal's bodyguard. Half-way there he picked up 200 Tungpei troops, and at 3 a.m. drove to the outskirts of Lintung. There they waited till five o'clock, when the first lorry, with about fifteen men, roared up to the hotel, was challenged by sentries, and opened fire.

Reinforcements soon arrived for the Tungpei vanguard, and Captain Sun led an assault on the Generalissimo's residence. Taken by complete surprise, the bodyguards put up a short fight—long enough, however, to permit the astounded Generalissimo to escape. When Captain Sun reached his bedroom he had already fled. Sun took a search-party up the side of the rocky, snow-covered hill behind the resort and conducted his man-hunt. Presently they found the Generalissimo's personal servant, and not long afterwards came upon the man himself. Clad only in a loose robe thrown over his nightshirt, his bare feet and hands cut in his nimble flight up the mountain, shaking in the bitter

cold, and minus his false teeth, he was hiding in a cave beside
a great rock—a rock that marked the very spot where once stood
the grave of Ch'in Shih Huang Ti, builder of the Great Wall.

" Sun Ming-chiu hailed him, and the Generalissimo's first
words were, ' If you are my comrade, shoot me and finish it
all.' To which Sun replied, ' We will not shoot. We only ask
you to lead our country against Japan.'

" Chiang remained seated on his rock, and said with difficulty, ' Call Marshal Chang here, and I will come down.'

" ' Marshal Chang isn't here. The troops are rising in the
city; we came to protect you.'

" At this the Generalissimo seemed much relieved, and
called for a horse to take him down the mountain. ' There is
no horse here,' said Sun, ' but I will carry you down the
mountain on my back.' And he knelt at Chiang's feet. After
some hesitation, Chiang accepted, and climbed painfully on
to the broad back of the young officer. They proceeded
solemnly down the slope in this fashion, escorted by troops,
until a servant arrived with Chiang's shoes. The little group
got into a car at the foot of the hill, and set off for Sian.

" ' The past is the past,' Sun said to him. ' From now on
there must be a new policy for China. What are you going to
do ? . . . The one urgent task for China is to fight Japan.
This is the special demand of the men of the North-east.
Why do you not fight Japan, but instead give the order to
fight the Red Army ? '

" ' I am the leader of the Chinese people,' Chiang shouted.
' I represent the nation. I think my policy is correct.' "[1]

In this way, a little bloody but unbowed, the Generalissimo
arrived in the city, where he became the involuntary guest of
General Yang Hu-chang and the Young Marshal.

On the day of the coup all division commanders of the Tungpei
and Hsipei armies signed and issued a circular telegram addressed to the central Government, to various provincial
leaders, and to the people at large. The brief missive explained
that " in order to stimulate his awakening " the Generalissimo

[1] Part of an interview with Sun Ming-chiu by James Bertram, who was my
correspondent in Sianfu for the *Daily Herald*.

had been " requested to remain for the time being in Sianfu."
Meanwhile, his personal safety was guaranteed. The demands of
" national salvation " submitted to the Generalissimo were
broadcast to the nation—but everywhere suppressed. Here are
the famous eight points:

1. Reorganize the Nanking Government and admit all
parties to share the joint responsibility of national salvation.
2. End all civil war immediately *and adopt the policy of
armed resistance against Japan.*
3. Release the (seven) leaders of the patriotic movement in
Shanghai.
4. Pardon all political prisoners.
5. Guarantee the people liberty of assembly.
6. Safeguard the people's rights of patriotic organization
and political liberty.
7. Put into effect the will of Dr. Sun Yat-sen.
8. Immediately convene a National Salvation conference.

To this programme the Chinese Red Army, the Soviet Government and the Communist Party of China immediately offered
their support.[1] A few days later Chang Hsueh-liang sent to Pao
An his personal plane, which returned to Sian with three Red
delegates: Chou En-lai, vice-chairman of the military council;
Yeh Chien-ying, chief-of-staff of the East Front Army; and Po
Ku, chairman of the North-west Branch Soviet Government. A
joint meeting was called between the Tungpei, Hsipei, and Red
Army delegates, and the three groups became open allies. On
the 14th an announcement was issued of the formation of a
United Anti-Japanese Army, consisting of about 130,000
Tungpei troops, 40,000 Hsipei troops, and approximately
90,000 troops of the Red Army.

Chang Hsueh-liang was elected chairman of the United Anti-
Japanese Military Council, and Yang Hu-cheng vice-chairman.
Tungpei troops under General Yu Hsueh-chung had on the 12th
carried out a coup of their own against the central Government
officials and troops in Lanchow, capital of Kansu province, and

[1] Seven of the above eight points correspond exactly to the programme of
" national salvation " advocated in a circular telegram issued by the Communist
Party and the Soviet Government on December 1, 1936. Chang Hsueh-liang and
the Communists had already agreed on this programme at least that early, therefore, though the Communists did not anticipate that Chang was to adopt such
surprising measures in bringing it to the consideration of Nanking.

had disarmed the Nanking garrison there. In the rest of Kansu the Reds and the Manchurian troops together held control of all main communications, surrounding about 50,000 Nanking troops in that province, so that the rebels had effective power in all Shensi and Kansu.

Immediately after the incident, Tungpei and Hsipei troops moved eastward to the Shensi–Shansi and Shensi–Honan borders, on instructions from the new Council. From the same Council the Red Army took orders to push southward. In a week the Reds were in occupation of virtually the whole of north Shensi above the Wei River. A Red vanguard under Peng Teh-huai was located at San Yuan, a city only thirty miles from Sianfu. Another contingent of 10,000 Reds under Hsü Hai-tung circled around Sianfu and moved over to the Shensi–Honan border. The Red, North-eastern and North-western troops stood intersticed, shoulder to shoulder, along the Shensi border. But while these defensive arrangements proceeded, all three armies issued clear-cut statements declaring their opposition to a new internal war, reaffirming their purely political aims, and denying any intentions of attack.

Steps were taken at once to carry out the eight points—to which the Red Army scrupulously adhered, in its new territory, refraining from executing the programme of agrarian revolution. All orders for war against the Reds were cancelled. Over 400 political prisoners in Sianfu were released. Censorship of the Press was removed, and all suppression of patriotic (anti-Japanese) organizations was lifted. Hundreds of students were freed to work among the populace, building United Front organizations in every class. They toured into the villages also, where they began to train and arm the farmers, politically and militarily. In the army the political workers conducted an unprecedented anti-Japanese campaign. Mass meetings were summoned almost daily. At one of them over 100,000 people attended. At all, the slogans were to unite to resist Japan and to stop civil war—the latter a very realistic appeal to farmers whose grain and cattle had already been commandeered for the coming anti-Red drive.

But news of all these happenings was suppressed outside the provinces of the North-west. Editors who dared publish anything emanating from Sian, as even the highly respectable *Ta Kung Pao* pointed out, were threatened with instant arrest. Meanwhile Nanking's propaganda machine threw out a smokescreen that further confused an already befuddled public. Dumbfounded by the news, Nanking's first reaction was to call a meeting of the Standing Committee (of the Central Executive Committee and the Central Political Council), which promptly pronounced Chang Hsueh-liang a rebel, dismissed him from his posts, and demanded the release of the Generalissimo, failing which punitive operations would begin. People accepted the sensational news with varying reactions, some with jubilance at Chiang's arrest, others with consternation. Signs of disintegration appeared everywhere. Chiang Kai-shek was the pivot around which the contradictory forces in China had for a while found some degree of stabilization. With his removal from the central position all those forces were freed, and thesis and antithesis came into open conflict, to seek by necessity new alignments, new centralizing influences, new syntheses.

For three days nobody knew whether Chiang Kai-shek was dead or alive—except the Associated Press, which flatly announced that Chang Hsueh-liang had described over the radio how and why he had killed him. Nobody knew exactly what the rebels planned to do. Few fully realized the political significance of their position; even some of their sympathizers, misled by false reports, were inclined to condemn them. Nanking cut all communications with the North-west, and its papers and manifestos were burned by the censors. Sian broadcast all day long, over and over again, not attacks on the Government, but explanations of its actions, appeals for reason and peace; but Nanking's powerful radio station turned on a deafening siren which blotted out everything they said. Never before in China was the appalling power of dictatorship over all means of public expression so mightily demonstrated.

Hundreds of words were deleted from my own dispatches. I made several attempts to send out the eight demands of the North-west—which might have helped a little to clarify the enigma for Western readers—but the censors let out not a word. Many of the foreign correspondents were completely ignorant of recent happenings in the North-west, and glibly accepted as news every falsehood fabricated by the propaganda shops. For while real news and facts were rigorously suppressed, the Kuomintang and its adherents released to the world some puerile lies which made China appear much more of a madhouse than it really was. There were such yarns as these: the rebels had nailed the chief of police to the city gates; the Reds had occupied Sian, were looting the city, and flying Red banners on the walls; Chang Hsueh-liang had been assassinated by his own men. Almost daily it was stated by Nanking that riots were taking place in Sian. The Reds were abducting young boys and girls. Women were being "communized." The entire Tungpei and Hsipei armies had turned bandit. There was looting everywhere. Chang Hsueh-liang was demanding $80,000,000 ransom for the Generalissimo.[1] Japan was behind Chang Hsueh-liang. Moscow was behind him. He was a Red. He was a drug addict. He was an " ungrateful scoundrel for whom death was too good." He was a bandit.

Many of the wildest rumours circulated had their origin also with the Japanese Press in China, and even with high Japanese officials. Japanese were especially fertile with alarming " eye-witness " reports of the " Red menace " in Sian—although they, like everybody else, had no contact whatever with that city. The Japanese also discovered Soviet Russian intrigue behind the coup. But they met their masters in propaganda in Moscow's Press. *Izvestia* and *Pravda* went so far in their official disclaimers of responsibility, denunciations of Chang Hsueh-liang, and hosannas to Chiang Kai-shek, that they invented a story showing that the Sian affair was jointly inspired by the former Chinese premier, Wang Ching-wei, and " the Japanese imperialists "—a libel so antipodal to the facts that even the most reactionary Press in China had not dared to suggest it, out of fear of ridicule. " Prevarication is permissible, gentlemen," it was Lenin who once exclaimed, " but within limits ! "

The barrage of slander continued for days. But after the first week of Chiang's captivity Nanking's efforts to cork up the news behind the exciting events began to prove inadequate. Leaks occurred, and then big gaps. The eight-point programme was widely published in the surreptitious Press, and won adherents

---

Mme Chiang Kai-shek, deploring such rumours, wrote that " no question of money or increased power or position was at any time brought up."

among liberals and progressives, for it was really a liberal-progressive bourgeois programme. And the public began to realize that the North-west did not mean to make civil war, but to stop it. Sentiment slowly began to change from fear for the safety of an individual militarist into fear for the safety of the State. Civil war now could not save Chiang, but it might ruin China.

Intrigue for capture of the hegemony of power had begun in Nanking with the news of Chiang's capture. Ambitious War Minister Ho Ying-chin, closely affiliated with the pro-Japanese " political science clique " of the Kuomintang, then in high office at Nanking—and against whom the eight-point programme was primarily directed—was hot for a " punitive expedition." In this General Ho was fully supported (" instigated " is more probably the word, as General Ho is a man born to be " instigated ") by the pro-Fascist Whampoa clique, the Blueshirts, the Wang Ching-wei (out-of-office) faction, the Western Hills group, the " C. E." faction, and Nanking's German and Italian advisers. They all saw in the situation an opportunity to seize complete military power, relegating the liberal, pro-American, pro-British, pro-Russian, and United Front groups in the Kuomintang to political nonentity. General Ho promptly mobilized twenty Nanking divisions and moved them toward the Honan–Shensi border. He sent squadrons of aeroplanes roaring over Sianfu, and made tentative thrusts at the rebels' lines with his infantry. Some of the Nanking planes (anti-Japanese " birthday gifts " to the Generalissimo) experimentally bombed Weinan and Huahsien, inside the Shensi border, and killed a number of factory operatives. When he learned of the bombing, Chiang Kai-shek writes in his diary, he was " very glad."

But evidently not so Mme Chiang, who then understood the situation better than her husband. Angered and alarmed at these preparations for a " feast over the corpse " (people in Nanking then thought the Generalissimo would not come out of Sian alive), she called on General Ho and demanded an explanation. If he began a war, could he stop it ? Could he save her husband, whose safety, she wrote, " was inseparable from the continued existence of the nation itself " ? Did he want to kill her husband ? The General blanched. She insisted that he halt the hostilities and bend his genius to secure the release of M. Chiang. She

Oc

wanted him back still breathing. And she won her point—until Chiang's own envoy reached Nanking.

It became evident also that if war started on a big scale the North-west would be not without allies ! Military and political leaders in Kwangsi, Kwantung, Yunnan, Hunan, Szechuan, Shantung, Hopei, Chahar, Shansi, Suiyuan, and Ninghsia were all marginal cases, and it was almost certain none of them would lift a finger to help a war begun by Ho Ying-chin. Any one or even all of them might turn to with the rebels. Controlling political cliques in all those provinces would at best demand a big price ·for neutrality, and everyone would manœuvre to increase its power during the conflict. This became obvious on the 23rd, when a circular telegram was issued by powerful Generals Sung Cheh-yuan and Han Fu-chu (rulers of Hopei and Shantung), which urged a peaceful settlement, definitely warned against the opening of hostilities, and clearly intimated a lack of sympathy with General Ho's plans.

The big question now became this: whether Chiang Kai-shek could, even from his seat of captivity in Sian, still muster enough support in Nanking to prevent the outbreak of an exhausting war which was certain in any case to mean his own political, if not physical, demise. In Nanking and Shanghai his brothers-in-law, T. V. Soong, chairman of the Central Bank of China, H. H. Kung, acting premier, Mme Chiang, and even Chiang's sister-in-law, Mme Sun Yat-sen (whose bitter hatred for Chiang was well known), rallied Chiang's personal followers and worked frantically to prevent the more reactionary elements in Nanking from initiating an offensive in the name of an " anti-Communist punitive expedition."

Meanwhile, swift changes of heart were taking place in Sian. Soon after his capture the Generalissimo had begun to realize that perhaps his worst " betrayers " were not in Sian but in Nanking. Contemplating this situation, Chiang Kai-shek must have decided that he did not choose to be the martyr over whose dead body General Ho Ying-chin or anybody else would climb to dictatorial power. Descending from his Olympian perch, he promptly began in a very astute and realistic manner to deal with the common mortals who held his life in their hands. Even the Red-bandits.

3

Chiang, Chang and the Reds

THE story of the Generalissimo's ordeal in Sian has been written by no less an authority than the Generalissimo himself, with the able collaboration of his charming wife, Chiang Soong Mei-ling. Those who have not read their absorbing narrative of this turning-point episode in Chinese history are warmly urged to do so. I know of no more exciting and dramatic a document of recent times, and none which, for the reader equipped with some knowledge of China, throws into such sharp and vivid focus the character and mentality of its rulers.

The facts presented here, therefore, are offered in all humility merely as a meagre supplement to the efforts of the Premier-Generalissimo and his brave and talented wife. They saw the events at Sian as an outrage inflicted upon their own highly emotional assertions of personal destiny, and have given us the subjective account of their experiences. But the heavy impingement of those events on their own lives naturally imposed great restraints, and privately they would probably be the first to admit that reasons of politics, and the necessity of maintaining the dignity of office, obliged them to omit much material of value.

Here it must be emphasized that for most Chinese, a race of pragmatists, ethics were not primarily involved in judging the events at Sian. Chinese history is of course full of similar occurrences, especially in the ancient classics of feudal combat, which every Chinese general learns almost by heart. And there are plenty of recent precedents. In 1924 the "Christian General," Feng Yü-hsiang, arrested and held prisoner the then President of China, Tsao K'un, and forced him to accept his political demands. Public esteem for Feng very rapidly increased. He is to-day vice-chairman of Chiang Kai-shek's Military Affairs Commission. Other recent examples have been provided by Chiang Kai-shek himself. Not so long ago he "detained" the late Hu Han-min, his "elder brother," senior and rival in the

---

[1] *Sian, A Coup d'État*, by Generalissimo and Mme Chiang Kai-shek (Shanghai, 1937).

Kuomintang. Another instance was the kidnapping of General Li Chai-sum. Chiang kept him prisoner in Nanking until he had broken his political power.

Then it should be remembered that China is not yet a democratic country, and very often in politics it reverts to pure feudalism. With the Press completely stifled, and the populace disenfranchised, everybody knew quite well that there was but one effective way to censure Nanking, or alter its policies. That was by armed demonstration, or what the Chinese call *ping chien*—" military persuasion "—a recognized tactic in Chinese political manœuvre. Sentimentality discarded for a moment, it may be held that Chang Hsueh-liang chose the most humane and direct method conceivable by which to achieve his purpose, when he used direct action upon the head of the dictatorship. It cost a minimum loss of life, and a minimum of bloodshed. It was a feudal method, yes, but the Marshal was dealing with a personality whose pivotal rôle in semi-feudal politics he intuitively understood. His action was framed in terms of utmost realism, and to-day it is generally recognized that its objective historical effects were progressive.

But was Chiang Kai-shek's life ever really in serious danger ?

It appears that it was. Not from the Young Marshal, and not from the Reds. From Yang Hu-ch'eng, possibly. But most certainly from the radical younger officers of the North-eastern and North-western armies, from the discontented and mutinous soldiery, and from the organized and arming masses, all of whom demanded a voice in the disposal of the Premier. Resolutions passed by the young officers called for a mass trial of " Traitor " Chiang and all his staff. The mood of the army decidedly favoured the Generalissimo's immolation. Curiously enough, it fell to the lot of the Communists to persuade them that his life should be saved !

Communist policy throughout the Sian incident has never been clearly explained. Many people assumed that the Communists, in triumphant revenge for the decade of relentless war which Chiang Kai-shek had waged against them, would now demand his death. Many believed that they would use this opportunity to coalesce with the Tungpei and Hsipei armies, greatly enlarge their base, and challenge Nanking in a great new struggle for power. Actually they did nothing of the sort. They not only urged a peaceful settlement, and the release of Chiang Kai-shek, but also his return to leadership in Nanking. Even Mme Chiang says that, " quite contrary to outside beliefs, they [the Reds] were not interested in detaining the Generalissimo." But why not ?

Allusions have frequently been made to the demands of the Communists for cessation of civil war, a " national United Front " to oppose Japan, and the realization of a democratic political structure at Nanking. These slogans were absolutely honest, *simply because* they coincided with the dynamics of a strategy forced upon the Communists by all objective conditions. Economically, politically, militarily, in every way, they really needed peace, really wanted a representative, many-sided democracy, to achieve their immediate goals. They saw clearly that such a democracy was the only satisfactory formation under which it was now practicable to unite the whole nation in an anti-imperialist struggle for independence against Japan. And this struggle, they had fully convinced themselves, must precede, was inseparable from, indeed must simultaneously initiate, further efforts to achieve social revolution in China. They had learned empirically that continued revolutionary war, in the face of a foreign menace which promised extinction for the entire nation, would further weaken not only the national strength of resistance, but with it perhaps bury the potential forces of the revolution itself.

" The victory of the Chinese national liberation movement," said Mao Tse-tung, " will be part of the victory of world Communism, because to defeat imperialism in China means the destruction of one of its most powerful bases. If China wins its independence, the world revolution will progress very rapidly. If our country is subjugated by the enemy, we shall lose everything. *For a people being deprived of its national freedom, the revolutionary task is not immediate Socialism, but the struggle for independence. We cannot even discuss Communism if we are robbed of a country in which to practise it.*"[1]

Thus it was fundamentally on the conclusions of this thesis that the Communists based their peace proposals to the Kuomintang,

---

[1] In an interview with me at Pao An. Italics mine.

even before the capture of the Generalissimo. Throughout that crisis they adhered to their " line " with amazing steadiness, and a dispassionate objectivity unequalled in the highly personalized politics of China. Despite all the temptations which the situation obviously presented to them, they gave a demonstration of Party discipline which must profoundly impress any candid observer. From the very beginning they recognized that the central meaning of Sian was for them the opportunity to demonstrate the sincerity for their programme for a United Front. They had nothing to do with the arrest of Chiang Kai-shek. It astonished them as much as the rest of the country. But they had much to do with its *dénouement*.

Immediately after hearing of the event, the Soviet Government and the Communist Party called a joint meeting, at which it was decided to support the eight-point programme, and to participate in the United Anti-Japanese Council. Soon afterwards they issued a circular telegram[1] expressing the belief that " the Sian leaders acted with patriotic sincerity and zeal, wishing speedily to formulate a national policy of immediate resistance to Japan." The telegram strongly condemned Ho Ying-chin's punitive expedition, declaring that " if civil war is launched, the whole nation will be plunged into complete chaos, the Japanese robbers, taking advantage of this, will invade our nation, and enslavement will be our fate." To secure a peaceful settlement, the Reds urged that negotiations be opened on the basis of no war, and the summoning of a peace conference of all parties, at which would be discussed the programme of united national resistance to Japan. This telegram clearly indicated the policy followed out by the Red delegates whom Marshal Chang—he very largely relied upon them for political advice throughout the incident—summoned to Sian.

Shortly after his arrival, the head of the Communist delegation, Chou En-lai, went to see Chiang Kai-shek.[2] One can easily imagine the effect of this meeting on the Generalissimo. Still physically weak and psychologically deeply shaken by his experiences, Chiang is said to have turned pale with

[1] " Proposal for the Convention of a Peace Conference," Pao An, December 19, 1936.

[2] In his own account Chiang does not even mention having talked to Chou En-lai.

apprehension when Chou En-lai—his former political attaché, for whose head he had once offered $80,000—entered the room and gave him a friendly greeting. He must have at once concluded that the Red Army had entered Sian, and that he was to be turned over to it as captive! Such a fear also troubled the comely head of Mme Chiang Kai-shek, who says that she " felt the objective (if Chiang were removed from Sian) would be somewhere behind Red lines."

But the Generalissimo was quickly relieved of this apprehension by both Chou and the Marshal, both of whom acknowledged him as Commander-in-Chief, and sat down to explain the attitude of the Communists toward the national crisis. At first frigidly silent, Chiang gradually thawed as he listened, for the first time during his decade of war against it, to the Communist point of view. Between December 17 and 25 Chiang Kai-shek, Chang Hsueh-liang, Yang Hu-ch'eng, and the Reds held frequent conversations. As is well known, Chiang at first refused even to discuss the rebels' programme. But as he remained isolated from the environment provided for so long by his own satellites, as news came of the intrigues going on in Nanking, as his fears increased of the consequences of a big civil war, he became more convinced not only of the sincerity of his immediate captors, but also of the Reds, in their opposition to civil war and their readiness to assist in the peaceful unification of the country, under his own leadership, provided he defined a policy of positive armed resistance to Japan. Here in these meetings also the four points may have been discussed which eventually became the basis of a truce between Nanking and the Soviets.

Chiang naturally does not record the details of these discussions in his diary, for his position was, and had to be, that he never " bargained " for the peace that was achieved. There could be only " submission to the Government." The full content of these two weeks must remain obscure until Chang Hsueh-liang and others record their versions of the interviews—which, in view of present political formations, may not be for some time. From available facts, however, it is possible to reconstruct the outline of events after the 12th.

The first progress made toward an agreement was the arrival in Sian on December 14 of an Australian, Mr. W. H. Donald, the

Generalissimo's " foreign friend," a kind of unofficial adviser to Chiang, who had formerly served Chang Hsueh-liang in a similar capacity. Why did the Young Marshal invite Donald, of all people, to come to see with his own eyes and give the world " assurances of his [Chiang's] safety and comfort ? " The reason casts an interesting sidelight on Chinese psychology. Chang knew, and so did Nanking, that nobody would believe the word of any Chinese who went on such a mission, in such a crisis. But a foreigner, being an " outside party," would be trusted !

Donald returned to Loyang on the 15th, and telephoned his report to Nanking. Chiang was alive and well treated. He also brought word that the Generalissimo was sending General Chiang Ting-wen (one of his captured staff members) with an autographed letter to the War Ministry and the Government at Nanking. This news strengthened Mme Chiang's hand very much against the warmongers, as she now had definite proof not only that her husband still lived, but that there was " another way " (besides war), as Donald had put it. A peaceful settlement was possible.

On the 18th, General Chiang Ting-wen reached Nanking with the Generalissimo's letter, ordering a halt in War Minister Ho's " punitive expedition." General Chiang Ting-wen also had the delicate mission of returning to Sian with some delegates from Nanking. As first choice in " delegates," Chang Hsueh-liang had naturally enough suggested Dr. H. H. Kung, the heavy-jowled brother-in-law of the Generalissimo, who was then not only Finance Minister but, in Chiang's absence, also acting-Premier and head of the State. Dr. Kung demurred, for " doctors advised against Dr. Kung's flying to Sian," Mme Chiang relates. But the rest of Nanking also advised against it, for his trip would surely have been generally interpreted as the opening of official negotiations, and this, General Ho Ying-chin insisted, must be avoided, for the sake of the Government's prestige. As compromise, therefore, Chiang Kai-shek's other brother-in-law, Harvard-educated T. V. Soong, head of the National Economic Council, went in Dr. Kung's place. " T. V.," who belonged to the liberal elements in Nanking, the so-called " European-American " group in the Kuomintang (which was extremely anti-Japanese, and just now favoured the United Front movement), was *persona grata* in Sian, and the best possible mediator. With " T. V." flew General Ku Tsu-tung, the only important Nanking general, besides War Minister Ho, who had not been captured in the *coup d'état.*

T. V. Soong arrived in Sian by plane on the 20th. By this time a general agreement " in principle " seems to have already been reached. The Generalissimo makes no reference to it, but the following excerpts from the statement issued to the foreign Press by Marshal Chang Hsueh-liang on the 19th indicates that he, at least, regarded the settlement as virtually complete :

" The Generalissimo's prolonged stay here is not of our doing. As soon as Mr. Donald arrived last Monday, and the Generalissimo had somewhat recovered from his natural indignation, and his reluctance to talk, he calmly enough discussed the problems confronting us all, and by Tuesday had agreed in principle with the points we had in view for adoption of a defined national policy and the effecting of changes to permit the nation to develop logically and freely, both politically and materially, and in accordance with the will of the late Dr. Sun Yat-sen.

" I therefore telegraphed, welcoming anyone to come from Nanking to hear the Generalissimo's views, and arrange with him for the necessary safeguards to prevent the development of civil warfare. The Generalissimo naturally vigorously demanded that he be released to proceed to Nanking, but while I personally had full confidence that the Generalissimo would carry out his promises, it was impossible to risk his being persuaded after his arrival at Nanking to continue with the warfare. . . . He acquiesced in the view, however, and ever since then he has been waiting in vain, as have we, for someone to arrive from Nanking competent to deal with the matter (i.e. to offer adequate guarantees), so that the Generalissimo can return to the capital.

" That is all. It is a strange thing that there has been this delay. Had someone come, he could have returned some days ago. . . .

" CHANG HSUEH-LIANG."[1]

[1] This telegram was sent from Sianfu on December 19, addressed to Frazer, *Times* correspondent in Shanghai, with the request that it be given to other correspondents. Nanking censors suppressed it. A copy was also given to Mr. W. H. Donald, who is the source of this quotation.

But serious trouble was developing in the ranks of the radical younger officers of the Tungpei Army. They had acquired strong direct voice in the affairs of Chang's military council, and their views were now important. Infected by the temper of the strong mass movement now spreading throughout the North-west, they were at first fiercely opposed to the release of Chiang Kai-shek, until Nanking began to carry out the eight-point programme. The majority, in fact, insisted upon giving Chiang a " popular trial " for his life, before an enormous mass meeting which they planned to call.

The possibility of this public humiliation had also occurred to Chiang. No one knew any better than he the potentialities of the movement that had been set afoot in the North-west, for a similar rising had almost overwhelmed him in 1927. Chiang's whole career had been a struggle against the intervention in his well-ordered chain of events of that disturbing imperative which he calls " the mob." Talk of the " popular trial " was even on the lips of the sentries around him; Chiang tells of listening through the doorway to the conversation of his jailers, in which his fate was discussed. " When I heard [the words] ' the people's verdict,' I realized that it was a malicious plot to kill me by using the mob as their excuse."

But here the Red delegation was most effective. Following their own talks with Chiang, they had received enough assurances from him (aside from assurances now clearly to be inferred from the whole situation) to believe that if released he would be obliged to stop civil war, and in general to carry out the whole " United Front " programme. But to do so Chiang's position must be preserved, he must return to Nanking with his prestige still intact. They therefore saw clearly that if he signed any agreement, and this became known, or if he were submitted to the indignity of a " people's trial," these facts would irreparably injure him, and destroy his position of leadership. Worse still, if Chiang were killed, civil war inevitably would develop on an immense scale, the decade of stalemate in the Red-Kuomintang war would be very much prolonged, and the hopes of achieving an anti-Japanese national front would become remote indeed. From such a prospect no party could hope to benefit, only China could suffer, and only Japan gain. So, at least, the Reds argued.

Thus Po Ku, Yeh Chien-ying, Chou En-lai, and other Communists in Sian now spent many hours, often talking through an entire night, explaining and explaining the reasons for their policy. Their position was extremely confusing to the young Tungpei radicals, for they had expected the Reds to be the first to cry for Chiang's blood. Some of them actually wept in anger at the " betrayal "—for this group looked for political leadership to the Communists, who had as much influence with them as Chang Hsueh-liang himself. But though most of them—and Yang Hu-ch'eng with them—remained unconvinced of the wisdom of releasing Chiang, the demand for his death somewhat diminished. Gradually a more reasonable attitude prevailed. With less pressure upon him now for drastic action, Chang Hsueh-liang made more progress with his conversations.

Besides T. V. Soong, Donald, and two or three other arrivals from Nanking, there was already a big part of the Government in Sian, including the Governors of Shensi and Kansu, the Minister of Interior, the Vice-Minister of War, the President of the Military Advisory Council, the Chief Aide-de-Camp of the Generalissimo, and assorted members of the General Staff, who had been " detained " with Chiang Kai-shek. Most of them took some part in the parleys with Chang Hsueh-liang, Yang Hu-ch'eng, Chou En-lai, and high commanders of the Tungpei Army. When it came to actual negotiations, apparently none of the eight demands was accepted *per se*, for both sides recognized the necessity of upholding the prestige of the Government mechanism. But Chinese demands always begin with the *ne plus ultra*, not with any real notion that it is actually attainable, but because it erects a high point from which one can *coast* down to the sordid process of bargaining. Sian was no exception.

The substantial meaning of the eight demands to those who supported them was, in correct order of importance, as follows: (1) cessation of civil war and co-operation between the Kuomintang and the Communists; (2) a defined policy of armed resistance against any further Japanese aggression; (3) dismissal of certain " pro-Japanese " officials in Nanking, and the adoption of an active diplomacy for creating closer relations (alliances, if possible) with Great Britain, America, and Soviet Russia; (4) reorganization of the Tungpei and Hsipei armies on an equal footing (politically and militarily) with Nanking's forces; (5) greater political freedom for the people; and (6) the creation of some sort of democratic political structure at Nanking.

Those seem to have been the main points of agreement, between Chiang Kai-shek and Chang Hsueh-liang before they left Sian. Chiang also made a personal guarantee that there would be no more civil war. It is certain that Chiang Kai-shek is quite honest in saying that he signed no document, and there is no evidence to support any claims that he did. But although Nanking and the Generalissimo still had their " face," subsequent events were to show that the Young Marshal had not lost his entirely in vain.

The arrival of Mme Chiang on the 22nd no doubt hastened the termination of the interviews, and (as in the lively account of her three days in Sian she makes abundantly clear) her own importunity and scolding of Chang Hsueh-liang speeded up the Generalissimo's release. Just as her husband compared himself with Jesus Christ on the Cross, so also Mme Chiang recognized her own rôle as a biblical one, quoting, " Jehovah will now do a new thing, and that is, he will make a woman protect a man." On the 25th, when Mme Chiang was wistfully wondering if " Santa Claus would pass by Sian," old Nick himself at last appeared in the person of Chang Hsueh-liang, who announced that he had won all the arguments with his officers. He would that day fly them back to Nanking. And he did.

Finally, there was that last and flabbergasting gesture of face-saving. Marshal Chang Hsueh-liang, flying in his own plane, went with the Generalissimo to the capital to await punishment !

4

" *Point Counter Point* "

AND now there began the last act, and the most wonderful and
puzzling of all to novitiates (and even to some veteran observers)
in the art of Oriental make-believe and dissimulation. During the
next three months most of the political involutions created at
Sian were completely unravelled, and in the end the scene was
radically altered. Great conquests were made and victories won.
Great losses and retreats were recorded too. But the duels fought
were like those you see in a Chinese theatre between two warriors
of old. They fling out blood-curdling yells, viciously slashing the
air, but never actually touching each other, and in the end, after
the loser has acknowledged his demise by languidly draping
himself on the floor for a moment, he pulls himself together and
stalks from the stage under his own locomotion, with the gravest
dignity.

Such was the fantastic and yet completely fascinating shadow-
boxing that went on at Nanking. Everybody " won," and only
history was cheated—of a victim.

" Blushing with shame, I have followed you to the capital for
the appropriate punishment I deserve, so as to vindicate discipline," says Chang Hsueh-liang to the Generalissimo, immediately after reaching Nanking.

" Due to my lack of virtue and defects in my training of
subordinates," gallantly responds Chiang, " an unprecedented
revolt broke out. . . . Now that you have expressed repentance, I
will request the Central authorities to adopt suitable measures
for rehabilitation of the situation."

And what are the rehabilitation measures? Watch carefully
now to see how superbly all acts of severity are commuted by
acts of conciliation, note the fine adjustment of punishment and
compensation. Here is the work of master in the strategy of
compromise, of perfect knowledge of how to split the difference
between what the Chinese call *yu shih wu ming*, the " reality
without the name," and *yu ming wu shih*, the " name without
the reality."

What is Chiang's first move on returning to Nanking? He

issues a long statement confessing his inability to prevent the revolt, and his failure as Premier. He immediately orders the withdrawal of all Government troops from Shensi—thus fulfilling his promise to prevent civil war—and offers his resignation. He will repeat it the traditional three times. But in reality he takes his resignation no more seriously than does Nanking. For on December 29 he calls an emergency meeting of the standing committee of the Central Executive Committee, and " requests " this highest organ of the Kuomintang to do four important things. These are: to hand over to the Military Affairs Commission (of which he is chairman) the punishment of Chang Hsueh-liang; to delegate to the Military Affairs Commission the settlement of the North-west problem; to terminate military operations against the rebels; and to abolish (Ho Ying-chin's) " punitive expedition " headquarters. His recommendations are obeyed.

On December 31 Chang Hsueh-liang is sentenced by tribunal (at which Chiang is not present) to ten years' imprisonment, and deprivation of civil rights for five years. On the following day he is pardoned. And all the time he is the personal guest of Chiang Kai-shek's brother-in-law and recent envoy to Sian, T. V. Soong ! Then, on January 6, the Generalissimo's Sian headquarters for Bandit Suppression (Anti-Communist Campaign) are abolished. Two days later it is already known that the skids are under Japanese-speaking, Japanese-educated Foreign Minister Chang Chun, important leader of the " political science clique " in the Kuomintang. Chang Chun was the principal target of the North-west in its charges of " pro-Japanese " officials at Nanking. He is replaced by Dr. Wang Chung-hui, American-educated barrister, and a leader of the Ou-Mei P'ai, the anti-Japanese " European-American " clique of Kuomintang politicians, whom the North-west regards with favour.

Again at Chiang's request, a plenary session of the Kuomintang is summoned for February 15. This is only the third time in party history that such a session has been called. In the past its functions have been easily predictable, and confined to legalizing important changes in party policy decided in advance by the ruling cliques, which in coalition are the Chiang Kai-shek dictatorship. What is the important change of policy that is to be introduced now? Hundreds of resolutions are prepared for presentation to this august body. The great majority deal with " national salvation."

During January and early February, Chiang Kai-shek gets " sick leave." He retires, with Chang Hsueh-liang, to rest in the Generalissimo's country home near Fenghua, his native place in Chekiang. His first resignation rejected, Chiang repeats it. Meanwhile, ostensibly freed from official duties, he has complete command of the settlement of the North-west issue, complete control of the conversations now going on with the Tungpei, Hsipei, and Red Army commanders. Chang Hsueh-liang, " in disgrace," is at his side, still a virtual prisoner. And in Nanking, Chiang's lieutenants are busily gathering the information he needs in order to estimate the new balance of forces created by the incident for and against him, in order to re-evaluate his following, in order to ferret out the loyalists from the opportunists who were ready to bomb him in Sian. The Sian incident has indeed been, as Mme Chiang called it, " a blessing in disguise." In more ways than one.

On February 10 the Central Executive Committee of the Communist Party addresses to the National Government at Nanking, and to the Third Plenary Session, an historic telegram.[1] It congratulates the Government on the peaceful settlement of the Sian affair, and on the " impending peaceful unification " of the country. To the Plenary Session it proposes four important changes in policies: to end civil war; to guarantee freedom of speech, Press, and assembly, and to release political prisoners; to invoke a national plan of resistance to Japanese aggression; and to return to the " three principles " of Dr. Sun Yat-sen's will.

If these proposals are adopted, in form or in substance, the Communists state, they are prepared, for the purpose of " hastening national unification and resistance to Japan," to suspend all attempts to overthrow the Government, and to adopt the following policies: (1) change the name of the Red Army to the " National Revolutionary Army," and place it under the command of the Military Affairs Commission; (2) change the name of the Soviet Government to the " Special Area Government of

[1] Cf. *New China* (a Soviet publication) (Yenan, March 15, 1987).

the Republic of China "; (3) realize a completely democratic form of government within the Soviet districts; and (4) suspend the policy of land confiscation and concentrate the efforts of the people on the tasks of national salvation—that is, anti-Nipponism.

But the Plenary Session, when it convenes on February 15 takes no formal notice of the bandits' telegram. There is much more important business to be accomplished. Chiang Kai-shek in his first speech to the Session, once more recounts, in complete and (for him) impassioned utterance, the whole story of his captivity in Sian. Dramatically he describes how he refused to sign any pledge to carry out the rebels' demands. He tells also how the rebels were converted to his own point of view, and were moved to tears by the revelations of patriotism in his confiscated diary. And not until he has said all this does he at last, in a very off-hand and contemptuous manner, submit the rebels' eight demands to the Session. Reiterating its complete confidence in the Generalissimo, the Session rejects his third resignation, condemns Chang Hsueh-liang, and just as casually and contemptuously rejects the impertinent demands.

But look ! Meanwhile, in its well-trained way, the Central Executive Committee is accomplishing things on its own initiative. Significant above everything else, perhaps, is the opening statement of Wang Ching-wei, second only to Chiang Kai-shek in party leadership. For the first time since the beginning of the anti-Red wars, Comrade Wang makes a speech in which he does not say that " internal pacification " (eradication of Communism) is the most important problem before the country, in which he does not repeat his famous phrase, " resistance *after* unification." The " foremost question " before the country now, he says, is " recovery of the lost territories." Moreover, the Session actually adopts resolutions to begin by recovering east Hopei and northern Chahar, and abolishing the " autonomous " Hopei-Chahar Council. Of course, this does not mean that Nanking is to launch a war against Japan. Its significance is simply that from now on any further Japanese military aggression on Chinese territory will meet with armed resistance from Nanking. But that is a real leap forward.

Secondly, the C.E.C., again on the Premier's recommendation, decides to convene the long-delayed " People's Congress," which is supposed to inaugurate democracy in China, on November 12. No more postponements; this time it is final. More important, the standing committee is authorized to revise the organic laws of the Congress to increase representation of " all groups." The Generalissimo—through Wang Ching-wei again—announces that the second great problem before the nation is the speedy realization of democracy.

Finally, on the last day of the Session, Chiang Kai-shek makes a statement in which he promises greater liberty of speech to all but traitors—and he says nothing about the " intellectual bandits "—and this is the first time anyone ever heard the Generalissimo defending freedom of the Press. He also promises " release of political prisoners who repent." Very quietly an order goes out to the Press that no longer are the epithets " Red-bandit " and " Communist-bandit " to be used. A few prisons begin to pour out a trickle of their less important victims.

Then, as if in afterthought, on the very last day of the historic Session, a long manifesto is issued, ostensibly to denounce the Communists. The history of ten years of crime and vandalism is recapitulated. That is, the Kuomintang's version of the decade. How is it possible, it is asked, for human beings who were once decent citizens, even the allies of the all-virtuous Kuomintang, to have descended so low ? Is it not obvious that any talk of " reconciliation " with brigands, thieves, and murderers is out of the question ? But all this explosion of wind, it turns out, is actual preparation for the terms of peace which, to the extreme distaste of Tories who still oppose peace at any price, conclude the manifesto.

What are these proposals ? The Session offers the Communists a chance " to make a new start in life," on four conditions: (1) abolition of the Red Army and its incorporation into the national army; (2) dissolution of the " Soviet Republic "; (3) cessation of Communist propaganda that is diametrically opposed to Dr. Sun Yat-sen's " three principles "; and (4) abandonment of the class struggle. Thus, though phrased in terms of " surrender " instead of " co-operation," the Kuomintang decides after all to accept the Reds' basis for negotiation of a " reconciliation." Note that those terms still leave the Reds in possession of their little autonomous State, their own army, their organizations, their Party, and their " maximum programme " for the future. Or so, at least, the Reds can hope ! And so, indeed, they do. For on March 15 the Communist Party, the Soviet Government and the Red Army issue a long manifesto requesting the opening of negotiations with Nanking.

What was the purpose of all these complex manœuvres by Chiang ? Obviously they were skilfully interwoven in such a manner as to conciliate the Opposition without weakening the prestige either of himself or of Nanking. Read in their proper sequence, his orders and statements, and the resolutions of the Plenary Session, show that he *partly* satisfied the political demands of all groups of the Opposition—just enough to shatter their solidarity and resolution in defying him, but not enough to cause a revolt in the Kuomintang. Civil war had been stopped, and it was clear that Nanking had at last shouldered the task of armed resistance to Japan. Promises of greater political freedom had been made, and a definite date had been set for the realization of " democracy." Finally, a formula had been proposed by which the Kuomintang and the Communists might at least live together in armed truce, if not in " co-operation." At the same time the Government had nominally rejected the rebels' demands, and the Communists' proposals for " co-operation." It was all very wonderful.

One should not fail to note that these conciliatory gestures were forced through by Chiang Kai-shek in the face of considerable antagonism to them in Nanking, and at the conclusion of a terrific personal shock which might have embittered and unbalanced a man less gifted with foresight, and hastened him into precipitate actions of revenge—which, in fact, Chiang's outraged followers in Nanking demanded. But Chiang was shrewder than they. The tremendous popular demonstration on his safe return from captivity was not merely a personal ovation, but a mighty demand of the people for peace against civil war, and unity in resistance to Japan. Chiang understood that perfectly, and knew that any punitive action he took against the North-west might result in deflation of his popularity overnight.

More important, the incident had revealed deep fissures in

his own edifice of power. He knew how easily these might enlarge into fatal cracks, bringing down the whole scheme in ruins. And he saw now with clear vision the great advantage to himself of a peace in which the last of those fissures could be obliterated. It was real genius of political strategy that he did not ignore the promises made in Sian, that he took no immediate overt revenge against his captors, that he tactfully employed a policy combining just the right weight of threat with the necessary softening of concession. In this way he eventually succeeded in breaking up the North-west *bloc* (his first objective), and peacefully transferred the Tungpei Army from Shensi into Anhui and Honan, while the Hsipei Army of General Yang Hu-ch'eng was reorganized under the central command. In February, Nanking troops were able to occupy Sian and its environs without disturbance or opposition, and in the following month negotiations were opened with the Communists.

5

Auld Lang Syne ?

FOR the Communists, too, were much impressed by Chiang's friendly gestures, his abolition of the Bandit Suppression Headquarters, his cancellation of plans for a new Anti-Red Campaign, and various other orders and resolutions already mentioned. All fighting ceased. Nanking troops and Red troops were actually in joint peaceful occupation of several border regions. Chiang had demonstrated his readiness to reconcile himself to the Reds' existence, temporarily at least, provided they adhered to the promises of their telegram of March 10.

During the Sian incident the Red Army occupied big new areas. In Shensi it now held the greater part of the province, including nearly everything north of the Wei River. In their some fifty counties—an area between 60,000 and 70,000 square miles, or roughly twice the size of Austria—the Reds controlled the biggest single realm they had ever ruled. But it was economically poor, very limited in its possibilities of development, and thinly populated, with perhaps less than 2,000,000 inhabitants.

Strategically, the area was extremely important. From it they could, if they chose, block the trade ways to Central Asia, or perhaps later themselves make direct connections with Chinese Turkestan (Sinkiang) or Outer Mongolia. The organic value of this frontier in terms of a hypothetical war with Japan is obvious. It is one of only two Chinese frontiers, and sources of supply, which Japan cannot blockade. More than half of Chinese Turkestan, which is roughly 550,000 square miles in area, is already under a semi-Socialist form of government sympathetic to the Chinese Reds, semi-independent of Nanking, and a loose affiliate of the U.S.S.R. North-east of it, the Autonomous Outer Mongolian Republic, another 900,000 square miles of former dependency of China—and the Chinese suzerainty of which is still nominally recognized, even by Russia—is now definitely under the Red banner, as a result of the military alliance (Mutual Defence Pact) concluded with the U.S.S.R. in 1936.

These three regions of Communist control in what may still be called " Greater China " total in area roughly a third the size of the former Chinese Empire. Separating them from physical contact with each other are only politically ambiguous buffer districts inhabited by Mongols, Moslems, and frontiersmen whose ties with Nanking are fragile, and against whom the threat of Japanese conquest is a deepening reality. Those areas might later on be brought into the orbit of the " Anti-Japanese United Front," and under Soviet influence. That would close in an immense future Red base extending from Central Asia and Mongolia into the heart of North-west China. But all this realm is backward, some of it barren steppe and desert, with poor communications, and sparsely populated. It could become a decisive factor in Eastern politics only in close alliance with the advanced industrial and military bases either of the U.S.S.R. or Central China, or both.

Immediate gains of the Chinese Reds were confined to these categories: the cessation of civil war, a certain degree of liberalization and tolerance in Nanking's internal policies, a stiffening toward Japan, and a partial release of the Soviet districts from their long isolation. As a result of negotiations conducted between General Chang Chung, the Generalissimo's envoy in Sian, and Chou En-lai, the Reds' delegate there, a number of important changes took place during April, May, and June. The economic blockade was lifted. Trade relations were established between the Red districts and the outside world. More important, communications between the two areas were quietly restored. On the frontiers the Red Star and the Kuomintang White Sun were crossed in symbolic union.

Mail and telegraph services were partly reopened. The Reds purchased a fleet of American lorries in Sian, and operated a bus service connecting the principal points in their region. Needed technical materials of all sorts began to pour in. Most precious to the Communists were books. A new Lu Hsun Memorial Library was established in Yenan, and to fill it Communist comrades throughout the country sent in tons of new literature. Hundreds of young Chinese Communists migrated from the great cities in Yenan, the new Red capital in north Shensi. By May over 2,000 students had been accepted for enrolment in the

Red Academy (renamed the " Anti-Japanese University "), and some 500 were in the Communist Party School. Among them were Mongols, Moslems, Tibetans, Formosans, and Miao and Lolo tribesmen. Scores were also studying in a number of technical training institutes.

Enthusiastic young radicals as well as veteran Party workers rolled in from all parts of China, some walking over great distances. By July, despite the rigours of student life, and the well-known starvation diet of millet and vegetables, there were so many applicants that no more could be accommodated. Scores were turned back, to wait for another term, when the Reds prepared to receive 5,000. Many trained technicians also arrived, and were given work as teachers, or in the " construction plan " which was now begun. In this, perhaps, lay the biggest immediate benefit of peace: a base in which freely to train, equip, and discipline new cadres for the ranks of the revolution and the anti-imperialist movement.

Of course, the Kuomintang continued strictly to supervise the Reds' connections with the outer world. There was less restriction on the movement of Communists now, but there was as yet no open acknowledgment of the fact. Many parties of non-Communist intellectuals also arrived in Red China to investigate conditions there—and many of them stayed on, to work. In June the Kuomintang itself secretly sent a semi-official group of delegates, headed by Hsiao Hua, to visit the Red capital. They toured the Soviet districts and made appropriately rufescent anti-Japanese speeches before huge mass meetings. They acclaimed the return to the anti-imperialist United Front between Communists and the Kuomintang. Nothing of this was allowed to appear in the Kuomintang Press, however.

Conditions in the Kuomintang areas also improved for the followers of Lenin. The Communist Party was still nominally illegal, but it became possible to extend its influence and widen its organization, for the oppression somewhat diminished. A small but steady stream of political prisoners was released from the jails. The special gendarmes (so-called Blueshirts) continued their espionage on Communists, but kidnappings and torturing ceased. Word was sent out that Blueshirt activities henceforth should centre primarily on " pro-Japanese traitors." A number of the latter was arrested, and for the first time several Chinese agents in Japan's pay were actually executed.

By May, in return for these concessions, the Soviets were ready to adopt the name of " Special Area Government," and the Red Army had petitioned to be included in the national defence forces as part of the " National Revolutionary Army." Great " all-China " meetings of the Party and Army delegates were called in May and June. Decisions were made on measures by which the new policies, calling for co-operation with the Kuomintang, could be realized. At these meetings the portraits of Lenin, Marx, Stalin, Mao Tse-tung, Chu Teh, and other Red leaders appeared beside those of Chiang Kai-shek and Sun Yat-sen.

These phenomena reflected a general disposition on the part of the Reds to make necessary changes in form and nomenclature, while retaining the essential content of their doctrine and programme, and their autonomous existence. Sun Yat-sen's San Min Chu I—the " three principles " of democracy, nationalism, and livelihood to which the Kuomintang pays specious homage—were once more honoured by the Communists, as during the Great Revolution. They were not the San Min Chu I of Chiang Kai-shek, for the Reds brought to them their own Marxist interpretation. Marxism, and the basic tenets of social revolution, it was quite clear, they would never give up. Every new step taken, every change made, was examined, debated, decided, and integrated in terms of Marxism—and the proletarian revolution, which the Communists did not abandon as their ultimate purpose.

The most important changes in Red policy were the cessation of the practice of confiscation of the landlords' land, the cessation of anti-Nanking, anti-Kuomintang propaganda, and the guarantee of equal rights and the voting franchise to all citizens, regardless of their class basis in society. Of these, the one which most directly affected Red economy was, of course, the cessation of land confiscation. This did not mean the return of land to the landlords in areas where redistribution had already been realized, but an agreement to abandon the practice in new districts under Red control.

To augment the deficiency in income resulting from this

retreat, Generalissimo Chiang tacitly—though not officially—agreed to consider the Soviet districts part of the "national defence area," and pay accordingly. The first payment to the Reds ($500,000) was delivered shortly after Chiang Kai-shek's return to Nanking. Some of the Kuomintang money was used to convert Soviet currency, to buy manufactures for their co-operatives—now well stocked—and some to purchase needed equipment. None of it was wasted on salaries. The Commissioner of Finance continued to exist on five dollars a month! The exact monthly allowance from Nanking was still under negotiation as these paragraphs were written, as, indeed, was the whole definitive working agreement for future co-operation.

In June the Generalissimo sent his private plane to Sian for Chou En-lai, the Reds' chief delegate, who flew to Kuling, China's summer capital. There Chou held further conversations with Chiang Kai-shek and members of the Cabinet. Among points discussed was the Communists' demand for representation in the People's Congress—the Congress which is scheduled to adopt a "democratic" constitution—in November. It was reported that an agreement was reached whereby the "Special Area" would be permitted to elect nine delegates on a regional basis.

However, these delegates in all probability would not be known as "Communists." Nanking had not openly acknowledged the so-called "remarriage." It preferred to regard the relationship rather as the annexation of a concubine whose continence had yet to be proved, and one about which, for diplomatic reasons, the less said outside family circles the better. But even this furtive *mésalliance* was an astounding and open defiance of Japan, unthinkable a few months previously. Meanwhile Japan's own offer (through Matchmaker Hirota) of a respectable bourgeois "anti-Red" marriage with Nanking was finally spurned. In this was perhaps a last and definite indication that Nanking's foreign policy had undergone a fundamental change.

Now, all this must seem to be an utterly incomprehensible *dénouement* to the innocent Occidental observer unskilled in Chinese politics, and he is likely to make serious errors of judgment in analysing its significance. Certainly it could happen nowhere else in the world but China. After a decade of the

fiercest kind of civil war, Red and White suddenly burst into
" Auld Lang Syne." What is the meaning of it ? Have the Reds
turned White, and the Whites turned Red ? Neither one. But
surely someone must have won, and someone lost ? Yes, China
has won, Japan has lost. For the last decision in this profoundly
complicated two-way struggle has been postponed once more
by the intervention of a third ingredient—Japanese imperialism.

It is therefore in terms of the rôle of imperialism in the
Chinese revolution that we must seek an outline of the future
against Red horizons.

6

Red Horizons

To " explain " the Chinese revolution, to explore its rich mines
of social and political experience, these are the tasks of quite
other books than the present one. But even in these few remaining pages it may be possible to suggest a general chart of understanding for the voyager down the hurrying stream of this
many-channelled history.

There was an accomplished social scientist named Lenin.
" History generally," he wrote, " and the history of revolutions
in particular, is always richer in content, more varied, more
many-sided, more lively and ' subtle,' than the best parties and
the most class-conscious vanguards of the most advanced class
imagine. This is understandable, because the best vanguards
express the class consciousness, the will, the passion, the fantasy of tens of thousands, while the revolution is made, at the
moment of its climax and exertion of all human capabilities,
by the class consciousness, the will, the passion, and the fantasy
of tens of millions who are urged on by the very acutest class
struggle."[1]

The observation is apposite to China. What Lenin admitted
in one sense was simply the fallibility of Communist prog-
nostication, the tendency of the Communist very often to con-
fuse his emotional wish-fancy with reality, to suffer from
delusions that identify " class-consciousness " of the " thousands " with the " fantasy " of the " millions." And this may
be no proof of the frailty of the method of dialectical materialism, but of the frailty of the dialectician. It explains why
Inprecorr, the organ of the Communist International, or the
New Masses, for example, are sometimes as mistaken in their
analysis of given historic possibilities as are *The Times* or
Popolo d'Italia.

In what ways has Chinese history to be " richer in content,
more varied, more many-sided, more lively and ' subtle ',"
than the Communist theoreticians foresaw a decade or so ago ?

[1] " *Left-Wing* " *Communism: An Infantile Disorder*, by V. I. Lenin (London,
1934).

To be specific, why has the Red Army failed to win power in China, despite its heroic and exhausting struggle? Before answering this, one must recall again, and keep clearly in mind, the Communist conception of the Chinese revolution, and of its main objectives.

A popular and never-dying notion of the Communist movement in China is that it is anti-capitalist in the sense that it does not see the necessity for a period of bourgeois or capitalist economy, but wants right away to proclaim Socialism. This is rubbish. Every pronouncement of the Communists has shown clearly that they recognize the " bourgeois character " of the present revolution. The struggle has been not over the nature of the revolution so much as over the nature of its leadership. The Communists recognize that the duties of that leadership are to realize, as quickly as possible, two primary historic tasks: first, to overthrow foreign imperialism and establish national independence (that is, liberate China from its semi-colonial status); second, to overthrow the power of the landlords and gentry, and establish democracy (that is, liberate the masses from " semi-feudalism "). Only *after* those tasks have been accomplished, the Communists foresee, will it be possible to move toward Socialism.

But how can these victories be won? For a while the Communists hoped to win them *with* the bourgeoisie. But when the counter-revolution occurred in 1927, when the Kuomintang (the party of the landlords and bourgeoisie) abandoned the revolutionary method against both imperialism and " feudalism," they became convinced that " only a worker-peasant democratic dictatorship, *under the hegemony of the proletariat* " could lead the bourgeois revolution—which in China did not assume a definitive form immediately after the overthrow of the imperial monarchy, but only at the time of the Great Revolution, 1925-7.

All this may sound troublesome to anyone unfamiliar with the precise categories of Marxist logic. There is, of course, a tremendous body of literature behind the whole theory (for a starter, see Stalin's *About the Opposition*), if the reader cares to investigate it. Here I shall be content with the bare statement of the thesis. To put what has been said above in other terms, the

Communist conception of the revolution was this. A period of national capitalism in China was inevitable, but could only be achieved simultaneously with the elimination of foreign colonial power in the cities, together with the liberation of the peasant masses, by giving them land through the destruction of estates, and the landlords' economic, political, and social power in the villages.

The Communists saw that the Chinese capitalist class was not a true bourgeoisie, but a " colonial bourgeoisie." It was a " comprador class," with the character of an excrescence of the foreign finance and monopoly capitalism which it primarily served. It was too weak to lead the revolution. It could, in fact, achieve the conditions of its own freedom only through the fulfilment of the anti-imperialist movement, the elimination of foreign domination. But only the workers and peasants could lead such a revolution to its final victory. And the Communists intended that the workers and peasants should not turn over the fruits of that victory to the neo-capitalists whom they were thus to release, as had happened in France, Germany, Italy— everywhere, in fact, except in Russia. Indeed, they should retain power throughout a kind of " N.E.P." period, a brief epoch of " controlled capitalism," and then a period of State capitalism, followed at last by a speedy transition into Socialist construction, with the help of the U.S.S.R. All this is indicated quite clearly in *Fundamental Laws of the Chinese Soviet Republic*.[1]

" The aim of the driving out of imperialism, and destroying the Kuomintang," repeated Mao Tse-tung in 1934,[2] " is to unify China, to bring the *bourgeois democratic revolution* to fruition, and to make it possible to turn this revolution into a higher stage of Socialist revolution. This is the task of the Soviet."

But what, considering the alpine obstacles of which they were fully aware, made the Chinese Communists think in 1927 that they could succeed in such a mighty leap across a vast chasm of history ? Probably chiefly the example of the October Revolution. That tremendous pulsation hurled the Russian people from feudal monarchy right on to the plateau of Socialism. And it was made possible by two conditions which, it was argued, might be reproduced in China. Trotsky worded it most simply:

[1] Martin Lawrence, London, 1934.　　　[2] Cf. *Red China*, op. cit.

" a drawing together and mutual interpenetration of two factors, belonging to completely different historic species: a peasant war—that is, a movement characteristic of the dawn of bourgeois development—and a proletarian insurrection, the movement signalizing its decline."[1]

At the apex of the Great Revolution in China there was present the necessary revolutionary mood among both the peasant masses and the proletariat. But there were many differences from the situation which had produced the Russian revolution. One of these was very great. Survivals of feudalism were even more pronounced in Russia than in China, but China was a semi-colonial country, an " oppressed nation," while Russia was an imperialist country, an " oppressor nation." In the Russian revolution the proletariat had to conquer only a single class, its own native bourgeois-imperialist class, while the Chinese revolution had to contend with an indigenous enemy of dual personality—both its own nascent bourgeoisie and the entrenched interests of foreign imperialism. Theoretically, in the beginning, the Chinese Communists expected this dual nature of their enemy to be offset by the dual nature of their own assault, which would be aided by their " proletarian allies " of the world, and the " toilers of the U.S.S.R."

The reasons for the failure of the Communists to capture power after 1927 are essentially quite simple. The most important one lies in the character and conditions of existence of the Chinese industrial proletariat. Numerically very small—there are scarcely 4,000,000 industrial workers in China—inexperienced, poorly educated, enfiladed with disease, under-nourishment, and terror, further weakened by a preponderance in its midst of slave child and female labour, indescribably exploited by both native and foreign capital, this class would even in an independent China find it difficult to assert its political will. But the worst condition of its enslavement lies in the concentration of modern industry in China in zones of foreign control, and the isolation of the workers in these zones from each other.

Nearly a third of all the industrial workers of China huddle in Shanghai, under the gunboats of half a dozen of the world's

[1] Leon Trotsky, *History of the Russian Revolution*, vol. i, p. 70 (London, 1982).

great powers. In Tientsin, Tsingtao, Shanghai, Hankow, Hong-kong, Kowloon, and other spheres of imperialism are probably three-quarters of all the industrial workers of China ! Shanghai provides the classic prototype of them all. Here you can see British, American, French, Japanese, Italian, *and Chinese* soldiers, sailors, and police, all the forces of world imperialism combined with native gangsterism and the comprador bour-geoisie, the most degenerate elements in Chinese society, " co-operating " in wielding the truncheon over the heads of the hundreds of thousands of unarmed workers.

All rights of freedom of speech, assembly, or organization are of course denied these workers. Mobilization of the industrial proletariat in China for political action is utterly inconceivable as long as the dual system of native and foreign policing power is maintained. Only once in history has it been broken—in 1927—when for a few days Chiang Kai-shek made use of the workers to secure his victory over the northern warlords. But immediately afterwards they were suppressed in one of the most demoralizing blood-baths in history, with the sanctification of the foreign powers and the financial help of foreign capitalists.

All attempts at insurrection in the cities were thus doomed to failure. Nanking could and did count upon the security of the industrial bases held by the foreign powers in the treaty ports—and on their troops, their guns, their cruisers, and their inland police, the river gunboats, and on their wealth, their Press, their propaganda, and their spies. It does not matter that instances of the direct participation of these powers in actual warfare against the Red Army were few. They occurred on the occasions when such action was necessary. But their chief services were rendered by keeping the industrial workers immobilized, by furnishing Nanking with munitions and aeroplanes, and by entering into a conspiracy which complacently denied the very existence of civil war by the simple device of calling the Communists " ban-dits," so that the embarrassing question of " non-intervention committees " (as in present-day Spain) was never even allowed to arise.

With the workers thus powerless from the beginning, and unable to win a single important industrial base in the cities, the advanced leaders of the proletariat were obliged to fall back on the rural districts, where the Communist movement, while retaining the aims and ideology of Socialism, in practice assumed the economic character of an agrarian revolution. In the rural areas the Reds hoped eventually to build up sufficient strength to be able to attack Nanking first in urban bases where foreign influence was less firmly established,[1] and later—with the help, they hoped, of the world proletariat—to invest the citadels of foreign power in the treaty ports.

But while the imperialist powers were the objective allies of Nanking against Communism, the assistance expected from the world proletariat failed to materialize. Although in the *Communist International Programme*[2] it is clearly recognized that successful proletarian movements in semi-colonial countries such as China " will be possible only if direct support is obtained from the countries in which the proletarian dictatorship is established " (i.e. in the U.S.S.R.), the Soviet Union in fact did not extend to the Chinese comrades the promised " assistance and support of the proletarian dictatorship " in any degree commensurate with the need. On the contrary, the great help, amounting to intervention, which the Soviet Union gave to Chiang Kai-shek until 1927 had the objective influence of bringing into power the most reactionary elements of the Kuomintang. Of course, the rendering of direct aid to the Chinese Communists after 1927 became quite incompatible with the position adopted by the U.S.S.R.—and here is the well-known contradiction between the immediate needs of the national policy of the Soviet Union and the immediate demands of the world revolution, for to do so would have been to jeopardize by the danger of international war the whole programme of Socialist construction in one country. Nevertheless, it must be noted that the influence of this factor on the Chinese revolution was very great.

Deprived of an ally, the Chinese Communists continued to struggle alone for the " hegemony of the bourgeois revolution," believing that deep changes in internal and international politics would release new forces in their favour. They were quite mistaken. The result was a prolonged convulsion which brought to

[1] Yet even when in 1930 the Reds captured Changsha, a city far inland and comparatively unimportant to foreign imperialism, they were forced to give it up under a fierce bombardment of British, American and Japanese gunboats.
[2] London, 1929.

the Chinese masses all the anguish of political parturition, without the final consequence of an heir.

Nanking's power remained relatively secure in the great urban centres, for the reasons mentioned, but in the villages it developed only very slowly. Paradoxically—and dialectically— this rural bourgeois anæmia was traceable to the same source as Nanking's strength in the cities—to foreign imperialism. For while imperialism was eager enough to " co-operate " in preventing or suppressing urban insurrection, or possibilities of it, at the same time it was objectively engaged—chiefly through Japan, the focus of the system's point of greatest stress in the Far East—in collecting heavy fees for this service, in the form of new annexations of territory (Manchuria, Jehol, Chahar, and east Hopei), new concessions, and new wealth belonging to China. The great burdens placed upon Nanking by this newest phase of imperialist aggression made it impossible for the Kuomintang to introduce in the rural areas the necessary capitalist " reforms "—commercial banking, improved communications, centralized taxing and policing power, etc.—fast enough to suppress the spread of rural discontent and peasant rebellion. By carrying out the land revolution the Reds were able to satisfy the demands of a substantial peasant following, take the leadership of part of rural China, and even build several powerful bases on an almost purely agrarian economy. But meanwhile they could grow no stronger in the cities, on whom their enemy continued to be based.

In this situation, the Communists argued that the Kuomintang's attacks on the Soviets prevented the Chinese people from fulfilling their mission of " national liberation " in driving out the Japanese, and that the Kuomintang's own unwillingness to defend the country proved the bankruptcy of bourgeois leadership. The Communist thesis of the revolution was thus validated. But the enraged Kuomintang retorted that the Communists' attempts to overthrow the Government prevented them from resisting Japan, while the continued practice of " Red-banditry " in the interior, despite the grave national crisis, retarded the realization of internal reforms. The interesting—and again dialectical—thing about these two positions is that both were right and both were wrong. And here in essence was the peculiar stalemate, the fundamental impotence of this period of the Chinese revolution.

Over this decade the imperialist pressure gradually became so severe, the imperialists' price for the protection of the interests of the Chinese bourgeoisie in the cities became so excessive, that it tended to neutralize the class antagonisms between the Kuomintang, the party of the bourgeoisie and the landlords, and the Kungchantang, the party of the workers and peasants. It is precisely because of this—and because of the immediate events described in the foregoing chapters—that the Kuomintang and the Communist Party are thus able, after a decade of ceaseless warfare, to reunite in a synthesis expressed in terms of their essential unity on the higher plane of a common antagonism against Japanese imperialism. This unity, because of its inner contradictions, is not stable; it is not permanent; it may break up again whenever the internal denials outweigh the present external ones. But its achievement now definitely concludes an epoch of revolutionary warfare and begins a new era.

What is the chief significance of this decade of political experience ? Theoretically it is clearly this: that the Communists have been forced to abandon temporarily their thesis that " only under the hegemony of the proletariat " can the bourgeois democratic movement develop. To-day it is acknowledged that *only* " a union of all classes " can achieve those purposes. Its practical significance is the clear recognition of the *present* leadership— which is here synonymous with power—of the Kuomintang in the bourgeois revolution. For the Reds it must certainly be considered " a great retreat " (as Mao Tse-tung has frankly admitted) from the days in Kiangsi, when they fought " to consolidate the workers' and peasants' dictatorship, to extend this dictatorship to the whole country, and to mobilize, organize, and arm the Soviets and the masses to fight in this revolutionary war."[1] The immediate struggle for power has ceased. To-day Communist slogans are: to support the central Government, to hasten peaceful unification under Nanking, to realize bourgeois democracy, and to organize the whole nation to oppose Japan.

But in such periods " it is necessary," wrote Lenin, " to combine the strictest loyalty to the ideas of Communism with the

[1] *Red China*, etc., p. 11 (London, 1934).

Pc

ability to make all necessary compromises, to 'tack,' to make agreements, zigzags, retreats, and so on," and thus, although among the Chinese Communists there has been this great shift in strategy, still they believe it is now possible to conduct the contest in a much more favourable atmosphere than in the past. There has been this " exchange of concessions," as Mao Tse-tung says, and an exchange to which " there are definite limits."

He continues: " The Communist Party retains the leadership on problems in the Soviet districts and the Red Army, and retains its independence and freedom of criticism in its relations with the Kuomintang. On these points no concessions can be made. . . . The Communist Party will never abandon its aims of Socialism and Communism, it will still pass through the stage of democratic revolution of the bourgeoisie to attain the stages of Socialism and Communism. The Communist Party retains its own programme and its own policies."[1]

Practical gains resulting from these concessions have already been discussed. But what guarantees have the Communists that these gains can be held ? What guarantees are there that the present peace will be maintained, that the promised democracy will be realized, that a policy of resistance to Japan will last ?

Quite clearly the Kuomintang will utilize to the fullest extent the benefits of the new Communist policy to itself. With Nanking's authority now recognized by the only political party in China capable of challenging it, Chiang Kai-shek will continue to extend his military and economic power in peripheral areas where warlord influence is still strong, areas such as Kwangsi, Yunnan, Kweichow, and Szechuan. Improving his military position all around the Reds, he meanwhile extracts political compromises from them in return for his temporary toleration. Eventually, by skilful combination of political and economic tactics, he hopes so to weaken them politically that, when the moment is right for the final demand of their complete surrender (which he undoubtedly still aspires to secure), he may isolate the Red Army, fragmentize it on the basis of internal political dissensions, and deal with the recalcitrant remnant as a purely regional military problem.

[1] Report to the Communist Party (Yenan, April 10, 1937).

The Reds are under no delusions about that. Likewise they are under no delusions that the promise of democracy can be fulfilled, or the anti-imperialist movement, without a continued active opposition of their own. In upholding the slogans of a full democracy and anti-imperialism, which they will never give up, the Reds do not worry about minor political concessions, for they believe their fundamental political base is indestructible. Of course, no party of dictatorship in history ever yielded up one scrap of its power to the people except under the heaviest pressure, and the Kuomintang will prove no exception. The achievement of even the measure of " democracy " now in prospect would have been impossible without the ten-year presence of Communist Opposition. Indeed, without that Opposition no democracy would have been necessary, and no State power with the degree of centralization which we now begin to witness in China would have been conceivable. For the growth of democracy, like the maturing of the modern State itself, is a manifestation of the need for a power and mechanism in which to attempt to reconcile contradictions that are fundamentally irreconcilable in capitalist society—the basic class antagonisms. That is the simplest statement of bourgeois democracy.

These contradictions are not diminishing in China, but rapidly increasing, and, to the extent that they sharpen, the State must take recognition of them. The achievement of peace itself makes it inevitable, if that peace is to last, that Nanking reflect a wider representation of social stratifications. This does not mean that there is any likelihood of the Kuomintang quietly signing its own death-warrant by genuinely realizing bourgeois democracy, and by permitting the Communist Party to compete with it in open election campaigning (for it is everywhere conceded that the vote of the peasantry alone would give the Communists an overwhelming majority), although that is what the Communists and other parties demand, and will continue to agitate for. But it does mean that some recognition of the demands of the majority will have to be made by the tiny minority which now monopolizes the State economy and policing power. The concession of representation of the Soviets in the National Congress on a *regional* basis is an indication of that.

The centripetal spread of economic, political, and social

interests, the process of so-called " unification "—the very measures which create the system—at the same time require, for their own preservation, that ever-widening groups be focused in the centre in an attempt to resolve the insoluble—the deepening conflict of class interests. And the more Nanking tends to represent different and wider class interests throughout the country—the nearer it comes to achieving democracy—the more it is forced to seek a solution of self-survival through restoration of national sovereignty.

The guarantees of increased Communist influence, the guarantee against future " annihilation campaigns," therefore, are seen by the Communists to be inherent in the organic economic, social, and political relationships of the country— precisely those formations which have resulted in the present situation. These are, first of all, a wide popular demand among both the armed and unarmed masses for continued internal peace, for improved livelihood, for democracy, and for national freedom. Secondly, the Communist Party's " guarantees " lie in the leadership it can continue to give to the movement for those demands throughout the country, and in the actual military and political fighting strength of the Communist Party. Thirdly, they rely on the decade of political experience of the Chinese people, which has made manifest the necessity of an historically momentary sublimation of class differences in the bourgeois-proletarian struggle against imperialism.

In the spring of 1937 the temporary diminution in Japanese pressure on Nanking, the suspension of the invasion of Inner Mongolia, the opening of Anglo-Japanese conversations for " co-operation in China," and the hopes of the British Government to mediate a Sino-Japanese agreement and a " fundamental peace " in the Far East, caused some people to wonder whether the Communist estimate of the political scene was not in error. Was it not reckless gambling to pivot a strategy on the central inevitability of an early Sino-Japanese war ? Now that internal peace was established in China, now that the Reds had ceased their attempts to overthrow the Kuomintang, Japan was really turning a conciliatory face to Nanking, it was argued. Japan's imperialists realized that they had pushed the Chinese bourgeoisie too far and too fast along the road of surrender, with the result that China's internal duel was cancelled in the universal hatred of Japan. They now saw the wisdom of enforcing a new and friendly policy toward the Chinese bourgeoisie, in order to renew the freedom of internal antagonisms in China. And such a Tokyo-Nanking *rapprochement* would destroy the Communists' political influence, which was too heavily based on *k'ang jih*—the " resist Japan " movement.

But history in flood must seek its outlets according to the laws of dynamics. It cannot be forced back into its pre-flood channels. It was already too late for Japan to close the floodgates. The Communists understood that she could not carry out a static policy in China even though Japan's ablest leaders realized the imperative necessity for a halt. And this Red prescience seemed fully vindicated with the outbreak, on July 8, of the Liukochiao Incident, for here the brief pretence of a Japanese change of heart collapsed. Japanese troops, holding " midnight manœuvres " (quite illegally) on Chinese territory at the town of Wanping, about ten miles west of Peking, claimed to have been fired on by Chinese railway guards. The incident gave the Japanese Army the pretext; once more it demonstrated its real necessities. By the middle of July the Japanese had rushed over 10,000 troops into the Peking-Tientsin area, and made new imperialist demands, capitulation to which would mean virtually the establishment of a Japanese protectorate in North China.

The Communists' conception of this situation, and of the kindling events which it must set in motion, was that the growing pressure of the whole nation for resistance not only here, but everywhere that new acts of imperialist aggression were committed, compelled Nanking to take a position in which, if Japan did not reverse her policies and make amends for the past, there was no way out but war. Which meant that there was no way out but war. And remember that the Communists interpreted such a war not only as a struggle for national independence, but as a revolutionary movement, " because to defeat imperialism in China means the destruction of one of its most powerful bases " and because the victory of the Chinese revolution itself " will correspond with the victory of the Chinese people against Japanese aggression " (Mao Tse-tung). The war might open to-morrow. It might not occur for another year, possibly two years. But not for any important length of time, the Communists' analysis of the breaking-point politico-economic tension in Japan, China, and throughout the world informed them, could this settlement in human destinies be delayed.

They foresaw that in this war it would become necessary to arm, equip, train, and mobilize tens of millions of people in a struggle which could serve the dual surgical function of removing the external tumour of imperialism and the internal cancer of class oppression. Such a war, they conceived, could only be conducted by the broadest mobilization of the masses, by the development of a highly politicalized army. And such a war could only be *won* under the most advanced revolutionary leadership. It could be initiated by the bourgeoisie. It could be completed only by the revolutionary workers and peasants. Once the people were really armed and organized on an immense scale the Communists would do everything possible to establish a decisive victory over Japan. They would loyally march with the bourgeoisie as long as it led the resistance. But they would be prepared to take over this leadership whenever the bourgeoisie faltered, turned " defeatist " and exhibited a willingness to submit to Japan—a tendency which they anticipated would appear soon after the first great losses of the war.

Of course, the Nanking régime fully understood these objectives of the Communists, as did all men of power in China. And hence they would seek out every possible road of compromise; they would, if they could avoid the internal consequences, make further concessions to Japan, at least until the odds seemed very greatly in favour of the régime's ability not only to enter a war with power, but to emerge from it with that power still intact, and with the internal revolution still in abeyance. But the Communists were sufficiently content with their own analysis of the course of history behind them to be satisfied with the chart of direction which they had chosen for the voyage ahead, through events which would *compel* Nanking to make a stand for its own survival. They knew that Nanking would continue to vacillate, that Japan would continue to feint and manœuvre in a myriad ways, using now the soft voice of persuasion, now the mailed fist, as the hour demanded one or the other, until the utmost agony of antagonism was reached between the interests of Japanese imperialism and the national interests of China externally, and between the Chinese and Japanese masses and their bourgeois-landlord rulers internally, until the moment when all the physical restraints and oppressions became utterly intolerable, the barriers of history broke down, the mighty catastrophe bred by imperialism was set loose, Frankenstein-like, to destroy imperialism, and *le déluge* swept forward.

Thus only imperialism can destroy imperialism, in that only a great imperialist war, which is almost certain to assume the character of a world war, will release the forces that can bring to the Asiatic masses the arms, the training, the political experience, the freedom of organization, and the mortal weakening of the internal policing power which are the necessary accessories for any conceivably successful revolutionary ascent to power in the relatively near future. Whether or not, even then, the " armed masses " are likely to follow Communist leadership with final success depends upon many variable and now unpredictable factors—internal factors first of all, but such factors also as the policies in the East of America, Great Britain, France, Germany, and Italy.

But to the very greatest extent success will turn upon whether or not the U.S.S.R. is drawn into such a war, and the direction in which it throws the weight of its proletarian power during the various stages of its development. This means that the victory of the revolution in China may hinge on the ability of the U.S.S.R. (at the moment of the highest tension and deepest contradiction in its current position) to make the transition from a programme of Socialism in one country to Socialism in all countries, to world revolution, without undergoing a self-immolative counter-revolution within its present boundaries.

And that, I believe, is the contour of the Communist picture of the future. One may not follow all of it, but this at least seems certain—that what Lenin wrote over twenty years ago is still true to-day: " Whatever may be the fate of the great Chinese revolution, against which various ' civilized ' hyenas are now sharpening their teeth, no forces in the world will restore the old serfdom in Asia, nor erase from the face of the earth the heroic democracy of the popular masses in the Asiatic and semi-Asiatic countries."

And another thing is equally certain. Neither can the democratic Socialist ideas for which tens of thousands of youths have already died in China, nor the energies behind them, be destroyed. The movement for social revolution in China may suffer defeats, may temporarily retreat, may for a time seem to languish, may make wide changes in tactics to fit immediate necessities and aims, may even for a period be submerged, be forced underground, but it will not only continue to mature; in one mutation or another it will eventually win, simply because (as this book proves, if it proves anything) the basic conditions which have given it birth carry within themselves the dynamic necessity for its triumph. And that triumph when it comes will be so mighty, so irresistible in its discharge of katabolic energy, that it will consign to oblivion the last barbarities of imperialism which now enthral the Eastern world.

But here anyone who finds these conclusions too " alarming " is welcome to seek such dialectical comfort as may be derived—it cannot be denied—by recollecting the quotation that opened this chapter, for in the realm of speculation the subjective influence is of course very active.

THE END

FULL DESCRIPTION OF PHOTOGRAPHS
(which will be found between pages 224 *and* 225*)*

1. MAO TSE-TUNG, Chairman of the Central Soviet Government.

2. WORKERS' THEATRICAL TROUPE. These young dancers are photographed during an interpretative harvest-dance, a creation of their bright young Paris-educated director.

3. YOUNG VANGUARDS OF RED CHINA. One of the activities of the Red Vanguards, a youth organization found everywhere in the Chinese Soviet areas, is the recruiting and training of scores of youngsters to study dramatics and dancing and create theatrical troupes. These Shensi girls are shown in one of their plays called *United Front*, symbolizing the mobilization of all China's armed forces to resist the Japanese.

4. DANCE OF RED MACHINES. This is a movement in an inter- pretative dance created by the Director of Dramatics of the Young Vanguards.

5. RED CHORUS GIRLS. These child actors and dancers of a travelling troupe of the Anti-Japanese People's Theatre are all obliged to study characters and political subjects several hours a day, besides learning the latest dance steps of Red China. All these are children of the backward peasantry of north Shensi. (See Part III, Chapter 5.)

6. RED SCHOOLBOY. Not yet old enough to join the Young Vanguards, he belongs to the " Children's Brigade," which includes tens of thousands of very young boys and girls. They learn Marxism in " Little Red Schoolhouses " and perform auxiliary tasks for the Red Army. (See Part VI, Chapter 5.)

7. CHINESE SOVIET WORKERS' CLUB-ROOM, The workers' textbooks for their classes in school hang on the wall. The two portraits on the back wall are of Marx and Lenin in the workers' own rough rendering. Above these portraits is a pennant for first prize in a workers' literacy competition, and below it another award—the coveted " aeroplane banner " given to the workers' group ranking highest for one month in all competitions. These

include: character-study, wall newspapers, public health, political training, athletics, and factory efficiency. These, called "Lenin Club-Rooms," are found in all Red factories and in every regiment of the Red Army, as well as in Communist Youth headquarters, in Village Soviet headquarters, etc. This one is in the Arsenal in north Shensi.

8. CLASSROOM AND LENIN CORNER OF A RED ARMY DETACHMENT IN NORTH SHENSI. Characters on the back wall read "Struggle for the Peaceful Unification of China," a slogan of the United Front. (See Part VIII, Chapter 5.)

9. "ARISE, ARISE, YE SLAVES OPPRESSED BY HUNGER AND COLD," say the modernistic Chinese characters below this big canvas poster in Red China. This is the Chinese version of the "Internationale" song, which is often sung in the Red districts. The slogans at the bottom on the red posters are, left to right: "FIGHT FOR WORLD PEACE AND THE LIBERATION OF THE SMALL AND WEAK COUNTRIES!" Middle says: "DOWN WITH THE REACTIONARY RULERS WHO SUPPRESS THE REVOLUTIONARY MOVEMENT." On the right: "DOWN WITH FASCISM!" (In Chinese, "*Fa Hsi Ssu-t'i Chu I!*")

10. JAPAN THRUSTS A DAGGER THROUGH THE "OPEN DOOR." Chinese Red anti-Japanese propaganda corps are busy even in far Ninghsia, where this wall drawing was photographed. Japan is shown stabbing the "Open Door" of China, while thumbing her nose at America and England, looking on from their idle battleships. "You cannot come to Asia," says the Japanese, stepping over to China. "Asia for the Asiatics!" (English words written in by the photographer.)

11. WALL NEWSPAPER. This ingenious device is propaganda entitled "Build Up the National Defence Government." Each paper explaining various phases of the national defence programme is suppose to represent a brick in the "wall of defence"; two soldiers guard the archway of China. These wall newspapers are found in every part of the Soviet districts.

12. "NO SLAVES ARE WE!" say these Red Star-spangled girl-workers and Young Vanguards in the Soviet factories at Wu Chi-Cheng in north Shensi. Red factories operate twenty-four hours daily, but there are three shifts, each of which works but

eight hours. The workers are given food and lodging and receive salaries of from $10 to $15 per month; they get annual vacations, and have their own schools, theatres, and athletic associations.

13. RED CO-OPERATIVES have been established in the principal towns under Soviet control. Here villagers are examining the materials offered in Holienwan, Kansu. There are about 350 such co-operatives in the Soviet districts now, with a membership of some 500,000 peasants.

14. LIBRARY TABLE IN THE SOVIET DISTRICTS. Workers, soldiers, students, and the common people find magazines, newspapers, books, available in all Soviet centres. One of the books here is *Das Kapital* by Karl Marx. The Reds smuggle these papers in from the White areas of China as often as possible through devious ways and means, and keep very well informed on national and world affairs.

15. CHINESE REDS SALUTE THE SPANISH REPUBLICANS. Entrance to a meeting-hall where Communists assembled to hear news of Spain. Citizens of Red China take a keen interest in the development of the Spanish war, for they feel that the Spaniards are fighting for the same democratic ideals as they themselves have fought for during the past decade. (See Part XI, Chapter 3.)

16. RED FLAG AND KUOMINTANG FLAG crossed in union symbolic of the United Front, after the Sian incident, the cessation of civil war, and the opening of negotiations for Kuomintang-Communist co-operation. This is a building in the new Red capital, Yenan, north Shensi. (See Part XII, Chapter 5.)

INDEX

Printed in the United Kingdom
by Lightning Source UK Ltd.
117464UKS00001B/179